Open Source
XML Database Toolkit:

Resources and Techniques
for Improved Development

Liam Quin

Wiley Computer Publishing

John Wiley & Sons, Inc.

NEW YORK · CHICHESTER · WEINHEIM · BRISBANE · SINGAPORE · TORONTO

Publisher: Robert Ipsen

Editor: Cary Sullivan

Assistant Editor: Christina Berry

Managing Editor: Marnie Wielage

Associate New Media Editor: Brian Snapp

Text Design & Composition: Pronto Design, Inc.

Designations used by companies to distinguish their products are often claimed as trademarks. In all instances where John Wiley & Sons, Inc., is aware of a claim, the product names appear in initial capital or ALL CAPITAL LETTERS. Readers, however, should contact the appropriate companies for more complete information regarding trademarks and registration.

This book is printed on acid-free paper. ∞

Published by John Wiley & Sons, Inc.

Published simultaneously in Canada.

This publication is designed to provide accurate and authoritative information in regard to the subject matter covered. It is sold with the understanding that the publisher is not engaged in professional services. If professional advice or other expert assistance is required, the services of a competent professional person should be sought.

Library of Congress Cataloging-in-Publication Data:
Quin, Liam.
    Open source XML database toolkit : resources and technniques for improved
    development / Liam Quin.
p.   cm.
    ISBN 0-471-37522-5 (pbk. : alk. paper)
    1. XML (Document markup language) 2. Web databases. I. Title.

QA76.76.H94 Q56 2000
005.7'2—dc21   00-033022
                                                 CIP

Printed in the United States of America.

10 9 8 7 6 5 4 3 2 1

CONTENTS

ACKNOWLEDGMENTS

This book has been over a year in the making. During that time, the world changed: XML became popular; Perl and Python got XML support; Oracle announced support for Linux; books and magazines on XML, Linux, and Open Source software sprouted like teenagers. Originally, I had thought I would spend most of the book describing tools, but when the tools kept changing, I abandoned that plan, and concentrated on techniques.

Through all this, my editor at Wiley, Christina Berry, remained calm and helpful. I changed jobs; my partner Clyde went back to university; and work on the book dragged on. So thanks are due to Christina, and to Clyde, who insisted that I write this book in the first place. I also need to thank Christopher Cashell for his help with the "Resource Guide", Jerji (Jerry Herbert) for distracting me when I was close to despair, and, above all, Moonkitty and Cosmos for purring even in the darkest nights.

W elcome to *The Open Source XML Database Toolkit*. This book is not just for people who write code, but also for those who design and specify programs. There are chapters to introduce XML and databases of various types, and chapters to explain how to use them together, all in an open source environment.

Open Source

This book, as is obvious from its title, is about open source software. Most of the tools discussed are open source. Open source software is software that is distributed with its program source code, under a license that allows you to modify and redistribute that source code. In other words, if you don't like the way the program works, *you are free to change it*. People sometimes think that open source software refers to software that is free of charge, but that's not the case. Software in the context of open source is software that you are free to change and to use in any way you wish, as long as you don't try to restrict that freedom from other people.

That said, note that most open source software *is* distributed more or less free of charge, with development costs paid for by support fees, services, or even donations (there may be media and shipping charges, of course).

Also note that this book does mention software that is *not* open source, usually when the software is very significant or when there are no open source competitors. Even if the most appropriate tool is not free, it's better to use it than to be held back by ideology or dogma. Here are some examples of nonfree software mentioned in this book:

Oracle (www.oracle.com). The most widely used high-end commercial relational database.

Solaris (solaris.sun.com). The Sun Solaris operating system running on a Sun SPARC server is probably the best-engineered and most stable server platform today. The source code to Solaris *is* available for a small fee, but the license is restrictive.

SoftQuad XMetal (www.softquad.com). XMetal is a widely used editor for XML documents. It offers a documentlike interface, a structured interface, and a source code view. However, it's only available to run under Microsoft Windows.

Object Design's ObjectStore (www.excelon.com; www.odi.com). ObjectStore is one of the better-known object-oriented databases. Although there is a free version for Java (PSE), source is not available, and there are restrictions on its use.

Most of the software described in this book is free. In a few cases, you may need to pay royalties if you use the software as part of a product or service that you sell, so be sure to check the licenses. Here are a few examples of free software mentioned in this book:

FreeBSD (www.freebsd.org). FreeBSD is one of several open source and free operating systems mentioned in this book. The examples were tested on FreeBSD and Linux.

MySQL (www.mysql.com). MySQL is a freely available relational database, although royalties may apply for some uses. It lacks many of the features of a high-end commercial system such as Oracle's, but it is very widely used and fast, and will take you a long way.

XT (www.jclark.com). XT is an implementation of the XML Style Language Transformation specification, which is a complicated way of saying that it manipulates XML documents, for example to produce HTML or XHTML.

Apache (www.apache.org). Apache is the most widely used Web server on the Internet. In addition to being open source and free, it is also very powerful and robust.

NOTE Go to www.opensource.org for more information about the open source movement.

XML

The eXtensible Markup Language, XML, is a way of defining simple text-based representations of arbitrarily complex structured information. The term XML is also used to refer to data that's marked up in a format defined using XML.

This is a book about working with XML. You might have XML documents that you need to store in a database, or you might want to use XML as an interchange format.

Chapter 1 in Part One, "Just Enough XML", introduces the main concepts of XML.

Database

This is also book about using databases. You'll find an introduction to the Structured Query Language, SQL, in Chapter 3, "Just Enough SQL."

The book doesn't only address relational databases, though. You'll find descriptions of hashing (Chapter 12: "Dynamic Hashing: *ndbm*"), of object-oriented databases (Chapter 10, "Introduction to Object-Oriented Databases," and Chapter 11, "XML as Classes and Objects"), and of text retrieval databases (Chapter 13, "Text Retrieval Technology Overview").

In all cases, the emphasis is on using XML and databases together in an open source environment.

Toolkit

As in all the best toolkits, there are lots of toys to play with. Most of them are listed for reference in Part Five, "Resource Guide." The toolkit approach means that this book does not go deeply into any single product or tool, but instead focuses on using tools together. Chapter 2, "Client/Server Architecture," introduces network programming, but from then on, the idea of using applications together pervades the book.

The power lies in the way the tools work together. Not only are these open source tools, meaning you can change them to make them work together in the way you want, but they are also widely used and powerful tools, meaning you probably won't have to change them.

Welcome to the open source revolution.

About the Illustrations

The illustrations in printed books generally have to use crisp lines, as if everything was polished and perfect. But don't be deceived by this. A quick sketch on the back of an envelope, or on a whiteboard, can help people to understand the relationships between components where a textual description cannot. Never hesitate to draw pictures, and don't worry if they are not very polished.

Typographic Conventions

I've tried to keep things simple in this regard. In the few places where I've shown a session at an interactive terminal or shell, the prompt is given as the pound sign () if you need to be logged in as root, and as the dollar sign ($) otherwise. The text you type is in bold. Here's a brief example:

```
$ pwd
/export/home/liam
$
```

The dollar sign on the third line shows the prompt after the command (pwd, print working directory) completed.

If you are thinking that this looks suspiciously like a Unix (or Linux) shell, you're right. If you're using Microsoft Windows, don't despair—there's a lot you can learn from this book. But if you want to write reliable high-performance database applications, you should develop them on Unix if you can. Imagine going for a whole year of development without a single machine crash and you'll see why.

Source code is shown with function names in **bold** when they are defined. This is just for your convenience, since books don't have a search command. If you type the examples into the computer, or download them, they are plain text, with no formatting. In the same way, comments are shown in *italics*.

What's on the Web Site?

At the companion Web site for this book (www.wiley.com/compbooks/quin) you can find:

- The complete text of the "Resource Guide" in HTML, with links to all of the resources mentioned.
- All of the examples and source code from the book, along with complete or enhanced examples.
- The data for the BookWeb example, along with a simple shell script to create the sample database using MySQL under Linux/Unix.
- The BookWeb site.
- AutoLinker, with the Glossary and the Dictionary examples.
- The sample Web server, written in Perl.

Other XML resources are added from time to time, and the "Resource Guide" is updated occasionally. And note, you may need your copy of the printed book ready before downloading the examples.

Finally, feel free to contact me (liam@holoweb.net; http://www.holoweb .net/~liam/); I'm always interested in comments and suggestions for the next edition. You can also find me on the SorceryNet Internet Relay Chat network (irc.sorcery.net; its Web site is at www.sorcery.net).

Relational Databases and XML

P art One is for readers who have an existing relational database that they need to interface to an XML system, or who want to use XML as a medium to transport relational data. It also introduces important and useful concepts in XML, SQL, and Client/Server programming.

This book is aimed at readers using open source technology, therefore the examples have been tested on Linux and/or FreeBSD, and use open source tools wherever possible. Part Five, "Resource Guide," describes some of the tools that are available, and discusses their licenses.

The first three chapters in Part One offer introductions to the technologies we covered throughout the book:

Chapter 1, "Just Enough XML." Presents a solid background to XML without getting too bogged down in details you don't need to know at this stage. If you already know XML, you probably can skim the chapter quickly.

Chapter 2, "Client/Server Architecture." Primarily explores programming issues in a networked or multiprocess environment. It concentrates on C and Perl, since most people working with large relational databases today are likely to be using these languages.

Chapter 3, "Just Enough SQL." Another overview, this one covers enough SQL to enable you to understand the examples in this book.

The next three chapters show how to use XML and SQL together in a Client/Server architecture, combining the concepts introduced so far.

Chapter 4, "Generating XML from Relational Data." Discusses ways to represent your relational data in XML.

Chapter 5, "Reading XML into a Program." Demonstrates how to use an XML parser in C to read XML, and discusses other languages, including Perl and Java.

Chapter 6, "XML Database Applications." Explores a number of ideas about how to put these concepts together.

The example code for Part One can be found at www.wiley.com/compbooks/ quin; or you can contact me at liam@holoweb.net (www.holoweb.net/~liam/) or on Internet Relay Chat as Ankh on irc.sorcery.net.

## CHAPTER 1

Just Enough XML

I begin by describing the concepts and ideas behind XML, to give you enough of a technical understanding of XML to make you comfortable with the content of the rest of the book. (If you want to learn more about XML than I include here, choose from the books listed in Chapter 23, "Further Reading."

The best place to start is with an overview of XML, with a reference to its main features and syntax. This not intended to be complete, but it does cover all of the XML features used in this book. Those not described fully are mentioned so that you can make note of them to look up later in the online XML specification if you need to. (And note, a copy of the XML specification is included on this book's CD. Or you can download the specifications for XML and related standards by going to www.w3.org/XML/ and following the appropriate links.)

What Is XML?

XML is the acronym for the eXtensible Markup Language, a way of representing information that is, to some extent, self-describing. You can use XML to design miniature markup languages of your own that are tailored to specific problem domains. Less accurate is to say that XML is as a more elegantly designed and flexible version of HTML. The reason this is not accurate is that HTML is a fixed markup language based on ISO 8879:1986 SGML, whereas

XML is a subset of a later version of the Standard Generalized Markup Language (SGML). You can define HTML itself (more or less) using XML; in fact, this has been done by the World Wide Web Consortium with XHTML; see www.w3.org/ for details.

XML files, or *streams*, are called *documents*, even though they might not contain anything you would ever read or print. It may seem odd to refer to an authentication ticket for an electronic funds transfer as a document, but the term serves to emphasize an important point: XML is a text-based format, not a binary one.

Here is a quick example:

```
<?xml version="1.0">
<Book>
    <Title>The Silmarillion</Title>
    <Author>Tolkien, J.R.R.</Author>
    <Date>1980</Date>
</Book>
```

XML is based on the ISO standard language ISO 8879:1988 SGML. This is important because it means that XML, like SQL, is not vendor-specific, and is therefore likely to remain in use for a long time. XML was defined by the World Wide Web Consortium (W3C) as a subset of SGML, intended to be easier for programmers to implement. The XML specification has clearly met that goal, since at the time of writing there are already more XML implementations than anyone can count.

In the example just given, there are three kinds of elements:

- The beginning *XML declaration* identifies the document as an XML document.
- The year of publication and the author's name are examples of textual information.
- <Title> and <Date> are examples of *markup* that identifies the textual information.

Of course, markup can get more complex than this example shows. For example, textual information often contains *embedded markup* as well:

```
<Instruction>
    Clean your attach&eacute; case using the
    Soft Rag <PartNo>1991</PartNo>.
</Instruction>
```

In this example, there are two types of embedded markup. The first is a *general entity*. Note: The term entity is widely used both in the database world and in the XML specification, but their meanings are not the same. In this case, the reference to the general entity eacute is used to provide a textual platform-independent way of writing the character é (e with an acute accent). Although general entities are part of XML, this particular entity is not; XML provides a way of defining your own general entities, which is described in the *Document Type Definitions* section later in this chapter.

The second piece of embedded markup is the element called PartNo. If you are familiar with relational data, you may be used to thinking of information in terms of relationships between atomic units, but in fact a great deal of information is embedded in textual descriptions. Imagine trying to search a large collection of documents for part number 1991 without finding documents containing the date 3rd August 1991, and the advantage of *nested markup* becomes very clear. Or, one might say, <emphasis>very</emphasis> clear.

Nested objects, such as a part number inside an instruction, have often proved difficult to handle in a relational database world. In Part One, we'll look primarily at the sort of data you customarily find in a relational database, in which any markup intermingled with text in this way is either not allowed, or is treated simply as a sequence of characters. In later parts of the book, we'll look at ways to handle more complex XML data.

What XML Is Not

It's important to understand what XML is not, before we delve into what it is. Briefly, XML is not a programming language and it's not HTML. To elaborate XML is not:

A programming language. You can't declare variables, set triggers on events, loop 30 times, or *do* anything except use XML to describe information. XML does not have any built-in meanings for constructs such as if or else, and does not have any built-in scripting languages.

HTML. Despite the obvious superficial similarities, the basic HTML behaviors, such as the idea that <img src="bigben.jpg"> includes an image, or that <P> starts a paragraph, are not built in to XML. As described in the *Namespaces* section later in the chapter, you can access the HTML elements and their behavior from XML, if the application you are using supports HTML rendering (just as a database API might permit you to access SQL functionality from within a C program).

XML *is* SGML, however. That is, every fully conforming syntactically correct and valid XML document is also a valid SGML document, because of the way in which the XML specification was written. But XML is only a fairly small subset of SGML, which means that many SGML documents are not also XML documents.

NOTE This chapter is intended as a review. If you are not familiar with SGML, HTML, or XML, you may need to read an introductory book first, such as Kevin Dick's excellent *XML: A Manager's Guide* (Addison-Wesley, 1999).

XML Reference

The purpose of this section is to introduce all the features of XML. (For more detail, refer either to the specification itself or a book such as *The XML Specification Guide* by Ian S. Graham and Liam R. E. Quin (Wiley, 1999).) We'll begin with an explanation of how to read the XML specification, followed by a description of each part of an XML document, including the optional document type definition.

Reading the XML Specification

This section describes how to make the best use of the XML specification, the latest, authoritative version of which can be found at www.w3.org, the site of the World Wide Web Consortium, which published the XML specification. And if you'd like to read the specification in an annotated form, the *XML Specification Guide* is a good resource.

Before launching into how to use the specification, it's important to reiterate that this document is a specification, *not* a tutorial. It was not written to be easy to read. It was written to be precise enough to ensure that programmers all implement it in the same way. Hence, words were carefully chosen, making distinctions rarely acknowledged in colloquial English anymore, such as between the verbs *can, may,* and *must.* The most significant consequence of this is that if you are not used to reading specifications, you will probably find it tough going. Let's get started.

Grammatical Productions

The XML specification uses Extended Backas-Naur Form (EBNF, or BNF for short) to represent grammatical productions. For example, you might see:

```
[1]    Document ::= prolog element Misc*
[2]    Char ::= #x9 | #xA | #xD | [#x20-#xD7FF] | [#xE000-#xFFFD] |
[#x10000-#x10FFFF]
```

This means that a `Document` is defined as a `prolog`, followed by exactly one `element`, followed by zero or more things (indicated by the asterisk) that match the production `Misc`. The details of the *expression* on the right-hand side are basically the same as for *element content models,* which are described later in the chapter in the section entitled *Document Type Definitions.*

Numbered Productions

In the preceding code, the bracketed numbers [1] and [2] are Production Numbers; they are referred to frequently in the specification; you'll also find a cross-reference to them in the back cover of the *XML Specification Guide.*

XML Document Features

This section describes the XML features you'll find within a document.

Character Set

XML documents are plain text files, usually in U.S. ASCII, Latin 1 (also known as ISO 8859-1) or Unicode encoded with UTF-8 or UTF-16. You may encounter other variations, but these are the main ones, and for the purpose of this book, all XML documents will use either U.S. ASCII or ISO 8859-1, not because other languages are less important, but because multilingual issues are not central to using databases with XML.

If a document is in another character set, this will be indicated in the Prolog (see the following section, *Prolog*). A Unicode file may be stored with a Unicode *byte order mark* at the beginning of the XML document. Documents that begin with this mark are assumed to be in the corresponding Unicode encoding. If a part of a document is in another character set, that part must be stored as a separate *external entity*, and its character set must be identified. We'll discuss external entities in more detail later in the chapter.

Entire books have been written on the subject of character sets. If you are interested, or need to know how to represent languages that can't use the Latin 1 character set, go to www.unicode.org or read the character set appendix to the *XML Specification Guide.*

Prolog

XML documents begin with a Prolog that consists of an optional XML declaration and an optional document type declaration. There can be no blank lines, spaces, or comments preceding the XML declaration, although there can be comments and processing instructions following both the XML declaration and the document type declaration. The XML specification presents the Prolog like this:

```
Prolog ::= XMLDecl? Misc* (doctypedecl Misc*)?
```

Although the XML 1.0 specification says that the Prolog is optional, every XML file should start with one. This practice will aid interoperability, and help non-XML tools to identify XML files.

The XML Declaration

The XML declaration looks like this:

```
<?xml version="1.0" encoding="ISO-8859-1" standalone="yes"?>
```

Important points to note here are:

- The XML declaration begins with <?xml and ends with ?>. It is a common error to omit the question mark from the end of the declaration.

- The version, encoding, and standalone items must occur in the order shown.

- The version is "1.0", since that's the current version of XML.

- You can generally omit the encoding item if it's ISO-8859-1, and if that's the default processing character set in your environment. Other possible values are ASCII, UTF-8, UTF-16, ISO-10646-UCS-4, ISO-8859-2, Shift-JIS, EUC-JP, and ISO-2022-JP. If XML is transmitted over the Web, the HTTP Content-type header must match the encoding label in the XML declaration. Ian Graham's *HTML 4.0 Sourcebook* (Wiley, 1999) includes a useful summary of the HTTP protocol.

- The standalone declaration is set to "yes" if the XML processor does not need to read an external document type declaration. See the section *The Document Type Declaration* later in the chapter for more information.

NOTE When an XML document is served up over the Web using HTTP, the MIME Content-type header must be the same as the encoding given in the XML declaration in the document. If you're not sending your XML over the Web, you can ignore this. If you're not familiar with how HTTP handles character sets and encodings, refer to Ian Graham's *The HTML 4.0 Sourcebook* or the IETF HTTP documentation. Also note there is an overview of how HTTP works in Chapter 2, "Client/Server Architecture."

Comments

Comments start with <!-- and finish with -->. The optional comments that appear after the XML declaration use the same syntax as in HTML and SGML. You can't nest comments within comments or include -- in a comment. Nor can you start an XML document with a comment followed by an XML declaration, as in the following example:

```
<!--* illegal example: *-->
<?xml version="1.0"?>
```

You can have multiline comments, which I prefer to make distinct with asterisks, as follows:

```
<!--* This comment can easily be seen and
    * recognized as a comment.
    * That's especially important if you comment out markup,
    * <!ELEMENT eve (smile|insight)+>
    * because it's clear that the ELEMENT line is not a declaration.
    *-->
```

The declaration commented out here is explained in the section *Element Declarations* later in the chapter. For now, the important point is to make comments plainly visible.

The Document Type Declaration

The document type declaration is a line that identifies the type of document that follows (it's often called the DOCTYPE declaration because of the keyword it uses). Here is an example:

```
<!DOCTYPE children SYSTEM "http://www.holoweb.net/xml/children.dtd">
```

This says that the root element is called children, and that the definition for this sort of document can be found at the URL given. The keyword SYSTEM is optional, and, if present, must be followed by a valid URL. The URL is read relative to the document that contains it, so that if the XML document were to be stored at www.holoweb.xml/docs/c901.xml, the URL could have been "../xml/children.dtd" instead. Windows and MS-DOS users need to be careful to use the correct slash—/ and not \—here, as elsewhere in XML.

If you don't have an external document type definition (described later), you can use a simpler form:

```
<!DOCTYPE children>
```

But if you do that, you might as well omit the DOCTYPE declaration altogether.

There are several variations on a DOCTYPE declaration, including PUBLIC identifiers and the ability to include declarations. We will explore the second of these variations when we talk about entities, element declarations, and document type definitions. You would include definitions there if you wanted to define entities or if you wanted a self-contained document with no external DTD, but with the benefits of validation checking.

Here is an example of a document type declaration that includes some definitions, contained between square brackets, in what is formally called an *internal document type definition subset*, and informally called the *subset*, or the *DTD subset*:

```
<!DOCTYPE children SYSTEM "http://www.holoweb.net/xml/children.dtd" [
    <!ENTITY David "David Pilgrim">
```

```
<!ENTITY Ganny "Mithrandir">
<!ENTITY poem SYSTEM "http://www.holoweb.net/xml/poems/p12.xml">
]>
```

The declarations in this example are explained in the various sections on Entities later in the chapter.

The document type declaration declares where to find the document type definition. The similarity of the two terms is, however, still confusing.

Elements

The Prolog is followed by a single XML element. This element is called the *root element*, or the *document type element*, and it can contain other elements. The following is an example of an XML document with a Prolog and a single element:

```
<?xml version="1.0" encoding="ASCII"?>
<!DOCTYPE para>
<para>This is a document with only one element in it,
and some text.</para>
```

Elements are the fundamental building blocks of XML. An element can contain any mixture of other elements and text. It can also contain references to *entities*, which are described later in the chapter.

Tags

An element begins with a start tag, contains content, and finishes with an end tag. A start tag looks like this:

```
<para>
```

or like this, if it has attributes:

```
<para weight="3" writer="Liam Quin">
```

An end tag looks like this:

```
</para>
```

If an element has content, it goes between the start and end tags. Content is any mixture of text (as described later) and more elements.

An element with no content can have a special end tag: The following two forms are the equivalent:

```
<para></para>
<para/>
```

Element names are case-sensitive, so that the following fragment is in error:

```
<Para>incorrect</para>
```

NOTE

Elements whose names begin with `"xml"` (in any combination of upper- and lowercase) are reserved for use by XML; you should not define them yourself. You can use any sequence of letters, numbers, and Unicode name characters in a name, as long as it starts with a letter. You can also include underscore (_) and dot (.) characters in names.

The elements in a document build a tree, which is why the topmost element is called the root. Consider the following simple document:

```
<?xml version="1.0" encoding="ASCII"?>
<!DOCTYPE brats>
<brats>
  <brat><name>Simon</name><age>14</age><hair>Fair</hair></brat>
  <brat><name>Luthien</name><age>27</age><hair>Chestnut</hair></brat>
  <brat><name>Ben</name><age>17</age><hair>Fiery red</hair></brat>
</brats>
```

One possible tree for this document is shown in Figure 1.1. The figure does not emphasize that the order of the children elements (the three `brat` elements) is significant, but it does show the hierarchy.

If you come from a relational database world, you will need to keep reminding yourself that sequence and containment are fundamental to XML. Most authors would be upset if their paragraphs were returned in the wrong order! Also notice how one element can contain others. In a relational database, this might seem a little like one field containing an entire table; and although that's not usually a possible implementation, it's exactly the right way to look at it.

Since elements must form a tree, they must nest properly. The following example is illegal in both HTML and XML, but some HTML browsers try to patch it up transparently:

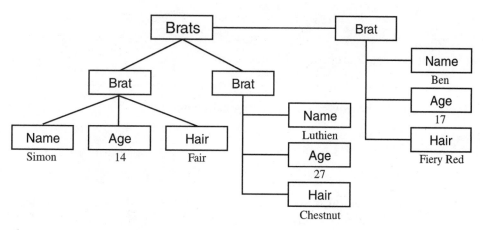

Figure 1.1 Document tree for the brats.

```
<P>David <I>loves <B>Simon</I> but Simon loves Julia</B></p>
```

Here is a possible interpretation, and a well-formed way to mark it up:

```
<P>David <I>loves</I> <B><I>Simon</I> but Simon loves Julia</B></P>
```

The following is another interpretation:

```
<P>David <I>loves</I> <B>Simon</B> but Simon loves <B>Julia</B></P>
```

The ability to catch this sort of error is a very important feature of XML.

Attributes

If elements *contain* text intermixed with other elements, attributes are *properties* of elements. Attributes appear inside start tags, like this:

```
<Student id="m31095" name="Simon Whitehead"
    DOB="19630228" instrument='Double Bass'>
Simon's Content appears here, perhaps <Disposition>Simon is
always a cheerful fellow</Disposition>
</Student>
```

If you are familiar with HTML, note that the quotes are *required* around the attribute values. You can use either double or single quotes around an attribute value, as long as they are both the same: Compare the *name* and *instrument* attributes.

Attributes can contain general entity references (described later in the *General Entities* section), but not elements. As a result, you should not use an attribute to contain structured data that will need to be broken down into components, such as Last Name and First Name. The *name* example just given would be better written like this:

```
<Student id="m31095" BirthDate="19630228">
    <FirstName>Simon</FirstName>
    <LastName>Whitehead</LastName>
    <Instrument>Double Bass</Instrument>
    <Disposition> Simon is always a cheerful fellow</Disposition>
</Student>
```

It is illegal to repeat attributes, as in:

```
<Teacher course="cs101" course="cs109">illegal</Teacher>
```

You can, however, repeat elements in content:

```
<Teacher>
    <teaches course="cs101" />
    <teaches course="cs109" />
</Teacher>
```

This example also shows how you can use attributes in an empty element: course has no content, so it has the slash at the end of its tag, and no end tag.

It is possible to exercise control over what goes inside an attribute (see the section *Document Type Definitions* later in the chapter for examples).

Attributes whose names begin with `"xml"` (in any combination of upper- and lower-case) are reserved for use by XML; you should not define them yourself.

Text Content

Most XML documents contain at least a little text, although any XML element that can have text content can also be empty. The `Student` example has a `first-name` element with text content of `"Simon"`. Wherever you can have text content, you can also have *white space*, *character references*, and *general entity references*.

When an element is declared to have text content in a document type definition (see the section *Document Type Definitions*), the keyword #PCDATA (for Parsed Character Data) is used, so you will sometimes hear the words used interchangeably. *PCDATA* is just a complicated way of saying text content!

White Space

In HTML documents, multiple blanks are generally treated as a single space, and spaces at the start and end of a paragraph or heading are ignored.

The rules governing white space are either very vague or almost impossibly complex, depending on how you look at it. In either case, XML needed to be simple, clear, and precise. The rule is that all white space in the input is passed on to the application reading it. An application is free to treat white space however it likes.

White space is difficult to get right in programs; it looks deceptively simple, but it isn't. You can hint in your document how you want white space to be treated: within any element bearing the attribute `xml:space='preserve'`, white space is to be treated as part of data and not discarded or collapsed. Within such an element, any subelement can in turn put things back how they were just within its own content, with `xml:space="default"`. Of course, an element with *that* could specify `xml:spce="preserve"` (there is no distinction between single and double quotes around the value).

Character References

You can refer to any Unicode character by number, wherever text or markup would be allowed. This is done with a *character reference*, which in decimal looks like `&#423;`, or in hexadecimal, `&#x1A7;`.

Character references are used to insert characters that otherwise would be treated as markup, or that one can't easily enter from a keyboard. Suppose you need to include a fragment of computer program source code in an XML document, such as `"if (a<b) then action(a) endif"`. You need to escape the less-than sign so that the XML parser won't see the `<b` as the start of an element called `"b"` and get confused. One way to do this would be to use `&a&#60;b`,

since the less-than sign is character 60 in ASCII and Unicode. A clearer way to write this is a<b, where < is the less-than entity described in the *General Entities* section, next. This gives us `"if (a&lt;b) then action(a) endif"`, which is now legal XML.

In a similar way, to refer to an e with an acute accent (é), you could use é since that's the number for an e with acute accent. If you're using the X Window system, you can see the Latin 1 (ISO-8859-1) character set in 16 pt Times Roman with this command:

```
$ xfd -fn '-*-times-medium-r-normal—*-160-100-100-p-*-iso8859-1' &
```

Another way is to run the xfontsel program, choose a font with the ISO-8859-1 character set, use the xfontsel Select button, and paste the resulting font name into a terminal window instead of typing it.

An even easier way is to use the é entity, as in HTML, but this entity is not defined in XML by default. In the next section, we'll learn how to define it ourselves.

General Entities

One of the most powerful differences between HTML and XML is the latter's support of "general entities". A *general entity* is a name that is replaced with a string or with the contents of a file. You can think of entities as simple macros.

C programmers are familiar with these concepts:

```
#define DEFAULT_HOST "localhost"
                /* connect here if no other host given */
#include <net/inet.h>
#include "mydefs.h"
```

In Perl, you might write this:

```
my $DEFAULT_HOST = "localhost";
use NET::INET;
use mydefs;
```

A Java programmer would use import and a String constant.

What's so special about this? Traditionally textual markup has been an area where programming and writing come together—the purpose of XML is to make information easier to process by computer. It's an area where scripting languages such as Perl, tcl, and Omnimark flourish. The idea of keeping *processing* separate from *information* is an important one. If you start putting fragments of programs inside your information, you turn it from information that can be used in numerous ways into a program that only does one thing.

So XML has *limited* support for inclusions and definitions, as follows:

- Use a *general entity* to define a replaceable text string.
- Use an *external entity* to include a fragment of XML.

General Text Entities

A general text entity is declared like this:

```
<!ENTITY name "replacement value">
```

Entity declarations go in the document type definition, or they can go in the *document type definition internal subset* in the document type declaration. In other words, you can define your entities in an external file (the DTD) or at the start of the document, in the DOCTYPE subset. We will return to this topic in the following section, *Document Type Definitions*. For now, let's assume you're putting the declarations at the start of your file, as in the document type declaration example discussed earlier.

You can use the entity within the body of your document like this:

```
<p>Anywhere you can have text, you can use &name;</p>
```

This is called an *entity reference*.

WARNING

Entity names are case-sensitive, meaning that Server and server are two entirely unrelated entities.

You can use the entity as many times as you like, but you can't change its value after the end of the DTD. If the same entity is declared twice, the second definition is ignored, as we'll discuss later in *Conditional Sections*.

There are five predeclared entities in XML:

ENTITY	RESULT
amp	&
apos	'
gt	>
lt	<
quot	"

You are not allowed to use the less-than (<) or greater-than (>) signs in entity values, so if you want to do that, you have to "escape" them; that is, you have to use markup that will prevent them from being seen as tags by the XML processor.

```
<!ENTITY Ptag "&lt;P&gt;">
```

Now, in text, &Ptag; will produce <P>.

If you want to include a double quote, either use single quotes around the value, or use " like this:

```
<!ENTITY FirstWay 'here are "quotes"'>
```

```
<!ENTITY SecondWay "here are &quot;quotes&quot;">
```

If you want to include both single and double quotes, you *must* use either entities or character references.

General text entities are most powerful when you combine them with an external DTD, which I will demonstrate later in the chapter.

External Entities

If you have written (or have read) any C or C++ programs, you will have encountered the two forms of file inclusion:

#include <stdio.h>. Includes a standard header file from a systemwide shared location (normally /usr/include on Unix systems).

#include "myfile.h". Includes a header file from the current directory, or by looking for the named file in a search path.

The ANSI C standard gives a set of C header files that you can include on any system.

In XML, there are also two standard forms of file inclusion, using SYSTEM and PUBLIC identifiers; but only the SYSTEM identifier is sufficiently well defined to be useful.

Including a file involves first declaring a named *entity*, and then referencing it where you want to include it.

Here is a declaration for an external entity:

```
<!ENTITY Poem SYSTEM "poem.xml">
```

Figure 1.2 shows the contents of the file `"poem.xml"`, Figure 1.3 shows the file `"arnold,m.xml"`, which gives a brief description of the poet, and Figure 1.4 shows an extract from the works of Matthew Arnold. You can see that the poems are stored in separate files for convenience in editing, and the information about the poet is stored in a single place so it can be included in every poem. Finally, Figure 1.5 shows how one program (SoftQuad Panorama, now sold by Interleaf) displays the resulting document.

Entities and Element Attributes

You can include entity references in attribute values too, like this:

```
<picture src="http://&server;/&imageDir;/sock.jpg" />
```

If the entity `server` is defined to be `"www.holoweb.net"` and `imageDir` is defined as `"xmlbook/images"`, the resulting URL is `"http://www.holoweb.net/xmlbook/images/sock.jpg"`.

NOTE You can only use general text entities in attribute values, not external entity references.

```
<Poem firstPublished="1852">
<Title>Morality</Title>
  <Verse>
    <Line>We cannot kindle when we will</Line>
    <Line>The fire that in the heart resides,</Line>
    <Line>The spirit bloweth and is still,</Line>
    <Line>In mystery our soul abides:</Line>
    <Line indent="2">But tasks in hours of insight will'd</Line>
    <Line>Can be through hours of gloom fulfill'd.</Line>
  </Verse>
  <Verse>
    <Line>With aching hands and bleeding feet</Line>
    <Line>We dig and heap, lay stone on stone;</Line>
    <Line>We bear the burden and the heat</Line>
    <Line>Of the long day, and wish 'twere done.</Line>
    <Line indent="2">  Not till the hours of light return</Line>
    <Line>All we have built do we discern.</Line>
  </Verse>
  . . .
</Poem>
```

Figure 1.2   An external entity: Morality Poem (morality.xml).

```
<Poet>
  <Name>
    <lastName>Arnold</lastName>
    <firstNames>Matthew</firstNames>
  </Name>
  <Dates>
    <born>1822</born>
    <died>1888</died>
  </Dates>
  <description>
    Matthew Arnold was born at
    <place long="51 20" lat="0 30">Laleham</place> in
    Surrey, England, on Christmas day in 1822.
    He went to school at Winchester and Rugby, and
    studied at Balliol College Oxford.
    . . .
  </description>
</Poet>
```

Figure 1.3   The `arnold,m.xml` file.

```
<?xml version="1.0" charset="ISO-8859-1"?>
<!DOCTYPE Writings [
    <!ENTITY MatthewArnold
        SYSTEM "bios/arnold,m.xml"
    >

    <!--* some poems *-->
    <!ENTITY poem001
        SYSTEM "morality.xml"
    >
]>
<Writings>
  <!--* include the description of the poet *-->
  &MatthewArnold;
  <!--* include a poem *-->
  &poem001;
</Writings>
```

Figure 1.4 Extract from the works of Matthew Arnold.

Processing Instructions

You can include processing instructions wherever you can put elements or text content (that is, inside the content of any element, but not inside tags or attributes). The intent is that you use processing instructions for proprietary information that is not part of the document. For example, at least one commercial XML editor (Arbortext Adept) stores the last cursor position as a processing instruction.

NOTE Processing instructions are not used in this book; they are mentioned here so that you can recognize them if you see them, and so that you can understand that the XML declaration at the start of a document is not, in fact, a processing instruction.

The syntax of a processing instruction is:

```
<?target data ?>
```

The target is the name of a notation declared in the DTD (see the following section).

The data cannot contain less-than or greater-than signs, and the XML parser does not expand entity references within it, so that <?myprog start-

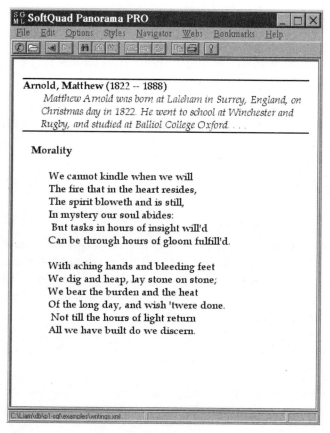

Figure 1.5 Resulting XML document.

`mode=46  display="&lt;bold&gt;"?>` is legal, but the application will have to expand `&lt;` and `&gt;` without any help from the XML parser.

WARNING

A processing instruction uses the same syntax as the XML declaration described earlier; don't confuse them!

Document Type Definitions

You can think of XML as being a markup language definition language. Where in HTML there is a fixed set of elements, in XML, you can define your own sets of elements. XML (like SGML) also provides a way to check that a document conforms to a set of rules. You can say that a `Person` element must contain a `lastName` element, and perhaps some `firstName` or `initials` elements, but nothing else. You can also: define which attributes are allowed for particular elements; comment about their contents; and define where Text Content is allowed.

Unfortunately, there are some things every database designer needs to do that XML does *not* permit. You can't, for example, say that a `firstName` can be no more than 35 characters long, or that textual content of an element cannot be empty. If you need to impose such limitations, you have to use an *XML Schema*, but since these are not yet defined (at the time of writing), you can go to www.w3.org/XML/ for more information.

NOTE This chapter doesn't describe all of the features of document type definitions. It does, however, describe those most often used, and the ones used in the examples in this book. Also, be aware that I have used the terms Declaration and Definition interchangeably in this book, *except* for Document Type Definition and Document Type Declaration, which are two very different things.

How a DTD Is Found

A DTD is a plain text file (it can be in Unicode) that contains declarations. A DTD can be empty, but that's not particularly useful. It makes life simpler to generate a DTD by program.

There are two kinds of DTD in XML: an *internal subset* and an *external* DTD. The only difference between them is in the way parameter entities are treated, as we'll discuss later in the chapter. The internal subset is found between the square brackets in the document type declaration, as shown earlier in the Children example. The external subset is mentioned at the start of the document type declaration (usually with the SYSTEM keyword) but is read at the end of it.

Suppose your XML document is called `http://www.leftfoot.org/docs/sock.xml` and that it uses a DTD called `http://www.leftfoot.org/dtds/hosiery.dtd`. A suitable DOCTYPE declaration at the start of `sock.xml` would be as follows:

```
<!DOCTYPE sock SYSTEM "../hosiery.dtd">
```

This works because the SYSTEM keyword is followed by a URL, and that URL is interpreted relative to the file containing it, in this case `sock.xml`.

If there were an entity declaration for sockColor in the DTD, we could override it like this:

```
<!DOCTYPE sock SYSTEM "../hosiery.dtd" [
    <!ENTITY sockColor "black">
]>
```

This works because:

- The internal subset (the part between the square brackets) is read *before* the external subset (hosiery.dtd).

- The first entity declaration that is seen "wins"; an entity cannot be redefined, so subsequent entity definitions for sockColor are ignored.

We revisit this example in the following section, *Parameter Entities*.

NOTE
More complex SGML systems sometimes use PUBLIC identifiers and something called an SGML OPEN Catalog, a file that maps public identifier strings into filenames. This is not part of XML.

Comments and Spaces

You can put a comment in a DTD wherever you can put a declaration. You cannot, however, put a comment *inside* a declaration.

The comment syntax in a DTD is the same as within the body of the document:

```
<!-- the contents of the comment go here -->
```

Although the comment starts with <!-- and ends with -->, you cannot include -- in a comment.

Comments can be as long as you like, but they do not nest. If you need to comment out a chunk of a DTD for some reason, use a *Conditional Section*, described later in this chapter. Here are two examples of long comments, to show the benefit of laying them out clearly, much as one might in a C program:

```
<!ELEMENT example              (z*)>
<!--
<!ELEMENT example (z+)>
The "example" element is used to contain zebras. -->
<!ATTLIST example color CDATA #required>        <--
The color attribute lets us have a blue zebra, but
what if the zebra is striped? -->
```

and

```
<!ELEMENT example              (z*)>
<!--*
```

```
    *   <!ELEMENT example (z+)>
    * The "example" element is used to contain zebras.
    *-->
<!ATTLIST example color CDATA #required>
<!--* The color attribute lets us have a blue zebra, but
    * what if the zebra is striped?
    *-->
```

In the second example, it's pretty clear that the second ELEMENT line is commented out. When you are maintaining a large DTD, this quickly becomes important. You can also see that the ATTLIST is *not* commented out, which is difficult to see at a glance in the first version.

Anywhere you can put a space in a DTD, you can put multiple spaces. Blank lines are legal, so you can use white space to group your declarations. Since a new line is a white space character, you can use indentation too.

Declaring Elements

XML does not require that you declare elements, but if you do, the XML processor can check that they are used properly. If you declare *all* of your elements, the XML processor can go one step further and check that the entire document is *valid* according to the rules you have given. This means that the document contains no undeclared elements, that all elements declared as being required are indeed in the right place, and that all attributes have legal values. If you read the XML Specification, you'll see that there are *Validity Constraints* throughout, and a valid document meets all of those formal requirements.

There are usually two parts to an element declaration: One part declares its name and what it can contain, using a *content model*; the other part specifies what attributes the element has. If there are no attributes, the attribute list declaration is not needed.

Element Content Models

You declare an element and its content model like this:

```
<!ELEMENT sock
    (foot)
  >
```

This declaration says that a sock element must contain a foot. It cannot contain any other sorts of elements, and it does not have text content. We'll see how to include text content in a moment.

Of course, this doesn't take empty socks into account, an unforgivable omission.

```
<!ELEMENT sock
    (foot?)
  >
```

Now we have marked the foot as optional. As you've probably guessed, the text between the parentheses is a *pattern*, or *regular expression*. When the XML processor validates a document, it does so by reading each element in the input in turn, and checking that the contents of that element match the pattern specified in the element declaration. This pattern is formally called the element's *content model*.

A content model can contain sequences with a comma (,) and choices with a vertical bar (|, pronounced *or*). You can also group parts of a content model with parentheses. Here are some examples:

```
<!ELEMENT Table
    (title, Head, Body, Foot?)
  >
<!ELEMENT Head
    (Title | Image | (ColumnDefinitions, Rows))
  >
```

We have already seen the question mark operator, which makes the value to its left optional. In the preceding example, a `Table` element in a document will match the content model for `Table` if it contains a `title` followed by a `Head`, followed by a `Body` element; a single `Foot` element may appear at the end or not, because of the question mark.

The other operators are the asterisk and plus sign (* and +). The asterisk means that the value to its left can appear any number of times, including not at all. The plus sign means that the value to its left must appear at least once, but can appear more times. There is no convenient notation to say that something must appear between 5 and 9 times.

The following examples illustrate some different content models:

```
<!--* simple model for Psalms, *-->
<!ELEMENT Psalm
    (Verse*)
  >
<!--* This example is not taken from any EDI standard,
    * since I wanted something simple
    *-->
<!ELEMENT FinancialTransaction
    (Buyer, Seller, (Item, Amount, Tax*)+, TotalAmount, TotalTax, Total)
  >


<!--* A Journey is a sequence of segments each using a
    * different mode of transport:
    *-->
```

Regular Expressions

If you are not familiar with regular expressions, or if you think the name itself sounds complicated, it's time to take another look. Relational databases are very weak when it comes to string manipulation, particularly when compared to the strong heritage of text-processing tools that grew up around the Unix operating system.

A regular expression is simply a pattern. For example, a regular expression that matches "ba!" "baa!" "baaaa!" and so on, might be written as `ba+!`. The plus sign (+) means that the pattern matches one ore more of whatever is before it: an "a" in this case.

Often, a few minutes of careful thought constructing a search and replace in an editor (even Microsoft Word has regular expressions!) can save hours of painstaking handwork. In a program, regular expressions can increase the flexibility and robustness of your code as well as saving a lot of code complexity.

Here are some more examples.

`^b`	Matches a string starting with "b"; the caret (^) *anchors* the pattern to the start of the string it's trying to match.
`t$`	Matches a string ending in "t." The dollar sign ($) anchors the pattern to the end of the string it's trying to match.
`^pattern$`	This pattern is anchored at both ends, so it only matches the word itself—pattern! It's not a very useful example, but when you use a more complicated pattern between the ^ and $, it's invaluable.
`b[aeiou]y`	A character class in square brackets matches any of the characters listed in it; this example matches bay, bey, biy, boy, or buy.
`[^aeiouy][aeiouy][^aeiouy]`	The ^ at the start of a character class indicates to match anything except the characters listed inside the brackets. This example matches a three-letter word that starts and ends with a consonant and contains a single vowel: boy, tub, cot, dig, lip, and so forth.
`[a-d][a-m][a-m]`	A hyphen (-) inside a character class represents a range, so that `[a-d]` is the same as `[abcd]`; this is just convenient shorthand.

This example matches bag but not bay, because y comes after m, the end of the range allowed for the third character.

ba*   The asterisk (*) means zero or more of whatever was immediately before it, so this example matches b (with no "a" at all), ba, baa, and even baaaaaaaaaaaaa.

ba+   The plus sign (+) means one or more. Not all tools support +, because you can always make ba+ by writing baa* instead. This example matches ba, baa, baaa, and so on, but not just b.

ba?   The question mark (?) means optional; this example matches "b" and "ba".

A *substitution* replaces whatever was matched by a regular expression with something else. For example, to change every *grey* or *gray* to *yellow,* we could use the *sed* or *vi* syntax:

```
s/gr[ae]y/yellow/
```

where s means to substitute.

This command, in *vi*, *sed,* or *perl*, might change:

```
The grays of the dawn were like a green grayhound
```

into

```
The yellows of the dawn were like a green grayhound
```

Notice that the second match on the line wasn't changed.

Let's try again:

```
s/gr[ae]y/yellow/g
The yellows of the dawn were like a green yellowhound
```

You will also see some examples that use parentheses, either for grouping or in a substitution. These (unfortunately) work differently in different programs; see the documentation for the specific program.

In the Unix *sed, vi, grep,* and *perl* commands, the idiom \(...\) is used to bring something into the replacement part of a substitution:

```
s/\(barefoot\) \([^ ]*\)/\2: \1/
```

turns

```
barefoot jim
booted Susan
barefoot Martin and Eve
```

into

```
jim: barefoot
booted Susan
Martin and Eve: barefoot
```

```
<!ELEMENT Journey
    (Car | Plane | Bus | Ship | Rickshaw | Motorcycle | Bike | Feet)+
>
```

Declaring Text Content

Most XML documents contain text content somewhere, so we need to know where it's allowed. You declare text content by putting the keyword #PCDATA at the start of the content model in which text is allowed:

```
<!ELEMENT Paragraph (#PCDATA|Emphasis)* >
<!ELEMENT Emphasis (#PCDATA)>
```

The #PCDATA keyword must be the first thing in the content model, and the content model must be a "repeatable or-group"; that is, it must either be a list of elements separated by a vertical bar (|), with an asterisk at the end, or be just #PCDATA by itself.

```
<Paragraph>The Paragraph above can contain <Emphasis>any number</Empha-
sis> of Emphasis elements interspersed with
any amount of text, <Emphasis>even no text at all</Emphasis>,
in which case it might be empty.</Paragraph>.
<Paragraph></Paragraph>
<Paragraph><Emphasis></Emphasis></Paragraph>
```

NOTE The #PCDATA keyword matches zero or more characters of text content. There is no way to use an XML DTD to say that an element must have text in it, only that it is *allowed* to have text in it.

The following are some legal and illegal examples:

```
<!--* illegal: #PCDATA not at the start: *-->
<!ELEMENT Para (Emphais|Misery|#PCDATA)*>
<!--* illegal: no * at the end *-->
<!ELEMENT BadBoy (#PCDATA|OtherStuff)>
<!--* illegal: wrong sort of connector *-->
<!ELEMENT Chapter (#PCDATA, Para)*
<!--* legal *-->
<!ELEMENT BadBoy (#PCDATA|Shout|GetDirty|Trick|Play|Eat|Sleep)*>
<!--* legal: special case *-->
<!ELEMENT Title (#PCDATA)*>
<--* legal: even more special case *-->
<!ELEMENT Text (#PCDATA)>
```

Attributes and Attribute-List Declarations

An attribute is simply a name-value pair, such as gender="male" or paidRent="no". Just as the content model of an element says what can appear inside that element, the *attribute-list declaration* says what attributes an element can have.

NOTE

XML gives you slightly more control over attributes than over elements. The XML Schema working group is trying to change that for the future, but for now, this is what we have. The latest draft for XML Schema can be found at www.w3.org/XML/; follow the links, as the exact location was not fixed when this book was written.

An attribute-list declaration is a list of attribute declarations, each of which declares a single attribute. You use this declaration to say which attributes a given element has, and to place some fairly basic limits on their values. Here is an example:

```
<!ATTLIST Publication
    Type (book|magazine|journal|essay|other) "book"
    Date CDATA #IMPLIED
    ID ID #REQUIRED
    Publisher IDREF #IMPLIED
>
```

This says that a Publication element can take up to four attributes.

The following is an example you might find in the main body of a document:

```
<Publication
    Type="journal"
    Date="19990901"
    ID="mt99vol01issue2"
    Publisher="p9103"
>stuff</Publication>
```

An attribute can be marked in the following ways:

- #REQUIRED, meaning that it must always be given:

      ID ID #REQUIRED

- #IMPLIED, meaning that you can leave it off:

      Date NMTOKEN #IMPLIED

- #FIXED, meaning it always has the same value (we will revisit this in the *Namespaces* and *Architectures* sections later):

      Version CDATA #FIXED "1.3"

- A string, meaning that if you omit the attribute, it is as if you gave it that value. Be aware that default attribute values won't work if you use an XML processor that doesn't read the DTD, since it won't recognize the defaults:

      Type (book|magazine|journal|essay|other) "book"
      Country CDATA "Botswana"

The attribute types are as follows:

CDATA. Contains *character data*; that is, text content with no elements inside it. This attribute type contains a mix of text and general entities only.

NMTOKEN. Must contain a string that would be valid as an element name.

ID. A name (like an NMTOKEN); but all ID attributes within a document must be unique, even if they occur on entirely different types of elements.

IDREF. A name that appears anywhere else in the document as an ID; some software, such as Interleaf's Panorama browser, automatically creates a link between an element with an IDREF and the element with the corresponding value in an ID-valued attribute. By convention, attributes of type ID and IDREF are normally called ID and IDREF, respectively.

ENTITY. Must take as its value the name of a general entity. This type is not used in this book.

Tokens. A list of possible name values, such as (boy|girl|child|petunia). If a default value is given, it must be one of the tokens in this list!

Note that NMTOKEN, IDREF and ENTITY can be pluralized to NMTOKENS, IDREFS and ENTITIES, in which case, the corresponding value is a space-separated list of values. There is no good reason why this list uses spaces, while other lists use commas or vertical bars—you just have to remember it.

You can have more than one attribute list for the same element. As long as you don't declare two different attributes with the same name, the result is to define all of the attributes:

```
<!ATTLIST Student
    StudentID ID #REQUIRED
>
<!ATTLIST Student
    EyeColor CDATA #IMPLIED
>
<!--* now a Student has both a Student ID and an Eye Color. *-->
```

Parameter Entities

A *Parameter Entity* is just like a general entity except that it occurs in the DTD. You can have a general entity, a parameter entity, an element, and any number of attributes with the same name: They are all different.

You declare a parameter entity just like a general entity, but add the percent (%) sign:

```
<!ENTITY % pubTypes "(book|magazine|journal|essay|other)">
<!ENTITY % moreStuff SYSTEM "morestuff.dtd">
<!ENTITY % isPubl 'IGNORE'>
```

WARNING

The space between the percent sign and the entity name is very important. If you forget it, you will get strange and unexpected error messages.

There is a restriction on how you can use parameter entities in the Internal Subset. For the purpose of this book, we'll say that you can only use external parameter entities and conditional sections in the internal subset (although you can define either sort of entity).

As with general entities, if the same entity is defined twice, the second definition is ignored.

Parameter Entities for String Reuse

One common use for parameter entities is to provide a layer of abstraction; that is, to be able to write element content models and attribute definitions using terms that reflect the problem rather than the implementation. This makes DTDs much easier to understand and maintain.

Here is a simple example that defines Block-Level elements (such as paragraphs and tables) in one place, and the Running Text that goes inside them in another:

```
<!ENTITY % Blocks "P|Table|Illustration|Poem|Address|BlockQuote">
<!ENTITY % RunningText "#PCDATA|Emphasis|CrossReference">
<!--* now use the entities
    * (this example is not complete; see the Exercises)
    *-->
<!ELEMENT Book
    (Title, Chapter+)
>

<!ELEMENT Chapter
    (Title, (%Blocks;)+)
>

<!ELEMENT P
    (%RunningText;)*
>

<!ELEMENT Emphasis
    (%RunningText;)*
>
```

Notice that it is clear that the `Emphasis` element contains regular running text, and consider how easy it would be to add a new inline element such as `Foot-NoteReference` or `InlineImage` to this DTD fragment.

NOTE

You cannot use parameter entities in this way in the Internal Subset, only in an external file.

Including a File with a Parameter Entity

You include a parameter entity by expanding it inline, much as with a general entity, but using a percent sign instead of an ampersand (&) to mark it as special:

```
<!ENTITY % myDefines "dtds/myDefines.dtd">
%myDefines;
```

As with an external general entity, the SYSTEM identifier in a parameter entity definition is a URL, and is treated as relative to the document containing it. Figure 1.6 shows a possible directory structure for storing some XML documents.

The file `"argyle.xml"` would start with a document type declaration like this:

```
<!DOCTYPE socks SYSTEM "../dtds/socks.dtd">
```

to include the `"socks.dtd"` file. The DTD itself might include a master file that defines general text entities, naming each of the files in the `"dealers"` directory. The DTD includes that master file, `"defs.ent"`, like this:

```
<!ENTITY % master SYSTEM "dealers/defs.ent">
%master;
```

Notice that the system identifier is `"dealers/defs.ent"` and not `"../dealers/ defs.ent"`, because it occurs inside `"socks.dtd"`; that's how to get from `"socks.dtd"` to `"defs.ent"`. If you are familiar with MS-DOS, Microsoft Windows, or other nonopen-source operating systems, notice also that the directory separator is the forward slash (/), not the backslash (reverse solidus) character (\). This forward slash is always used to separate components of a URL.

Now that we know how to include files with parameter entities, it's time to revisit Matthew Arnold. A third way to include the DTD is shown in Figure 1.7. Note that this way gives you complete control over the order in which the various components are read.

You might be wondering why anyone would use a SYSTEM identifier on the DOCTYPE line. There are two main reasons. The first is for the benefit of non-XML tools that might know how to ignore a simple DOCTYPE line, but get confused by more complex markup. The second reason is that some people believe that the system identifier in some way identifies the document as a whole. Neither of these seems satisfactory to the author. If you are serving XML documents up over the Web, the few bytes you save might be considered useful, perhaps, but the best reason is simply its convenience.

Overriding Content Models Using Parameter Entities

Recall that if a parameter entity is defined more than once, all but the first definition are ignored. Suppose the file "table.xml" contains the following snippet:

```
<!ENTITY % ThingsInCells "(#PCDATA)*">
<!ELEMENT TableCell
    %ThingsInCells;
>
```

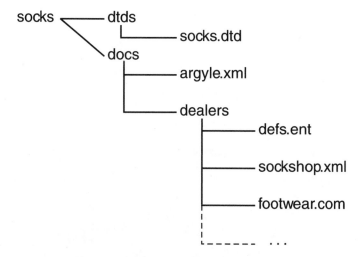

Figure 1.6 Directory structure for parameter entity inclusion example.

Now suppose we have a DTD (or internal subset) like this:

```
<!ENTITY % ThingsInCells "(#PCDATA|Squiggle)*">
<!ENTITY % TableFragment SYSTEM "table.xml">
%TableFragment;
```

Because `ThingsInCells` was defined in the DTD to be `"(#PCDATA|Squiggle)"`, and because that definition was encountered *before* the definition in "table.xml", the content model of the `TableCell` element will allow `Squiggle` elements intermixed with textual content.

Conditional Sections

A conditional section is a part of a DTD that is included only if a keyword is set to `"INCLUDE"`:

```
<![IGNORE[
<!--* All declarations are ignored inside
    * an IGNORED conditional section like this one
    *-->
    <!ELEMENT unused (not|ever|seen)*>
    <![INCLUDE[
    <!--* including this part here!
       * This is ignored too
       *-->
    ]]>
<!--* up to (and including) the closing delimiter: *-->
]]>
```

```
<?xml version="1.0" charset="ISO-8859-1"?>
<!DOCTYPE Writings [
    <!--* include the DTD: *-->
    <!ENTITY % theDTD
        SYSTEM "http://www.holoweb.net/xmlbk2/dtds/poems.dtd"
    >
    %theDTD;
    <!--* define external entities for the poems *-->
    <!ENTITY % Poems
        SYSTEM
"http://www.holoweb.net/xmlbk2/poems/arnold/poems.xml"
    >
    %Poems;
]>
<Writings>
    <!--* copy the rest from Figure 4 here *-->
</Writings>
```

Figure 1.7   Poems with parameter entities.

NOTE

Conditional sections nest. There is no way to escape the closing]] > string.

Conditional sections are most useful when they are combined with parameter entities. Suppose you have a fragment of a DTD that you include in several other DTDs. It looks like this:

```
<!ENTITY % UseBibliography "INCLUDE">
<![%UseBibliography;[
    <!ELEMENT Bibliography (BibEntry)*>
    . . .
]]>
```

If you define the parameter entity UseBibliography to be "IGNORE" *before* you include that DTD fragment, then the Bibliography element won't be defined. This is a bit like #ifdef in C, as mentioned, except that there is no #else, and you can't combine conditions in an elegant way.

If you find yourself wanting more complex conditional processing, consider writing a preprocessor to build DTD fragments on the fly, or use an XML Schema.

Additional XML Features

The additional features described here are not used directly in this book; they are mentioned for completeness.

Notations

Notations let you define a non-XML entity, such as a JPEG or PNG image, or an MP3 file. In a client-server environment, and in particular on the World Wide Web, you should use HTTP MIME Content Types to identify image formats, not notations. Notations are not used in this book.

Namespaces

Namespaces enable you to associate groups of XML elements with external authorities. For example, you might say that you are using bibliographical elements defined by the Library of Congress, even though the Library of Congress is entirely external to your organization. Each authority is a unique string (it's supposed to be a URL, but no one has defined what resource might be found at that location). The idea is that you associate a *Prefix* with a URL. Here is an example:

```
<Bibliography xmlns:bib="http://www.holoweb.net/xml/namespaces/bib1.3/">
    <bib:entry>
        <bib:a>Quin, Liam</bib:a>
        <bib:a>Graham, Ian. S.</bib:a>
        <bib:t>The XML Specification Guide</bib:t>
    </bib:entry>
</Bibliography>
```

It is possible to specify a default namespace, so that, for example, all a elements within a `Bibliography` would by default be for Author, and not the HTML Anchor element, even if the rest of the document used the HTML Namespace.

This is pretty powerful, and later specifications such as XSL (see the next section) use it heavily. Although XML 1.0 does not include Namespaces, they are already used frequently. The specification is at www.w3.org under XML.

Style Sheets

At the time of writing, there are two main ways to turn an XML document into a user-friendly format: *Cascading Style Sheets*, and the *XML Style Language* (XSL).

This book isn't about style sheets, however. If you want to know more about them, go to www.w3.org or see Chapter 23, "Further Reading," for further pointers. Style sheets are supported by most SGML, XML, and even HTML browsers.

Exercises

1. Type in one of the poetry examples and get it to work with Mozilla (www.mozilla.org) or Internet Explorer 5 or later.

2. Write a DTD fragment to represent tables, and test it.

3. Extend your sample table DTD to handle spanned rows and columns, table headings and footers. Make the content model of a cell a parameter entity as shown.

4. Read about other XML DTDs on the Web, such as the Text Encoding Initiative's DTD for representing academic texts, or an e-commerce DTD. The best way to learn about XML is to do it!

Summary

This chapter introduced XML. The next chapter moves on to address Client/Server programming and application architectures. Once we have that framework in place, we'll talk a little about databases and SQL. If you are already familiar with Client/Server programming, and understand how HTTP and the World Wide Web operate, you may choose to scan Chapter 2 and advance to Chapter 3.

2

Client/Server Architecture

The first half of this chapter uses code examples to illustrate the main concepts of Client/Server networking, and discusses some of the implementation and programming issues involved. The second half of the chapter describes the World Wide Web architecture, and points out the differences between traditional Client/Server networking and Web-based systems. If you have worked with databases or other networked systems before, but have not implemented a Web-based system, you will find the discussion particularly useful.

There are several kinds of Client/Server architectures in use, and it's important to understand the differences among them. Even if you are already familiar with Client/Server concepts, at least skim this section to make sure that this book uses the terms in the way you expect. Later, we will be using the information presented here, along with related concepts, and there are important differences between Web-based database systems and local area network systems, for example, that need to be considered.

Client/Server Systems

The first Client/Server systems had a single computer running a *server*; that is, providing some kind of service to other computers. The *client* computers used the service over a network, either local or wide area. An example of such a service might be a hospital patient record system or an airline booking system. Figure 2.1 shows this architecture.

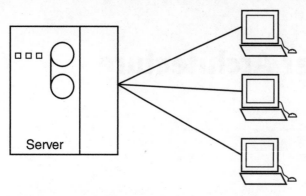

Figure 2.1 Computers as servers.

Later, particularly as multitasking systems such as Unix became more wide-spread, the idea evolved, and the terms *client* and *server* were used not just to refer to entire computers, but also to individual processes running on those computers. Today, a typical Unix system runs anywhere from a dozen to several thousand server processes at the same time. Figure 2.2 shows this slightly more sophisticated architecture. Notice how a client can run on the same computer as the server or on a different one.

Networks and Protocols

A *protocol* addresses the question of how the client and server communicate with each other. When the client and server are not on the same computer, some kind of network connection is needed, such as a serial cable or an Ether-

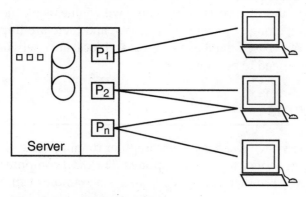

Figure 2.2 Processes as servers.

net link. This book isn't about networking hardware; it's important to point out that there is a physical connection that carries the communication language between the client and the server.

A simple example of a protocol might be:

```
client connects to server
server says HELLO
client says GET mail.txt
server says SENDING mail.txt size: 3091 bytes
followed by 3091 bytes of data
client says OK
client says GET some-other-file
and so on.
```

Protocols and APIs

The earliest protocols were all devised on a purely ad hoc basis. The programmers who wrote the server software would define a set of commands, sometimes in binary and sometimes in ASCII (or EBCDIC or BAUDOT). Any programmer working on client software would have to learn the protocol, often with little or no documentation.

Sometimes the server programmer would provide an object library for developers of clients to use. This library would define an *application programmer's interface* (API), a documented set of procedure calls, such as startConnection, getFile, listFiles, stopTransfer. These procedures would then handle the task of sending the proper protocol sequence over the connection.

Protocol Layers

The computing world advanced, slowly, and learned the concept of *layers*. The idea of a layer is that one API can be written entirely in terms of other APIs. The benefit is that programmers only have to change the lowest-level API if the underlying protocol changes (perhaps because of a new kind of network hardware).

With *dynamic linking* (for example, on Unix System V or SunOS in the mid-1980s, or on Microsoft Windows much later) the client programs might not even need to be changed at all—they automatically find the latest version of the library at runtime. This means that if, for example, I need to write a network protocol to allow clients to connect to my inventory system, I can provide an API with calls such as HowManyDoWeHave(partNumber). The code might use a lower-level API to send requests to the server such as QUANTITY. Of course, the lower-level API is itself sending data, such as 14 bytes follow, but when I write my API I don't need to think about that at all; my API still works if that lower-level protocol is changed completely.

We will be building on the idea of a layered protocol later in the book.

API Example

Let's look at an example of how to write a layered networking API. First we'll use a proprietary protocol; later we'll see how XML concepts affect our design.

We'll use the C programming language for this short (and incomplete) example, because it has traditionally been the language of choice for low-level APIs. Our example API lets a programmer write a client that connects to an inventory control system that keeps track of stock levels in a warehouse or department store. Our client will be a *second-class citizen*, meaning with read-only access; a full API would allow a client to change the database on the server.

Let's start by considering the operations that our client program might need to perform. We will need to start a connection to the server and to end it again. We will need to ask how many items there are for a given part. We might also want to search for a part number by entering its description.

When the client wants to connect to the server, our library has to be told the name of the server. For this example, we'll assume that the server name is sufficient to establish a connection, although if we were using a dial-up connection we might also need a telephone number.

The convention with a C API is to use a prefix in front of function names; we'll use SIP, for the Simple Inventory Protocol. Let's start by declaring these functions now.

NOTE
Strictly speaking, most C functions are actually *subroutines*, because they can have side effects, but the usual C terminology is to call them *functions*.

```
SIPstatus SIPconnect(const char *serverName, SIPhandle *result);
```

This declaration specifies a function called SIPconnect; the function is called with two parameters, serverName and result. The function returns a value, which is of type SIPstatus. This value will be a number either with 0, signaling success, or other numbers, indicating the error that occurred to prevent success. The function is only *declared* here; the code that *implements* the function will appear elsewhere.

After connecting, at some point, the client will need to disconnect:

```
SIPstatus SIPdisconnect(SIPhandle session);
```

Once the client is connected, it will want to ask how many socks are available in our warehouse:

```
SIPstatus SIPquantityAvailable(SIPpartNo partNo, int *result);
```

Notice that SIPquantityAvailable returns a success code; the actual value we are interested in is written into the integer whose machine address is passed as the last parameter, *result*. This is so all of the SIP functions can return a status in a form that's easy for the programmer to remember. A network programmer has to be aware that the network connection could be lost at any time (for example, the user unplugged the modem, or a remote server was struck by lightning). Returning a status code explicitly helps to remind programmers that the value they requested might not have been available, and hence to write more robust code.

A special type was defined to represent a part number, SIPpartNo. Although this isn't strictly necessary, it shows how to use the typing mechanisms in the C programming language to get a slightly more robust API. The type definition helps in two main ways:

- If a programmer tries to call SIPquantityAvailable with an integer instead of the correct type, most C compilers will generate a warning or error at compile time. The programmer is saved debugging time, and our library won't crash.

- We can change the way we represent a part number without changing our API. For example, we can start out using strings to hold part numbers, and later use pointers to complex structures, The user of the SIP API only has to recompile his or her code that calls our functions.

Of course, we need to supply the programmer with a way of obtaining a SIPpartNo object:

```
SIPpartNo SIPstringToPartNo(const char *theString);
```

Or, if we want to be fancy:

```
SIPstatus SIPgetPartNo(const char *theString, SIPpartNo *result);
```

This second form would let SIPgetPartNo connect to the server to perform the transformation, although it's hard to justify wanting to do that, so we'll go with the simpler form!

Finally, it would be useful for the programmer to be able to print out human-readable error messages based on our error codes:

```
const char *SIPgetStatusDescription(SIPstatus status);
```

We will put all of these function prototypes in a C header file, sip.h, along with definitions for the C types we have mentioned:

```
typedef enum {
    SIP_OK,
        /* OK: no error */

    SIP_ERR_HandleIsClosed,
        /* e.g. someone tried to use a connection handle after
         * they had called SIPcloseConnection on that handle
         */

    SIP_ERR_BadHandle,
        /* e.g. passing a null pointer instead of a handle.
         * Passing garbage as a handle will be more likely to
         * produce a core dump or a crash, but NULL is a pretty
         * common error and worth catching.
         */

    SIP_ERROR_NoReplyFromServer,
        /* The client library got bored waiting for the
         * server to respond. Perhaps networking is down?
         * Right now, there is no way to configure the timeout
         * without recompiling the source; it defaults to five
         * minutes.
         */
    SIP_ERROR_BadPartNumber,
        /* A null pointer, an empty string, or a value not
         * obtained by stringToPartNo was passed to a SIP
         * function.
         */

    SIP_ERROR_InsufficientMemory,
        /* There was not enough memory available to complete
         * the request. You might also get this error if you
         * replace the system malloc() function with one of your
         * own that has an incompatible calling convention.
         */

    SIP_ERROR_BadResultPointer,
        /* A NULL pointer for a result value was passed to a SIP
         * function; it is not generally possible to detect other
         * sorts of bad pointers, except that an unexpected area
         * of memory will be overwritten by the SIP function.
         */

    SIP_ERROR_OtherError
        /* An error occurred that was not categorized as one of
         * the above errrors.
         */
} SIPstatus;
```

An experienced network programmer will see at once that this protocol is *synchronous*; that is, these function calls will block until they get a reply from the server. This design is not suitable for use with a graphical user interface—while the program is waiting for a reply from the server, it is ignoring the user's mouse-clicks. We will address this issue later in the chapter, with the server example using `select()`.

The functions all use a single shared connection, so they cannot handle connections to multiple servers, except one at a time. This also makes the design difficult to use in a multithreaded environment, since one thread could try to open a new connection while another was still using the current one. We can fix this easily by adding an extra argument to the functions, the connection handle; and we'll do that in our implementation. The implementation may still not be thread-safe, but at least it *could* be made so with the improved design.

When a program calls one of these functions, a message will be sent to a server. The message is simply a string (a stream of bytes), since that is the nature of all network messages. It is tempting to say that the message should be in XML, but for an example this small, it would be easier to use plain text. We'll start with plain text and move to XML later.

For our purposes here, we'll implement just one function (the complete code is available from this book's companion Web site at www.wiley.com/comp-books/quin).

```c
#define SIP_PROTOCOL_GET_QTTY 'n'

SIPstatus
SIPquantityAvailable(
    SIPhandle h, /* handle to our network connection */
    SIPpartNo partNo, /* the part number */
    int *result /* number available stored here */
)
{
    /* First, check that the server handle we have been passed is
     * at least plausible:
     */
    SIPstatus status = SIP__handleIsOK(h);
    if (status != SIP_OK) {
        return status; /* fail, probably bad handle */
    }

    /* now check that the result pointer isn't NULL: */
    if (result == (int *) NULL) {
        return SIP_ERROR_BadResultPointer;
    }

    /* If the result pointer is OK, let's set the result to zero
     * before doing anything more. This may help an API programmer
     * to debug an error, since if the result pointer is invalid,
     * the program will crash (dump core on Unix) at this line,
```

```
        * not in the lower-level API that we are about to call.
        */
       *result = 0; /* default: none available */

      /* Check that the part number supplied is plausible;
       * although we didn't tell the programmer using our API,
       * the part number is really a pointer to a string right now.
       * We will simply check the pointer isn't NULL and that the
       * string pointed to is at least one character long:
       */
      if (!partNo || !*(char *)partNo) {
          return SIP_ERROR_BadPartNumber;
      }

      /* Ask the remote server to tell us how many are available;
       * one possible error here is that the server has
       * disconnected us.
       */
      status = SIP__Send(h,
          SIP_PROTOCOL_GET_QTTY, strlen(partNo), partNo
      );
      if (status != SIP_OK) {
          return status;
      }

      /* Now we sit and wait for the server to send a reply, and
       * when it does, pass that reply straight back to the caller.
       * SIP__Send and SIP__Await are internal functions, not visible
       * to the API programmer. If the server doesn't reply in a
       * reasonable time, or sends back an error code, SIP__Await
       * will return an error, which we simply pass back.
       */
      return SIP__Await(h, SIP_PROTOCOL_INTEGER, result);
  }
```

This example function, like most C code, consists of lots of error-checking, followed by a call to a couple of lower-level functions that actually do the work. These functions, in turn, will almost certainly start by checking their arguments before calling system-provided routines such as *sendto* or *read*. All this error-checking is very important: It's especially difficult to debug network code, because you have to determine whether the error is on our system, on the remote one, or somewhere in between. Worse, many network problems are time-dependent, and are thus hard to reproduce. The more carefully the library code checks for errors, the better chance the library has of catching a mistake that a programmer made, and the more robust the library will appear to be as a result.

The lowest-level functions have a double underscore in their names, since, unlike Java or C++, the C programming language does not have classes with private members. A C function can be declared static, but it cannot then be shared between the separate source files that implement a library. Our compromise is to use obscure names.

The code for SIP__Send probably looks a little like this:

```
SIP_Status
SIP__Send(SIPhandle h,
    int type,
    size_t nBytes,
    const char *data
)
{
    char *buf = malloc(nBytes + 4);
    if (!buf) return SIP_ERR_INSUFFICIENT_Memory;

    /* build up a string to send: */
    (void) snprintf(buf, nBytes + 4, "%uc%c%s\n",
        nBytes, type, data
    );

    /* send the string over the socket */
    if (sendto(SIP__FD(h), buf, nBytes + 4) == nBytes + 4) {
        return SIP_OK;
    } else {
        /* not shown: check the result of write() and return an
         * error if approriate.
         */
    }
}
```

This code sends a single byte containing the number of bytes in the data, followed by the byte indicating the kind of message, followed by the data (the part number in this case, which is represented as a string). The code that waits for a reply tries to read a single byte, and uses that to determine how many bytes of data will follow, reading exactly that many bytes.

The protocol is very simple, but the binary-length count byte means that you can't easily use the server with telnet; most modern protocols use plain text so that they can be debugged more easily.

The single byte-length count means that we can only cope with messages no longer than 255 bytes; and using a single byte as the command, we can have at most 256 different messages. That's more than enough for this example, but it could be extended fairly easily, by using the character x to indicate an extended format message type, followed by the real message type. Then the protocol would start to get more complex than this example warrants!

The implementation shown here has the very unfortunate property that a call to any of the SIP functions could block awaiting data from a remote server. If the server is down, or if it crashes while we're connected to it, some networking libraries can wait several *hours* before recovering. A better implementation would use the *poll* or *select* functions to read data only when it was available, and use asynchronous callbacks to supply results back to the caller when they were available. The server code works asynchronously; it is described in the next section.

If you download the complete sample SIP client and server, you can compile them and run them like this on Linux, Solaris 2, FreeBSD, or other Unix-style systems:

```
$ gzip -d < sipsample.tgz | tar xvf -
(this will extract files into a new sipsample directory)
$ cd sipsample
$ make
```

You will see the program being compiled here. If you see errors at this stage, or if the next step fails with a message such as `sipclient: no such file or directory`, or `cannot execute`, consult the readme file for possible solutions.

You can now start the server, and then run the client:

```
$ ./sipserver &
SIP Server waiting on localhost port 5103
$ ./sipclient "Argyle socks"
sipclient: connected to server localhost on port 5103
sipclient: requested quantity for part "Argyle socks"
sipclient: received reply from server: SIP_OK
sipclient: quantity available: 4,005
sipclient: closing connection to server
$
```

The server is still running, and you can connect to it again. The server occasionally reduces the quantity of socks available, as if they are being shipped out of the warehouse, so a different number may be reported the second time.

When you get bored of this exercise, here's how to stop the server:

```
$ ./sipstop
sipstop: connected to server localhost on port 5103
sipstop: requested server shutdown
sipstop: received reply from server: SIP_OK
```

If you are paranoid, you can test that the server stopped:

```
$ ./sipclient "Argyle socks"
sipclient: could not connect to server localhost on port 5103
sipclient: error: connection refused (no server running?)
$
```

In the next section we'll see how the World Wide Web architecture addresses some of these issues and differs from the traditional Client/Server model described here.

Asynchronous Networking

This section describes *asynchronous networking*, and discusses the main programming issues involved in implementing and using it.

The SIP example client in the previous section is synchronous: The code is always in control, and the control flow is fixed. The client sends a request to the server, then waits for a reply. But suppose we want to implement a message that the server could send to all connected clients, perhaps to say that a new part was available. The clients would not be expecting to receive this message and would not be listening to the network connection. When they sent a message to the server and looked for a reply to it, they'd find an unexpected message instead of the one they were waiting for.

Another problem with the synchronous design is that the program can do only one thing at a time, and cannot respond to mouse clicks, for example. While it is waiting for input, control flow is *blocked*: the program is said to be locked waiting for input. An *asynchronous* network client handles messages from the server whenever they arrive, even if the client wasn't expecting a message. To do this, the client must avoid blocking while it is waiting for input. Since an asynchronous client never blocks waiting for input, it can also respond to user events quickly, such as a mouse click or a screen refresh. To do this, our sample program will use two main techniques: an *event model* and *callback functions*.

Event Models

The idea behind the event model is that a single piece of code—usually hidden in system-supplied library functions—reads and interprets user actions such as mouse-clicks and keyboard presses, along with window system actions such as resizing a window or bringing up a menu. That code then presents all of these things to the programmer as a stream of generated objects called *events*. The programmer then has to learn only about a single type of structure (the event) and how to handle it.

An event-driven program might contain a routine that looks like this:

```
while (e = getNextEvent()) {
    switch (e) {
    case Ev_UserPressedQuitButton:
        handleQuit();
        break;
    case Ev_KeyPress:
        if (e->getkey() == KEY_F1) {
            handleHelpKey();
        }
    . . .
```

```
    }
}
```

In this example, the code normally sits waiting in the getNextEvent() call. When an event happens, the switch statement then handles the event appropriately and returns to listen for the next event. Since this is the only way the program responds to the Quit button, it's important that handleHelpKey(), for example, returns quickly. It might bring up a dialog box, for example, and return. The user's interactions with that dialog box would be reported as events in the loop shown here.

From this discussion, it should be no surprise that a program with a graphical user interface could use the same event mechanism to handle network I/O. It could in principle use the same mechanism to read XML, although in practice it's unusual to have a window event loop that also reads XML. It *is* common to read XML using that same user interface event loop to detect when XML data becomes available on a network connection (a socket) and to pass that data to an XML parser or other handling routine. That parser would in turn be quite likely to use an event model of its own. XML events might include ElementStarted, ElementEnded, Comment, ProcessingInstruction, and many others. We will return to this topic in Chapter 4, "Generating XML from Relational Data."

Callbacks and Hooks

A *callback* is a function or piece of code that is given by a programmer's code to a library or system routine. Later, the library calls the programmer's function. Most windowing systems make heavy use of callbacks, and networking programs also often use this model.

A *hook* is a function that a programmer can override by redefining it. This technique is more rarely used, because it gives the library designer less control.

With a callback-based API, the event loop sequence is replaced entirely; instead, the programmer registers a handler function for each event. The handler is a callback:

```
main()
{
    initialize();
    . . .
    RegisterHandle(Ev_UserPressedQuitButton, handleQuit);
    RegisterHandle(Ev_KeyPress, handleKeyPress);
    . . . .
    runTheMainEventLoop();
    cleanup();
    exit(0);
}
```

The handler for the keypress, HandleKeyPress, might look like this:

```
int
HandleKeyPress(
    Event ev
)
{
    if (ev->getjey() == KEY_F1) {
        handleHelpKey();
    }
}
```

This function isn't actually called anywhere in the programmer's code! Instead, we pass the name of the function (or, strictly speaking, its address) to the `RegisterHandler` function, which stores it in a table. Whenever the code in `runTheMainEventLoop` generates a keypress event, it looks in its table and calls the appropriate function. The library's event handler calls our routine back for us, hence the name *callback*.

Asynchronous Networking Example

Our synchronous example was the SIP client. Clearly, we don't want a server to be synchronous, because probably it has to listen to multiple clients at the same time. Now we'll discuss an example for an asynchronous server.

Our server will handle network events, but not window system events. Integrating the code into a windowing library is usually very easy, but it is a little different on the X Window system than under Microsoft Windows or the Macintosh. Furthermore, our server has no need for a user interface.

The server needs to handle incoming connections, and then process requests on each connection. We will use the BSD Networking API, with its `select( )` function, mostly because it's simpler to describe than the most common alternative, *poll*.

The code will tell `select( )` which network connections (sockets) to monitor, and how long to wait. The call to select will then block waiting for input on one or more socket, or until the timeout happens. If `select()` tells us that input is available on the main server socket, it means that a new connection has arrived.

If you have access to Linux or Unix, try looking at the manual page for *select* in Section 2 or 3 of the Unix Programmer's Manual:

```
$ man 2 select
```

Or, on Solaris 2, you may need to do:

```
$ man -s 3n select
```

The pseudocode for our server might look like this:

```
handleIncomingConnection(c)
{
    socket newConnection = accept(c);
    arrange to listen for incoming data on newConnection
}


server
{
    for (;;) {
        int nReady = select(incoming, outgoing, errors, timeout);

        if (nRead == 0) {
            /* handle a timeout here */
            . . .
            continue; /* loop again */
        }

        /* check for an incoming connection */
        if (FD_ISSET(incoming, mainSocket)) {
            nReady-; /* it was counted in the total */
            handleIncomingConnection();
        }

        /* now loop through each file descriptor,
         * processing incoming messages where they are
         * available
         */
        for (i = 0; nReady > 0; i++) {
            if (FD_ISSET(incoming, i)) {
                -nReady;
                processRequest(i);
            }
        }
    }
}
```

Here is a brief fragment of a working (but fairly minimal) World Wide Web server written in Perl. The full server is called webserver.pl, which you can download from this book's companion Web site at www.wiley.com/compbooks/quin.

The complete Web server supports directory listings and the Common Gateway Interface (CGI), but has no access control, no user directories, and minimal logging. There is a status page (/status) and a reload page (/reload) that restarts the server. The code is written using select() directly so that you can see how it works, probably in conjunction with the manual page for select() on your computer, along with the Perl documentation (run the perldoc perlfunc command). A shorter and easier-to-read example in Perl would use the IO::Socket package, but that would hide the very details this example is intended to illustrate. Tom Christiansen and Nathan Torkington's excellent book *Perl Cookbook* (O'Reilly, 1998) has more on this topic especially for Perl.

The fragment here prints out the request you give it; the complete example is on the book's Web site. This short example is sufficient to demonstrate what's going on:

```perl
use Socket;
use Fcntl;
use English;
use FileHandle;

my $NewNameID = 0;
sub getNewName
{
    ++$NewNameID;
    return "nn$NewNameID";
}


sub addPort
{
    # This code adds the given port to $rbits, which is a binary
    # string with the nth bit set if we want to listen to
    # file descriptor n. It also saves the bit mask in $fdMap,
    # to simplify processing later.
    my ($port, $func, $argument) = @_;
    my $fd = fileno($port);
    vec($rbits, $fd, 1) = 1;

    # now build the reverse map:
    my $tmp = "";
    vec($tmp, $fd, 1) = 1;
    $fdMap{$tmp} = $port;
    $funcMap{$tmp} = $func;

    # Finally, make a place to store network input:
    $bufferPlace{$tmp} = "";
    return $tmp; # in case the caller wants it, return it
}


sub printLine
{
    # a routine for testing
    my ($text, $arg, $fh) = @_;
    print "    **** $arg: [$text]\n";
    return 1; # 1 means OK, undef means disconnect
}


sub server
{
```

```perl
    my ($ServerBit) = @_;
    my $timeout = 300; # time in seconds to wait

    $errbits = ($rbits | $wbits);

    for (;;) {
        my $nfound;
        my $pattern;
        my ($rout, $wout, $eout);

        # the following call to select() will block until
        # (1) input is available, or
        # (2) the timeout happens, or
        # (3) a socket that was blocked for writing becomes free, or
        # (4) an error occurs.
        $nfound = select(
            $rout=$rbits,
            $wout=$wbits,
            $eout=$errbits,
            $timeout
        );

        if ($nfound == 0) {
            print STDERR "timeout after $timeout seconds\n";
            next;
        }

        my $buffer;

        for $pattern (keys(%fdMap)) {
            if ($pattern eq $ServerBit) {
                # Either an incoming connection is there,
                # or in some versions of perl, there seems
                # to be a bug, whereby this bit gets set when
                # there is nothing to read.
                if (($pattern & $wout) ne "") {
                    print STDERR "eek: the wout case happened\n";
                } else {
                    # either there is a connection,
                    # or the call to listen will not block
                    acceptConnection($fdMap{$pattern});
                }
            } elsif (($pattern & $rout) ne "") {
                # There is data available for reading.
                # Since the network can split up data en route,
                # we might not have a complete message yet,
                # so we save up what we've got in $bufferPlace
                # until we have a complete line.
                my $nRead;
                $nRead = sysread($fdMap{$pattern}, $buffer, 4096);
                if (!defined($nRead)) {
```

```perl
        # print STDERR "nothing to read\n";
        next;
    }
    if ($nRead == 0) {
        print STDERR "eof on port\n";
        close($fdMap{$pattern});
        delete $fdMap{$pattern};
        $rbits &= ~$pattern;
        $errbits &= ~$pattern;
        $wout  &= ~$pattern;
    } else {
        # convert DOS-style CR LF to a single line feed:
        $buffer =~ s/\r\n/\n/gmsx;
        $buffer =~ s/\r/\n/gmxs;

        # Append what we have just read to the
        # data we've already read, that's waiting
        # for us to receive a complete line
        $bufferPlace{$pattern} .= $buffer;

        # process any complete lines received,
        # one line at a time:
        while ($bufferPlace{$pattern} =~
                        /^([^\n]*)\n(.*)$/){
            my $str = $1;
            $bufferPlace{$pattern} = $2;
            # note: using $1 and $2 is much more
            # efficient than using $`

            # Fetch the callback function associated
            # with this network connection:
            my $func = $funcMap{$pattern};

            # call the function:
            if (! &$func(
                $str,
                $arguments{$pattern},
                $fdMap{$pattern}
            ) ) {
                # If the function returns false (undef),
                # we close the socket...
                close($fdMap{$pattern});

                # ... and stop listening on it:
                delete $fdMap{$pattern};
                $rbits &= ~$pattern;
                $errbits &= ~$pattern;
                $wout  &= ~$pattern;

                # ... and stop looking at the data we read
                last;
```

```
                    }
                }
            }
        }
    }
}
}

# This short subroutine is just for testing:
sub test
{
    addPort(\*STDIN, \&printLine, "STDIN");
    server();
}

# When an incoming connection is received, we accept
# it here and arrange to read incoming data:
sub acceptConnection
{
    my ($Server) = @_;
    my $paddr;

    my $Client = getNewName();

    $paddr = accept($Client, $Server);
    if (!defined($paddr)) {

        return;
    }
    my ($port, $iaddr) = sockaddr_in($paddr);
    my $name = gethostbyaddr($iaddr, AF_INET);
    if (!defined($name)) {
        $name = inet_nota($iaddr);
    }

    print STDERR "connection from $name [" .
            inet_ntoa($iaddr) . "] port $port\n";

    # set the socket to nonblocking so that sysread() in the
    # server routine will return whatever data has already
    # arrived, instead of blocking until
    # the amount we request becomes available:
    fcntl($Client, F_SETFL, O_NONBLOCK()) or die "fcntl failed, $!";

    # turn off perl's output buffering (this is
    # often written as $| = 1; if the "English" package was
    # not used):
    autoflush $Client 1;

    # get ready to listen for incoming data
    my $clientNumber = $#clients + 1;
```

```
        addPort($Client, \&ircCommand, $clientNumber);
    }

    # now try it:
    test();
```

If you run this rather long example, it will simply sit and wait for you to type lines, then print them. You may find it does not work on non-Unix-like operating systems that treat input devices such as keyboards radically differently from network connections. There is no real reason for such bugs: `select()` and `read()` should work with every kind of file, but some operating systems are broken.

Note that this example omits some declarations to save space. The version for download is complete; there is also another more complex example that is rather more interesting to experiment with. All the versions, however, work in the same way: They collect incoming network data, and then, whenever they receive a complete line, they process it. If you try the longer example, the World Wide Web HTTP server, you can test it using the telnet program, or with any standard Web browser, connecting to your local computer on port 5103.

NOTE

Although the Web server example is complete and functional, it is *not* intended for production use on an Internet site. It is slow, possibly insecure, and may not fully conform to the HTTP specification. I have used it on an internal Solaris 2 system for several months without problems, however.

The main difference here from the synchronous networking is that the code is no longer organized around a clear control flow. Instead of "when the user does this, do these actions," we have a list of actions to be taken when each individual event occurs.

World Wide Web Architecture

In this section, we use the concepts introduced so far in this chapter to discuss the architecture of the World Wide Web. The previous two sections showed a "traditional" Client/Server architecture, in which one or more clients stay connected to a server for an entire session, performing multiple transactions.

The World Wide Web uses a very different, and much simpler, architecture. A *Web client* (a browser like Netscape Communicator, for example) connects to a *Web server* and makes a single request. The server responds, either refusing or satisfying the request, and then disconnects the client.

The protocol used is the HyperText Transfer Protocol (HTTP). Since HTTP uses ASCII (or ISO 8859-1/Latin 1), you can connect to a Web server with a program such as telnet and try it yourself. Web servers usually listen on IP port number 80, which you'll need to specify. Then type the following HTTP request followed by a blank line (press Return or Enter twice). The blank line ends the HTTP request:

```
$ telnet www.holoweb.net 80
GET / HTTP/1.1
Accept: */*
Host: localhost
        (then press RETURN twice to make a blank line)
```

You should see a reply like this:

```
HTTP/1.1 200 OK
Date: Sat, 09 Sep 1999 22:52:15 GMT
Server: Apache/1.3.6 (Unix)  (Red Hat/Linux)
Last-Modified: Wed, 07 Apr 1999 21:17:54 GMT
Content-Length: 177
Content-Type: text/html

<HTML>
 <HEAD>
    <TITLE>This is my home page</TITLE>
 </HEAD>
<BODY>
 <H1>this is my jolly little home page</H1>
 <P>You can read this if you like.</P>
 </BODY></HTML>
```

The code 200 following HTTP indicates that the request was successful, and that the reply follows. As soon as the reply data has all been sent, the server closes the connection, and that's the end of the transaction. In this mode, there is no possibility of continuing to interact with the server. If you want to get a second file, such as an image, you must make a separate HTTP connection. HTTP 1.1 supports a *keepalive* mechanism, whereby a single connection can be used for multiple requests, but this is not widely used.

The sequence is as follows:

1. Client connects to Web server.
2. Client issues HTTP request (usually GET or POST).
3. Client issues HTTP headers (at least Accept, and usually others).
4. Server issues response.
5. Server sends data.
6. Server disconnects.

The data is normally sent with carriage return and line feed (CR LF) at the end of each line, and the Content-Length header in the reply reflects this.

MIME Types

The HTTP response example just given included the following line to indicate that the result was a file in the HTML format:

```
Content-Type: text/html
```

The *Multipurpose Internet Mail Extension* specification (MIME) specifies how these work. The registry of MIME content types includes text/html, text/xml, text/plain, image/jpeg, and many others. In the Macintosh environment, each file is marked with the signature of the application that created it. On the Microsoft Windows system, file types are determined by looking up the last few characters (after a dot) of the filename in the Windows Registry. On Unix systems, generally either the first few bytes are examined or the file suffix is used.

On the Internet, when you are fetching a remote document, it's important that the person who maintains the file can change its format. As a result, World Wide Web clients determine the format of data not by the filename (to which they usually don't have access) but by the Content-Type header. The client then looks up the content type in a table to see how to process the data. You can see such a table by looking in Netscape's Applications preference box, or by looking for a `mime.types` file on a Unix system.

By working through this, it should be clear that a Web client can be either synchronous or asynchronous, depending on its other needs. A Web server will always be asynchronous, in order to deal with multiple incoming connections. The Perl example in the previous section could be extended to make a Web server, and this is a useful exercise. There are many easy-to-use Web server modules available for download from the Comprehensive Perl Archive Network, CPAN (www.cpan.org) and elsewhere (see the Resources section at the end of the book for more information). The architecture shown in the Perl example is the most efficient for a single-processor Unix system handling many small requests. For other architectures, see Chapter 23, "Further Reading."

If you are working in a multithreaded environment such as Java, or have multiple processors, you may prefer to use a separate thread to handle each connection. This simplifies the programming, although if you only have one processor, the overhead of switching threads will generally make the result less efficient. For most applications, efficiency is unlikely to be a major issue.

URLs and Gateways

It seems safe to assume that most people have seen a Uniform Resource Locator by now. In case you haven't (!), here is an example:

```
http://www.valinor.sorcery.net:81/search/glossary?term=irl
```

This URL contains five parts:

- The name of protocol (http)
- The server to which to connect (www.valinor.sorcery.net)
- The network port to which to connect (81)
- The path to fetch (/search/glossary)
- An argument (term=irl)

In fact, /search is a program, so that there is no /search/glossary file on the server. Instead, the Web server passes /glossary as a parameter to the search program, along with the argument term=irl. The search program is acting as a gateway to a database, and the Web server uses the CGI to communicate with the search program.

NOTE

You may sometimes hear the term CGI scripts, implying that CGI is a programming language. In fact, although most CGI programs seem to be Unix shell or Perl scripts, a CGI program can be written in any language, including a complete C++ database client.

For more on CGI, see Chapter 23, "Further Reading," particularly *HTML 4.0 Sourcebook* by Ian Graham (Wiley, 1999).

From the point of view of the XML database programmer, the important thing to know is that you have the flexibility to write a standalone program that can be called by a Web server or by a dæmon that stays running and works like a simplified Web server itself, responding to requests, or even a module loaded into an existing Web server.

Web 401 Authentication

A World Wide Web client will usually make a new connection to the Web server for each separate object to be fetched. This is very simple, but it means that there is no good way to track a user's session. Most databases use this model: first log in, do a number of operations, then log out. Clearly, this is incompatible, since logging in would be one Web transaction, and then you'd be disconnected again!

To support some kind of login, the Web supports a response called 401 Authentication. The client connects and requests a URL as normal, but the server replies with 401 instead of the normal 201 (OK). The client disconnects from the Web server, prompts the user for a password, and, if the user gives one, tries again, this time supplying the password (lightly encrypted). If the password is correct, the Web server responds with 201 as if nothing had happened. Each time the client requests a URL with the same prefix as the first in which the password was requested, it sends the password to the server.

For example, suppose www.valinor.sorcery.net/admin/index.html is password-protected. An attempt to fetch this URL results in a 401 Authentication Required reply. If the client supplies a valid username and password, however, the fetch succeeds. If the client then attempts to fetch www.valinor.sorcery.net/admin/opertalk/, it will see that this URL begins with the same www.valinor .sorcery.net/admin/ prefix and automatically supply the username and password, to save time. The username and password combination, however, is not retained between browser sessions.

Web Cookies

A *cookie* is a piece of data stored locally by a Web client. The idea is that a Web server can send a small piece of data (up to 4000 bytes in most implementations) to the client, which will store it. The next time the client connects to that URL, or to that prefix (as in 401 Authentication), the client sends the cookie back to the server along with the HTTP request.

People running Web sites can use cookies to keep track of user preferences, or to manage login sessions that span long periods. Unfortunately, perhaps because of misunderstood or misdirected media coverage in the early 1980s, many people believe that cookies are an invasion of privacy and so disable them, or even purchase software that automatically deletes them. As a result, cookies should not generally be used on the Web, although they are fine in a corporate intranet where one might be able to control the clients and setting that people can use.

Exercises

1. Download and compile the SIP client and server program. Modify the client to remain connected, asking about the part number supplied once every five seconds.

2. Add a SIP_SHIP message to the low-level protocol that tells the server to deduct a given number of items of the specified part number. You may find it helpful to stop the server from changing quantities in stock itself! Make a SIPship client program that uses this, and experiment with running multiple copies of the SIPclient at the same time sipship runs. This exercise should help you get a solid idea of exactly what's going on inside the client and server protocols.

3. Make an asynchronous version of the client. A good way to test it would be to make a graphical user interface and make sure that the program

responds while waiting for a reply. Add a 10-second delay in the server to test this.

4. Investigate another Client/Server protocol, such as Internet Relay Chat (IRC) or the File Transfer Protocol (FTP); you'll find references for these in Chapter 23, "Further Reading." You might also want to download the irc++ example code and try it.

5. Read the IETF specification for HTTP used by Web browsers. Write a Perl script that connects to a Web server and downloads an HTML document to a file.

6. Write a simple Web server in a language of your choice. Support GET to fetch files from a specific directory, then add either CGI or Java servlet support. Using your server, can users access files they shouldn't? How would you test the performance and security of the server?

Summary

This chapter was intended as a quick overview of how Client/Server systems work, including some working examples in C and Perl that you can use for experiments. The World Wide Web uses a model in which the client does not stay connected, but connects separately for each request using the HyperText Transfer Protocol, HTTP.

The next chapter introduces Structured Query Language, SQL. If you are already familiar with SQL, you might want to skim it for the XML perspective.

Just Enough SQL

I f you have not used the Structured Query Language (SQL) before, or are not familiar with relational databases, you may find this chapter helpful. The first half is an introduction to SQL and relational databases; the second half is a worked example (BookWeb). If you already understand Third Normal Form, SELECT and JOIN, you can skip the first half this chapter. But note that Book-Web is mentioned in other chapters, so you will probably find it useful to give it at least a quick glance.

Introduction to Relational Databases

Relational databases store *tables* of data. Here is a typical example, used perhaps by a schoolteacher who has difficulty in identifying his or her pupils:

PUPIL	NAME	HEIGHT (CM)	HAIR	EYES	AGE	GENDER	MARK
1	Andrew	96	Brown	Brown	12	M	45
2	Julia	112	Blonde	Green	11	F	61
3	Simon	120	Fair	Blue	12	M	81
4	Joy	?	Green	?	11	F	0
5	Alan	110	Black	Brown	11	M	79
6	Dawn	106	Red	Green	12	F	94

Neither Joy's height nor her eye color are listed yet, perhaps because she only joined the class yesterday.

The main characteristics of this table are:

- It has lots of small pieces of information.

- The information in the cells is *atomic*—a single number, for example, not both a height and a weight. You should not have a value such as "height 5′8″, weight 120; instead maintain two separate columns in the table, one for each value.

- Every row of the table is more or less complete: Every column heading applies to everyone in the table, and very few entries are missing.

This is the kind of data traditionally associated with a relational database. In some ways, you can think of a database as a sort of glorified spreadsheet.

Object Properties

Another way to look at the information in this table is as a descriptor of a number of schoolchildren: A child has an age, a hair color, and a test score. From this viewpoint, we could draw a diagram, as shown in Figure 3.1.

This notation is used in a standard database entity relationship diagram to show an *entity*. (Note: XML uses the term entity to mean something different entirely, so this book refers to a database entity as an *object*, but you'll see them called entities if you read anything about databases or SQL.)

The heading, Pupil, names the object; the remaining fields give attributes. It is common to see more detail in entity relationship diagrams, as in Figure 3.2. The problem here is that, in implementing this object as a relational database table, I have used a numerical ID to identify each pupil. This lets me refer to

Figure 3.1   The Pupil object.

```
┌─────────────────────────┐
│ Pupil                   │
├─────────────────────────┤
│ Name CHAR(12)           │
│ Height INT              │
│ Hair CHAR(12)           │
│ Eyes CHAR(12)           │
│ Age INT                 │
│ Gender BYTE             │
│ Mark INT                │
└─────────────────────────┘
```

Figure 3.2   The Pupil object, with attribute details.

the pupils reliably. Some methodologies include the ID in the diagram, and some don't. I have omitted it, but I now have nowhere to put the name and type of the attribute. For this reason, it's more often shown.

A more notable problem is that this notation muddles up the *implementation*. For example, I am using a single byte to store Gender with the *design*, and I want to capture that information. For this reason, it's often better to stick to the simpler form of the diagram, with more detailed information kept separately. An entity relationship diagram for a large business application often includes hundreds of separate entity types, and spans dozens of sheets of paper. Keeping the individual boxes as simple as possible helps to make the diagram readable.

Relationships among Objects

The primary raison d'être of a relational database is to help people manage the relationships among different sorts of information, not simply to store data.

Databases describe relationships in two ways: the kind of relationship, and its *cardinality*. Let's draw a slightly more complex example, so we can talk about some of the objects and relationships found in it. Figure 3.3 shows an entity relationship diagram for a database that represents books.

Types of Relationships

A book has a title; the title is an *attribute* of the book. A book also has a publisher, but we have modeled a publisher as a separate object. The relationship between a book and a publisher is *published*; that is, the publisher *published* the book. We will return to this concept of relationship types, or roles, in Part Four, "Links and Metadata."

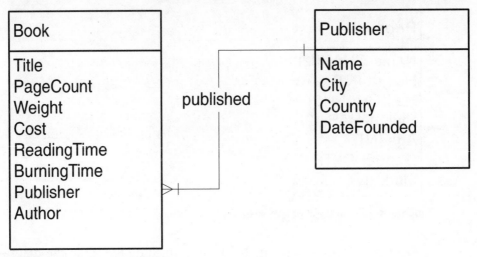

Figure 3.3 Books and publishers.

Cardinality

The *cardinality* of a relationship is the number of entities that are related to each other. There are three possible cardinalities:

- One-to-one
- One-to-many
- Many-to-many

In our model, a book has exactly one publisher (although a single *edition* of a book can have one or more publishers). One publisher, though, might publish more than one book, and almost certainly does in order to stay in business! The relationship is one publisher publishes many books, and is thus a *one-to-many relationship*. The "crow's foot" on the line connecting the two boxes shows this relationship.

The relationship between a book and its title is *one-to-one*. A one-to-one relationship is the only one that can be represented as either an attribute or a separate table. A one-to-one relationship between two separate objects is drawn as a straight line with no "feet" at the ends.

The relationship between authors and books is *many-to-many*, because a book might have multiple authors, and an author might write multiple books. This relationship is drawn with a crow's foot at each end of the line. This relationship must be represented as a separate database table. An example of such a table, `Wrote_tbl`, is in the BookWeb database at the end of this chapter.

Cardinality affects the layout of a database, so it's important to get it right.

The Structured Query Language

The Structured Query Language, universally referred to by its acronym, SQL, is a language for interacting with a database. It is pronounced either as three separate letters or as "sequel." SQL traces its origins to IBM in the late 1970s and early 1980s, but the main version in use today is the one defined by the International Organization for Standardization (ISO). ISO SQL is commonly called SQL/92, although there have been revisions since 1992.

You can use SQL in a number of ways. For the most part, the examples in this chapter use a standalone SQL interpreter called mysql. This is a program for Unix (including Linux) that reads SQL commands, or *statements*, as you type them, and sends them to the MySQL database.

In the next chapter we'll discuss SQL embedded in Perl, C, or Java programs.

NOTE
If you have installed MySQL, and need help with it, check out the tutorial included in the manual. Look in /usr/doc/MySQL-3.22.25 **(or whichever version you have installed) for manual.html. There are also numerous SQL tutorials available on the Web, as well as useful books.**

Creating a Database

We'll start by creating a database to work with. It will be empty at first, of course. (Although this chapter is written for MySQL, almost everything *except* creating a database uses standard SQL. If you're not using MySQL, you may need to create the database by connecting as the database administrator. The default administrator name for MySQL is *root*, although this has nothing to do with the root user on Unix or Linux.)

NOTE
In this and other examples, the dollar sign ($) is my Unix shell prompt, and text shown in boldface indicates what I typed. Most SQL statements can be entered in either upper- or lowercase.

```
$ mysql -h localhost -p -u root
Enter password: enter your password here
Welcome to the MySQL monitor. Commands end with ; or \g.
Your MySQL connection id is 2 to server version: 3.22.25
Type 'help' for help.
mysql> create database books;
Query OK, 1 row affected (0.00 sec)
mysql> quit
$
```

You can also use the *mysqladmin* command to create a database:

```
$ mysqladmin -u root -p create boys
Enter password:
Database "boys" created.
$
```

This is especially convenient if you must be the database administrator to *create* a database, but a regular user to work with it.

Deleting a Database

If you make a mistake and create a database with the wrong name, or if you've finished working with a database, you can delete it. Deleting a database removes all the tables and associated data. *There is no undelete command*, so you must be very careful before doing this.

```
$ mysqladmin -u root -p drop boys
Enter password:
Dropping the database is potentially a very bad thing to do.
Any data stored in the database will be destroyed.
Do you really want to drop the 'boys' database [y/n]
y
Database "boys" dropped
$
```

It's also possible to delete a table with the SQL command "drop database books," but this will delete the database without warning, so it's best not to get into the habit of using it!

The following sidebar shows the output of `mysqladmin -?` to give you an idea of its features.

SQL Data Types

A database contains one or more tables, and these tables contain the data. When you create a table, give it a clear name that's easy to remember. Though it's tempting to sketch on a piece of paper, number the boxes, and create tables like t1, t2, t3, you'll hate yourself later for doing this when you're trying to debug errors in your SQL queries.

When you create a table, you assign a table name and a list of column names and *types*. Every field—that is, every entry in the column—must be of the correct type. You can't put a person's name into a column that's defined as an Integer, for example. Table 3.1 summarizes the most common types you can use.

Modifiers

There are a number of *modifiers* you can use to change the meaning of the basic data types. Modifiers are added to the line in the CREATE statement;

MySQL Administration

The `mysqladmin` command has the following options:

```
$ mysqladmin -?
mysqladmin  Ver 7.11 Distrib 3.22.25, for pc-linux-gnu on i686
TCX Datakonsult AB, by Monty
This software comes with NO WARRANTY: see the file PUBLIC for details.
Administer program for the mysqld demon.
Usage: mysqladmin [OPTIONS] command command....
  -#, —debug=...        Output debug log. Often this is 'd:t:o,filename'.
  -f, —force            Don't ask for confirmation on drop table. Continue.
                        even if we get an error.
  -?, —help             Display this help and exit.
  -C, —compress         Use compression in server/client protocol.
  -h, —host=#           Connect to host.
  -p, —password[=...]   Password to use when connecting to server.
                        If password is not given it's asked from the tty.
  -P —port=...          Port number to use for connection.
  -i, —sleep=sec        Execute commands again and again with a sleep
                        between.
  -s, —silent           Silently exit if one can't connect to server.
  -S, —socket=...       Socket file to use for connection.
  -t, —timeout=...      Timeout for connection.
  -u, —user=#           User for login if not current user.
  -V, —version          Output version information and exit.
  -w, —wait[=retries]   Wait and retry if connection is down.
Where command is a one or more of (commands may be shortened):
  create databasename   Create a new database.
  drop databasename     Delete a database and all its tables.
  extended-status       Gives an extended status message from the server.
  flush-hosts           Flush all cached hosts.
  flush-logs            Flush all logs.
  flush-status          Clear status variables.
  flush-tables          Flush all tables.
  flush-privileges      Reload grant tables (same as reload).
  kill id,id,...        Kill mysql threads.
  password new-password Change old password to new-password.
  ping                  Check if mysqld is.
  processlist           Show list of active threads in server.
  reload                Reload grant tables.
  refresh               Flush all tables and close and open logfiles.
  shutdown              Take server down.
  status                Gives a short status message from the server.
  variables             Prints variables available.
  version               Get version info from server.
```

Table 3.1   SQL Data Types

TYPE	DESCRIPTION	EXAMPLE	SAMPLE VALUES
INT, INTEGER	A whole number	FridgeCount INT(2)	01, 02, 36
FLOAT	A floating-point number; you can specify length and the number of decimal places, as in the example.	`FLOAT Height(4,3)`	0.6, 9999.99
YEAR	A year between 1901 and 2155.	RenewalDue YEAR	1936
CHAR(len)	A fixed-length string of text; values are padded with spaces, or truncated as necessary.	`City CHAR(14)`	"Lower Lemingto", "London "
VARCHAR(len), VARBINARY(len)	A case-insensitive text string or binary data; values can vary in length up to *len* bytes, which cannot be more than 255.	City VARCHAR(120)	"Lower Lemington", "London"
TEXT, BLOB	A text or binary field (respectively) that can be up to 65,536 bytes long. Although this data type is widely supported, it's not very useful.	(varies by database vendor)	(any data)
LONGTEXT, LONGBLOB	A text or binary field that can be up to 4 Gbytes in size. There may be a slight overhead in size for each of these (for MySQL, a LONGTEXT field uses 4 bytes to store the length, in addition to the data).	Chapter LONGTEXT (1000000000)	(e.g., the text of this chapter)
ENUM	One of an enumeration, or an integer, or possibly NULL.	`Gender ENUM("male", "female", "trans")`	1, "male"

in the following example, the words NOT NULL and PRIMARY KEY are modifiers:

```
CREATE CREATE TABLE Author_tbl (
    Pupil_id INT NOT NULL PRIMARY KEY,
    Name VARCHAR(35) NOT NULL
    Height INT
);
```

The most important modifiers are listed here:

NOT NULL. A value must always be supplied for this item. For example, in:

```
PlaceOfBirth VARCHAR(255)
```

a row could omit `PlaceOfBirth`; MySQL will show this as \N. If instead you use:

```
PlaceOfBirth VARCHAR(255) NOT NULL
```

every row must provide a value for `PlaceOfBirth`.

DEFAULT something. If no value is given for this column when you insert a row, the default value *something* will be used.

UNIQUE. The value for this field must be different in each row. You should probably combine this with NOT NULL for portability, because some databases allow NULL values, others might say you can't have more than one NULL field in a UNIQUE column, and still others don't allow UNIQUE values to be NULL at all.

NOT NULL UNIQUE PRIMARY KEY. This field will be indexed and can be used to identify a row in the database. There is a more formal meaning, but it is beyond the scope of this chapter.

REFERENCES Table. This field refers to another table. Although MySQL does not implement this, other databases (such as Oracle) do. See the upcoming description of UPDATE and DELETE. The REFERENCES modifier is an important part of *database integrity*, that is, making sure your database is internally consistent.

Creating a Table

Now that you understand data types, let's create a table:

```
$ mysql -p
Enter password:
Welcome to the MySQL monitor. Commands end with ; or \g.
Your MySQL connection id is 12 to server version: 3.22.25
Type 'help' for help.
mysql> use tutorial;
Database changed
mysql> create table pupils (
    -> Name VARCHAR(30) NOT NULL PRIMARY KEY,
    -> Age INT,
    -> Height INT,
    -> Hair VARCHAR(15),
    -> Marks INT
    -> );
Query OK, 0 rows affected (0.31 sec)
mysql>
```

Notice that you can spread out an SQL statement over several lines, to the ending semicolon (;).

Inserting Data

Now that we have created a table, we can insert some data into it. One way to do this is a single row at a time:

```
mysql> insert into pupils VALUES ('Max', 19, 178, 'reddish', 15);
Query OK, 1 row affected (0.34 sec)
mysql>
```

We can also load data from a file with the following, rather wordy, syntax:

```
mysql> LOAD DATA LOCAL INFILE 'authors.tbl' INTO TABLE Author_tbl
            FIELDS TERMINATED BY '|'
            (LastName, FirstNames, Sortkey, Author_id);
```

The `authors.tbl` file has to be an ASCII (Unix-format) text file with a vertical bar (|) between the fields, like this:

```
Abbott|Edwin A.|Abbott, Edwin A.|10
Adams|Douglas|Adams, Douglas|20
Adams|Richard|Adams, Richard|30
Aldiss|Brian|Aldiss, Brian|40
Allegro|John|Allegro, John|50
Amis|Kingsley|Amis, Kingsley|60
Anderson|Poul|Anderson, Poul|70
Asimov|Isaac|Asimov, Isaac|80
Asprin|Robert|Asprin, Robert|90
Bailey|Paul|Bailey, Paul|100
Ballard|J. G.|Ballard, J. G.|110
Banks|Iain|Banks, Iain|120
Banks|Iain M.|Banks, Iain M.|130
Bannon|Mark|Bannon, Mark|140
Barker|M.A.R.|Barker, M.A.R.|150
Bates|Brian|Bates, Brian|160
Baudino|Gael|Baudino, Gael|170
Bayley|Barrington|Bayley, Barrington|180
Beagle|Peter|Beagle, Peter|190
```

The commands to create the BookWeb database are given in the worked example later in this chapter; the data is available on the companion Web site at www.wiley.com/combooks/quin.

Using SELECT to Print an Entire Table

You can print all or part of a table using the SQL SELECT statement:

```
mysql> select * from pupils;
+------+------+--------+---------+-------+
| Name | Age  | Height | Hair    | Marks |
+------+------+--------+---------+-------+
| Max  |  19  |   178  | reddish |   15  |
+------+------+--------+---------+-------+
1 row in set (0.00 sec)
mysql>
```

In the next section I'll demonstrate how to print out only certain rows of interest.

Using WHERE to Limit the Query

Using SELECT with WHERE is what makes relational databases start to look interesting. Let's print all authors whose names start with a C:

```
mysql> select * from Author_tbl where LastName LIKE 'C%';
+-----------+-------------+--------------+----------------------+
| Author_id | LastName    | FirstNames   | Sortkey              |
+-----------+-------------+--------------+----------------------+
|       390 | Cabell      | James Branch | Cabell, James Branch |
|       400 | Callenback  | Ernest       | Callenback, Ernest   |
|       410 | Cameron     | Eleanor      | Cameron, Eleanor     |
|       420 | Campbell    | John W       | Campbell, John W     |
|       430 | Campbell    | Jon          | Campbell, Jon        |
|       440 | Campbell    | Marion       | Campbell, Marion     |
|       450 | Campbell    | Ramsey       | Campbell, Ramsey     |
|       460 | Capek       | Karel        | Capek, Karel         |
|       470 | Card        | Orson Scott  | Card, Orson Scott    |
|       480 | Carroll     | Lewis        | Carroll, Lewis       |
|       490 | Carter      | Angela       | Carter, Angela       |
|       500 | Carter      | Lin          | Carter, Lin          |
|       510 | Chalker     | Jack L.      | Chalker, Jack L.     |
|       520 | Chant       | Joy          | Chant, Joy           |
|       530 | Churchward  | James        | Churchward, James    |
|       540 | Clark       | Douglas W.   | Clark, Douglas W.    |
|       550 | Clarke      | Arthur C.    | Clarke, Arthur C.    |
|       560 | Clayton     | Jo           | Clayton, Jo          |
|       570 | Clute       | John         | Clute, John          |
|       580 | Comyns      | Barbera      | Comyns, Barbera      |
|       590 | Coney       | Michael      | Coney, Michael       |
|       600 | Constantine | Storm        | Constantine, Storm   |
|       610 | Cook        | Robin        | Cook, Robin          |
|       620 | Cooper      | Edmund       | Cooper, Edmund       |
|       630 | Cooper      | Louise       | Cooper, Louise       |
|       640 | Cowper      | Richard      | Cowper, Richard      |
+-----------+-------------+--------------+----------------------+
26 rows in set (0.01 sec)
mysql>
```

SQL supports quite complex expressions in a WHERE clause. Table 3.2 lists some of the expression syntax and examples.

Joining and Sorting

The complex WHERE example is an example of an *inner join*. The idea of a join is that you create a new table by taking rows of several other tables that match a WHERE clause. We won't need more complex joins than that in this book.

You can sort output with the ORDER BY clause to SELECT; the optional DESC modifier sorts items in descending order:

```
mysql> Select * from Author_tbl
    -> where LastName LIKE 'C%'
    -> order by SortKey;
```

Returning Multiple Columns

You can return any number of columns in a SELECT clause, and you can give them names for use within the expressions, either to save typing or to make the output headings easier to read.

Here is an example from the BookWeb application described later in the chapter:

Table 3.2   SQL Expressions

EXPRESSION	RESULT
name	The value of the corresponding field; for example, "IS" in SELECT * from Author_tbl where ID < 100.
e + e, e - e	The sum (or difference) of two expressions.
*e * e, e / e*	Multiply or divide two fields.
NOT *e*	1 if *e* is 0, and 0 otherwise.
e OR *e*	1 (true, if you will) if either expression is nonzero.
e AND *e*	1 if both expressions are nonzero; 0 otherwise.
e = e	1 if the two expressions are equal; 0 otherwise.
e < e	1 if the left-hand expression is less than the right-hand expression. The other relational operators include <=, >=, > and <> (or != if you prefer).
REGEXP *s*	True if the field is a text (or vartext) field that matches the regular expression *s*; this is a MySQL extension to SQL.
LIKE *pattern*	True if the field matches the given *pattern*, in which % is a wildcard that matches any sequence of characters (like the C% in the earlier example), and the underscore matches a single character.

```
SELECT
    Author_tbl.LastName as Author,
    Author_tbl.FirstNames as firstName,
    Book_tbl.Title as Title,
    Book_tbl.Book_id as Book_id
FROM
    Wrote_tbl, Author_tbl, Book_tbl
WHERE
    Author_tbl.LastName REGEXP "Tolk[ei]+n"
    AND Wrote_tbl.Author_id = Author_tbl.Author_id
    AND Wrote_tbl.Book_id = Book_tbl.Book_id
    AND Author_tbl.Author_id = Wrote_tbl.Author_id
;
```

The result of this query is a table with four columns: `Author`, `firstName`, `Title`, and `Book_id`. These values did not originally come from the same table, but from the tables `Author_tbl` and `Book_tbl`.

Using UPDATE and DELETE to Change Data

You can change values in a table with the `UPDATE` statement:

```
UPDATE Author_tbl
SET firstNames = "Michael Greatrix"
WHERE Author_id = 590;
```

will change

```
590 | Coney        | Michael         | Coney, Michael
```

to

```
590 | Coney        | Michael Greatrix | Coney, Michael
```

You can also delete rows (but only entire rows; if you want to delete a single field, set it to NULL):

```
DELETE FROM Author_tbl WHERE Author_id = 590;
and Michael Coney is no longer listed.
```

If you try this on the sample BookWeb database, you may find that there are books written by Michael Coney. The `Books_tbl` contains a field created with the `REFERENCES Author_tbl` modifier, so that the database "knows" you can't delete an author if there are books referring to that author. In fact, at the time of writing, MySQL doesn't perform this checking; and since it lacks transaction support, it might not support this sort of constraint for quite some time. Most other databases support this sort of constraint checking, as part of *referential integrity checking*, which makes sure that the database "makes sense."

Normal Forms and Database Design

Two important principles in designing a database are to avoid duplication of data, and to store *absolute* rather than *derived* values, those computed from other values. For example, if you store my birthdate, you should not also store my age, because that's derived from today's date and my birthdate. The birthdate is an example of an absolute value. This is referred to as putting a database into *normal form*.

First Normal Form

To describe normal forms, we must go back to looking at a database as representing objects with attributes. A book, for example, is an object; the title is an *attribute* of that book. (Recall that proper relational database terminology calls the objects *entities*, but to avoid confusion with XML, I'm using the term objects instead.)

A database in *first normal form* does not have any attributes with repeating values, and a unique key identifies every object. For example, a book may have two authors, but you can't directly represent that in a normalized database. Repeating data like this is not a good idea, because if you make a mistake, for example, by writing "Ananxi" instead of "Anansi", the database has no idea that the values are supposed to be related.

```
The Descent of Anansi | Larry Niven
The Descent of Ananxi | Steven Barnes
```

Instead, we need to store separate tables to represent Book and Author objects. A book has a single title, and an author has a single name. We then use a separate table (`Wrote_tbl`) to represent the relationship:

```
Author_ID | Name
1         | Larry Niven
2         | Steven Barnes


Book_ID   | Title
1         | The Descent of Anansi
```

Then the Wrote table relates the two:

```
Author_ID | Book_ID
1         | 1
2         | 1
```

This tells us that book 1 was written by authors 1 and 2.

The Wrote table indicates we no longer have duplicated attribute data, and therefore don't need to worry abut which version is correct (look carefully at *Anansi* and *Ananxi* in the previous example).

Second Normal Form

In *second normal form*, all attributes of an object depend entirely on the object's identifying attribute. Translated into English, this means that you shouldn't store a publisher's name in the Book table, because the same publisher probably has published more than one book. The book title is different for every book (unless we have two books with the same title, but that sort of coincidence is acceptable because the titles still refer to different books). The publisher is not different for every book, and so it should be in a separate table with a `Publisher_ID` stored in the Book table to refer to it.

A database in second normal form must also already be in first normal form.

Third Normal Form

In *third normal form*, a database is already in second normal form. In addition, no nonidentifying attributes can depend on any other nonidentifying attributes.

In our Author table, the ID is the identifying attribute. Suppose we wanted to record the city in which each author lived, along with the time zone so we don't telephone an author in the middle of the night. The time zone depends on the city: If an author moves, we have to update both fields. This means we have a possible integrity problem if we update one field and not the other.

In third normal form, we use a separate table for the city with its time zone, and give it a City ID:

```
City_ID | Name          | TimeZone
1       | Toronto       | EST
2       | Swansea       | GMT
3       | San Francisco | PST
```

Now in our Author table, we refer to these by ID:

```
Author_ID | Name         | City_ID
1         | Larry Niven  | 3
2         | Daffyd Jones | 2
```

If your database is in third normal form, the chances are good that you have avoided the most common errors, and that your queries can have a reasonable chance of running efficiently.

Worked Example: BookWeb

This section presents the simple example that we'll use throughout the rest of the book. The BookWeb database represents novels and keeps track of names of characters mentioned in those books. I developed BookWeb because I wanted to be able to keep a database of names of characters and places in books, and to search for them.

Later, we will add more features to this, and integrate it with a text retrieval package. The completed application and source can be found at www.holoweb .net/~liam/bookweb/.

Start with a Book

A book has a title, a publisher, and a publication date. We could add a page count, perhaps, and an author. Since many books share a single publisher, we'll make that a separate table. The first attempt is shown in Figure 3.4.

Normalize

This database design has some problems. The first is that an author can write more than one book. And we don't want to type the author's name in more than once, because if we make a mistake, or put Michael G. Coney in one place and Michael Greatrix Coney in another, the database would treat them as two different people. The Author table is shown in Figure 3.5.

This still isn't quite right, as you might have guessed. One book might have two authors—Ian Graham and Liam R. E. Quin wrote *The XML Specification Guide*, and although that isn't fiction, plenty of fiction books were written by more than one writer.

To implement the many-to-many relationship between author and book, we need a separate table, `Wrote_tbl`, in which each row simply contains an asser- tion, "This author (ID) wrote this book (ID)". If there are multiple rows with the same author, that author wrote more than one book. If there are multiple rows with the same book ID, that book had multiple authors. To correct the

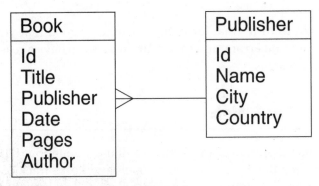

Figure 3.4 A book has a publisher.

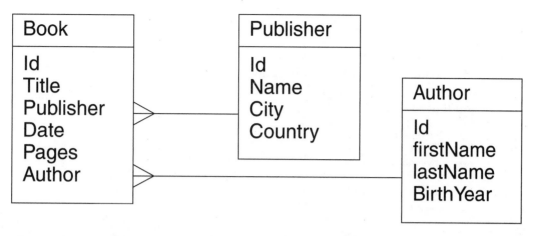

Figure 3.5 A book has many authors.

diagram, we can draw a crow's foot on the right-hand end of the Book-Author relationship, and write "Wrote" over it.

Names and Roles

A book can mention any number of names, and a name can appear in any number of books. Bilbo Baggins the Hobbit appears in several books, and so does Rand al'Thor. We need another table to represent the many-to-many relationship between a name and a book. This time, I add an extra field, Role, to the table. This is so that I can say that Bilbo is the *protagonist* in *The Hobbit* and *appears* in *The Lord of the Rings* (where the protagonist is Frodo Baggins). Figure 3.6 shows the final diagram.

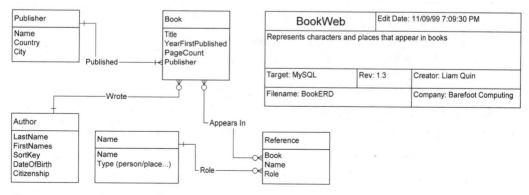

Figure 3.6 BookWeb entity relationship diagram.

Creating the BookWeb Database in MySQL

The following script is available at www.holoweb.net/~bookweb/ and can be downloaded freely. You can also play with the sample database there. If you are typing this in from a book, sample input files are given after the script, and you'll need those, too.

```
# create a "book" database
#
# Copyright, Liam Quin, 1999
#
# see the Barefoot License at http://www.holoweb.net/~bookweb/ or in
# Chapter 19, "Licenses," for copying restrictions.
```

A couple of user notes:

- If you have a MySQL account `emily` and your computer is called `crispin`, you can type the script into a file called `bkcreate` and then run it like this:

  ```
  $ mysql -h crispin -u emily -p < bkcreate
  ```

- If you are using Oracle, you may need to change VARCHAR to VARCHAR2 everywhere.

Let's start by creating the database. You may need to get the database administrator to do this for you, and then grant you access to it (see the section title *Creating a Database*, and the documentation for your database, if necessary).

```
CREATE DATABASE books;


USE books;
#
# First, an author
CREATE TABLE Author_tbl (
        # identify the author; the Author_id refers to the Author table;
        # note that two authors with the same name might be entirely
        # different people.
    Author_id INT NOT NULL PRIMARY KEY,
    LastName VARCHAR(35) NOT NULL,
    FirstNames VARCHAR(40),
    Sortkey VARCHAR(25)

);


# Now load some authors
LOAD DATA LOCAL INFILE 'authors.tbl' INTO TABLE Author_tbl
            FIELDS TERMINATED BY '|'
            (LastName, FirstNames, Sortkey, Author_id);
```

```
#
# Next, a publisher
CREATE TABLE Publisher_tbl (
    Publisher_id INT NOT NULL PRIMARY KEY,

        # name, e.g. Wiley, truncated if necessary because SQL,
        # unlike XML, is not really too happy about fields of
        # unrestricted length:
    Name VARCHAR(50)
);


# load some publishers
LOAD DATA LOCAL INFILE 'publishers.tbl' INTO TABLE Publisher_tbl
            FIELDS TERMINATED BY '|'
            (name, Publisher_id);


#
# Now a book and its attributes:
CREATE TABLE Book_tbl (
        # id: unique id for identifying each book
        # (ISBNs are not suitable as they refer to a specific edition)
    Book_id INT NOT NULL PRIMARY KEY,

        # title, truncated if necessary because SQL, unlike XML,
        # is not really too happy about fields of unrestricted length:
    Title VARCHAR(150) NOT NULL,

        # identify the publisher:
    Publisher_id INT REFERENCES Publisher_tbl(Publisher_id),

        # When the book was first published
        # we'd like to make it a DATE, but we usually only have
        # a year, not a day/month/year, so we just use a number:

    Date INT,

        # Number of pages in some particular unspecified edition.
        # We might use that to give thicker books bigger icons, perhaps.
        # Strictly speaking this might belong in an EDITIONS table,
        # but that's more detail than we need!
    Pages INT
);


# load some books
LOAD DATA LOCAL INFILE 'books.tbl' INTO TABLE Book_tbl
            FIELDS TERMINATED BY '|'
            (Book_id, Title, Publisher_id, Date);



#
# who wrote which book?
```

```
CREATE TABLE Wrote_tbl (
    Author_id INT NOT NULL REFERENCES Author_tbl,
    Book_id INT NOT NULL REFERENCES Book_tbl
);


# load the relationship
LOAD DATA LOCAL INFILE 'wrote.tbl' INTO TABLE Wrote_tbl
              FIELDS TERMINATED BY '|'
              (Author_id, Book_id);



#
# A character or place seen in a book
CREATE TABLE Name_tbl (
    Name_id INT NOT NULL PRIMARY KEY,

    Name VARCHAR(50) NOT NULL,

    # city|region|country|person|creature|plant|food|other
    Type CHAR(12) NOT NULL,

    Description VARCHAR(250)

);


# load some names
LOAD DATA LOCAL INFILE 'names.tbl' INTO TABLE Name_tbl
              FIELDS TERMINATED BY '|'
              (Name_id, Name, Type, Description);



#
# Where the name was referenced
CREATE TABLE References_tbl (
    Name_id INT NOT NULL REFERENCES Name_tbl,
    Book_id INT NOT NULL REFERENCES Book_tbl,

    # Record the role a particular name plays in a given book.
    # for example, Bilbo is "protagonist" in the Hobbit,
    # but in The Lord of the Rings he is secondary.
    Role VARCHAR(100) NOT NULL
);

# load some references
LOAD DATA LOCAL INFILE 'references.tbl' INTO TABLE References_tbl
              FIELDS TERMINATED BY '|'
              (Name_id, Book_id, Role);

# done — now we can use the database!
```

The following are some sample files you can use if you don't want to implement the longer ones on the companion Web site (www.wiley.com/compbooks/quin).

authors.tbl

This file is greatly truncated; I have given you enough of C to get the 24 lines of output in the tutorial, and a few other authors used in other examples. The fields are `lastName`, `firstNames`, `sorktKey`, ID.

```
Abbott|Edwin A.|Abbott, Edwin A.|10
Adams|Douglas|Adams, Douglas|20
Benford|Gregory|Benford, Gregory|210
Bester|Alfred|Bester, Alfred|220
Brin|David|Brin, David|330
Cabell|James Branch|Cabell, James Branch|390
Callenback|Ernest|Callenback, Ernest|400
Cameron|Eleanor|Cameron, Eleanor|410
Campbell|John W|Campbell, John W|420
Campbell|John W.|Campbell, John W.|430
Campbell|Marion|Campbell, Marion|440
Campbell|Ramsey|Campbell, Ramsey|450
Capek|Karel|Capek, Karel|460
Card|Orson Scott|Card, Orson Scott|470
Carroll|Lewis|Carroll, Lewis|480
Carter|Angela|Carter, Angela|490
Carter|Lin|Carter, Lin|500
Chalker|Jack L.|Chalker, Jack L.|510
Chant|Joy|Chant, Joy|520
Churchward|James|Churchward, James|530
Clark|Douglas W.|Clark, Douglas W.|540
Clarke|Arthur C.|Clarke, Arthur C.|550
Clayton|Jo|Clayton, Jo|560
Clute|John|Clute, John|570
Comyns|Barbera|Comyns, Barbera|580
Coney|Michael|Coney, Michael|590
Constantine|Storm|Constantine, Storm|600
Cook|Robin|Cook, Robin|610
Cooper|Edmund|Cooper, Edmund|620
Cooper|Louise|Cooper, Louise|630
Cowper|Richard|Cowper, Richard|640
Jordan|Robert|Jordan, Robert|1230
Niven|Larry|Niven, Larry|1620
Noon|Jeff|Noon, Jeff|1630
Zelazny|Roger|Zelazny, Roger|2360
Zindell|David|Zindell, David|2370
```

publishers.tbl

This version of the file has a City field added to it. It's up to you to decide whether to type in that field and add it to the example or to leave it out of the data file.

```
Abacus||USA|10
Ace||USA|20
Arrow|London|UK|30
Avin Books||USA|40
```

```
Axolotl Press||USA|50
Bantam||USA|60
Dell||USA|70
Doubleday||USA|290
Futura||USA|80
Grafton|London|UK|90
Guild/Bantam||USA|100
Legend||USA|110
Methuen||USA|120
Millennium|London|UK|290
New Directions||USA|130
Orbit||USA|140
Pan||USA|150
Penguin|Oxford|UK|160
Picador||USA|170
Random Century||USA|180
Ringpull||USA|190
Signet||USA|200
Sphere||USA|210
Tor||USA|220
Unicorn||USA|230
Unwin||UK|240
Unwin Hyman||UK|250
Victor||UK|260
Victor Gollancz SF||UK|270
Women's Press||UK|280
```

book.tbl

This, too, is a very small extract. The notation \N is used to represent a NULL
field; some databases may simply require that no data be present, or have some
other mechanism. The last two fields, when not NULL, are the number of pages
and the first publication date, respectively.

```
10|Flatland|\N|\N
20|Dirk Gently's Holistic Detective Agency|\N|\N
30|Life, the universe and everything|\N|\N
40|The Long Dark Tea-Time of the Soul|\N|\N
50|The Restaurant at the End of the Universe|\N|\N
700|The Demolished Man|\N|\N
710|Tiger! Tiger!|\N|\N
720|Virtal Unrealities: The Short fiction of Alfred Bester|260|1997
990|Earth|60|1990
1000|Startide Rising|\N|\N
1010|The Postman|\N|\N
1020|The Practice Effect|\N|\N
1030|The River of Time|\N|\N
1040|The Uplift War|\N|\N
1050|Glory Season|\N|1993
1060|Otherness|\N|1994
1260|The Wonderful Flight to the Mushroom Planet|\N|\N
```

```
1270|The Moon is Hell|\N|\N
1280|The Thing|\N|\N
1290|The Dark Twin|\N|\N
1300|Ancient Images|\N|\N
1310|The Hungry Moon|\N|\N
1320|War with the Newts|\N|\N
1330|A Planet Called Treason|\N|\N
1340|Alvin Maker 1: Seventh Son|\N|\N
1350|Songmaster|220|1978
1360|Speaker for the Dead 1: Speaker for the Dead|220|1986
1370|Speaker for the Dead 2: Ender's Game|\N|\N
1380|Speaker for the Dead 3: Xenocide|220|1991
1390|Speaker for the Dead 4: Children of the Mind|220|1996
1580|BRONTOMEK!|\N|\N
1590|Cat Karina|\N|\N
1600|Charisma|\N|\N
1610|Fang, The Gnome|\N|\N
1620|Gods of the Greataway|\N|\N
1630|King of the Scepter'd Isle|\N|\N
1640|Pallahaxi Tide|\N|\N
1650|The Celestial Steam Locomotive|\N|\N
3220|The Wheel of Time 1: The Eye of the World|220|1990
3230|The Wheel of Time 2: The Great Hunt|220|1990
3240|The Wheel of Time 3: The Dragon Reborn|220|1991
4500|Protector|\N|\N
4510|The Integral Trees|\N|\N
4520|The Smoke Ring|\N|\N
4530|Pollen|190|1995
6170|Isle of the Dead|\N|\N
6180|Lord of Light|\N|\N
6190|The Dream Master|\N|\N
6200|Neverness|90|1988
```

wrote.tbl

This file indicates who wrote which book. This is an extract from a much larger file; you may want to add more rows.

```
1230|3320
2370|6200
220|700
220|710
220|720
590|1580
590|1590
590|1600
590|1610
590|1620
590|1630
590|1640
590|1650
```

name.tbl

This file identifies the names of characters that appear in the books. The fields are ID, Name, Type, and Description.

NOTE Not all of the names in this sample file are actually mentioned in books that occur in the books.tbl file given, because this is just a subset of the full data.

```
0010|Ba'alzamon|person|One of the Forsaken, leading the forces of
     Darkness
0020|Dr Talos|person|
0030|Emereck|person|
0040|Flindarin|person|
0050|Foila|person|
0060|Jack|person|
0070|Jonas|person|
0080|Kim|person|
0090|Lan|person|Warder to Moraine
0100|Lanfear|person|One of the Forsaken, leading the forces of Darkness
0110|Mairelon|person|the wizard himself!
0120|Malito|person|
0130|Mat|person|a shepherd boy who likes tricks and gambling
0140|Minathlan|person|
0150|Moraine|person|An Aes Sadai who dedicated her life to finding and
     manipulating the Dragon Reborn
0160|Nessus|person|
0170|Egwene|person|a girl from the Two rivers
0180|Nynaeve|person|a bad-tempered unpleasant shrew from the Two Rivers
0190|Perrin|person|a blacksmith who gains a liking for wolves.
0200|Rand al'Thor|person|Just a farmer's boy. Or possibly the Messiah.
0210|Severian|person|The executioner, or lictor, in his meanderings
0220|Tar Valon|city|The home of the White Tower, where the Aes Sadai
     train their novices to manipulate the world
0221|Colin|Just a schoolboy
0222|Susan|Just a schoolgirl
0223|Fenodyree|a dwarf
0224|Durathror|One of the huldrafolk
0225|Atlendor|
0226|Gowther|A Lancashire farmer
0227|The Morrigan|spellweaver|A Witch
```

references.tbl

Finally, this identifies which names appear in which books, and the primary role the character plays in each book.

```
0010|3220|Adversary
0010|3230|Adversary
0010|3240|Adversary
```

```
0020|6030|Secondary
0020|6040|Secondary
0030|6030|Advisor
0040|6030|Protagonist
0050|5940|Secondary
0060|6100|Companion
0070|5920|Secondary
0080|6100|Protagonist
0090|3220|Secondary
0090|3230|Secondary
0090|3240|Secondary
0090|3250|Secondary
0090|3260|Secondary
0100|3230|Adversary
0100|3240|Adversary
0100|3250|Adversary
0100|3260|Adversary
0110|6100|Central
0120|5940|Secondary
0130|3220|Central
0130|3230|Central
0130|3240|Central
0130|3250|Central
0130|3260|Central
0140|5970|Place
0150|3220|Advisor
0150|3230|Advisor
0150|3240|Advisor
0150|3250|Secondary
0150|3260|Secondary
0160|5940|Secondary
0170|3220|Secondary
0170|3230|Secondary
0170|3240|Central
0170|3250|Central
0170|3260|Protagonist
0180|3220|Secondary
0180|3230|Secondary
0180|3240|Central
0180|3250|Central
0180|3260|Protagonist
0190|3220|Central
0190|3230|Central
0190|3240|Central
0190|3250|Protagonist
0190|3260|Central
0200|3220|Protagonist
0200|3230|Protagonist
0200|3240|Protagonist
0200|3250|Central
0200|3260|Secondary
```

```
0210|6030|Protagonist
0210|6040|Protagonist
0210|6050|Protagonist
0210|6060|Protagonist
0220|3220|Visited
0220|3220|Visited
0220|3220|Described
0220|3220|Visited
0220|3220|Visited
```

Exercises

1. Get the sample database working in whichever database you use. Try to construct queries to find which names were referenced in which books.

2. Find a tutorial for the database you have, and work through it.

3. If you are using the code supplied with this book, get the BookWeb sample application working.

4. The BookWeb sample is not fully normalized. Determine what needs to be done to put it into third normal form.

5. Figure out how to model the fact that characters in books inhabit often imaginary lands?

Summary

This chapter has given a quick introduction to SQL, exemplified by some sample data you can use. The next chapter shows how to get that sample data back out of a relational database, and how to create XML versions of the information.

## CHAPTER 4

Generating XML from Relational Data

I n this chapter you'll learn several ways to generate XML from an existing relational database. We'll start by examining how to represent relational data in XML, then discuss the most common strategies for generating XML, and finally check out some specific tools. We'll look at three different methods: Perl's DBI module, PHP, and a Java servlet. If you are not already familiar with XML and SQL, you may want to review the previous two chapters.

Why Generate XML?

Before delving into how to generate XML, let's consider why we might want to do so. There are several reasons you might want to take a relational database and generate an XML version of some or all of the contained data.

Mobility of Data

An XML representation of a complete or partial database could be used for a vendor-independent backup, or to move data from one database to another. You would have to write code to load the XML back into the chosen destination database, but the advantage of a single central *hub* format is that adding a new database format only involves adding two new converters. Figure 4.1 illustrates database-to-database translations, and Figure 4.2 illustrates a central hub format.

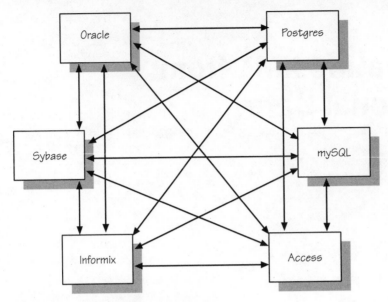

Figure 4.1   Six databases need 30 filters.

Browser Views

You might want to serve up information on the World Wide Web, taking advantage of browser-specific XML features such as the support in Mozilla or

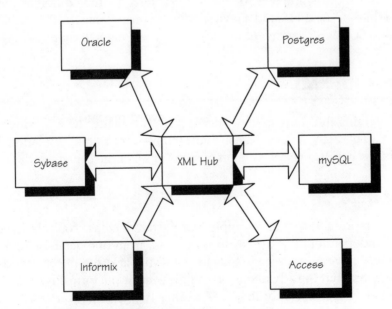

Figure 4.2   Six databases and a hub need 12 filters.

Internet Explorer. Since not all browsers support XML at the time of writing, this option is most appealing on an intranet, where you can control the software people are using. There's no point in telling people to use Microsoft Internet Explorer if they are using Linux or are sight-disabled and use a screen reader or a Braille terminal.

As more browsers support XML directly, however, this option becomes more interesting. A PHP script could generate different output depending on whether the client sent an HTTP Accept header for `text/xml`, for example. The PHP discussion in this chapter will help you in this regard. Better yet, it could offer the user a choice and track a session variable. Chapter 21, "XML Parsers, Editors, and Utilities," lists some browsers and gives pointers to getting started on this route.

Currently (Spring 2000), the most common way to display XML on the Web is to use the XML Style Language Transformation (XSLT) to convert the XML to HTML on the fly. The technology has been changing very rapidly, however, and this method isn't covered directly in the book, so I refer you to the book's companion Web site at www.wiley.com/compbooks/quin for more details.

Databases into Documents

For interoperability with a document-based system, such as the environments we will consider in Part Two, you could generate XML documents from a relational database and then load those documents into a document repository or an object-oriented database.

XML Tools

Exporting information as XML lets you use standalone XML-based tools, such as formatting or typesetting packages, data analysis or statistics packages, or XML-aware tools such as spreadsheets and word processors. In this chapter, we'll consider methods and tools that are suitable for all of these operations.

Representing Tables

For convenience here, we will use the BookWeb example from Chapter 3, "Just Enough SQL." Figure 4.3 displays a complete entity relationship diagram for the BookWeb example. Now let's consider this as an XML document.

Chapter 1, "Just Enough XML," described some of the ways XML can represent relationships. We'll consider several approaches for representing our sample data in XML, then discuss how to get the data from the database to XML.

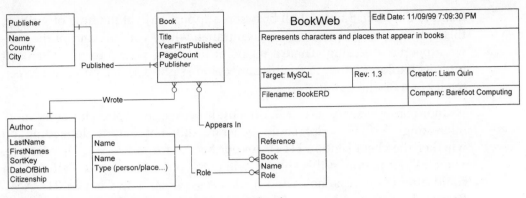

Figure 4.3 Entity relationship diagram for BookWeb.

The examples here are well formed; we'll present a DTD after the discussion. In Part Four, "Links and Metadata," we will consider how to represent this same database relation using an XML schema.

Let's look first at the Reference relation. The following is some sample data, with a single author and two books. First, here's an extract from `Author_tbl`:

ID	Author.lastName	Author.firstName
183	Tolkien	J. R. R.

Next, here are two (incomplete) rows from `Book_tbl`:

ID	Book.Title
901	The Hobbit
902	The Lord of the Rings

Now we show that Tolkien wrote those books. This is a many-many relationship, so we have a separate table for it:

Wrote.Book	Wrote.Author
901	183
902	183

Here is a character that appears in these books:

Name.ID	Name.Name	Name.Description
12	Bilbo	A hobbit, or halfling, a barefoot adventurer.

Bilbo appears in both of the books listed here, but plays different roles in each of them:

Reference.Book	Reference.Name	Reference.Role
901	12	Advisor
902	12	Protagonist

Since this relation contains references to two other tables and a string, we might use something like the following XML fragment to represent the Reference table:

```
<?xml version="1.0" encoding="ISO-8859-1"?>
<Reference_tbl>
  <Reference>
    <Book ref="book901" />
    <Name ref="name12" />
    <Role>Advisor</Role>
  </Reference>
  <Reference>
    <Book ref="book902" />
    <Name ref="name12" />
    <Role>Protagonist</Role>
  </Reference>
</Reference_tbl>
```

In general, when you first start exporting data from relational tables, you'll see this model a lot: a single row from a table forming a single element in a table. If your purpose is primarily to represent the table or tables, this is actually about as good as you can get—and all you need. It describes the data clearly, and it has not introduced any new concepts. We will use this model again when we consider reading XML in the Chapter 5, "Reading XML into a Program."

If you wanted to display this information to a user in a Web page, he or she would probably be a little disappointed. You would need to do a JOIN or a more complex SELECT, and capture the Name fields from the Book, Author, and Names tables as well:

```
<?xml version="1.0" encoding="ISO-8859-1"?>
<Reference_tbl>
  <Reference>
    <Book ref="book901">
      <Title>The Lord of the Rings</Title>
      <Author>Tolkien, J. R. R</Author>
    </Book>
    <Name ref="name12">Bilbo</Name>
    <Role>Advisor</Role>
  </Reference>
  <Reference>
    <Book ref="book902" >
      <Title>The Hobbit</Title>
      <Author>Tolkien, J. R. R</Author>
    <Name ref="name12">Gandalf</Name>
    <Role>Protagonist</Role>
  </Reference>
</Reference_tbl>
```

This example is much more readable for humans, but it is emphatically *not* suitable for data archiving or for transfer. It is not in normal form because data is duplicated. If you edited this little XML document and then saved it, you might easily make a mistake, such as spelling an author's name differently in two places. We return to this topic again later, because it's very central, but for now, let's say that you should use a reference to content when a relational table uses a foreign key. Use #PCDATA content (such as Bilbo) only when the data actually appears in the table directly, whether as an INTEGER, VARTEXT, or CHAR.

If we were trying to export the whole database, we would represent each of the tables as a sequence of elements, just as in the References example. We would end up with a section defining publishers, another defining authors, another books, another names, another relating authors and books, and a final section relating names and their appearances in specific books.

Here is a sample XML file; we'll use it again in the next chapter with more discussion and a real XML DTD:

```xml
<?xml version="1.0" encoding="ISO-8859-1" ?>
<Catalogue>
    <AuthorList>
        <Author id="a001">
            <LastName>Benford</LastName>
            <FirstNames>Gregory</FirstNames>
        </Author>
        <Author id="a002">
            <LastName>Coney</LastName>
            <FirstNames>Michael Greatrix</FirstNames>
        </Author>
        <Author id="a003">
            <LastName>Brin</LastName>
            <FirstNames>David</FirstNames>
        </Author>
    </AuthorList>
    <PublisherList>
        <Publisher id="p001">
            <Name>Bantam</Name>
            <Country>USA</Country>
        </Publisher>
        <Publisher id="p002">
            <Name>Futura</Name>
            <Country>UK</Country>
        </Publisher>
    </PublisherList>
    <BookList>
        <Book EarliestDate="1983" Publisher="p002">
            <Title>The Celestial Steam Locomotive</Title>
            <AuthorRef Role="Wrote" Who="a002" />
            <Blurb>Alan-Blue-Cloud is pure intelligence, immortal,
                ineffable, a being who remembers not only what
                was, but what will be. This is his story, set in the
                year 143,624 Cyclic, in a future so distant that . . .
            </Blurb>
```

```
      </Book>
      <Book EarliestDate="1986" Publisher="p001">
          <Title>Heart of the Comet</Title>
          <AuthorRef Role="Wrote" Who="a001" />
          <AuthorRef Role="Wrote" Who="a003" />
      </Book>
      <Book EarliestDate="1998" Publisher="p001">
          <Title>Heaven's Reach</Title>
          <AuthorRef Role="Wrote" Who="a003" />
          <Notes>The final book of the second Uplift trilogy</Notes>
      </Book>
    </BookList>
  </Catalogue>
```

This example does not reduce the publisher to a normal form, and does not include any names, but it's enough to illustrate the examples in this chapter. This book's companion Web site, www.wiley.com/compbooks/quin, includes a fuller example, with several hundred books described.

A very different approach is to generate an entire document. For example, given the Tolkien data earlier, we could generate something like this:

```
<BookDescription>
  The writer J. R. R Tolkien wrote both <title>The Hobbit</title> and
  <title>The Lord of the Rings</title>. Bilbo appears as protagonist
  in <title>The Hobbit</title> but as advisor in <title>The Lord
  of the Rings</title>.
</BookDescription>
```

This sort of text generation requires a lot more thought, and the techniques are beyond the scope of this book, but if you are trying to generate human-readable reports or documents, you should consider the possibility.

Generating XML with DBI

Now that we have seen some ways to represent XML, let's look at ways to generate it from a database. First, let's write a simple Perl script that connects to a database and prints out a single table. (Note: If you type this example yourself, you may need to change the first line to reflect the location of Perl 5 on your system; on FreeBSD, for example, it's probably /usr/local/bin/perl5 instead of /usr/bin/perl.) Comments starting with # [...] are intended to help readers of the book; there's no need to type them. You can leave out all the comments except the very first line, if you like, but that's not usually a good idea, as they are there to make the program easier to read.

```
#! /usr/bin/perl -w
use strict;
```

The `"use strict"` declaration turns on stricter error checking. Although it will take longer to get your program to run, because you have to fix all the errors, those errors would probably have made the program run incorrectly.

```
# This program requires the DataBase Interface package, DBI:
use DBI;
```

If you are not using MySQL, you will need to change the next two lines. Try running the Unix command `perldoc DBI` for more information. The Perl DataBase Interface (DBI) supports a wide range of databases, both free and commercial.

```
my $driver = "mysql";
my $port = 629; # default for mySQL


# Specify the computer running the database.
```

You can use `"localhost"` if it's running on the same machine as this Perl script. If `"localhost"` appears not to work, try "127.0.0.1", then go to www.localhost.com/ for information on how to fix your domain name server (DNS) configuration.

```
my $host = "localhost";
```

The script will try to connect to the database using the user and password given here. In a shared environment, the script should prompt the user for a password instead.

```
my $password = "n0tshown";
my $user = 'liam';
```

NOTE

The variable $user represents a database user, *not* a Unix user. They can be the same, but often they aren't. And even when they are, the passwords might be different. A common error is giving an incorrect username or password.

```
# The name of the database to connect to:
```

The database name is case-sensitive in some implementations, including mySQL on Unix. You should always refer to a database by exactly the same name you used when you created it, even if your database doesn't distinguish between upper- and lowercase. Your scripts will then work on other systems if you have to move them.

```
my $database = "books";
# Now let's connect to the database
my $dbh = DBI->connect(
    "DBI:$driver:database=$database;host=$host;port=$port",
    $user,
    $password
```

```
    );

    if (!defined($dbh)) {
        die "could not connect to database $database on $host:$port - $!";
    }
```

Now we are connected. Though production code might do better error handling, such as waiting for a few seconds and trying again, or maybe trying a secondary database, perhaps analyzing the error to determine what to do, this example leaves out most error checking. Otherwise, the code would be too long, and no one would read it. Just be aware that 70 percent or more of production code is often taken up by error handling.

```
    # Now build an SQL query and run it

    # First make a query. This is a pretty simple query!
    my $sth = $dbh->prepare("SELECT * FROM books.Author_tbl;");

    # run the query:
    $sth->execute;
```

Note the lack of error checking here!

```
    # now let's find out some things about the result...
    # the number of rows in the result:
    my $numRows = $sth->rows;

    # fetch the names of the columns:
    my $names = $sth->{'NAME'};
```

Though innocuous-looking, this statement requires an explanation. We are calling the NAME method of the $sth object. This method is documented as returning a reference to an array. If you are not familiar with references in the Perl language, try running "perldoc perlref" to get started. The idea is that $names now holds a representation of the name of an array (actually a pointer), so that @{$names} is the actual array. This means that ${$names}[0] is the first element of the array in question. Perl lets us write that as $$names[0].

```
    # How many columns are there in the result?
    my $numFields = $sth->{'NUM_OF_FIELDS'};

    # Print out a container for the result:
    print "<Result rows=\"${numRows}\">\n";
    # Now print out the data, one row at a time.
    while (my $ref = $sth->fetchrow_arrayref) {
        # Since this is Author_tbl, we could use <Author> for
        # the rows, or we can just use <row>, as here.
        print "    <row>\n";

        # Now the individual fields.
```

```
    for (my $i = 0;  $i < $numFields;  $i++) {
        if (defined($$ref[$i])) {
            print "    <$$names[$i]>$$ref[$i]</$$names[$i]>\n";
        }
    }
    print "  </row>\n";
}
print "</Result>\n";

# now free the resources used by that query:
$sth->finish;

# finally, disconnect from the database:
$dbh->disconnect;
```

When objects go out of scope, and there are no more references to them, Perl's "garbage collection" automatically deletes them. You could rely on this to disconnect from the database, but if someone changed your program to keep a reference to $dbh, or you needed to reuse the code, this assumption might surprise you later when the connection wasn't closed. It's therefore good practice to disconnect explicitly, as done here.

This is a pretty simple example. When it is run on the sample database, it produces output like this:

```
<Result rows="239">
  <row>
    <Author_id>10</Author_id>
    <LastName>Abbott</LastName>
    <FirstNames>Edwin A.</FirstNames>
    <Sortkey>Abbott, Edwin A.</Sortkey>
  </row>
  <row>
    <Author_id>20</Author_id>
    <LastName>Adams</LastName>
    <FirstNames>Douglas</FirstNames>
    <Sortkey>Adams, Douglas</Sortkey>
  </row>
  <row>
    <Author_id>30</Author_id>
    <LastName>Adams</LastName>
    <FirstNames>Richard</FirstNames>
    <Sortkey>Adams, Richard</Sortkey>
  </row>
  . . .
  lots more output
</Result>
```

If you have loaded the sample database from the companion Web site, you got several hundred rows of output from running this script; the actual output may differ slightly from that shown here, however. The fields you see may also differ slightly if you took the sample from the Web page, since it is a live project.

If you are looking at this and thinking it's much larger than a comma-separated-value (CSV) file, or a tab-delimited one, you're right. But if you compress this file with Unix *bzip2* or *gzip*, you'll find the difference in size is negligible, often less than 5 percent, because the adaptive compression programs can represent the repeating sequences of markup very compactly.

Size is much less important than quality. The explicitly named start and end tags in XML mean that a transmission error can often be detected automatically, which is very important when you're dealing with databases. If you gave each *row* element a sequence-number attribute, you could detect missing rows, too.

One possible error *not* dealt with in this example is when a field contains a less-than sign. Clearly, if an author's name were to contain "</row>", all sorts of havoc would break loose. One way to deal with this is to change the inner loop of the Perl script from:

```perl
# Now the individual fields.
    for (my $i = 0;  $i < $numFields;  $i++) {
        if (defined($$ref[$i])) {
            print "      <$$names[$i]>$$ref[$i]</$$names[$i]>\n";
        }
    }
```

to

```perl
# Now the individual fields.
for (my $i = 0;  $i < $numFields;  $i++) {
    if (defined($$ref[$i])) {
        print "      <$$names[$i]>" .
              xmlquote($$ref[$i]) . "</$$names[$i]>\n";
    }
}
```

and supply an extra function:

```perl
sub xmlquote($)
{
    my $input = shift;
    # quote XML markup characters in the input
    $input =~ s/\&/\&amp;/g;
    $input =~ s/</\&lt;/g;
    $input =~ s/>/\&ht;/g;
    return $input;
}
```

This xmlquote subroutine is general enough to be used in other programs, too. Coincidentally, it also works for quoting HTML.

Generating XML for a Web Browser: CGI

The example Perl script in the preceding section is very close to a working CGI script, so let's finish it off and try it!

Just Enough CGI

If you are not familiar with the Common Gateway Interface (CGI), this brief summary will help. There is nothing mystical or complex about it, but if Rob McCool had not given it a name, perhaps it would never have been popular! If, on the other hand, you have experience writing CGI scripts, skip to the section *DBI and CGI*.

The idea is simply this: A Web server such as Apache can be configured so that when a client connects and requests a particular URL, instead of looking for a file, the server runs a program and returns to the client the output of that program. The program can be written in any language and can do anything it likes. *This is not the same as letting external users run any program on your computer!* The Web server's configuration file lists which programs can be run; usually, it's files with names ending in `".cgi"` or that are in a directory whose name is `"cgi-bin"`.

When the Web server, httpd, runs the CGI script, it sets a number of environment variables. The important variables are listed here. We'll assume that the CGI program is called *classmates* and the following (fictional) URL was requested:

```
http://www.holoweb.net/~lee/classmates/1974/boys?name=simon&wantpic=yes
```

REMOTE_ADDR. The Internet address (IP) of the client making the request, as an ASCII string in dotted format (e.g., 127.0.0.1).

HTTP_USER_AGENT. The name of the software the client is using, if the browser sent it.

SERVER_PROTOCOL. The protocol part of the requested URL, usually http.

SERVER_NAME. The name of the machine running the Web server or its Internet address.

SERVER_PORT. The Internet port number used to connect to the server, usually 80.

SCRIPT_NAME. The URL of the script on this server, in this case, `/~lee/classmates`.

PATH_INFO. The part of the URL following the program name, in this case, `/1974/boys`. Notice how the user (and the browser) can't tell from the URL whether the CGI program is `classmates`, `1974`, or `boys`, or maybe even none of the above.

QUERY_STRING. The query part of the URL; that is, everything that follows the question mark. In this case, that's `name=simon&wantpic=yes`.

If the URL was fetched with an HTTP GET request, there is a limit of approximately 2000 bytes on the length of the URL, including all query parameters. For sending longer data to the server, you have to use a POST or PUT method; the method used is available as `REQUEST_METHOD`.

If a POST method was used, `CONTENT_LENGTH` contains the number of bytes that the CGI program can read from its input.

NOTE

A *fragment identifier* (in the form of #xxx at the end of a URL) is never passed back to the Web server. Instead, the browser removes the #xxx, fetches the document, and then searches for `<a name='xxx'>` in the document.

The output of the script should normally be an HTTP header followed by a blank line, followed by data. The following Unix shell script is a useful example:

```
#! /bin/sh

# print the header:
cat <<EOF
Content-type: text/html

<head><title>CGI Example</title></head>
<body
    bgcolor="white"
        text="black"
        link="blue"
>
EOF

# deduce and then print our URL:
URL="http://${SERVER_NAME}"
if [ ! -z "${SERVER_PORT} -a "$SERVER_PORT" -ne 80 ]
then
    URL="${URL}:${SERVER_PORT}"
fi

URL="${URL}${SCRIPT_NAME}"

if [ ! -z "$PATH_INFO" ]
then
    URL="${URL}${PATH_INFO}"
fi

if [ ! -z "$QUERY_STRING" ]
then
    URL="${URL}?${QUERY_STRING}"
```

```
fi

# print the result:
cat <<EOF
 <p>The URL of this script is:</p>
 <form method="$REQUEST_METHOD" ACTION="$URL">
   <pre>${URL}</pre>
   <input type="text" name="name" value="simon">
   <input type="SUBMIT" value="Try Again">
 </form>

 <hr>

EOF

if [ ! -z "$*" ]
then
    echo "<h2>Arguments:</h2>"
    for i
    do
     echo "<pre>    \"$i\"</pre>"
    done
fi


echo "<h2>Environment</h2>"

echo "<pre>"
set
echo "</pre>"

# end the HTML document:
echo "</body></html>"
```

Figure 4.4 shows the output you might see.

Debugging CGI Scripts

It would be unfair of me to introduce you to CGI scripts without warning you that they are easy to get wrong. If you are working with CGI, Perl, a database, SQL, XML, and an HTTP client, a number of factors are present. Therefore, the first trick is to try to eliminate as many sources of error as possible.

Testing CGI Scripts

If you already have a copy of the try.cgi program, run it by telnetting to the machine running httpd and type an HTTP request. My Web server is running on port 8080, so that's the port I'll use in the example:

Figure 4.4 Possible output from sample CGI script.

```
$ telnet 127.0.0.1 8080

Trying 127.0.0.1...

Connected to 127.0.0.1.

Escape character is '^]'.

GET /~lee/cgi-bin/try.cgi HTTP/1.1

Accept: */*

Host: 127.0.0.1
```

Note: Press Return twice to make a blank line.

You should see some output like this:

```
HTTP/1.1 200 OK
Date: Mon, 20 Sep 1999 02:55:16 GMT
Server: Apache/1.3.9 (Unix) PHP/4.0B2
Connection: close
Transfer-Encoding: chunked
Content-Type: text/html
193
Content-Type: text/htm
<head><title>CGI Example</title></head>
<body
     bgcolor="white"
        text="black"
        link="blue"
>
124
 <p>The URL of this script is:</p>
 <form method="GET" ACTION="http://hp7100_1.dehavilland.ca/~lee/cgi-
bin/try.cgi">
    <pre>http://www.holoweb.net/~lee/cgi-bin/try.cgi</pre>
    <input type="text" name="name" value="simon">
    <input type="SUBMIT" value="Try Again">
 </form>
 <hr>
15
<h2>Environment</h2>
```

And so forth. The numbers indicate the number of bytes to follow. As this is an optional feature of HTTP 1.1, you may not see them. What's important is to verify that you get the right output. If it works, this test shows that the Web server is listening on the right port; if you get the correct output, it also shows that any problems you are having might be in your Web browser configuration, not at the server end.

404 Forbidden, or Not Found

If you get this error, make sure your CGI script file has the right modes. If it is in a scripting language such as Perl, it must be readable to the user running the Web server (usually nobody) as well as executable.

```
$ ls -l try.cgi
-rwxrwxr-x  1 lee      lee             947 Sep 19 22:37 try.cgi
```

Make sure that the directory has the same modes, too. You can use:

```
$ chmod 755 try.cgi
```

to fix them if necessary.

If it still doesn't work, check the server error log. This is a text file where error messages are logged; for FreeBSD, it's usually in /var/log/httpd-error-log, and for Red Hat Linux, it is usually in /var/log/httpd/error-log. It's useful to run tail -f /var/log/httpd/error-log in a separate window while you're developing CGI scripts, because then you'll see the errors as they happen.

The following error shows you that you've put the CGI script in the wrong place (it probably needs to be in $HOME/public_html/):

```
[error] File does not exist: /home/lee/public_html/try.cgi
```

You might also see a "not found" error if you got the first line of the script wrong. Try running the script at the command line to see that it works properly:

```
$ cd public_html/cgi-bin
$ ./try.cgi
```

You should see the HTML output, but if you don't, you need to fix the errors in try.cgi.

NOTE

Go to www.apache.org or consult the documentation for your Web server for additional error messages you might see when debugging CGI scripts.

I See the Source!

If your Web server returns the source of the CGI script instead of running it, you need to edit the server configuration file. There, usually comments will tell you what to do. Look in /etc/apache, /etc/httpd or /usr/local/apache for a directory called conf, and edit the file httpd.conf to add the option ExecCGI to your CGI directory.

Malformed Errors from Script

This error almost always means that your script produced an error message on *standard error,* or that it printed something (perhaps a debugging message) before the Content-type line. You also get this error if you forgot to insert the blank line between the header and the actual data.

DBI and CGI

Enough talk about CGI! Let's write a simple CGI script that will return any table in the Books database. The Web server will call our program, which is written in Perl and uses the DBI module to contact MySQL. Figure 4.5 shows this architecture.

The first version of the script always prints the same table. (See the *Exercises* section at the end of the chapter, and the CGI specification, for ways to make

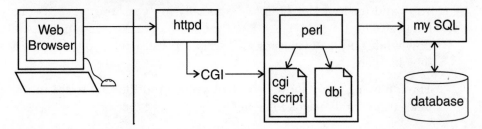

Figure 4.5 CGI architecture.

the script understand an option to specify which table to print. If you do this, remember that you may want to restrict the choices for security by having the CGI script check its input very carefully!)

Here is the simpler CGI script; it's very similar to the previous standalone script:

```perl
#! /usr/bin/perl -w
use strict;
use DBI;

my $startedHTML = 0; # set to 1 after we begin the header

sub header($$)
{
    my ($title, $bgcolor) = @_;

    print "Content-type: text/html\r\n";
    $startedHTML = 1;
    # blank line at end of HTTP header:
    print "\r\n";
    print <<EOF;
<html>
 <head>
  <title>${title}</title>
 </head>
 <body
  bgcolor="${bgcolor}"
      text="#000000"
      link="#3333FF"
     vlink="#666699"
     alink="#FFFFFF"
 >
EOF
}

sub fail($)
{
    my $errorMessage = shift;
```

```perl
    if (!$startedHTML) {
     header("Error", "red");
    }
    print <<EOF;
<h1>Error</h1>
<p>${errorMessage}</p>
EOF
    # although there was an error, we exit(0) because the script
    # actually ran OK, and we don't want the http server to
    # log an error in the httpd-errors log file. (Not all do)
    exit(0);
}

sub xmlquote($)
{
    my $input = shift;

    $input =~ s/\&/\&amp;/g;
    $input =~ s/</\&lt;/g;
    $input =~ s/>/\&gt;/g;
    return $input;
}



# config parameters:
my $driver = "mysql";
my $port = 629; # default for mySQL
my $host = "localhost";

my $database = "books";

my $password = "YourPasswordHere";
my $user = 'lee';

my $table = "Author_tbl";

my $dbh = DBI->connect(
    "DBI:$driver:database=$database;host=$host;port=$port",
    $user,
    $password
);

my $sth = $dbh->prepare("SELECT * FROM books.Author_tbl;");
$sth->execute;

my $numRows = $sth->rows;
my $numFields = $sth->{'NUM_OF_FIELDS'};

# We've already shown generating XML, so we will
# generate an HTML table this time.
```

```perl
# When you've got this working, you can change the
# Content-type to text/xml and start changing the tags...

header("XML Book Example/${table}", "white");

print "<h2>Result for ${table}, rows=\"${numRows}\"</h2>\n";

print "<table>\n";

# a table heading
my $names = $sth->{'NAME'};
foreach (@$names) {
    print "<th lign='left' bgcolor='#CCCC99'>";
      print "<b>$_</b>";
    print "</th>";
}

while (my $ref = $sth->fetchrow_arrayref) {
    print "  <tr>\n";
    for (my $i = 0;  $i < $numFields;  $i++) {
      if ($$ref[$i]) {
          print "    <td>";
          print xmlquote($$ref[$i]);
          print "</td>\n";
      }
    }
    print "  </tr>\n";
}
print "</table>\n";

$sth->finish;
$dbh->disconnect;

exit(0);
```

Figure 4.6 shows the sample output.

Using PHP

Now that you've seen how easy it is to use a CGI script, we'll move on to look at PHP—which doesn't seem to stand for anything useful, by the way. PHP is a language for writing active Web pages. It's a bit like Cold Fusion, except that it's nonproprietary, open source, freely available, and without glossy marketing literature and slick development environments. PHP normally runs as a module inside Apache, as shown in Figure 4.7.

There are some significant advantages to using PHP over using Perl with CGI, and a couple of disadvantages.

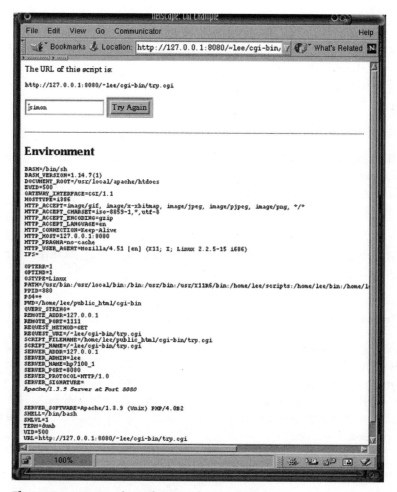

Figure 4.6 Output from the sample CGI script.

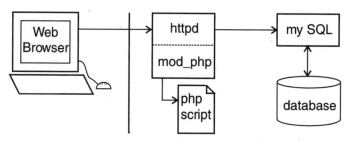

Figure 4.7 PHP architecture.

ADVANTAGES

- Since PHP is a module that's resident inside the Web server, it's much faster than starting Perl for each request.

- The PHP language is smaller than Perl, and therefore may be easier to learn.

DISADVANTAGES

- PHP is not in as widespread use as Perl. At the time of writing, there are only one or two books on PHP (one of which appears to do little more than reprint the documentation that you probably already have in /usr/doc or that's on www.php.org/).

- PHP is not as powerful as Perl.

- CGI scripts can be in any language. Earlier, you saw an example that was a Unix shell script; a C program could also be used.

Example Code

The code given here is similar to the Perl script in functionality, but uses PHP. Before trying it, make sure that you have a version of PHP configured to use MySQL. The example should be saved in a file called names.php (or, if you are using PHP 3, the previous release of PHP, the file should be called names.php3 until you upgrade). Run the example by fetching the file from a Web browser.

```php
<html><head><title>books</title></head>
<body>
<?php

$host = getenv("HTTP_HOST");

if (!$host || strcmp($host, "") == 0 ) {
    $port = getenv("SERVER_PORT");
    if (!$port) {
     $port = 80;
    }

    $server = getenv("SERVER_NAME");
    if (!$server) {
     $server = getenv("SERVER_ADDR");
    }
    if (!$server) {
     $server = "localhost";
    }
    $host = "${server}:${port}";
}
```

```php
$scriptpath = getenv("SCRIPT_NAME");
$url = "${host}${scriptpath}";

function cell($result, $row, $name)
{
    echo "    <td valign=\"top\">";
    echo mysql_result($result, $row, $name);
    echo "    </td>";
}


function book_details($book_id)
{
}

function find_name_info($name, $name_id)
{
    if ($name_id != "") {
     $where = "Name_tbl.Name_id = $name_id";
    } else {
     $where = "Name_tbl.Name REGEXP '$name' ";
    }

    $query = "SELECT
     Name_tbl.Name as Name,
     Name_tbl.Type as Type,
     Name_tbl.Description as Description
     FROM
     Name_tbl
     WHERE
     $where
    ";

    $result = mysql_db_query("books", $query);

    if (!$result) {
     echo "name lookup for [$name/$name_id] failed.";
    } else {
     $count = mysql_numrows($result);

     echo "<h3>result count: $nums</h3>\n";

     echo "<table>\n";
     for ($i = 0; $i < $count; $i++) {
         echo "  <tr>\n";
             $type = mysql_result($result, $i, "Type");
             echo "<td>\n";
             echo "<img src=\"icons/${type}.gif\" width=\"32\"
height=\"32\" alt=\"${type}:\">";
             echo "</td>\n";
             cell($result, $i, "Name");
```

```
            cell($result, $i, "Description");
        echo "   </tr>\n";
    }
    echo "</table>\n";
}


}

function find_books($author, $author2, $title, $eariest, $latest)
{
    # mode==booksearch
    # the following variables might be set:
    # author
    # author2 (not done)
    # title
    # earliest
    # latest
    # name
    $where = "";
    $and = "";

    if ($author != "") {
     if (ereg("(.*) *, *(.*)", $author, $names)) {
         $where = "Author_tbl.LastName REGEXP '$names[1]'
                 AND Author_tbl.FirstNames REGEXP '$names[2]'";
     } else {
         $where = "Author_tbl.LastName REGEXP '$author'";
     }
     $and = "AND \n";
    }

    if ($title != "") {
     $where = "$where $and Book_tbl.Title REGEXP '$title'";
     $and = "AND \n";
    }

    # if ($earliest != "") {
     # $where = "$where $and Book_tbl.date >= $earliest";
     # $and = "AND";
    # }

    # if ($latest != "") {
     # $where =  "$where $and Book_tbl.date <= $latest";
     # $and = "AND";
    # }

    # make sure $where is not null:

    $query = "SELECT
     Author_tbl.LastName as Author,
     Author_tbl.FirstNames as firstName,
```

```
 Book_tbl.Title as Title,
 Book_tbl.Book_id as Book_id
 FROM
 Wrote_tbl, Author_tbl, Book_tbl
 WHERE $where $and Wrote_tbl.Author_id = Author_tbl.Author_id
 AND Wrote_tbl.Book_id = Book_tbl.Book_id
 AND Author_tbl.Author_id = Wrote_tbl.Author_id
 ";
echo "<h2>books!</h2>\n";

echo "<pre>$query</pre>\n";

$result = mysql_db_query("books", $query);

if (!$result) {
 echo "query failed.";
} else {
 $count = mysql_numrows($result);

 echo "<h3>result count: $count</h3>\n";

 if ($count <= 0) {
     echo "<p>There were no matches for ";
     if ($name_id != "") {
         echo "name id $name_id";
     } else {
         echo "name $name";
     }
     echo "</p>\n";
 }
 echo "<table>\n";
 for ($i = 0; $i < $count; $i++) {
     echo " <tr>\n";
         echo "<td valign=\"top\">";
             $r_name = mysql_result($result, $i, 'Author');
             echo "<b>$r_name</b>";

             $r_first = mysql_result($result, $i, 'firstName');
             if ($r_first != "") {
                 echo ", $r_first";
             }
             echo ":";
         echo "</td>\n";

         echo "<td valign=\"top\">";
             $r_title = mysql_result($result, $i, 'Title');
             $r_id = mysql_result($result, $i, 'Book_id');
             $info = "<a
href=\"http://${url}?mode=book&bookid=${r_id}\">[details]</a>";
             echo "<i>$r_title</i> $info";
         echo "</td>\n";
```

```
            echo "</tr>\n";
            echo "<tr><td> </td>";
        echo "   </tr>\n";
     }
     echo "</table>\n";
    }


}

function find_books_with_name($name, $name_id)
{
    # the following variables might be set:
    # name
    # name_id

    if ($name_id) {
     $where = "References_tbl.Name_id = $name_id
              AND Name_tbl.Name_id = $name_id";
    } else {
     $where = "Name_tbl.Name REGEXP '$name'
              AND Name_tbl.Name_id = References_tbl.Name_id
              ";
    }

    $query = "SELECT
     Author_tbl.LastName as Author,
     Author_tbl.FirstNames as firstName,
     Book_tbl.Title as Title,
     Book_tbl.Book_id as Book_id,
     Name_tbl.Name as Name,
     Name_tbl.Type as NameType,
     Name_tbl.Description as NameDesc,
     References_tbl.Role as Role
     FROM
     References_tbl, Wrote_tbl, Author_tbl, Book_tbl, Name_tbl
     WHERE $where
     AND References_tbl.Book_id = Book_tbl.Book_id
     AND Wrote_tbl.Author_id = Author_tbl.Author_id
     AND Wrote_tbl.Book_id = Book_tbl.Book_id
     AND Author_tbl.Author_id = Wrote_tbl.Author_id
     ";

    # echo "<pre>$query</pre>\n";

    $result = mysql_db_query("books", $query);

    if (!$result) {
     echo "query failed.";
    } else {
     $count = mysql_numrows($result);
```

```
echo "<h3>result count: $count</h3>\n";

if ($count <= 0) {
    echo "<p>There were no matches for ";
    if ($name_id != "") {
        echo "name id $name_id";
    } else {
        echo "name $name";
    }
    echo "</p>\n";
}
echo "<table>\n";
for ($i = 0; $i < $count; $i++) {
    echo "  <tr>\n";
        echo "<td valign=\"top\">";
            $r_name = mysql_result($result, $i, 'Author');
            echo "<b>$r_name</b>";

            $r_first = mysql_result($result, $i, 'firstName');
            if ($r_first != "") {
                echo ", $r_first";
            }
            echo ":";
        echo "</td>\n";

        echo "<td valign=\"top\">";
            $r_title = mysql_result($result, $i, 'Title');
            echo "<i>$r_title</i>";
        echo "</td>\n";

        echo "</tr>\n";
        echo "<tr><td> </td>";
        echo "<td>";
            $r_name = mysql_result($result, $i, 'Name');
            $r_role = mysql_result($result, $i, 'Role');
            $r_type = mysql_result($result, $i, 'NameType');
            $r_desc = mysql_result($result, $i, 'NameDesc');
            if (strcmp($r_type, "person") == 0) {
                echo "Role of $r_name in this book: $r_role";
            } else if (strcmp($r_type, "wizard") == 0) {
                echo "Role of $r_name in this book: $r_role";
            } else {
                echo "$r_name, $r_desc, is ${r_role}.";
            }
        echo "</td></tr>\n";
    echo "  </tr>\n";
}
echo "</table>\n";
}
}
```

```
?>

<!--* possible dumb mode section if mode is unset *-->
<?php if ($name == "" && $name_id == "" && $mode == ""): ?>
<?php echo "<form action=\"http://$url\" method=GET>\n"; ?>
<table>
  <tr valign=top>
   <th align=right>Character or Place:</th>
   <td><input width=20 size=20 name=name></td>
  </tr>
  <tr>
   <td> </td>
   <td><input type=submit value="search"></td>
  </tr>
</table>
<?php endif ?>
<!--* end of dumb mode section, if present *-->

<--* results section *-->

<?php
    mysql_connect("localhost", "lee", "Your PasswordHere");

    if (strcmp($mode, "booksearch") == 0) {
     find_books($author, $author2, $title, $eariest, $latest);
    } else if (strcmp($mode, "book") == 0) {
     book_details($book_id);
    } else if ($name != "" || $name_id != "")  {
     echo "<h1>Books mentioning $name</h1>";
     find_name_info($name, $name_id);
    }

    if ($name != "" || $name_id != "") {
     find_books_with_name($name, $name_id);
    }

?> .

</body></html>
```

Java

This section gives a brief overview of using Java and the Java DataBase Connection (JDBC) to export data. This is not primarily a Java book (there are many of these), but if you are in a Java environment already, you might find the strategies presented here useful. I have not included a *Just Enough Java* section in this book, so if you are not already using Java, go to your local bookshop and get a tutorial on Java. One to look for is Mary Campione's and

Kathy Walrath's *The Java Tutorial Second Edition: Object-Oriented Programming for the Internet* (Addison-Wesley, 1998).

The techniques in Java are the same as for Perl; you print pointy brackets around elements. Another possibility is to write a class that builds objects in memory, perhaps using a SAX-compatible interface (SAX is described in the next chapter) so that you can use an off-the-shelf Java class to print out the result as XML.

Using a Java Servlet

The following simple Java servlet is roughly equivalent to the CGI script shown earlier, except that it doesn't take a parameter to return a particular table. You can find the original version of this example at the URL given in the comment.

This version generates HTML. You only need to change the Content-type to text/html and alter tags as appropriate to make XML. Save the resulting XML to a file and check it with a parser such as XP to make sure it's well formed.

```
/**
 * Servlet to query Books database by author.
 *
 * The original sample code was by Daniel.Schneider@tecfa.unige.ch
 * 1999 TECFA, and was freeware. In the same spirit, this example
 * is in the public domain.
 * See http://tecfa.unige.ch/guides/java/staf2x/ex/jdbc/coffee-break/
 *
 */

import java.io.*;
import javax.servlet.*;
import javax.servlet.http.*;

import org.gjt.mm.mysql.*;
import org.gjt.mm.mysql.Connection;
import org.gjt.mm.mysql.Statement;
import org.gjt.mm.mysql.Driver;
import org.gjt.mm.mysql.ResultSet;
import org.gjt.mm.mysql.ResultSetMetaData;

import java.sql.*;

public class BookAuthorServlet extends HttpServlet {
    Connection con; // The database connection
    Statement stmt; // The statement
    String queryString = null; // The queryString

    public void init(ServletConfig conf) throws ServletException {
      super.init(conf);
```

```
        String username = "nobody";
        String password = "xxx";

        // Syntax: jdbc:TYPE:machine:port/DB_NAME
        String url = "jdbc:mysql://localhost:3306/Books";

        try {
            Class.forName("org.gjt.mm.mysql.Driver");
            // Connect to the database at URL with usename and password:
            con = (Connection)
                    DriverManager.getConnection(url, username, password);
        } catch (Exception e) { // ClassNotFoundException + SQLException
            throw(new UnavailableException(this, "db conenct failed"));
        }
    }

    /**
     * service() method to handle user interaction
     */
    public void service(HttpServletRequest req, HttpServletResponse res)
        throws ServletException, IOException
    {
     res.setContentType("text/html");
     PrintWriter out = res.getWriter();

     try {
         String title = "Books by Author";
         out.println("<html>");
         out.println("<head><title>Books by Author</title></head>");
         out.println("<body><H1>BookWeb demo: Books by Author</H1>");
         String queryString = req.getParameter("QUERYSTRING");

         if ((queryString != "") && (queryString != null)) {
             out.println("<table border>");
             Statement stmt = (Statement) con.createStatement();
             ResultSet rs = (ResultSet) stmt.executeQuery(queryString);
             ResultSetMetaData rsMeta = (ResultSetMetaData)
rs.getMetaData();
             // Get the N of Cols in the ResultSet
             int noCols = rsMeta.getColumnCount();
             out.println("<tr>");
             for (int c=1; c<=noCols; c++) {
                 String el = rsMeta.getColumnLabel(c);
                 out.println("<th> " + el + " </th>");
             }
             out.println("</tr>");
             while (rs.next()) {
                 out.println("<tr>");
                 for (int c=1; c<=noCols; c++) {
                     String el = rs.getString(c);
                     out.println("<td> " + el + " </td>");
```

```
                }
                out.println("</tr>");
            }
            out.println("</table>");
        }
    } catch (SQLException ex ) {
        out.println ( "<P><PRE>" );
          while (ex != null) {
              out.println("Message:   " + ex.getMessage ());
              out.println("SQLState:  " + ex.getSQLState ());
              out.println("ErrorCode: " + ex.getErrorCode ());
              ex = ex.getNextException();
              out.println("");
          }
          out.println ( "</PRE><P>" );
    }

    out.println ("<hr>You can now try to retrieve something.");
    out.println("<FORM METHOD=POST
ACTION=\"/servlet/BookAuthorServlet\">");
    out.println("Query: <INPUT TYPE=TEXT SIZE=50
NAME=\"QUERYSTRING\"> ");
    out.println("<INPUT TYPE=SUBMIT VALUE=\"GO!\">");
    out.println("</FORM>");
    out.println("<hr><pre>e.g.:");
    out.println("SELECT * FROM Author_tbl");
    out.println("SELECT * FROM Name_tbl");
    out.println("<pre>");

    out.println ( "</body></html>" );
    return ;
    }
}
```

Exercises

1. Study the `xmlquote` function given near the end of the first code section in this chapter. It first replaces every `"&"` with `"&amp;"` in the input. What would happen if it did this last instead of first?

2. Figure out how to change either the Perl CGI script or the PHP code to add a facility for users to enter new books.

3. Make a provision for handling users who enter incorrect data (typing, perhaps, that Heinlein wrote *The Lord of the Rings*) or malicious data (4000 authors all with a rude word as their name)? One approach might be to have your program write an XML file with the new entry, and ask a human to approve it, but that still doesn't help the moderator who gets 4000 mail messages.

4. The Java servlet lets users send an arbitrary query. You could encode a fixed set of choices in a Web page, but people could get around that simply by editing the URL or by saving a local copy of the HTML and changing it. How would you code the servlet to be secure? (The Servlet API at http://java.sun.com/ may help you answer this.)

Other Approaches

The approaches described here all have one major failing in common: They do not validate the generated XML or HTML. Alternative approaches that do more stringent checking include:

- Using the XML Style Language Transformations (XSLT, www.w3.org) to convert generated XML to HTML, validating on the way.

- Using commercial tools such as Omnimark (www.omnimark.com) or Balise (www.balise.com), which offer SGML/XML-aware scripting languages.

- Using complete development environments such as Bluestone's Visual XML (see Chapter 22, "Databases, Repositories, and Utilities," for more database tools).

All of these tools require more specialized knowledge; the general technique of printing with less-than and greater-than signs works in all languages and is easy to understand.

Summary

This chapter has described some brute-force approaches to generating XML from databases. As hinted at in the preceding section, there are many other approaches possible, but they are increasingly specialized. Perl, PHP, and Java all have support for connecting to a database, either from a Web server or standalone.

The next chapter discusses how to read XML back into a program.

## CHAPTER 5

Reading XML into a Program

This chapter describes how to incorporate the capability to read XML into a program, whether that program is written in C, C++, Java, Perl, Python, or some other language. We'll start by showing simple ways to manipulate XML in a program. We'll then explore various ways to read XML by interfacing with a parser, either external or internal.

The XML example we'll use in this chapter is a description of my science fiction and fantasy book collection, represented as a catalogue. We will return to this example in Part Two, but our focus here will be on the information as a document rather than a database. It is important to consider the differences that result from these two world views: the document versus the database. These differences will emerge gradually over the course of this chapter, then be discussed further in Part Two.

XML Example: Book Catalogue

I chose this example because aspects of it are applicable to all the major topics covered in this book: documents, databases, information retrieval, and metadata. The programs I will show you how to develop in this chapter will enable us to put this science fiction and fantasy book catalogue up on the Web, make automated changes to it, or read it in software.

The catalogue will, at least for now, be held in a single XML file. This isn't a good long-term choice, as you'll see when we talk about storing XML in a repository in Part Three; nevertheless, it's a good place to start.

Let's use the following as a first attempt to represent a single book:

```
<book>
    <title>The Celestial Steam Locomotive</title>
    <author>Michal Greatrix Coney</author>
    <publisher>Futura</publisher>
    <city>London, UK</city>
    <pages>302</pages>
    <date>1983</date>
</book>
```

There are some problems with this example. First, my collection contains a number of books by Michael Coney (many of them with equally strange titles), and if I have to retype the author's name for each of them, I will certainly make mistakes. Subsequently, I won't be able to find all books by Michael Coney, because the name will be wrong in some of them. If you're thinking, "Why don't you just proofread more carefully," consider that once I've put this up on the Web, I might want to allow other people to search or update entries; hence, I'll quickly have what database people call an integrity problem. For example, I could end up with three entries for the same book, all with slightly different spellings.

Another problem is that this code sample doesn't represent multiple editions very well. But for the purposes of this discussion, I'm going to ignore this problem, because it raises issues that aren't relevant to reading XML in a program, although they are certainly important (Part Four, "Links and Metadata," gives some ideas on representing information about objects such as books). For now, we'll use the copyright date for the earliest publication of each book and pretend it's the only edition.

We might also want to store other types of information, such as pictures of the cover, extracts, reviews, or even the blurb on the back of the book cover. The following is a richer DTD that will let us represent the catalogue more thoroughly, although it still isn't up to use by a real library. Most libraries use the MARC format, mentioned in Part Four.

Finally, it's very difficult to know how to sort a name like Michael Greatrix Coney; should we list it under M, G, or C? Should we mark the Last Name and the First Names separately, or use an explicit sort key?

Let's start by defining separate sections for authors, publishers, and actual titles:

```
<!ELEMENT Catalogue
    (AuthorList, PublisherList, BookList)
>
```

```
<!ELEMENT AuthorList
    (Author*)
>

<!ELEMENT PublisherList
    (Publisher*)
>

<!ELEMENT BookList
    (Book*)
>
```

The use of the asterisk (*) in the various lists means that we can start editing without any books (for the production DTD, we'll use a plus sign instead of an asterisk).

We will use the XML ID/IDREF linking facility to represent the relationship between a book and its authors and publisher. We will also allow multiple authors, and admit the possibility of editors as well as authors. A book in our simplistic model has only a single date and publisher, so these are attributes.

```
<!ELEMENT Book
    (Title, AuthorRef*, Blurb?)
>
<!ATTLIST Book
    EarliestDate NUMBER #IMPLIED
    Publisher IDREF #IMPLIED
    id ID #REQUIRED
>

<!ELEMENT Title
    (%RunningText;*)
>
<!ELEMENT AuthorRef
    EMPTY
>
<!ATTLIST AuthorRef
    Role (Wrote|Edited) "Wrote"
    Who IDREF #REQUIRED
>
```

We could have used an IDREFS attribute on the Book element instead of separate subelements, but that would make it difficult to determine whether the person referenced wrote the book or edited it. With one more book added, our code now looks like this:

```
<Catalogue>
    <AuthorList>
        <Author id="a001">
            <LastName>Benford</LastName>
            <FirstNames>Gregory</FirstNames>
        </Author>
```

```
        <Author id="a002">
            <LastName>Coney</LastName>
            <FirstNames>Michael Greatrix</FirstNames>
        </Author>
        <Author id="a003">
            <LastName>Brin</LastName>
            <FirstNames>David</FirstNames>
        </Author>
    </AuthorList>
    <PublisherList>
        <Publisher id="p001">
            <Name>Bantam</Name>
            <Country>USA</Country>
        </Publisher>
        <Publisher id="p002">
            <Name>Futura</Name>
            <Country>UK</Country>
        </Publisher>
    </PublisherList>
    <BookList>
        <Book id="b001" EarliestDate="1983" Publisher="p002">
            <Title>The Celestial Steam Locomotive</Title>
            <AuthorRef Role="Wrote" Who="a002" />
            <Blurb>Alan-Blue-Cloud is pure intelligence, immortal,
                ineffable, a being who remembers not only what
                was, but what will be. This is his story, set in the
                year 143,624 Cyclic, in a future so distant that . . .
            </Blurb>
        </Book>
        <Book id="b002" EarliestDate="1986" Publisher="p001">
            <Title>Heart of the Comet</Title>
            <AuthorRef Role="Edited" Who="a001" />
            <AuthorRef Role="Wrote" Who="a003" />
        </Book>
        <Book id="b003" EarliestDate="1998" Publisher="p001">
            <Title>Heaven's Reach</Title>
            <AuthorRef Role="Wrote" Who="a003" />
            <Notes>The final book of the second Uplift trilogy</Notes>
        </Book>
    </BookList>
</Catalogue>
```

Reading the Example in Perl

The easiest way to read this example is to start at the end. Consider the last book in the example, *Heaven's Reach*. The AuthorRef tells us that author a003 wrote the book (wrote because Role is *wrote*). If we look up in the AuthorList section, we see that author a003 is David Brin. Similarly, publisher p001 published the first edition of this book, and we can look up to the PublisherList section to see that this is Bantam, in the United States. I have also noted that

Heaven's Reach is the last book in David Brin's second *Uplift* trilogy. This data is *normalized*: There's no repetition of data, although the model of publishers is oversimplified, and I should probably represent the idea of trilogies a little more carefully. It's enough for now, though, since our real goal is to read this into a program, not to write a book catalogue!

Unfortunately, there is an error in the sample. *Heart of the Comet* was co-authored by Gregory Benford and David Brin; Gregory Benford is listed incorrectly as an editor. Let's see how to fix that, in Perl first, with a simple text substitution:

```
if (m@<AuthorRef Role="Edited" Who="a001" />@) {
    s@Edited@Wrote@;
}
```

That wasn't so bad!

Unfortunately, if Gregory Benford had edited any other books, this Perl fragment would change those, too, so let's fix that, then discuss when to use a simple Perl script like this before moving on to more XML-specific tools.

```
#! /usr/bin/perl -w
# perl script to change the role of an author $1 to $2 in
# the books whose Ids are $3, $4, etc

if ($#ARGV < 2) {
    die "usage: $0 author-id new-role book-id [book-id...]"
}

my ($author_id,$new_role) = ($1, $2);

# remember which books we have to change in an array:
my %books;

{
    my $i;

    for ($i = 2; $i <= $#ARGV; $i++) {
        $books{$ARGV[$i]} = 1;
    }
}
# perl hackers might use this slice instead:
# %books{@ARGV[2 .. $#ARGV]} = @ARGV[2 .. $#ARGV];

my $changeThisBook = 0;

while (<>) {  # for each line of input

    # see if we found a book and want to change it:
    if (/<Book [^<>]*id=['"]([^'"]+)"/) {
        $changeThisBook = $books{$1}; # true if we want to change it
```

```
    }

    # if we see the author, and we're changing things...
    if ($changeThisBook && /<AuthorRef [^<>]*Who="${author_id}"/) {
        s/Role="[^"]*"/Role="${new_role}";
    }

    # print the (possibly changed) line:
    print;
}
```

This Perl example will do the job: Let's put it in a file called newrole.pl, and run it with

```
newrole.pl a003 Wrote b001 b003
```

to make the change.

If you're used to working with relational databases, you are probably thinking that this is utterly insane compared with:

```
UPDATE Wrote_tbl
    SET Role = "Wrote"
    WHERE Book_id = "b001" AND Author_id = "a003"
        ;
```

You're right, it is. But what if we change the question to "I seem to have written Teh instead of The a lot, and it's never right in a book title; can you change them all for me?" Now, we have something we can't do in SQL, because although we can use LIKE to match Teh and teh and TEH and maybe even tEh, we can't directly change the value in SQL.

With Perl, it's very easy:

```
if (/<Title>/ .. /<\/Title>/) {
    s/teh/the/ig;
}
```

The trailing i tells Perl that the substitution is case-insensitive, so that it will match all of the possible variations; the g means that the substitution should be performed throughout the entire input line, not just on the first match found.

Desperate or Dirty?

The Perl fragments shown so far all have one serious failing: They do not check that the XML they are given is well formed. This means that if they are given malformed input, they'll merrily pass it along as malformed output. The scripts also assume that separate book elements will be on separate lines, although that's fairly easy to fix using Perl's *slurp* mode to read an entire file at once:

```
my $textfile;
{
    local $/; # enable slurp mode
    $textfile = <INPUT>; # read the entire file into $textfile
}
```

These fragments are perfect when you need to make a quick change, but they are probably not suitable for production code. That doesn't mean that can't use Perl in a production system, but rather that production code has to be robust against errors.

The fact that these scripts are even possible is due to careful design on the part of the XML Working Group; it is not just a happy coincidence! Let's look at the XML design features that help Perl programmers.

EMPTY Elements Are Distinguished

In SGML, from which XML was derived, an EMPTY element such as Author-Ref has a normal start tag and no end tag. Consider this SGML example:

```
<Book>
    <Title>Heart of the Comet</Title>
    <AuthorRef>
```

You have no way to know whether there will be an end tag for AuthorRef or if it's EMPTY, except by fetching and parsing the DTD. In XML, though, the tag is written with a /> instead, thus: <AuthorRef/>. This was done so that text-processing tools would not need to look at the DTD to handle EMPTY elements.

Attributes Cannot Contain Markup Characters

An attribute value is not allowed to contain less-than or greater-than signs, so that the regular expression <[^>]+> will always match a tag. Without this rule,

The Desperate Perl Hacker

During the development of XML, one of the editors of the specification, John Bosak, wanted to describe a technical writer who was given a task such as: replace part number 1996 by part 1996B without affecting dates, in all 150,000 pages of documentation. The writer would know some Perl but not be a programmer, and the deadline would be by the end of the afternoon.

The person thus described was desperate to get the job done, was a hacker in the sense of someone writing "quick-and-dirty" code to get a job done, and used Perl because it's the most commonly used language for jobs like this.

A lot of issues were decided in the design of XML based on how hard they would be for the so-called Desperate Perl Hacker, and it should come as no surprise that Perl and XML go very well together.

a start tag like `<expr value="a > 4 and b < 12">` would not be possible; the regular expression would only match `<expr value="a >`.

NOTE

If you need to put a less-than or greater-than sign into an attribute value, use `&lt;` or `&gt;` as appropriate.

Tags Cannot Be Omitted

In HTML, and in many other SGML applications, it's possible to leave out tags if a sufficiently intelligent parser can determine exactly what you omitted. This is called the OMITTAG feature of SGML, but XML doesn't have it. Consider the following HTML example:

```
<table>
 <tr>
  <td><p>This is a table cell.
      <p>It contains two paragraphs
  </td>
</table>
```

In XML, it must be written like this (the extra markup is in bold):

```
<table>
 <tr>
  <td><p>This is a table cell.</p>
      <p>It contains two paragraphs</p>
  </td>
 </tr>
</table>
```

Not So Dirty

There are many other similar ways that XML has been made amenable to Perl or other text-based languages, but these are the essential ones to understand; the others are important only if you are working with SGML as well as XML.

Later in this chapter, you'll see that it's possible to use Perl together with XML well-formed checking, and even validation, but you can do a lot with simple scripts like this, given well-formed XML input.

External Parsing and the ESIS

In addition to knowing how to read XML in Perl using regular expressions, there are two other important approaches that we must cover. The first is to use an external program to "parse" the XML and convert it into a format that's easier to handle. The second approach is to use a parser that's built into your program. This section describes the first of those two approaches, using an external program, or *parser*, to read the XML, in this case, the Element Structure Information Set (ESIS).

What Is ESIS?

ESIS was defined in ISO 13673, Reference Application for SGML Testing, so that the output of two SGML parsers could be compared. When most people refer to ESIS, they mean the output of James Clark's freely available *nsgmls* tool, which also conforms to the ISO 13673 standard. The format is documented (at the time of writing) at www.jclark.com/sp/sgmlsout.htm.

Table 5.1 gives a summary of the ESIS format. The first character on each line determines the meaning of the rest of the line. There are other possible codes, but those listed in this table are the most important. Consult the documentation if you need the full set.

You will also see some *escape sequences* within the text, such as those listed in Table 5.2.

Figure 5.1 illustrates the ESIS output from the book catalogue sample earlier in the chapter. It was produced by running the following command:

```
$ nsgmls xml.dcl bokcatalogue.xml > esis.txt
```

where xml.dcl is found in the /pubtext directory of the SP 1.3 (or later) distribution from www.jclark.com.

Table 5.1 ESIS Format Summary

CHARACTER	MEANING
(name	Start of element called name; if the element has attributes, they are on A-lines before this one.
Aname type [value]	The element about to start will have an attribute called name of the given type, with the given value (if present). The type is one of IMPLIED (in which case there is no value), CDATA, NOTATION, ENTITY, TOKEN, or ID.
)name	End of element called name.
-text	Textual content of an element; there can be more than one of these lines for a single element.
?procinst	A processing instruction or XML declaration.
e	The next element to start was declared as EMPTY, and would therefore have a tag like `<name atts../>` with the /> at the end. You get this only if you run nsgmls with the -oempty option.
C	This is the last output line, and is issued only if the document was valid.

The trailing C at the end of the code in Figure 5.1 shows us that the document is conforming to its DTD—that is, it's *valid*. In this case, *nsgmls* also returns to the Unix shell an exit code of 0, signifying success. This means you can write a test in a shell script as follows:

```
# /bin/sh
# esis -- generate ESIS from an XML file,
# just a wrapper to show how to incorporate
# nsgmls into a shell script
# Liam Quin, Barefoot Computing, 1999
# This shell fragment is public domain.

input="$1"

if test ! -f "$input"
then
    echo "usage: esis file.xml" 2>&2
    exit 1 # fail
fi

decl="/usr/local/pubtext/xml.dcl"

esis=/tmp/xx.$$
# arrange for the temporary file to be removed on exit:
trap '/bin/rm -f $esis; exit' 0 1 2 3 15

if nsgmls -oempty $decl $input > $esis
then
    # process valid output in $esis in some way:
    /bin/ls -l "$esis"
else
    echo "$input is not valid" 1>&2 # error messaage
    exit 1
fi
```

Table 5.2 Escape Sequences

ESCAPE SEQUENCE	REPRESENTATION
\n	This represents a newline character in the input, ASCII LF (10 in decimal, 012 in octal, or 0A in hex; also control-J). You will normally see this only where #PCDATA was allowed in the DTD.
\ddd \#nnnnnn;	Represents the input data character whose character code is *ddd* in octal. For example, an A might be represented as \101 because it's 65 in decimal, 101 in octal. The alternate decimal form \#65; is used for Unicode characters whose codes are too large to be represented by three octal digits.
\\	Represents a literal \ that was found in the input.

```
?xml version="1.0" encoding="iso8859-1"
(Catalogue
(AuthorList
Aid TOKEN a001
(Author
(LastName
-Benford
)LastName
(FirstNames
-Gregory
)FirstNames
)Author
Aid TOKEN a002
(Author
(LastName
-Coney
)LastName
(FirstNames
-Michael Greatrix
)FirstNames
)Author
Aid TOKEN a003
(Author
(LastName
-Brin
)LastName
(FirstNames
-David
)FirstNames
)Author
)AuthorList
(PublisherList
Aid TOKEN p001
(Publisher
(Name
-Bantam
)Name
(Country
-USA
)Country
)Publisher
Aid TOKEN p002
(Publisher
(Name
-Futura
)Name
(Country
-UK
)Country
)Publisher
)PublisherList
```

continues

Figure 5.1   ESIS output from the book catalogue.

```
(BookList
AEarliestDate TOKEN 1983
APublisher TOKEN p002
(Book
(Title
-The Celestial Steam Locomotive
)Title
ARole TOKEN Wrote
AWho TOKEN a002
(AuthorRef
)AuthorRef
(Blurb
-Alan-Blue-Cloud is pure intelligence, immortal,\n\012
              ineffable, a being who remembers not only what\n\012
              was, but what will be. This is his story, set in
the\n\012
              year 143,624 Cyclic, in a future so distant that . .
.\n\012
)Blurb
)Book
AEarliestDate TOKEN 1986
APublisher TOKEN p001
(Book
(Title
-Heart of the Comet
)Title
ARole TOKEN Wrote
AWho TOKEN a001
(AuthorRef
)AuthorRef
ARole TOKEN Wrote
AWho TOKEN a003
(AuthorRef
)AuthorRef
)Book
AEarliestDate TOKEN 1998
APublisher TOKEN p001
(Book
(Title
-Heaven's Reach
)Title
ARole TOKEN Wrote
AWho TOKEN a003
(AuthorRef
)AuthorRef
(Notes
-The final book of the second Uplift trilogy
)Notes
)Book
)BookList
)Catalogue
C
```

Figure 5.1 ESIS output from the book catalogue (*continued*).

Reading ESIS

If you have used *awk* or *perl*, you can probably see how to make use of this format at once. Even in C it's pretty easy. I am not going to show you much sample code, because a better approach is to use a higher-level library that reads ESIS and returns events to your program. When you can, it's better to incorporate an XML processor directly into your program, as we'll discuss in the next section. When you can't recompile the code you're working with, for example, reading ESIS is often a painless option. If you use C or C++, remember that there is no fixed line-length limit and no maximum length for an XML element name, so you'll need to use *malloc( )* for all the strings you see, instead of fixed-size arrays.

David Megginson's NSGMLS.pm

This oddly named software, also called SGMLS.pl, is a Perl library that reads ESIS and returns a sequence of events. You provide Perl functions to handle element starts, ends, and other events, and the library builds up all the attributes into a hash table and calls your code as appropriate. It's mentioned here because it reads ESIS and is sometimes your best option. The Simple XML API, SAX, described later, is much more likely to be what you're looking for, though (It also was written by David Megginson, so you don't need to feel disloyal). More important, there are open source SAX-style modules for Perl, Java, C, Python, C++, and other languages.

Why Keep nsgmls?

James Clark's *nsgmls* tool can produce an ESIS form of an XML (or SGML) document, and it can check a document's validity and warn about errors. This turns out to be very useful; and since *nsgmls* is fast, it's pretty handy to have around. There are versions for Linux, Solaris (Intel and SPARC), Windows, Free BSD, and other operating systems. (See Chapter 21, "XML Parsers, Editors, and Utilities," for more details.) The *nsgmls* package also includes a program called *spam* that can remove unwanted whitespace from SGML and XML files, add missing SGML end tags, and generally clean up (or normalize) the data.

Using an Internal Parser

Using an external parser can involve the fewest source changes, particularly on Unix where running an external process is fast and easy. If you need better performance, or control over error messages, you will need to compile a parser into your application directly.

The parser we will use for both C and Perl is *expat*, also from James Clark, because expat is most difficult in C and most common in Perl. We will start by using expat directly, with Clark's C interface.

Again, the purpose of this chapter is to give you an understanding of the strengths and weaknesses of the various approaches to reading XML so you are encouraged to try the examples.

The expat API

This section and its example are intended to give you enough documentation to get started. It is included partly because at the time of writing there aren't any other books that discuss it usefully; but primarily it is included because expat is the easiest way to integrate XML into an existing C or C++ program. There are also Perl and Python interfaces to expat. If you are using Java, you should look at SAX instead; it is covered in a later section.

NOTE Much of the material describing expat comes from comments in James Clark's C code or from the Perl documentation from the modules that Larry Wall and Clark Cooper wrote.

The expat parser defines a set of callbacks and some functions for you to call. The general model is this:

1. Create a parser object with XML_ParserCreate().
2. Your program registers callbacks with XML_SetElementHandler(), XML_SetCharacterHandler(), and so on for each sort of function you're interested in (element start, text, element end, processing instruction); the functions to do this are described in the *Using Expat Functions in C* section.
3. Hand the data to XML_Parse() as it becomes available.
4. Destroy the parser object with XML_ParserFree().

Using expat in Perl

Larry Wall and Clark Cooper have provided a Perl interface to expat, XML::Expat. There is also a higher-level interface called XML::Parser.

The following Perl example shows the XML::Parser in Tree mode; it also supports an API very similar to that shown in the *Using expat Functions in C* section, later.

Though the online manual (perldoc XML::Parser) describes the expat-style API, it is very terse about the Tree style, so this example uses a Tree. Save it in a file such as xmltree.pl, and run it with:

```
$ chmod +x xmltree.pl
$ ./xmltree.pl somefile.xml
```

The program prints its input; a more useful example might store the input in a relational database a row at a time. The following C example shows how to build up a structure in memory from the expat-style API, and that technique could be used in Perl, too.

```perl
#! /usr/bin/perl -w
use strict;

use XML::Parser;

sub parseFile($)
{
    my ($fileName) = @_;

    my $parser = new XML::Parser(
        Style => 'Tree',
        ErrorContext => 2,
        ProtocolEncoding => 'ISO-8859-1'
    );
    open(INPUT, "< $fileName") ||
        die "could not open input file $fileName: $!";

    my $data;
    {
        local $/; # slurp mode: read entire file
        $data = <INPUT>
    }
    close(INPUT);

    my @result = $parser->parse($data); # convert the XML to a Tree
    # The parser returns an array whose only element
    # is a reference to the result.  So we return just that:
    my $realresult = $result[0];

    return $realresult;
}

sub printTree($$$)
{
    my ($name, $tree, $level) = @_;
    my $atts = $$tree[0];

    # An element is represented as an array
    # if tree[i] is 0, tree[i+1] is text data
    # if tree[i] is a string, it's the name of an element, and
    # tree[i + 1] is the contents of the children.
    # The first item of the child array is the element's attributes;
    # the rest are the childern in the same format.
```

```perl
# A good way to see what's going on is to use Data::Dumper.

# The arrays are actually all references to arrays, because
# that's the only way Perl can nest arrays.

my $prefix = " " x ($level * 2);

# Start tag with attributes:
print "<$name";
my ($key, $value);
foreach $key (keys %$atts) {
    print " $key=$$atts{$key}";
}
print ">";

my $i;
my $max = $#$tree;

# Content (handled recursively); Item zero is a reference
# to a hash of XML attributes, and the children are the remaining
# items. Alternate items in the child array are the type of what
# follows, and the value. Currently, the only two types are
# 0 for PCDATA and a string representing the name of an element, if
# it's a child element.  The children are thus elements
# 1 and 2, 3 and 4, up to $max - 1 and $max, since $max is the
# highest legal subscript for the array, $#$tree.

# perldoc perlref
# is a good way to learn more about using references in Perl.

for ($i = 1; $i < $max; $i+= 2) {
    my $what = $$tree[$i];

    if ($what eq '0') { # text context
        print $$tree[$i + 1];
    } else {
        printTree($what, $$tree[$i + 1], $level + 1);
    }
}

# Finally, print an end tag:
print "</$name>";
}

sub main
{
    foreach (@ARGV) {
        my $tree = parseFile($_);

        printTree($$tree[0], $$tree[1], 0);
```

```
       }
    }

    main();
```

Using expat in Java

If you have determined that you really need the performance, it *is* possible, using native methods, to use expat in Java (see the archives of the xml-dev mailing list to get started). Make sure you've used Java profiling tools and are certain that more than 10 percent of your program's runtime is spent XML parsing code directly, not in calling your own methods to handle things found in the XML; if this is not the case, you won't be able to get enough speed to make your effort worthwhile. Even then, you may do better using a cache of recently parsed documents, or perhaps storing the XML in an object-oriented database, as described in Part Three.

NOTE

Try to avoid using native methods for as long as possible. They are difficult to debug, make it harder to use profiling tools, and make it almost impossible for your code to work on multiple platforms.

Using expat Functions in C

This section describes the functions that the expat API exports.

Creating a Parser

Begin by creating a new parser with `XML_ParserCreate`, as here:

```
XML_Parser
XML_ParserCreate(
    const XML_Char *encoding
);
```

This generates a new parser object and returns a handle to it. Keep the handle, as you'll need it for future calls.

The encoding parameter is a string, which, at the time of writing, should be one of those listed in Table 5.3.

Encodings

Suppose that you supply a different encoding parameter, or that you supply a NULL pointer, and the document contains an XML declaration with a different encoding, like this:

Table 5.3 Encoding Parameters

PARAMETER	USE
(NULL)	A NULL pointer passed as an encoding tells expat to use the encoding given in the XML declaration in the input document. If that declaration is unknown, the Unknown Encoding Handler will be called.
ISO-8859-1	Also known as Latin 1, this is the encoding most widely used for HTML documents; it is also the default character encoding on the X Window System in most Western countries.
US-ASCII	This is a 7-bit encoding (the eighth, top, bit in each byte must always be 0), and since it's essentially a subset of ISO-8859-1 without the accented characters, you probably don't want to use it.
UTF-8	This is the most common encoding for Unicode in Western countries.
UTF-16	This is an alternative encoding of Unicode, which is much more efficient for Kanji and other non-Western character sets, but which is not so useful if you are mostly dealing with English or other Latin-alphabet languages, since it uses 2 bytes for each character.

```
<?xml version="1.0" encoding="iso8859-1"?>
```

Here, the encoding is not an exact match for any in Table 5.3. If you have called XML_SetUnknownEncodingHandler(), the function you gave as an argument to it will now be called with two parameters, the encoding string "iso8859-1", and a structure that your function must fill in.

```
typedef int(* XML_UnknownEncodingHandler)(
    void *encodingHandlerData,
    const XML_Char *name,
    XML_Encoding *theEncoding
);

void
XML_SetUnknownEncodingHandler(
    XML_Parser parser,
    XML_UnknownEncodingHandler handler,
    void *data
);
```

In our example, expat already knows how to handle the encoding, though it has a different name for it. We can handle that easily by filling in the XML_Encoding structure that is passed to our callback function, and returning 1:

```
typedef struct {
    int map[256];
    void *data;
    int (*convert)(void *data, const char *s);
    void (*release)(void *data);
} XML_Encoding;

static int
handleMisspeltEncoding(
    void *encodingHandlerData,
    const XML_Char *encodingName,
    XML_Encoding *result
)
{
    /* always use the current C locale setting; this
     * may be wrong, so you should write code to check that
     * encodingName looks like iso8859-1 or Latin1 first.
     */
    int i;

    for (i = 0; i < 256; i++) {
        result->map[i] = i;
    }

    /* We won't set the handler functions for the encoding,
     * because this is a one-byte encoding. If you need to handle
     * multibyte encodings other than UTF16, for example
     * ISO2022 escape sequences, you'll need to fill in the other
     * components of the structure.
     */


    return 1;
}
```

Installing Callbacks

Once you have created an XML_Parser object, you probably want to arrange to see the data. You supply a number of functions, of which the most important are handlers for when an element starts, when an element ends, and when character data is seen:

```
typedef void (* XML_StartElementHandler)(
    void *userData,
    const XML_Char *name,
    const XML_Char **atts
);

typedef void (* XML_EndElementHandler)(
```

```
        void *userData,
        const XML_Char *name
);

void
XML_SetElementHandler(
        XML_Parser p,
        XML_StartElementHandler start,
        XML_EndElementHandler end
);


typedef void (* XML_CharacterDataHandler)(
        void *userData,
        const XML_Char *s,
        int len
);

void
XML_SetCharacterDataHandler(
        XML_Parser p,
        XML_CharacterDataHandler handler
);
```

The example code shown later in this chapter uses these callbacks.

NOTE

When a *dataLength* parameter is supplied, the given string is *not* nul-terminated. This means that you can't use functions like `strcmp()`, `strcpy()`, or `strdup()` on it: You must use `strncmp()`, `strncpy()`, and `malloc()` instead. If you are using Unicode data, you may have to consult the Unicode specification at www.unicode.org for information on how to compare strings, unless you have a library to do it for you.

Other XML features for which you can set callbacks include CDATA sections, comments, external entity references, namespaces, notation declarations, processing instructions, unparsed entities (that is, non-XML objects such as images), and the XML standalone declaration.

Other Functions

There are a number of other expat functions whose names start with XML_, but you should probably avoid declaring any global (nonstatic) functions or variables whose names start with that prefix, to avoid confusion and the generation of frustrating bugs.

Installing and Building expat

Chapter 20, "Installing and Configuring Downloaded Software," includes notes on how to build software on Unix. It's not difficult, but if you are not used to software development on Unix, the absence of a Makefile for *expat* causes it to be more difficult than it should be, at least at the time of writing.

A Sample expat Program

Here is the sample program. It builds a linked list of authors by reading from bookcatalogue.xml, and, at the end, prints them all out.

```c
/* authors.c
 *
 * Liam Quin, Barefoot Computing, 1999
 *
 * This source code is in the public domain.
 *
 * Authors -- read an XML book catalogue and fill in a data
 *     structure for them.
 *
 */

#include <stdio.h>
#include <string.h>
#include "xmlparse.h"

typedef struct s_Author {
    struct s_Author *Next;
    char *id;
    char *LastName;
    char *FirstNames;
} t_Author;

typedef struct {
    t_Author *Authors;
        /* hold the list so far */
    t_Author *Current;
        /* pointer to the author element we're updating right now */
    int Saving;
        /* non-zero if we are inside an Author element */
    char **SavePointer;
        /* where to put text we save */
} t_State;

static void
startElement(
    void *userData,
    const char *name,
```

```
        const char **atts
    )
    {
        t_State *State = userData;

        if (strcmp(name, "Author") == 0) {
            /** A new Author element, so make a new structure
             ** to hold it, and start to fill it in
             **/
            t_Author *neo =
                (t_Author *) malloc(sizeof(t_Author));

            if (!neo) {
                /** out of memory;
                 ** handle this better in real code
                 **/
                fprintf(stderr, "author: out of memory, sorry\n");
                exit(1);
            }

            neo->Next = 0;
            neo->id = neo->LastName = neo->FirstNames = 0;

            if (State->Current) {
                State->Current->Next = neo; /* bug: see Exercises */
            }
            State->Current = neo;
            if (!State->Authors) {
                State->Authors = neo;
            }
            State->Saving = 1;
            State->SavePointer = 0;

            /** Save the ID attribute, if set
             ** Attributes are supplied in an array, with alternate
             ** values being the attribute name, then the value
             **/
            if (atts && atts[0]) {
                char *AttName, *AttValue;

                int n;
                for (n = 0; atts[n]; n += 2) {
                    if (strcmp(atts[n], "id") == 0) {
                        State->Current->id = strdup(atts[n + 1]);
                    } else {
                        fprintf(stderr, "unexpected attribute %s\n",
atts[n]);
                        /* see Exercises for ideas about this one */
                        exit(1);
                    }
                }
```

```
            }
            return;
        }

        if (!State->Saving) {
            return;
        }

        /* arrange to save text if it's wanted:
         * we do that by setting SavePointer to point to the field we
         * want to fill in
         */

        if (strcmp(name, "LastName") == 0) {
            State->SavePointer = &State->Current->LastName;
        } else if (strcmp(name, "FirstNames") == 0) {
            State->SavePointer = &State->Current->FirstNames;
        } else {
            fprintf(stderr, "element %s found inside Author! Urk!\n", name);
            /* see Exercise about using validation */
            State->SavePointer = 0;
        }
    }

static void
endElement(void *userData, const char *name)
{
    t_State *State = userData;

    if (State->Saving) {
        /* stop saving  text until the next element */
        State->SavePointer = 0;
    }

    if (strcmp(name, "Author") == 0) {
        State->Saving = 0;
    }
}

static void
textHandler(void *userData,  const char *theText, int len)
{
    t_State *State = userData;
    char **destination = State->SavePointer;

    /* since the expat callback does not tell us which element
     * we are in, we look at the saved state and see if we're saving.
     * If we are, we use SavePointer to tell us where to store the data.
     */

    if (!State->Saving || !State->SavePointer) {
```

```
            return;
    }

    *(State->SavePointer) = (char *) malloc(len + 1);
                                        /* see Exercises */
    memcpy(*destination, theText, len);
    (*destination)[len] = '\0';
}

static void
printAuthors(t_Author *List)
{
    while (List) {
        printf("%s: %s",
            List->id,
            List->LastName
        );

        if (List->FirstNames && *List->FirstNames) {
            printf(", %s", List->FirstNames);
        }

        printf("\n");

        List = List->Next;
    }
}

/** Now a main() that will use all these functions we've defined!
 **/
int
main(int argc, char *argv[])
{
    XML_Parser parser = XML_ParserCreate(NULL);
    char buf[BUFSIZ];
    int finished;
    FILE *f;

    t_State *State;

    if (argc <= 1) {
        fprintf(stderr,
            "%s: supply an XML file as an argument.\n", argv[0]
        );
        exit(1); /* fail */
    }

    f = fopen(argv[1], "r");
    if (!f) {
        perror(argv[1]);
        exit(1);
```

```
    }

    State = (t_State *) calloc(1, sizeof(t_State));

    /** Register the callbacks so that expat will call these
     ** functions when the appropriate events occur:
     **/
    XML_SetUserData(parser, State);
    XML_SetElementHandler(parser, startElement, endElement);
    XML_SetCharacterDataHandler(parser, textHandler);

    /** Now read the input a block at a time, passing each
     ** block to expat. Expat will call our functions.
     ** It would be more efficient to use stat() and read the
     ** whole file into memory, I expect, but this way works if
     ** we're reading chunks of data from a network socket too.
     **/
    do {
        size_t len = fread(buf, 1, sizeof(buf), f);
        finished = len < sizeof(buf);

        /* If we read fewer bytes from the file than we asked for,
         * this is probably the last chunk of data in the file.
         * A return of -1 from fread() means an error occurred.
         * Some implementations set an error or EOF condition too,
         * but it's not necessary to test for EOF in more than one way.
         * If you used sockets and read(2) you'd test for EINTR or
         * EAGAIN here, probably; see the man page for read(2).
         */
        if (!XML_Parse(parser, buf, len, finished)) {
            fprintf(stderr,
                "%s at line %d\n",
                XML_ErrorString(XML_GetErrorCode(parser)),
                XML_GetCurrentLineNumber(parser)
            );
            exit(1); /* fail */
        }
    } while (!finished);

    /* We have finished with the parser now: */
    XML_ParserFree(parser);

    /* We've finished with the input file: */
    fclose(f);

    /* now print the resulting data structure
     * An important note: if we encountered a parse error, we called
     * exit() above. Since expat passes objects back as soon as it finds
     * them in the input, you must think carefully about error handling.
     * An error in the input means that the elements you have seen so
     * far should be discarded. In this example, we call exit() on an
```

```
 * error, so that's not an issue, but for a real program it might be!
 */
if (State->Authors) {
    printAuthors(State->Authors);
}

exit(0);
}
```

SAX: Ælfred Was a Saxon

David Megginson was heavily involved in the XML initiative; he was one of a number of people who decided to write his own XML processor. It quickly became clear that lots of people were writing parsers, particularly for use from Java, and the APIs were all incompatible. The JUMBO XML browser that Peter Murray-Rust was developing for the biochemical industry could use any of a number of parsers, but at the expense of difficult-to-modify code.

The solution was, of course, for everyone involved in writing parsers to agree on one interface. This usually takes either coercion or chutzpah, and, fortunately, David Megginson had the latter. Megginson's own parser was called Ælfred, named after the Saxon king. The Simple API for XML (SAX) continued the theme.

SAX is an event-based API, rather like *expat* discussed in the previous section. Like expat, a SAX parser does not build up a data structure in memory for you, but rather hands back fragments of XML to your application as soon as it sees them.

The full SAX API is documented at www.megginson.com/SAX/. There is also a tutorial at http://java.sun.com/xml/docs/tutorial/, and pointers to more information in Chapter 23, "Further Reading."

Exercises

1. The comments in the sample *expat* program mention several bugs. Can you figure out what they are? What would happen if the text handler were called more than once for the same element, perhaps for a piece of text that was longer than the input chunk? How could you test this? How could you make the program robust against this situation?

2. The sample *expat* program might not run correctly if you handed it a document based on another sort of DTD, one in which an Author element was empty, for example. You could help matters along by enforcing the

use of the right DTD. At the time of writing, *expat* did not have an interface to do this. How might you extend *expat* in this way? What if *expat* doesn't validate its input? Investigate the SP validating parser.

3. How could you handle database update from an *expat* program in the face of possible syntax errors in the input? One approach would be to use a database transaction around the call to `XML_parse()` in `main()`, if the database you are using supports transactions (MySQL does not). Another is to build a complete data structure in memory and check it for completeness before performing any database operations. What would be the memory and performance trade-offs?

Summary

This chapter showed several ways to read XML into a program. You can use regular expressions (or write brute-force C code), or you can use an XML parser that someone else has written. Parsers are available for most languages; this chapter gave examples in both C and Perl. You can use a parser written in the language you're using or built in to a library or interpreter, or run an external process.

Chapter 6, "XML Database Applications," combines all of the techniques and tools mentioned in the book so far, and shows various ways of building XML database applications.

XML Database Applications

The purpose of this chapter is to give you the information you need to combine the techniques described in the first five chapters of the book, choosing architectures and strategies, and making your own complete XML-based applications with relational backends. A sample application, an XML transcription of a dictionary, is used as an example.

NOTE This chapter example is expanded on later in the book. You can download the code from the companion Web site at www.wiley.com/combooks/quin. You'll need your copy of this book to log in if you want to try updating the database.

Understanding Requirements

The best way to begin is by writing down some requirements; word them clearly, and, if necessary, get everyone involved in the project to agree to them. Though determining who should be involved can be difficult, it's very important to get right.

To help you formulate your requirements, the following sections are presented as questions, to prompt you to address the main points you need to consider.

Who are your users?

Are your users primarily technically adept, only marginally computer-literate, or somewhere in between? If, for example, you are writing an interface to a school timetable for 7-to-10-year-olds, your user interface will be different than if it's for tie-and-suit-clad executives of Fortune 500 businesses.

A related question is: How much do you trust your users? If the answer is that you give them complete read/write access to the relational database, your application will probably be a lot simpler than if you have important security concerns to address. (Note: This book is not about dealing with program security; so if this is an important issue for you [as it often is], I recommend that you hire a very good consultant to help you.)

Where are your users?

If your users are all on your local machine or are all users of your departmental internal network, you have a number of immediate advantages:

- You may know what software they are going to use; you may even be able to tell them what to use.

- You can ask them what they want, or need, and respond to their needs directly.

- You know whether you will need a multilingual interface or other special capabilities.

If your users are on an *extranet*, that is, a virtual network that includes more than one organization, you probably have less control than if they are on a corporate intranet or local area network (LAN).

If the users of your application are on the Internet, and the application is public, you will probably need to cater to a fairly wide range of people. You may also have to cope with automatic search engines visiting your site to index all the pages. Part Four, "Links and Metadata," discusses this topic in more detail.

Finally, if your users are culturally diverse or physically impaired, you may need to ensure that the application is accessible to people who, for example, can't use a mouse; are using a text-based Web browser, such as Lynx (if it's a Web application); or use a screen-to-voice reader or a Braille terminal. Users who are directed to "click on the image for more information" will become frustrated quickly if they are using a character-based browser that supports neither images nor a mouse! And in some parts of the world, laws require that business applications or information be made accessible to users with disabilities or physical differences. The Yuri Rubinsky Insight Foundation (www.yuri.org) is a good starting point for information about how to do this.

Why do the users want the data?

If the information you provide will be loaded into spreadsheets, word-processing applications, and users' own databases, a choice you might consider is to use the XML data as a *hub format* and convert to other formats either nightly or on the fly. The *XML as a Hub Format* section later in this chapter describes this process in more detail.

If you are building XML export so that your users can run other tools on the data, as is done at the SlashDot Web site (www.slashdot.org/) with its daily summaries, plain XML output is fine. Chapter 4, "Generating XML from Relational Data," contains most or all of what you need.

If you're planning on using the new Web Browser XML-specific client features to make a "truly dynamic site" (as marketers might say). You'll probably use Java or JavaScript, but depending on who your users are, you may also need to provide HTML as well.

If you are generating XML to someone else's specification, start by asking them for a DTD (see Chapter 1, "Just Enough XML") or an XML Schema, together with sample marked-up documents or data, and any other design documents and specifications they have. If it's an industry standard DTD, such as the Text Encoding Initiative's XML TEI DTD, the aircraft industry's ATA series, or the Word Wide Web Consortium's Resource Description Framework (RDF), you'll probably find Web sites with examples and specifications galore.

Finally, make a list of specific features that are requested. Usually, it's a good idea to ask users why they are requesting a specific feature, because often you'll find a much simpler-to-meet requirement emerges. It's always worth talking to the end users, the actual consumers of your product.

What does the database look like?

Can you can draw a picture of the database, whether with a formal entity relationship diagram or an informal pencil sketch? You should be able to do so. And make sure that you also have a complete listing of the tables, their keys, and what they mean.

Can you change the relational database to make your project easier? If so, you should think about the project more carefully, and perhaps read Part Three for other ideas.

How large is your database, and what are you exporting? If you have 15 terabytes of corporate sales information to transfer every hour, you might need a distributed cluster of high-end servers with OC48 links just to move the data.

A more likely scenario is the difference between a few hundred and a few million records. You will need to make sure you don't force the server to do too much work. This means dividing up the work between client and server.

If you have a lot of *mixed content*, that is, if you have paragraphs and running text with embedded elements, you may be better off with one of the hybrid solutions offered in Part Three. If you have a deeply nested structure, and most of your queries are going to involve finding a document or element and navigating around—for example, "go left one element, along two, and take the first child"—then you should consider an object-oriented database.

The fastest relational database is the one with the fewest items in it—the fastest query runs against the smallest table. This means that you'll get better performance if your database has a reasonable number of reasonable-sized tables, not one huge, long, skinny one or thousands of tiny ones. That said, what is "reasonable" depends mostly on your database software and your hardware.

What will the XML look like?

The nature of the XML you have to produce can make a significant difference both to the database requirements and to the architecture you use. The simplest XML is a direct reflection of your relational data, one table at a time. If your database supports it (MySQL does not), an SQL cursor is probably the most efficient approach. If not, you can use a join such as those shown in Chapter 3, "Just Enough SQL."

If you need to build numerous cross-references, you may need auxiliary tables, intermediate data structures, or even multiple passes over the input.

Usually, the data in a relational database ends up becoming very straightforward XML, if you can apply the simplest possible transformations. If you have to do complex textual transformations, consider using a text-processing language such as Perl. If performance is a major issue, sometimes it's cheaper to buy more hardware than to spend a lot of time programming around the problem. Almost every program can be made faster by a good, experienced programmer; hiring a consultant to help may be appropriate here, since optimization may not be a skill that you need every day.

Who will be writing the code?

The purpose of XML is to make information more accessible to computer programs. That means if you have XML, you will need computer programs. And if you don't have the programs, you'll need programmers. If, however, the primary coders are two Omnimark programmers and a part-time Perl hacker, you probably shouldn't be attempting a 300,000-line C++ project.

In a text-processing environment, a Unix Perl script, five *sed* scripts, and a bit
... often go further than several months of dedicated C or
... more proprietary operating systems. If you don't have
... consider hiring some, at least to get you started. The
... is that you can automate lots of tasks you used to do
... that way involves listening to programmers, even if
... bare feet.

... erlooked factor, and forgetting to address it is one of the
... project failure. Your project is more important than your
... staff; if you can't, choose the right project for the staff

... ue?

... two weeks, try a Unix shell script, a Java servlet, a Perl
... you already know how to do. If you have six months,
... something new.

... s are massively over-budget and long overdue. The main
... specifying deadlines are usually managers who don't
... icalities involved, or tend to gloss over them if they do.
... n's book, *Death March: The Complete Software Developer's
... ssion Impossible' Projects* (Prentice Hall, 1997), for ways to
... nd scheduling problems.

... ered the questions raised in the previous section, you will
... aluate the best approach to take for your project. This sec-
... are commonly used, together with some pitfalls to avoid.

... ata Transfer

... possible architecture in which a database is exported in
... back on another system. Companies such as Data Mirror
... m) claim to have very efficient software to transfer data
... another, but they generally use proprietary intermediate
... restore from a five-year-old backup, you'd better use open
... kup was written for a tool that no longer exists, you can at
... to read it if you have the specification of the data format,

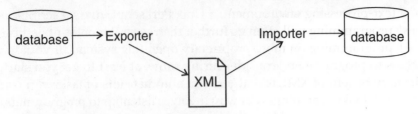

Figure 6.1 XML for backup or data transfer.

and it was publicly available; and more likely than not, there are still products available that you can use.

It's tempting to try to keep the generated XML as terse as possible, using short element names. Don't give in to this temptation. Use good compression software; *gzip* and *bzip2* on Unix are free and give very good results. If you have to decipher complex table names five years from now, you'll thank yourself.

Make sure that your backup is *complete*. You might test for completeness by restoring to a clean database, then using the database's own dumping mechanism to dump both databases. Compare the dumps carefully. If you have additional documentation over and above the database schema, consider including that in a backup.

Finally, remember that the dumped database should not be made available to people who aren't supposed to have read access to the database itself!

XML as a Hub Format

If you have a lot of different databases or applications, you may be able to define a single XML document that can be read by any of them. Such a central document is usually called a *hub*, by analogy to the center of a wheel, with radiating spokes corresponding to the applications that share the central document. Figure 6.2 illustrates this.

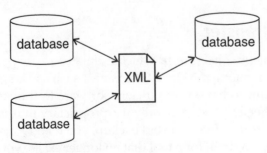

Figure 6.2 XML as a hub format.

If you can't institute a hub, you might end up with platform-specific information in a single file which is still easier to generate and maintain. You might then write separate filters to convert into and out of this format for each database or application that can't use XML directly. See the XML Style Language Transformation (XSLT, www.w3c.org/Style) and other XML and SGML transformation tools listed in Chapter 21, "XML Parsers, Editors, and Utilities."

XML for Interchange with Other Organizations

All over the world companies and organizations exchange product data. Many industries have their own XML or SGML formats that they have defined, usually by forming a consortium. Here are some examples:

Semiconductor industry (Pinnacles). Documents conforming to the Pinnacles DTD are used to store and exchange data sheets that document electronic components in detail.

Aircraft industry (ATA 2100). Even a small aircraft needs tens or hundreds of thousands of pages of documentation. There are flight manuals, training manuals, repair manuals, in-flight fault-isolation manuals, documentation for scheduled maintenance, wiring manuals, mechanics' task cards, even notes on what to do if the coffee machine won't brew. And it's all in SGML. The ATA is likely to move to XML in the future.

The humanities (Text Encoding Initiative). The Text Encoding Initiative (TEI) is an attempt to provide a framework for marking up texts with sufficient richness to facilitate scholarly study. The TEI Project (www.tei-c.org/) has been enormously successful, and the XML version of the "TEI Lite" DTD is already in wide use. If you are working in any field that involves applying markup to existing texts, the TEI should be one of the first places to look for inspiration.

Technical documentation. The DocBook DTD is widely used for technical publishing, both of manuals and books. Software tools to format Docbook-conformant SGML or XML documents using TEX, automatic conversion to RTF for Word, electronic browsers, and other tools are freely available.

Other industries. The newspaper industry, the footwear industry, the automobile industry, scientific journals…the list goes on. If the thought of XML-based shoes and socks surprises you, it's a good reminder of the extent to which XML is changing our technical infrastructure.

Getting Involved

If your organization is part of an industry that has a standard interchange format, *use it*; don't invent your own. If the interchange format doesn't support your business practices, ask the question, *should we change?* The difference between using off-the-shelf software, or free software that other people are also using, and taking a commercial package and customizing it, is rarely less than a factor of 10 in cost.

If there is a consortium, join it. You will learn a lot about how your partners and competitors work, and whether the interchange format is something just for show or is really central. Of course, by using it yourself, you help to make it more mainstream and to spread the interchange of free information.

If there is no consortium, consider starting one. Starting an open mailing list can be enough, together perhaps with an announcement on the Usenet comp.text.xml newsgroup or on the xml-dev mailing list. There is more information on these forums in Chapter 23, "Further Reading."

Many organizations use their own internal formats, and convert to an interchange format. This is often because they carry extra proprietary information in their documents and don't want to give that information out. Figure 6.3 shows such an architecture.

XML for Paper-Based Publishing

At the time of writing, the best ways to go from XML to paper involve either very expensive ($50,000+) commercial SGML-based packages or complex but free solutions. You can use TEX together with either a DSSSL engine such as Jade (most complex) or write your own Perl script to convert XML to TEX and write macros. If you use someone else's DTD, there is a chance that the macros are already available—Norm Walsh's package for the DocBook DTD is a good example.

Figure 6.4 illustrates one way to publish a view of a database on paper and on the Web, using open source tools.

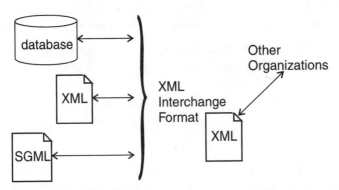

Figure 6.3 XML for interchange with other organizations.

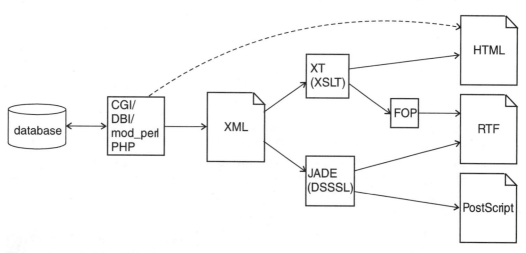

Figure 6.4 XML for paper-based publishing.

XML for Interchange between Applications

This is a variation of the hub format described earlier, combined with the idea of an interchange format. For example, you might want to save output from a database and insert it into a spreadsheet, check the results, then use a 3D graphics rendering package to make a stunning representation to hand to someone who isn't very numerate. You might be able to use a "comma-separated value" file to go from the database to the spreadsheet, but then you'll probably lose information, such as the names of column headings, data types, and relationships. A Web-based approach (even on a single computer) might be to have a CGI-script that can read your XML hub format and generate data for the spreadsheet and for the rendering engine; that way, you can't doctor the figures in the spreadsheet before rendering them! Figure 6.5 is a diagram of such a system.

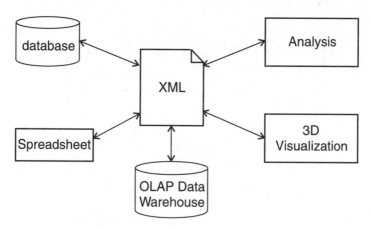

Figure 6.5 Saving time and money with CGI and XML.

XML-Aware Web Browsers

Some of the newer Web browsers are already XML-aware, others are not. On an intranet, you can mandate that everyone has access to Mozilla (www .mozilla.org/) or, with somewhat weaker standards compliance and *definitely* not open source, Internet Explorer 5.

On the Internet, many people are using older software or newer software that isn't XML-aware. It has been written that "on the Internet, no one can hear you scream," but you still have to deal with it. One approach is to generate XML but with the capability to convert it to HTML on the fly, perhaps using XSL. The next section, *XML as an Intermediate Format for Advanced Web Pages*, expands on this theme.

Another approach is to generate HTML that's also XML-conformant, and use Cascading Style Sheets (CSS) to give some of your readers a better deal. You can use the HTML SPAN element and the CLASS attribute to preserve a lot of the XML information, although you lose the benefit of using a DTD or schema to provide structure validation specific to your application.

Figures 6.6 and 6.7 show these two options, and Figure 6.8 is a screenshot of Mozilla running with the Enlightenment window manager under Unix, and running under Microsoft Windows 98 to show that it's downward-compatible.

XML as an Intermediate Format for Advanced Web Pages

This section makes a subtle distinction from the previous example. The approach here is to generate an XML document, then process it to create part or all of a Web site.

The following example reappears in full in Part Three, where we'll talk about cross-references and show the source code that was used. To formulate the

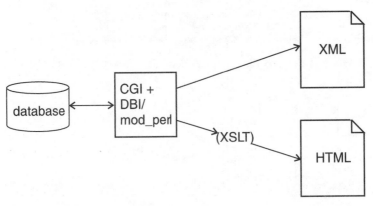

Figure 6.6 Generating XML and converting where needed.

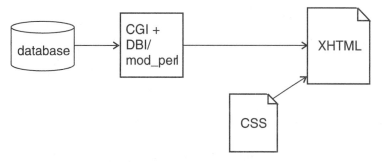

Figure 6.7   Generating HTML that happens to be XML.

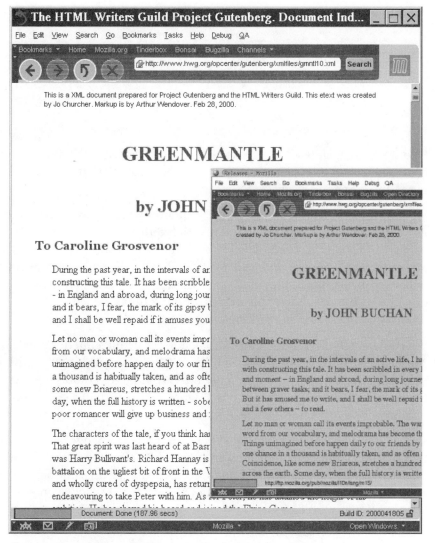

Figure 6.8   Mozilla on Windows and Unix (Red Hat Linux).

example, I typed in samples from the *Eighteenth-Century Dictionary of the Canting Language* by Nathan Bailey. This language comprises slang terms used by thieves, criminals, and wandering beggars. For now, let's suppose that the dictionary is loaded into a relational database table, perhaps like this:

```
CREATE TABLE canting (
    headword VARCHAR(30) PRIMARY KEY;
    definition VARTEXT;
);
```

Here are a couple of sample entries:

```
mysql> SELECT * FROM canting;
+------------+-----------------------------------------------------------+
| headword   | definition                                                |
+------------+-----------------------------------------------------------+
| ABRAM-COVE | a lusty Rogue, with hardly any Cloaths on his Back:       |
|            | a Tatterdemallion.                                        |
+------------+-----------------------------------------------------------+
| AMBIDEXTER | one that goes snacks in Gaming with both Parties; also    |
|            | a Lawyer that takes Fees of Plaintiff and Defendant at    |
|            | once.                                                     |
+------------+-----------------------------------------------------------+
```

One way to generate an HTML version of this dictionary would simply be to have a form that allows users to search for entries; but that's not very interesting. A browsing interface is a lot more fun.

We'll develop a main dictionary page containing some notes about the dictionary and links to a separate page for each letter (A, B . . . Z). Each of those pages will list all the words starting with that letter, and have a link to a separate page for each word and its definition. Finally, the pages for the definitions will each have Next, Previous, and Up links, so users can move around quickly. Figure 6.9 shows this organization; a quick pencil sketch like this is often a good first step in working out a design.

We could easily design the page for each letter using something like `SELECT * FROM canting WHERE headword LIKE 'A%'`; and so forth; this is very easy with the perl DBI module. The individual pages could be generated on the fly with PHP. Such a scheme will work well, but will place a load on the database for every fetch. Worse, it's wrong.

Why is it wrong? Because the data isn't ever going to change, apart from fixing typos. The dictionary was printed in 1736 and it's finished. The database might be useful for other reasons, and this is supposed to be an example, so let's pretend we need the dictionary in a relational database. But let's generate a single static XML file, a bit like this:

```
<entry><title>ABRAM-COVE</title>
<p>a lusty Rogue,
```

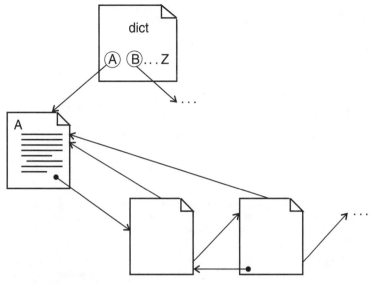

Figure 6.9 Diagram of Web layout for a dictionary.

```
with hardly any Cloaths on his
Back: a Tatterdemallion.</p></entry>
```

This is slightly more markup than you might expect, but some of the entries turned out to be several paragraphs long.

NOTE

For easier proofreading, I inserted a hard return wherever the input line ended in the printed book. I typed the XML using the vi editor, and included a comment at every page and column boundary.

Now that we have the whole dictionary in XML, we can read it into a Perl associative array; generating the title pages is simply a question of iterating through the keys of that array, using Perl's sort and grep functions.

More interestingly, we can handle implicit cross-references: Wherever a word occurs that's defined elsewhere in the dictionary, we'll surround it with an HTML link to the generated page for that definition. This is lots of fun and really helps people look around the dictionary. Who would ever have guessed that a File was someone who helped a pickpocket?

Generating the links to the cross-references is easy with the intermediate file. If the Perl script had to go to the database for each word in the input to see if it was there, you'd wait forever. Furthermore, even though the Perl script takes a couple of minutes to run through the whole dictionary, the HTML files don't change often, and the resulting pages are very fast. Figure 6.10 shows a screenshot of

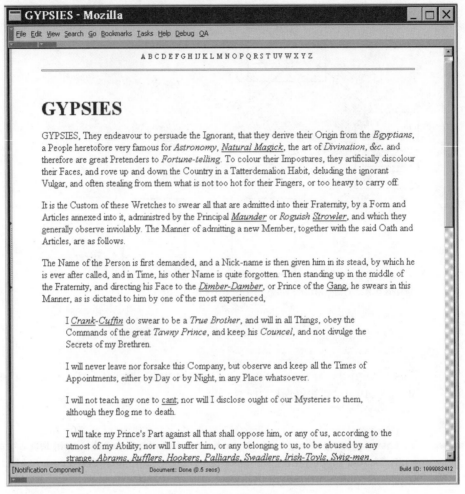

Figure 6.10 Gypsies (a somewhat fanciful description).

part of the entry for "Gypsies," so you can see the cross-references in place. If your data doesn't change often, static intermediate files can be very useful.

Summary

Part One addressed reading and writing XML, Client/Server architectures, and SQL. It also described some ways of combining these techniques to make complete applications. In Part Five, "Resource Guide," you'll find pointers to working tools that you can use.

Before you get started, though, read through Parts Two and Three, because though a relational database may be a familiar and solid tool, it is not always the *best* tool.

XML and Databases

Part One addressed readers who have an existing relational database that they need to make available as XML documents or who want to use XML to transport data. But what if you are working with XML documents and want to put them in a database? That's what we discuss in Part Two.

Chapter 7, "What Is a Document?" Looks at different sorts of XML documents, and in particular explores issues surrounding mixed content, where XML elements contain a mixture of text and other elements.

Chapter 8, "XML Repositories and Databases." Explores different strategies for storing XML in relational databases, and talks about some of the benefits and drawbacks of each approach.

Chapter 9, "Implementation Strategies." Gives additional specific implementation information aimed at programmers.

Unless you are *very* committed to using a relational database, I recommend that you also read Part Three, which explores other types of databases (in particular, hybrid approaches). But if you want to store part of your documents as fields in a relational database and part of them elsewhere, skim this part to get a feel for some of the ideas, then go on to Part Three.

## CHAPTER 7

What Is a Document?

This chapter expands on a few central aspects of Chapter 1, "Just Enough XML." It is primarily intended for people from the database world who may not be used to working with textual documents.

The main ways that an XML document differs from the sort of data you find in a "typical" relational database include:

- Fields and data are normally intermixed (mixed content).
- Any document can have its own schema, or DTD.
- Fields do not have length restrictions.
- Fields can nest arbitrarily.
- Fields have a sequence.

The next few sections describe each of these in turn.

Mixed Content

Mixed content occurs where a mixture of text and elements is allowed, as in:

```
<!ELEMENT Paragraph
    (#PCDATA|Emphasis)*
>
```

Here, a paragraph is defined as containing an arbitrary mixture of textual content (#PCDATA) and Emphasis elements. The following are some examples:

```
<Paragraph>Welcome to my caf&eacute;.</Paragraph>
<Paragraph></Paragraph>
<Paragraph>This is <Emphasis>Much</Emphasis> more interesting.</Para-
graph>
<Paragraph><Emphasis></Emphasis><Emphasis></Emphasis></Paragraph>
```

Notice how #PCDATA matches the empty string, so that the empty paragraph and the empty Emphasis elements are perfectly valid. There is no equivalent of the SQL "NOT NULL" clause in an XML element's content model. This absence was one of many of the driving forces behind the XML Schema movement, but at the time of writing, XML Schemas (or Schemata) are in a draft stage.

There can be any number of Emphasis elements in our Paragraph. It is not possible to allow text inside the Paragraph yet also restrict the number of times in which Emphasis can occur. Therefore, if you are storing XML documents in a database, you will probably have to deal with multiple elements occurring within mixed content.

Of course, Emphasis is quite likely to have a mixed content model, too, which we'll discuss in the following section.

An element need not start or end on a word boundary: It's not <Emphasis> im</Emphasis>possible to embed markup within a word.

The XML Specification states that wherever you have mixed content, the declaration must be in the form of an optional repeatable or-group whose first component is #PCDATA. In other words,

```
<!ELEMENT illegal-example
    (Emphasis|#PCDATA)+
>
```

is illegal because it uses a plus sign (+) instead of an asterisk (*), and because #PCDATA is not at the start. The following:

```
<!ELEMENT also-illegal
    (#PCDATA, Emphasis)*
>
```

is illegal because the comma (,) is used instead of the vertical bar (|).

NOTE

This second content model is called a *pernicious mixed-content model* in SGML because of the way whitespace is treated within it. It is sufficiently complex to get right in SGML, and therefore was disallowed in XML.

Per-Document Schemata

Any XML document can contain its own Document Type Definition, and can define elements.

```
<!DOCTYPE boy [
    <!ELEMENT boy (noise|dirt|grin)*>
    <!ELEMENT noise (#PCDATA|grin|dirt)* >
    <!ELEMENT dirt EMPTY>
    <!ELEMENT grin EMPTY>
]>
<boy>
    <noise>shuffling <dirt/> feet <grin/></noise>
    <noise>SHOUT!</noise>
</boy>
```

If you want to store this document in a database, you might end up creating a table on the fly, with columns for each element type, or you might use a generic schema that copes with XML elements whatever they are called.

What you could not do is have a fixed schema that said that a boy element contained noise, dirt, and grin elements, because you may then get a document that defines boy differently, and your database would not function properly.

Unrestricted Field Length

The boy in the previous example can make just as much noise as he likes, or he can be silent: #PCDATA matches *any* amount of data, from none at all to millions of terabytes or more. In a data entry form for a relational database, you might restrict a telephone number to 10 digits and a postal code to 9 characters. But an XML document is not generally bound by such rules. This isn't always a bad thing: To telephone my father in England from where I live in Toronto, I have to dial 15 digits, and fairly often I want to give an extension number as part of a phone number. In the United States, zip codes can be longer than nine characters, too.

It does mean that you will need to experiment and determine the storage overhead of VARTEXT in your database. Some implementations always use a fixed-size block and pad it with spaces internally. Of course, adding trailing spaces to elements would also be unacceptable if you were representing textual information! An emphasized word in the middle of a sentence might have a space inside the Emphasis element and not outside, or one after it:

```
1. This is <Emphasis>very</Emphasis> important.
```

```
2. This is <Emphasis>very </Emphasis> important.
3. This is <Emphasis>very        </Emphasis> important.
```

Example 1 is marked up correctly. If you used underline for emphasis (perhaps for an ASCII computer screen), example 2 would show the space after the *very* as underlined, which would be bad. Example 3 is obviously wrong. When you are working with text, whitespace becomes very important.

Some databases place a maximum length restriction on a field; you may need to use multiple BLOBs to store a paragraph, which can make searching difficult. We'll return to searching in Part Three, but for now, note that some databases don't let you search BLOBs with wildcards or patterns. The publicly available MySQL database, however, supports both SQL wildcards and Unix regular expressions on VARTEXT fields.

Arbitrary Field Nesting

Consider the following content mode:

```
<!ELEMENT emphasis
    (#PCDATA|emphasis)*
>
<!ATTLIST emphasis
    type (automatic|ripple|flash|smell|bold|italic) "automatic"
>
```

The following is a valid example of an emphasis element instance in a document:

```
<emphasis>very, <emphasis type="ripple">very, <emphasis
  type="smell">very</emphasis></emphasis></emphasis>
```

There could be hundreds of nested emphasis elements in there, and it would still be legal. Since this is the fundamental nature of XML, if you are storing XML documents in a database, you probably have to live with it. Recursion like that is very common in XML. Here is an example from HTML, too:

```
<ul>
  <li><p>First item</p></li>
  <li><p>Second item</p></li>
  <li>
    <ol>
      <li><p>here is an li within an ol within an li</p></li>
      <li><p>here is another one.</li>
    </ol>
  </li>
</ul>
```

A good database design avoids making the server do all the work, so when you come to implementing nested elements, resist the temptation to use a complex JOIN. Oracle has implemented some extensions to its database to help with storing XML, but there is still a fundamental disconnect between the flat field in the relational world and the complex nesting field in XML.

Field Sequencing

A chapter probably contains a title followed by paragraphs of text. If you store the chapter in a database and then extract it, you want the paragraphs to reappear in the right order! This seems pretty obvious, but to implement it, you might end up giving each paragraph a sequence number and using an ORDER BY clause or an SQL cursor. It's hard to do that efficiently: More than once I have seen a design that seems correct to a database engineer who is unfamiliar with textual documents, and yet can take half an hour or more to paste a single 5-megabyte document on half a million dollars' worth of hardware.

It's sometimes tempting to offload some of this work onto the author by assigning each paragraph a required Sequence Number attribute. If you do this, consider that an author who wants to reverse the order of two paragraphs, or copy part of a chapter and edit it, will probably forget to change the attributes. Your routine that imports the chapter into the database should therefore reassign all of the sequence numbers at that time, so that the export routine can sort the data.

Sorting items in the database client can be one good way of splitting up the work so that the database server doesn't grind to a halt and start issuing purchase orders for bigger SPARC Servers.

If all this sounds a bit drastic, consider that most relational databases were not really designed for this sort of data, and generally work best with integers rather than paragraphs. You may be able to reconfigure your database to use larger blocks in its BTREE or ISAM physical storage layer to help performance, but whatever else you do, you will need to deal with storing explicit sequences of elements.

Summary

Though this is a short chapter, all the points it makes are very important. The differences between a relational database and a text document database are in how you look at the data, not just the nature of the data. These differences will pervade all the work you do with XML.

I'll leave you with some illustrations I've used in presentations to managers, who are often very intelligent people but have little technical knowledge or experience with XML. Sometimes simple illustrations like this can be very effective. Figure 7.1 shows a relational table as a rectangular grid; Figure 7.2

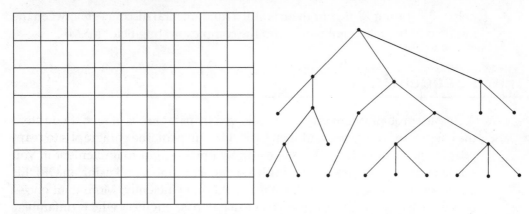

Figure 7.1 A relational data model.　　　**Figure 7.2** An XML document.

shows how an XML document is a tree; and Figure 7.3 shows how the tree isn't a rectangle.

In the next chapter, "XML Repositories and Databases," we look in more detail at storing XML in databases as part of a larger document management system.

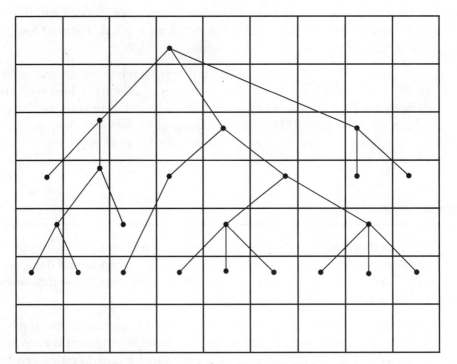

Figure 7.3 An XML document stored in a relational database.

XML Repositories and Databases

P art One explained how to read an XML document with a view to extracting information to store in a relational database. In this chapter we'll consider the problem of storing a document in a database in such a way that it can be extracted (in whole or in part) again later as well as be the subject of database queries.

There are several ways to do this, but choosing the most suitable for any given application and environment is not always easy. To help you choose, this chapter presents sample scenarios, and strategies for dealing with each. Chapter 9, "Implementation Strategies," aimed at programmers, describes how to implement each strategy.

Sample Scenarios

There are many possible scenarios in which databases may be used. Those discussed in this chapter are intended to be representative of a wide range of applications, and have been carefully chosen to illustrate the various issues that come up during implementation. It may be useful to outline your own situation as I have done in the scenarios here so that the various strategies for addressing them will be more directly applicable to your needs.

Scenario Characteristics

The following characteristics are typical of each scenario. In some cases, you'll find pointers to implementation strategies and notes discussed in Chapter 9. The main characteristics are:

Resource discovery. This term is used to refer to the problem of finding things. If the single biggest problem you are trying to solve is that people can't find documents, consider a text retrieval system or the implementation of the Central Access scenario. Often, additional requirements emerge *after* you solve the most pressing problems.

Cooperation and communication. The needs of a solitary worker differ from the needs of numerous employees working together in a corporate environment. The most important aspect of this characteristic often is how well the software supports the business or work processes in an organization. The more important this is to you, the more likely you are to lean toward using a database.

Update. In most environments, documents are read tens, hundreds, or even thousands of times more often than they are changed. But that isn't always true. An environment in which saving a document is complex or slow may be perfectly acceptable at one end of the spectrum and entirely unacceptable at the other.

Configuration management. Since XML documents are potentially composed of multiple *entities,* or files, you will need to keep track of sets of things, not just individual things. If you do versioning, you may need to track relationships that change, too. (What if, for example, the DOCTYPE declaration was changed in a document, so that it used a different DTD in a particular version? What if that DTD has changed in the meantime?)

Access control. Any organization with more than one person must decide who can do what, with what, to what. If you are putting up a commercial encyclopedia for pay-per-use viewing on the Internet, you'll need fairly secure access control. If you are a group of writers working on a book at a university, you may be more concerned with preventing two people working on the same chapter at the same time.

Historical archiving. If you need to keep track of old versions of information, or be able to compare versions, you will need to think carefully about a number of related issues. Configuration management, access control, update, compound objects composed of many interrelated files, and even treatment of whitespace are all fraught with peril.

Examples

The examples for each scenario have been chosen to highlight the fact that these categories are blurred. If you take a few moments to think about them, you may decide to move them to other scenarios or ask why other solutions weren't chosen to deal with them.

Central Access Scenario

In this scenario, your job is to make sure that everyone who needs to can find any document, without having to search users' home directories or networked computers.

In this scenario, searching is clearly important. People might need to find a document for which they do not know the document name. For example, someone may need to search for all documents written by Simon Whitehead between 1994 and 1996 that contain the word Helicopter in the title. If you make it a lot easier for people to access information, you change their world, either because they waste less time looking through filing cabinets or because they find things that they would never otherwise have seen.

A browsing interface, perhaps where documents are arranged into categories and subcategories, is often useful, and easy to set up with a Web server such as Apache. This strategy, at its implies, consists of nothing more than setting up an internal Web site with your documents organized into separate directories.

Characteristics

Resource discovery. Locating information.

Cooperation and communication. Sharing notes and information.

Update. Documents are read much more often than they are changed, and are usually changed only by the author.

Example: Research Project

A university research project places all the design documents on a spare i486 PC that is running FreeBSD and Apache. Project members use the same system to run a mailing list for the project, and archives of the list are made available with the free HyperMail software. Later, as the project becomes more popular, they run an Internet Relay Chat (IRC) server on the machine, and use it for online meetings. The logs are posted on their Web site.

Example: Design Agency

A small design agency has a team of five people working on a promotional campaign to explain to people living in a small city how health care changes will affect them. The team uses a Macintosh FTP server to share their notes, and PhotoShop, Gimp, and Adobe Illustrator to design sketches.

Shared Authoring Scenario

Several people writing and maintaining a large XML document, such as an aircraft manual. You need to make sure, one, that everyone can find out which parts are complete, and, two, that no two authors work on the same section at the same time.

The simplest way to handle this might be to have everyone agree to share a single folder on a networked file server. If everyone uses tools that lock files while they are being worked on, there may not be too much confusion; nevertheless, this does not seem very secure.

In fact, there are a number of problems with this solution. For example, someone could easily delete a file by mistake, or two people could create a new file of the same name at the same time. If you use file permissions to control this, you start increasing the overhead and complexity of managing the environment.

Simple and free solutions to real problems are very valuable, and if this is your scenario, you should consider carefully whether you need a database. If you decide that you do, it might be because the fragility of shared files is unacceptable, or because filenames aren't appropriate for searching, or perhaps because you have too many documents to manage.

Characteristics

Resource discovery. Locating information.

Cooperation and communication. Sharing notes; up-to-date status information.

Access control. Document locking for exclusive access.

Update. Documents are changed frequently, often by people other than the author, or by a group of authors.

Example: Software Production

A small software company has about a dozen programmers who tend to arrive late in the morning and work for 18 hours at a stretch, pausing only to eat. They communicate with each other using email and Internet Relay Chat; but to make sure two people don't overwrite the same file, their source is held in a repository using the Central Versioning System (CVS) on a central Sun SPARC server. The CVS system also lets them compare differences between any two versions of any source file, and they can revert to older versions.

The company's documentation team tends not to be working at 3:00 A.M. when the best discoveries are made, so the programmers use email to let the documentation and support teams know about changes that had to be made, or to ask about new ideas. The documentation is also kept in CVS so that the programmers can look at it easily but not change it.

After a few years, the code becomes rather large, and the company implements a *text retrieval system* to maintain an automatic up-to-date index so the staff can search the software easily. The GNU *mkid* tools are one example of such software that's freely available (see Chapter 13, "Text Retrieval Technology Overview," for more on text retrieval).

Example: Aircraft Company

An aircraft company has more than 100,000 pages of documentation for a small aircraft, much of which is mandated by complex safety regulations. The staff writers write the documentation in XML and store individual chapters as objects in an object-oriented database, using a relational database to store metadata such as authoring information, dates, versions, and *effectivity* (where different customers order planes that differ slightly, and hence have different manuals).

Revision Control Scenario

In this scenario, let's assume your job is to issue a document that is frequently updated, such as a technical manual, and you need to know which versions of the document people are using, and to track the differences among versions. This scenario is a combination of Central Access and Shared Authoring. You may need to enable shared authoring, for example, so that writers can easily see what they have changed, and so that they can be sure that they are always working on the latest version of a document.

A common problem is that one writer might copy a file to a working directory and edit it for a week, while another author, blissfully unaware, copies the same original file and works on it at the same time as the first. The first author finishes his or her work on it and returns the file to central storage. The next day, the second author finishes his or her work, and overwrites the central file, losing all the work that the first author had done. This problem can be prevented if the first author *checks out* the file *locked for editing*, so that when the second author goes to fetch the file, it's marked as unavailable.

Revision control tools such as CVS, RCS, SCCS, MKS Anywhere, Briefcase, and many others address this problem; see Chapter 22, "Databases, Repositories, and Utilities," for more details. CVS in particular is very widely used for open source projects.

Characteristics

Access control. Centralized management.

Historical archiving. Tracking previous versions.

Configuration management. Tracking groups of objects that belong together.

Update. Documents are updated by more than one person, possibly over a long span of time.

Example: Writer's Revisions

A single author is working on a large XML document and needs to be able to compare versions, similar to the case where a single programmer uses RCS or CVS to track code revisions. If a problem is introduced in a new version of software, the programmer can review the changes that were made to the code to try to see how the problem was introduced.

Example: Configuration of Compound Documents

An XML document consists of multiple parts: a schema or Document Type Definition, included fragments, images, external files that define character entities, and more. A revision system for XML that stores each version of the document is severely limited if it doesn't store the corresponding document type definitions and documentation. You might be able to retrieve an older version of your document, but if the DTD has changed so that the old document cannot be validated with the new DTD or schema, you have a problem. If your software relies on validation in any way (for example, it uses an SGML tool that require a DTD, or it reads a schema to perform additional checking before importing data to a database), it is essential to track the two components together.

Information Reuse Scenario

In this scenario, we assume you are planning to take one set of information in XML and derive several other publications from it, perhaps even virtual online publications. For example, you might have a database of recipes and want to publish a CD-ROM or book of just recipes whose ingredients all contain ham, anchovies, and custard. Or you might have an encyclopedia or dictionary, and want to make a pocket reference book of terms used by biochemists or by athletes.

In this scenario, the capability to generate multiple views and subsets of your data is important. This means that the nature of your information must be static enough that you benefit from taking the time to define database queries, views, and style sheets.

It is important here not to let dogma stand in the way of common sense. It is perfectly reasonable to include separate information for each format in a single XML document. You might, for example, include a summary of each article, together with a short title that's intended only for the World Wide Web, since HTML places fairly severe limits on what can go inside a document's `title` element.

On this book's companion Web site at www.wiley.com/compbooks/quin, you can see a dictionary of thieving slang from the eighteenth century that has been formatted from XML in multiple ways, including as HTML and PDF. The HTML pages were created using a simple Perl script, also available at that site.

Characteristics

Configuration management. Tracking groups of objects that belong together.

Update. There may be a master set of XML documents that are static or change only very rarely; or there may be a continuous stream of articles coming in over a newswire, but the nature of the information probably does not change too fast. Though it can take weeks to set up style sheets to typeset complex documents, once it has been done, it has been done for all documents.

Example: Online Newsfeed

A newsfeed is a good example of this scenario. The content of the stories is constantly changing but the format the stories are presented in is more or less the same. You might filter the news articles by subject, sending some to other news agencies, some to a Web page, others to journalists or story editors for a printed newspaper. At the same time, you might generate summaries by extracting the abstract, byline and headings, and perhaps the first paragraph.

Example: Encyclopedia Publisher

Most encyclopedias consist of a (very long) sequence of articles, or entries, all of which are in essentially the same layout. The publisher could make a

CD-ROM edition, a printed edition, and an online edition. Perhaps more interestingly, the publisher might take all of the entries that are marked as relating to a specific field, such as biochemistry, together with all of the biographical entries that are mentioned in those entries, and make a special dictionary of biochemistry. The dictionary might also exclude introductory-level material, a process made possible by the XML markup. Some encyclopedia and dictionary publishers have already been doing this for years, using SGML.

Distributed Access and Technology Reuse Scenario

If you are part of a large organization, you may already have data warehousing software in place that copies oodles of data every night all over the globe. It might seem very attractive to take advantage of that replication technology to distribute your documents.

If you have large numbers of users, you may need to support a very wide range of editorial and browsing software, and a distributed database may be appealing for that reason.

Alternate free tools include automatic mirroring of Web sites, "push" delivery such as Usenet News (or Lotus Notes or Open Text's Livelink), perhaps combined with good old-fashioned couriers. You can't beat the bandwidth of a truck filled with CD-ROMs, although the access time is poor.

Characteristics

Resource Discovery. Locating information across the entire organization.

Update. Documents change slowly; or it rarely matters that someone view the latest version. Otherwise, you may need some other replication technology.

Access Control. Centralized management.

Example: Telephone Repair Manuals

A large telephone company has a lot of XML and SGML telephone manuals. Its support staff and engineers need access to the data, so they use a mixture of overnight replication and online access. They store their data in flat files on a Unix file server; but the access control and metadata to support resource discovery are held in a relational database. An external text retrieval package makes a nightly index to assist searches, and the entire database can be replicated automatically.

Other Issues

This chapter has concentrated solely on reasons for storing XML. A good document management system would also address many other issues. Some of these are described briefly here, although they are not directly related to XML.

Workflow. A workflow system keeps track of who should handle a document next, or of the sequence of processes that a document goes through in its lifetime. Some commercial SGML- and XML-based workflow systems have very attractive and easy-to-use interfaces, while others contain a morass of error-prone dialog boxes. If the system is to support users, a clean user interface is the single most important aspect of a workflow system. Without it, people will revert to using pencil and paper to keep track of their files if they have to.

Conversion. Documents originating from another organization will generally need to be converted into a format that you use. You may need to store the unconverted data, too, so that you can tell the supplier what you changed, or so that when you receive a new version you can compare it with the old one and assess the impact of the changes. You may also need to store converted *output* documents in your repository.

Effectivity. This is the term given to the situation in which you have different customers who each receive a different version of a document. Whenever you issue a new version of a manual, you need to keep track of which customers receive which changes. You might also need to keep track of repairs and configuration changes that have been made to a unit over time, such as a railway engine or an aircraft. A railway engine might have been built in one city, repaired in another, and refitted with new driver controls in another. The repair manual has to reflect the current state of the locomotive even though it might be the only one with that specific combination of parts.

Summary

There are many reasons to consider storing generic XML in a database. There are also many reasons not to. The sample scenarios in this chapter were intended to raise some of these issues. For a small environment, you are usually better off *not* using a database unless you have database programmers available. In a large environment, the physical storage is one part of a much larger picture.

The next chapter introduces some ideas about how to implement an XML repository using a relational database. The best advice I offer, however, is *don't do this*. Use the notes to help you buy one that someone else wrote. I have seen systems that take a fraction of an hour to copy a 500-page document on *very* expensive hardware. The features provided by the system in question may be worth it for that particular installation, but they are constantly looking for alternative software.

Part Three discusses other sorts of databases, as well as hybrid solutions, such as that hinted at in the telephone repair manual example in the last scenario. Hybrid solutions usually have the best performance, and are also often the most robust.

## CHAPTER 9

Implementation Strategies

This chapter introduces several strategies for implementing XML databases. No single solution is best; you will need to choose the one that works for your environment. The best solution for you is the one you can write, get working, document, and maintain. The system with twice as many features takes between four and eight times longer to produce, and costs many times more.

The major strategies discussed are as follows:

Documents as BLOBs. Store each entire document as a BLOB and keep separate metadata.

Paragraphs as BLOBs. Break down the document into fixed units, such as paragraphs, and store the structure above that level in the database, keeping the fixed units as BLOBs.

Elements as fields. Break down the document and store every element separately.

Metadata only. Store only information about each document in the database, and use another system to handle the actual data.

Elements as objects. Use an object-oriented database, representing elements as objects and attributes as properties, and store the individual objects.

Text retrieval. Use an information retrieval system (usually file-based) to locate documents, either in conjunction with another strategy or alone.

Hybrid approaches. Use a combination of techniques.

Each of these strategies has its strengths and weaknesses. This chapter will help you to understand when each strategy is most useful. Later chapters describe how to work with systems using these strategies in turn, and give technical guidelines both for integrating systems and for coding them yourself from scratch. Object-oriented and hybrid solutions are the subject of Part Three.

General Implementation Issues

When you are reading about these strategies, you may want to consider the issues described in the following sections. Many a sailor has been shipwrecked and stranded as a result of not heeding the maps, and the sharks of materialism are as brutal to the small business as sea-monsters were to the barefoot mariner of legend.

Round-Trip Identity Transform

If you store a document in the database and then retrieve it, in what ways might it have changed? If no changes are acceptable at all, you will probably end up using either the Documents as BLOBs approach or a hybrid strategy. Another common compromise is when the documents may be changed in certain ways when they are first stored in the database, but cannot change if you extract them again later. In other words, the process of storing a document may change it (by removing all XML comments, for example), but once the document has had its comments stripped, it won't change if it's loaded again.

The most common sorts of changes you might see are as follows.

Very Minor Changes

These changes are so minor that many XML processors don't even support giving the information back to the application. It's very hard to avoid them, and for most purposes not worth worrying about.

- Changes in whitespace within markup, such as losing the trailing space in `<Paragraph >`, or losing extra spaces between attribute specifications.
- Changes in the order of attributes.

Minor Changes

These changes can be reported by XML processors, but are unlikely to affect the meaning of the data.

- Loss of XML comments. This often doesn't matter at all, although some applications might use "significant comments" instead of processing instructions, to track editing information. If you are an author with comments that say "TO DO; rewrite paragraph," you might have to start using an authorNote element instead.

- Loss of processing instructions. This could be a potential problem if software removed the XML declaration, which looks much like a processing instruction. If you have an application that uses processing instructions to track information in a document, you'll have the same sorts of problems that arise when comments are removed.

Frustrating Changes

These changes cause constant irritation and interoperability problems, but usually no loss of data.

- Loss of `DOCTYPE` lines. Certain older SGML software is very particular about having a `DOCTYPE` declaration, and a few applications even require it in places where it isn't allowed, such as inside an external document type declaration subset.

- Comments in the wrong place. An XML document cannot have comments before the XML Declaration (`<?xml version="1.0">`, at the start of the document).

- Converting tags or attribute names to uppercase. Element and attribute names are case-sensitive in XML, but most older SGML software automatically converts the names to uppercase. If you avoid element or attribute names that contain accented characters, such as café, or stick to uppercase names, this won't be a problem, but not everyone can do that. You may be able to change an SGML application's SGML declaration to say NAMECASE NO to stop the application from mapping element names to uppercase. The SP package from www.jclark.com/ includes an SGML declaration for XML that does this.

Major Changes

Any change that causes loss of information or that can render a valid or well-formed document invalid or badly formed is obviously unacceptable. At the very least, the system must provide a warning before the data is lost.

Removing extra spaces. An XML application must not do this where the `xml:space="preserve"` attribute is given, and an XML processor must give all whitespace back to the application regardless.

Inserting or removing line breaks in the data. This causes problems with "verbatim" elements such as code listings, and makes it difficult to track changes in documents using the Unix *diff* program or other text-based comparison tools.

Figures 9.1 and 9.2 show a short XML document that was loaded into an XML system and then saved or retrieved back out. This particular system was pretty buggy, but many of the changes that were made to the document are perfectly legal, and are not prohibited by the XML Specification.

Documents as BLOBs Strategy

With this strategy, you consider a document to be an indivisible opaque object: You make no attempt to store or represent any structure within the document, and you don't let users access the information in any way other than to view or edit an entire document.

NOTE
This is the easiest to implement of the strategies we discuss, but it is also the least useful.

```
<?xml version="1.0">
<!DOCTYPE Recipe SYSTEM "Recipe.dtd">
<Recipe
    category="Salad"
    season="Spring, Summer"
    cost="low"
>
<Picture
    src="images/salads/491.tif"
    role="supporting"
>
<shortdesc>The Vicar tastes the salad</shortdesc>
<caption>
    The author's salad in use at a vicarage garden party
</caption>
<copyright>
    © 2001 Floppy Fish Marketing Corporation
    <!-- Jamie, please check this is right. -->
</copyright>
</Picture>
&Ingredients;
&Steps;
<Author>Ande&eacute; J. Müeller</Author>
></Recipe>
```

Figure 9.1 An XML document before the various changes.

```
<!DOCTYPE Recipe SYSTEM "Recipe.dtd">
<RECIPE CATEGORY="Salad" COST="low" SEASON="Spring, Summer"
><PICTURE ROLE="supporting" SRC="images/salads/491.tif"
><shortdesc>The Vicar tastes the salad</shortdesc
><caption
>The author's salad in use at a vicarage garden party</caption
><copyright>&copyr; 2001 Floppy Fish Marketing Corporation</copy-
right
></PICTURE>
&Ingredients;
&Steps;
<Author>Ande0 J. M eller</Author>
></Recipe>
```

Figure 9.2   An XML document after various undesirable or problematic changes.

An extreme example would be a system that gave every document a unique number, and required users to enter the document number in order to view the corresponding information. I encountered such a system in use at a major financial institution in 1989. The operators maintained paper binders that contained listings of all of the documents so that they could be located by title. When the system was upgraded, all of the document numbers changed, and the operators couldn't find anything. Needless to say, they stopped using that system at the first available opportunity!

Using filenames is only a slightly better alternative than this strategy is in a shared environment, because you have to guess at the names your colleagues used for documents you want to see.

The next improvement is to store information, such as the date a document was created, when it was last changed, and who wrote it. This is more or less as good as a Unix file system (even better if your date representation can extend past the year 2038, a limitation of many 32-bit Unix systems).

```
interlog> ls -l
File modes Owner     Size   Changed      Filename
-rw-r--r-- liamquin 129599 Oct 27 1997 1997-awanibiisaa.html
-rw-r--r-- liamquin   9124 Oct 23 1997 ankle5.xml
-rw-r--r-- liamquin  36464 Oct 23 1997 ankle5.gif
-rw-r--r-- liamquin   4753 Sep 25 1999 index.html
-rw-r--r-- liamquin 235848 Oct 23 1997 men-with-fish.jpg
-rw-r--r-- liamquin   1147 Oct 23 1997 millais-treasure-tn.gif
-rw-r--r-- liamquin  46438 Oct 23 1997 millais-treasure.gif
-rw-r--r-- liamquin    974 Oct 23 1997 millais-treasure.xml
drwxr-xr-x liamquin   4096 Jan  9 1999 pictures
```

You can go a little further by storing classification information, document titles, and maybe even searchable abstracts, summaries, or keywords. We will explore this in more detail in the section *Hybrid Solutions* later in this chapter, and again in Part Three.

The Approach

Storing an entire file in a single database entry is fairly easy technically. Depending on your database, you can use a BLOB or a LONG TEXT field, and simply slurp in the data. It might be a good idea, however, to check that the XML you are handed is well formed, and issue a warning or refuse to accept faulty input. Images, Document Type Definitions, and MPEG sound files tend not to be well-formed XML documents, but you might want to check that those, too, are at least plausible.

You should be aware that some databases (especially closed commercial ones) only allow one BLOB column per table, or per database, and even then may impose artificial limits on the data size. Check that your database isn't one that always allocates a multiple of 64 Kbytes for a BLOB (MySQL doesn't do that, but others might). Database query languages generally won't let you search a BLOB with the SQL "LIKE" clause either.

Luckily, every XML document can be represented in ASCII, using character entities like `&#255;` (y dieresis, ÿ), so you can use a `LONG TEXT` or `VARTEXT` field if that works better with your database.

There are few good reasons to choose the Documents as BLOBs approach, and lots of reasons not to, but as an interim solution before you get something more complex going, it's better than not storing anything at all.

Specific Tools and Alternatives

Reading a file into a BLOB is obvious and straightforward; but if it is an XML file, you should check it first to ensure that it is well formed. One of the advantages of this approach over many others is that you can store invalid files; and if someone has not yet finished writing a document, it may well not yet be valid. On the other hand, you will do your users a major disservice if you don't warn them that they are trying to save garbage.

Why not just use files? See in particular the Concurrent Versions System (CVS) described in Chapter 22, "Databases, Repositories, and Utilities." It's free. If you're using the database because you believe that it is in some way more stable than a Unix file system, consider carefully, especially if your database actually stores tables on your file system. That said, most databases are more stable than a Windows VFAT file system, simply because Windows isn't very stable.

NOTE

The MySQL database is freely available (but not for commercial use); Postgres is also free. Chapter 22, "Databases, Repositories, and Utilities," gives pointers to free and commercial database tools, many of which also have specific support for XML.

Advantages and Drawbacks

Using the Documents as BLOBs approach, you can have centralized control over who can edit, view, and save documents. Unless you store metadata, such as the document title in a separate database field, however, searching may be a problem.

Since the database does not represent document structure, you can't ask it to handle queries about that structure. The most common query people want to be able to ask is, "Find me *this string* inside *this element*"; if that applies to you, read the *Text Retrieval and Hybrid Approaches* section at the end of this chapter, or choose another strategy.

Some databases have size limits on BLOBs, so you may need to use a linked list, and pay a slight but noticeable performance penalty.

A common variant on the Documents as BLOBs approach is a hybrid solution in which you only store information *about* the document in the database, and use some other mechanism for storing the actual data, such as a Unix file system or a full text database. In my experience, this is the most effective way of using a relational database to store information about XML.

Paragraphs as BLOBs

With this strategy, you break down the document into fixed units such as paragraphs, and store the structure above that level in the database, keeping the fixed units as BLOBs.

Unlike the Documents as BLOBs strategy, you can now do revision control within a document, and you can also do structured queries about the element hierarchy above paragraphs. You still can't search within paragraphs directly, however.

This approach works best for booklike documents, where there are subdivisions such as chapter and section, each containing any number of paragraphs. The more different kinds of paragraphlike elements you have (such as lists, tables, definitions, pull quotes, poems, or verses), the harder this approach becomes to manage.

If you have a recursive content model, such as the nested lists shown in Chapter 8, you will have to choose whether to handle only the outermost list as a BLOB and make the rest invisible or do something more complex. In the former case, you will no longer be able to do queries to count the number of lists you have; in the latter, you may end up programming all the complexity of the next strategy, Elements as Fields.

If you are trying to manage or search on elements such as a part number or cross-reference embedded in a paragraph, you'll have to extract the necessary information whenever a paragraph is inserted or updated, and store it separately. See Chapter 14, "XQL, XLink, XPath, and XPointer Explained," for more on this topic.

The Approach

The most obvious approach here is to give every paragraph a sequence number and a parent ID to identify the containing chapter or section, thus linking the structure. The first problem you might find with this approach is performance. Consider the following pseudocode:

```
SELECT paragraph from paragraph,chapter
WHERE paragraph.parent = chapter.id
SORTBY paragraph.sequenceNumber;
```

The problem with this code is that if you have 5 million paragraphs in your documents, it's going to be very slow, even if you use `paragraph.parent` as a primary key for the `paragraph` table. You could have a separate table for every document, but that may cause other performance problems, and will make it harder to search across documents.

Editing the higher-level structure may be trickier. You will probably need a way to make sure no one is editing a paragraph when you delete the section it's in, along with a way to edit a paragraph someone was working on just before leaving for a four-month vacation in Bermuda. In order to accommodate these requirements, you'll have to find out who is currently editing what—and for that, you'll need to generate reports.

Specific Tools and Alternatives

You'll need to parse the incoming XML, and implement software to split up a document into individual fields and then to recombine the document, even if only for import and export. Some databases include an XML parser, but in most cases you can simply use a free one. Part One offered some ideas for doing that, and Chapter 21, "XML Parsers, Editors, and Utilities," lists some of the better-known XML parsers.

A Web browser communicating with a server running PHP, CGI scripts, or a Java servlet would work to retrieve and store individual paragraphs and their XML attributes. Although any XML editor should be able to handle a single paragraph, you'll need a way to create, edit, destroy, copy, and paste higher-level structures.

You probably don't need complex transactions for this strategy, so MySQL would work fine, as long as you lock tables (or the whole database) while you actually do an update. This is likely to be many times faster than using a heavy-weight commercial database such as Oracle or Sybase, but is perhaps less robust.

Advantages and Drawbacks

There are a number of commercial XML and SGML repositories that use this strategy. Two advantages are that you can arrange to display a single paragraph at a time, and multiple authors can be working on the same document, but with far less overhead than the Elements as Fields strategy discussed next.

The Paragraphs as BLOBs strategy is often best combined with a *link database* (described further in Part Four) to store information about cross-references. You have to ask yourself, however, whether it's a good idea to have two people working on adjacent paragraphs of the same document at the same time. In some environments, it's perfectly acceptable, but it might make a pretty disjointed final product.

Elements as Fields Strategy

This is an extreme version of Paragraphs as BLOBs, in which you break down the document and store every element separately. This is the most powerful and, in some ways, the most elegant strategy, but you will face a difficult challenge to achieve acceptable performance.

The Approach

You might keep a table of elements, each with an identification number, a sequence number, and a parent number. Reassembling the document will require traversing this structure using selects and joins.

With this strategy, you can do arbitrary, interesting queries; and if your database supports searching for text substrings you can do powerful searching. Unfortunately, most databases are not good at text searching, so you will probably need to use a hybrid approach with text retrieval, described in more detail later in the chapter.

The major complexities with this approach involve the handling of entities and of mixed-content models. Consider storing `<para>This is <emph show="italics">very</emph> interesting</para>` as six separate objects:

- The `<para>` with three children, `"This is"`, `<emph>`, and `"interesting"`
- The `<emph>` with two children, `"very"` and `"show="`
- The attribute `"show"` with a single child, `"italics"`
- The text string `"This is"`
- The text string `"very"`
- The text string `"interesting"`

You can see how difficult reassembling can become.

It's tempting to create a separate column for each element type (`emph`, `para`, and so forth), but you have to be careful that your underlying database schema doesn't depend on the document structure of your data, as changing your data will otherwise become prohibitively expensive. One day, your DTD may change, and you will need to store `emph` elements that contain paragraphs, or maybe rename an element.

On the other hand, if you put all the elements in a single column called `"element"`, performance will probably suffer. One compromise is to use separate columns for each element, but to manage the resulting schema dynamically. That's more programming, but it might actually work.

In addition to elements, you'll need to store attributes. The ability to display and search for attribute values is often important, especially if you are handling hypertext links. For example, users can ask, "Which documents link to this paragraph?"

Specific Tools and Alternatives

The same tools apply here as for the previous Paragraphs as BLOBs strategy. Before following this approach, however, consider some alternatives. In particular, object-oriented databases already provide support for sequence (linked lists) and containment (pointers, references, and object containment).

Chapter 22, "Databases, Repositories, and Utilities," gives some pointers to object-oriented databases.

Advantages and Drawbacks

The main advantage of this approach is that it gives you fine-grained access to your documents. You might use this access to connect specific elements to other databases, such as parts inventories or ordering systems. You can also perform very precise searches, and even edit documents with SQL.

The biggest disadvantage is that such systems are often very slow. I've seen a commercial database like this used on high-end hardware, and I've seen users waiting 45 minutes or more to copy a document. Admittedly, the documents they were working with were several thousand pages long, but a file copy took under a minute.

Metadata Only Strategy

This strategy uses the database for what it's best at; but it doesn't solve the problem of storing XML in a database. Instead of storing documents, you store information *about* documents, or *metadata*. You might store the author, title, creation date, size, and other information that can be useful for searches. You may also need to store information about access permissions and perhaps a revision history. The actual data is stored elsewhere—in a database owned by another department, or on the file system, for example.

The Approach

The approach for the Metadata Only strategy is pretty straightforward. You can parse an XML document as it's saved, in order to fish out the author and title information (since the author of a document isn't always the typist).

The two big questions are:

- Where do I store the data?
- How do I handle data integrity?

If you store the data in the file system, you must make sure that only your database tools can alter files. You might store modification date and file checksum in the database, to warn of any differences. If files are restored after a system crash, you may also need to rebuild their view in the database.

If you store the data in another database, integrity between the two databases will raise a more serious question. The best way to deal with this is to make all of the data in the relational database derived by inspecting the documents. If this isn't possible, it might be better to avoid this strategy.

If you are used to considering a relational database as the primary repository of your data, and a file system as a sort of cheap alternative that can't be trusted, this strategy may seem very odd. Nonetheless, it's used commercially by some of the fastest document management packages available, and can be very effective. It's especially useful if your database lacks fast and efficient support for large VARTEXT fields, or if you want the files to be accessible to an external process (indexing or external searching, for example).

This strategy can be considered a variant of the Hybrid XML database approaches explained in Part Three, but it is important that it gets its own place in this discussion.

Specific Tools and Alternatives

If the Metadata Only strategy appeals to you, read Parts Three and Four in detail. In addition to flat files, you can use text retrieval databases, revision control systems such as CVS, and search tools such as *sgrep* and *perl*—all with no extra work.

You may end up building a sort of server, perhaps in Perl or Java, or, if performance is a major issue, in C or C++. The discussion on Client/Server architectures in Part One might be of use to you. Before writing a server, however, consider using one that's already written. Apache with mod_perl or PHP will get you a long way. If you have a team of Java programmers instead of a team of Unix Perl scripters, consider using servlets.

Advantages and Drawbacks

One way we can distinguish between an elegant open architecture and a horrible kludge is to consider how error messages are reported to the end user. A system bolted together from disparate parts can be terribly difficult to configure and maintain, and if the errors are misleading, it can be almost impossible. One colleague used a system that claimed, "You may be running too many processes" whenever a subprocess failed for any reason (for example, because

A Real-World Example

I encountered a large-scale commercial document management system that used the Metadata Only strategy. Metadata was stored in a relational database, and accessed either by a proprietary client or through a Web browser using CGI scripts. The database server delivered the files to the client (or to the CGI scripts) using the Network File System (NFS) with a modified client to hide the filenames! It smelled of duct tape at first, but it actually worked very well, supporting some 30,000 users; and the open architecture made it possible to add extra features on the side, such as context-sensitive searching by element and alternate document viewers.

of a full disk). We all wished that we had access to the source code, or even a binary executable that included symbols for debugging.

Storing files on disk can be very simple and avoids a great many complications. Even if you abandon this strategy later, it's very useful in the early stages of development, because it's likely to be easier to debug.

With this strategy, you still get the advantage that you can use SQL to reason about your documents ("Find all documents modified by James in the last two weeks," for example). A smart implementation hides the SQL behind query windows or Web forms, and a smarter one hides it from the programmer, too, so you can easily change the way your data is represented; but the power is still there.

You can also get by with a less sophisticated database. This is significant because it means you can use a free database such as MySQL, which, lacking full transaction and rollback support, can be 10 or even a 100 times faster than a large commercial installation such as Oracle. It is also freely available and complete with source code, as is Postgres.

Elements as Objects Strategy

This is the first nonrelational strategy mentioned so far, and it is covered in more detail in Part Three. The idea is to use an object-oriented database to store XML elements as objects, with their attributes perhaps represented by properties of those objects, or as contained or referenced objects.

The Approach

In brief, there are three main approaches you can take:

- Create a generic "element" class.
- Create a separate class (or object type) for each different element type.
- Use a commercial object-oriented XML store.

The danger with the first approach is that you will probably end up with lots of code, as here:

```
if (element.name == "TickerSymbol") {
    // look up the symbol and generate a share price
} else if (element.name == "SharePrice") {
    // replace content with current share price
} else if (element.name == "ArtGallery") {
    // Jim's art gallery demo,
    // check for the gallery on the web and insert URL
}
```

This is exactly the sort of code you're not supposed to have to write in an object-oriented language. It's hard to maintain and hard to understand.

The art gallery demo crept into this example because there were documents from two DTDs in the database at one point; Jim left the company a year ago and no one remembers how to run the demo now, but removing the code makes some obscure things break.

If you use generic element classes, clearly you need a higher level of abstraction, such as an `ArtGalleryDemo` class whose instances make use of the `Element` class.

The second approach makes an XML Schema or DTD correspond closely to a database schema. One problem with this approach is that a DTD change can involve recompiling your code, exporting the database, and reloading from scratch, so it's best for specific applications.

A variation is to have a generic element class that creates a specialized element-specific class on the fly, perhaps by reading an XML Schema and applying that with a technique such as Introspection in Java. This gives you many of the advantages of both approaches, but it is harder to code, and not all languages support it. However, it might be a good way to start in Java, Python, or Perl. It's harder to create classes on the fly in a static compiled language like C++, but this presents a good opportunity for an embedded scripting language.

Specific Tools and Alternatives

A number of commercial object-oriented vendors sell XML data stores; some of these are freely available or very inexpensive (see Chapter 22, "Databases, Repositories, and Utilities," for additional information). There are some freely available object-oriented databases as well.

Advantages and Drawbacks

A major drawback of object-oriented databases in the past has been a lack of a standard query language. The Object Database Management Group (www.omg.org) has produced the Object Query Language (OQL), and this is gaining increasing support.

The work involved in creating an object-oriented XML repository is significant, and requires a high level of programming expertise. If you don't have a good steady supply of programmers, you should look instead at using an off-the-shelf solution such as those from Astoria, Poet, and Object Design, Inc.

Text Retrieval and Hybrid Approaches

Text retrieval and other nonrelational techniques form the subject of Part Three. Text retrieval approaches use a system outside the database to do queries and searching or to help with it; hybrid systems use a combination of text retrieval, object-oriented databases, relational databases, and other technology.

The Approach

Text retrieval systems generally make an index to files or database fields, and can then find any file or field very quickly based on words that are listed. This is the technology that AltaVista uses for its Web index, for example. Text retrieval software can take many hours to build an index to a few gigabytes of data, and the index may need to be rebuilt if the data changes. The resulting capability to find information, however, makes the overhead worthwhile in almost all textual applications.

Relational database programmers often try to implement a text retrieval system of their own using the database. *Do not do this.* Your index will be many times larger than your data (3 to 10 times larger is considered good for such an approach) and (partly as a result) much slower than either free or commercial text retrieval systems. My text retrieval database achieves more than 100,000 separate database stores per second on moderately inexpensive hardware, and can make an index of hundreds of megabytes in an hour.

Text retrieval systems do not necessarily address document management, versioning, or collaborative authoring. To do that, you need to combine the text retrieval database with other software, such as the CVS or a relational database with some management code, as described in the previous *Metadata Only* section.

Hybrid approaches might combine a text retrieval system with a relational database system to augment searching, or use an object/relational database to store both structure and metadata together. There are too many possible hybrid systems to list, and often they are the most powerful and fastest.

Part Three discusses a number of other techniques, including dynamic hashing (*ndbm*), that are worth understanding.

Specific Tools and Alternatives

Chapter 22, "Databases, Repositories, and Utilities," lists examples of text retrieval software, as well as version management software such as RCS and

CVS; a search on www.freshmeat.net/ will provide others, and there are Web sites devoted to lists of text retrieval databases. My *lq-text* open source text retrieval package can be downloaded from www.holoweb.net/~liam/ but is not (at the time of writing) XML aware.

There are so many ways to store XML in nonrelational databases that it would be impossible to list them all—OLAP, DB2 hierarchies, anything that can represent sequence and containment can generally be used. You can even expand XML files and use a separate file system folder for each element!

Advantages and Drawbacks

As just noted, often, using a mixture of tools builds the best system available. The main disadvantages can be in increased maintenance cost and the complexity of integration.

The biggest disadvantage of hybrid systems is that it is difficult to give clear error feedback to the user, meaning these systems are often very complex to configure and manage.

Summary

This high-level chapter described a number of approaches to storing XML in databases, moving quickly over a number of important concepts.

Part Three, "Nonrelational Databases," describes different sorts of databases that you might want to consider in conjunction with the strategies discussed here.

Nonrelational Databases

P arts One and Two focused on relational databases because they are the most widely used. They are not the only type of database, however; more to the point, in many cases, they are not the most suitable for use with XML. I have seen a number of attempts to store XML and SGML in relational databases. Most of these attempts have failed miserably. Part Three offers alternatives to relational databases. To avoid the failures, read the chapters here, which will help you to build working software supporting same day response (SDR).

Chapter 10, "Introduction to Object-Oriented Databases." Discusses object-oriented databases.

Chapter 11, "XML as Classes and Objects." Explains ways to use object-oriented databases to store XML.

Chapter 12, "Dynamic Hashing: *ndbm*." Introduces simple but powerful databases, in particular, the Dynamic Hashing package (*ndbm*, *sdbm*, *gdbm*), which is freely available both under Unix and other operating systems.

Chapter 13, "Text Retrieval Technology Overview." Provides an introduction to XML-aware text retrieval.

Chapter 14, "XQL, XLink, XPath, and XPointer Explained." Introduces standards related to XML and that are particularly useful in conjunction with nonrelational databases.

Chapter 15, "Hybrid Approaches." Returns to the topic of hybrid systems, where you keep parts of your information in one type of database, and other parts in another type of database.

## CHAPTER 10

Introduction to Object-Oriented Databases

The purpose of this chapter is to introduce the basic concepts of object-oriented databases, to help you understand how they work, which will then help you to decide whether you should investigate such products further.

Main Features

Object-oriented databases generally provide *persistent storage* for objects. That is, they allow a program to create objects in one run and to refer to them later in some other invocation, possibly even on a different computer. In addition, they may provide one or more of the following: a query language, indexing, transaction support with rollback and commit, and the possibility of distributing objects transparently over many servers. These features are described in the following sections. Some object-oriented databases also come with extra tools such as visual schema designers, Integrated Development Environments (IDEs), and debuggers. But note, some database vendors may charge separately for these features.

Context

Unlike a relational database, which usually works with SQL, an object-oriented database works in the context of a regular programming language such as C++, C, or Java. An object-oriented database may be host-specific or it may be able to read the same database from multiple hosts or even from multiple *kinds* of hosts, such as a SPARC server under Solaris 8 and a PC under Linux. Some object-oriented database servers can support *heterogeneous* clients, so that the SPARC system and a PC and a Macintosh (for example) might all be accessing the same database.

Persistence

With a relational database, you store information explicitly in tables, and get it back later with queries. Although you can use an object-oriented database in this way, it's not the only way. Consider a computer-aided design application (CAD) in which the user can save and load complex engineering drawings into memory. With a file-based system, loading a drawing might involve reading a large external file into memory and creating tens of thousands of objects before the user can start working. With a relational database, the software would run database queries to create those same objects.

With an object-oriented database, the software calls a database function to load the illustration, but objects are not created in memory until they are needed. Instead, they are stored in the database; only references are loaded into memory.

When an object is changed, the database silently writes the changes to the database, keeping the in-database version up to date at all times. When the user presses Save, all the application does is commit to the current transaction; since the database is already up to date, this is generally a very fast process. The code no longer needs to be able to read or write the proprietary save file format, and may also run faster.

Accessing Data

Most of the time, an application using an object-oriented database accesses data by *navigation*: In C or C++, this is done by following pointers, and in Java by following references. For example, the following code illustrates a C++ class that represents a tree:

```
class Tree {
    private:
        int Value;
        Tree *LeftChild;
        Tree *RightChild;

    public:
        Tree *Tree(int Value, Tree *Left, *Right) {
            this->Value = Value;
```

```
            this->LeftChild = Left;
            this->RightChild = Right;
            return this;
        }

        Tree *getLeft() { return LeftChild; }
        Tree *getRight() { return RightChild; }
        int getValue() { return Value; }

        Tree *setLeft(Tree *Left) {
            return LeftChild = Left;
        }

        Tree *setRight(Tree *Right) {
            return RightChild = Right;
        }

        int setValue(int V) {
            return Value = V;
        }

};

// recursive function to visit a tree and add up the values:
int Tree::getTotal()
{
    int Result = Value;

    if (LeftChild) {
        Result += getTotal(LeftChild);
    }

    if (RightChild) {
        Result += getTotal(RightChild);
    }

    return Result;
}
```

We might use this as follows:

```
Tree *myTree = getTree("tree one");

cout << "Total for tree one: " << myTree->getTotal() << "\n";
```

The getTree function could be implemented by reading a file from disk, but in this chapter, the implementation would probably be something like this:

```
Tree *Tree::getTree(const char *Name)
{
    return (Tree *) database::get(Name);
}
```

This creates a single in-memory `Tree` object, by restoring a memory image from the database. The object-oriented database (OODB) will also initialize the two pointers, `LeftChild` and `RightChild`, but it generally will not load the corresponding objects into memory. When `getTotal()` accesses or dereferences a child pointer, passing it to `getTotal()`, the database loads the corresponding object into memory and adjusts the pointer in the tree as necessary.

This pointer manipulation can be achieved in several ways, depending on the database software. The most common way in C and C++ is to use the `memprot` system function. On Unix, this sends the process a signal whenever a process tries to access unallocated memory. The database runtime support library intercepts the signal, looks to see if the address in question was a database address, and, if so, loads the object into memory and makes the address legal by changing permission on the corresponding page. Figure 10.1 shows memory before `Left-Child` is accessed, and Figure 10.2 shows memory after `LeftChild` has been accessed but before `RightChild` has been accessed. In Figure 10.1, the two blank Tree objects are in a block of hardware-protected memory. When that memory is referenced, the tree is filled in and the permission is changed. The pointers in the newly filled-in object are set to point to a new protected area of memory.

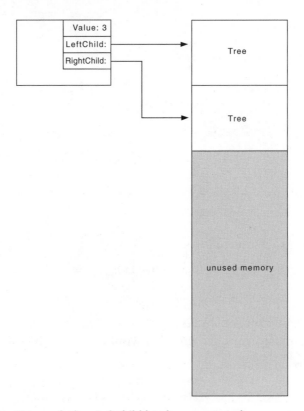

Figure 10.1　Memory before LeftChild has been accessed.

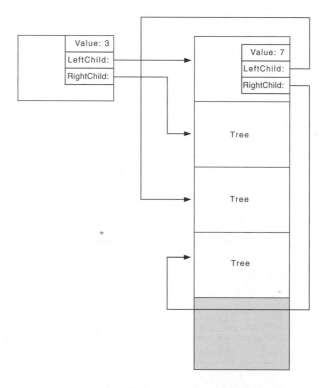

Figure 10.2 Memory after LeftChild has been accessed.

The hardware memory protection used most often relies on the computer's page table; this is the same table that the operating system uses to control virtual memory, and is usually very efficient. Although the figures show only a single object being initialized, in practice, an entire page worth of objects is usually loaded at the same time for efficiency reasons. A page may be anywhere from a kilobyte to 64 Kbytes on some systems. The consequence is that it can be tricky to get good performance.

To store objects in the database and to manage them, you may need to subclass from a `Persistent` class. Objects that are members of classes not derived from a suitable superclass are *transient*, meaning they are not stored. When objects containing pointers or references to transient objects are loaded back from the database, the transient pointers may be set to NULL; some databases may force the transient data to persist.

In Java, there is no control available over hardware memory access (unless native methods are used). Instead, references might be created to empty *stub objects* with methods that first load the data and then call the correct object method. For this to work properly, these stub objects may need to be the same physical size as the actual objects.

At the time of writing, at least one commercial object-oriented database for Java uses a different policy; it reads all reachable objects into memory whenever an object is loaded. In either case, you need to watch the memory footprint of your application carefully.

Binding to Objects

The previous example code assumes that the database runtime support can map from a string to an object. To do this, you have to connect the string to the object, an operation referred to as *binding*. You can then retrieve the object later using the string. The string you use is similar in function to a filename. Because some databases have a noticeable time and space overhead if you start binding thousands (or millions) of objects, you should bind only a few top-level objects. In fact, you only need to bind a root-level object—you can follow pointers from that to get to other data.

Saving Objects

Most object-oriented databases save your objects automatically when you finish using them. You may need to delete unwanted objects explicitly, however. Some schemes (especially in scripting languages such as Perl) are more likely to require that you call a `save` method on objects to write them to disk. If you have to save and load objects yourself, you might ask yourself what other database features you are using, and consider switching to a dynamic hashing package such as *ndbm*, described in Chapter 12, "Dynamic Hashing: *ndbm*."

Queries

You will get the best performance from an object-oriented database if you use a lot of pointer-style navigation and relatively few queries. There is no standard query language for an object-oriented database; the industry consortium Object Database Management Group (ODMG) has defined the Object Query Language (OQL), and some vendors (including Poet, www.poet.com) support this. A few other vendors, including Object Design Inc. (www.odi.com), one of the founders of the ODMG, use proprietary query languages instead.

To use queries, you may need to give each class a method to print its searchable values. Some systems support queries embedded in C or C++ code, others allow runtime queries.

The following is an example of an OQL query that appears in the published ODMG 2.0 standard. It's pretty similar to a SQL query, and this is of course by design.

```
select c.address
from Persons p,
p.children c
where p.address.street="Main Street" and
count(p.children) >= 2 and
c.address.city != p.address.city
```

This assumes that a Person object contains a child reference (`children`) that points to another Person instance. The dot notation works rather like a C or Java field selection. The query will make the database server (or library) look at every single instance of a Person to see if it has two children, and has a street address of Main Street, and has a child whose address city field differs from that of its parent.

This query might require a very large amount of memory in some implementations, as it may involve loading every Person object into memory. If you can build in an index on the `Persons.address.street` field, that might help. You must be careful how you design your objects to work with the object-oriented database you are using, as switching from one such system to another can involve a lot of unexpected work. Make sure that you hide the implementation of persistence as much as possible. This is also a good idea because it means you're less likely to make a mistake, such as forgetting to save an object.

NOTE

In C, the inequality operator "`!=`" might use the address of the city object or, in a language like C++, an overloaded method; in Java, it might use object identity. A detailed introduction to the Object Query Language is beyond the scope of this book (see the Object Database Management Group's published book at www.odmg.org for more information).

Object Design, Inc., Poet, and Ardent all provide XML parsers and/or XML storage facilities, as do many other vendors. Chapter 22, "Databases, Repositories, and Utilities," lists pointers to object-oriented database vendors.

Indexing

Just as with a relational database, an object-oriented database can often create an index to enable rapid access to a particular field. In the `Tree` example, we could build an index on the `Value` member, and then use that index to find `Tree` objects with a specific value very quickly. For this to be useful, you'll need to have upward and downward pointers in each tree node so that once you find a node, you can find the top of the tree containing that node.

Some databases support both hashing and b-trees; others support only one or the other. Some databases can create indexes based on multiple fields and can return pointers to complex objects. These are usually the databases that also support a query language.

Object Design, Inc.'s PSE database for Java is an example of a database that supports multiple types of memory access behavior with its indexing; it has an index that can be searched without loading all of the corresponding objects into memory.

Transactions

Like a relational database, a *transaction* is a sequence of database operations that either must all complete or all fail. If any of them fails, or if the program calls an *abort* method or raises an exception, the entire transaction will be aborted. Only when the transaction finishes can other database clients see any of the changes. Some databases may lock other threads trying to access data that is being changed in another transaction; this means that there may be a possibility for *deadlock*, where multiple threads (or programs) are all waiting for each other.

NOTE

The ODMG specification does not allow nested transactions, although some vendors support them. Again, this can increase the chances of deadlock, but it can also simplify programming and design.

If you have multiple threads within an application, each thread might get its own transaction, or you might be restricted to a single transaction per application, depending on the database software.

Transactions can be very expensive to implement, and enabling them can result in a noticeable performance degradation. This is true with some relational databases as well. The rule of thumb is, use transactions if you need the capability to undo (or roll back) a sequence of operations; if all you want is exclusive access for a short time, you might find that the database provides a locking mechanism that's faster and simpler.

For many applications, it is acceptable to allow multiple readers but only a single writer; sometimes all of the readers can happily wait for a single writer to finish. This is most likely to be true if the write operations are fast and relatively infrequent. If you have a lot of small write operations and a few that take longer, consider using a mixed strategy, whereby the write operations allow readers between them, but longer operations use a separate transaction so that readers can continue independently in other parts of the database. An example is a database backup, where you need to disable changes, and where you mark certain objects (top-level nodes, for example) as having been archived. These changes won't affect most readers, so you could allow other readers in between each write operation, but not allow other writers to come in and confuse your backup state.

Distributed Objects

Some object-oriented databases permit objects to *migrate* from one database server to another. For example, objects might move to the server that requested them most recently. If servers are running different operating systems on different CPU architectures, the database rewrites the objects as necessary. This may happen automatically, perhaps with a global cache manager, or you might need to request remote objects explicitly.

Databases that support this feature may use a lot more disk space to store the same data because they have to store information about which server contains the master copy for each object.

Summary

An object-oriented database is entirely different from a relational database. It seems like a natural fit for storing XML objects, although if you decompose your XML to individual elements, it's hard to get good performance.

Many relational database programmers are startled and puzzled when they first encounter object-oriented databases: From the perspectives of the database programmer and of the user, the two kinds of databases are very dissimilar. An object-oriented database may seem too simple, prompting the disturbing feeling at first that you have missed a hidden catch. But they really *are* that simple.

The next chapter discusses using object-oriented database with XML.

## CHAPTER 11

XML as Classes and Objects

This chapter describes various ways of using an object-oriented database to store XML and to get XML out of an existing object-oriented database. It's a lot easier to start using an object-oriented database than it is to write fast (time-efficient) code that does not use too much memory (space-efficient). This chapter will explain how to store XML efficiently.

NOTE

Before reading this chapter, you should have at least a basic understanding of object-oriented programming. Dave Taylor's book *Object Technology: A Manager's Guide* (Addison-Wesley, 1997) is a good introduction. This chapter does not assume that you are familiar with object-oriented databases, nor with object-oriented programming methodologies. Some of the diagrams in the literature use the Unified Modelling Language (UML), which you can learn more about at www.rational.com. You may also want to read *Design Patterns: Elements of Reusable Object-Oriented Software* by Erich Gamma, Richard Helm, Ralph Johnson, and John Vlissides (Addison-Wesley, 1995) but a knowledge of patterns is not necessary to understand this chapter. There is only pseudocode in this chapter, because you have to take too many other things into account for actual classes to be useful.

We will start by considering some of the relationships among the various components of XML documents. I make no attempt in this chapter to model a DTD because, at the time of writing, an XML Schema draft is emerging, and since an

XML Schema is an XML representation of a DTD, hopefully, you'll be able to use those instead.

After looking at the relationships we need to represent, we'll look at how to represent them. There are many ways to do this, and the one that's best for you will depend on the object-oriented database you use, as well as your goals and design constraints, much more so than with relational databases. For that reason, it doesn't make sense to give large examples. If you find yourself wanting boilerplate code to copy, ask yourself whether you wouldn't be better off using an off-the-shelf product or hiring someone who has done this sort of work before. Poorly designed-object oriented applications can be unpleasant to work with. On the other hand, a well-designed object-oriented system can be a positive delight.

The question most relational database people have when they first encounter object-oriented databases is, "Where's the code?" Object-oriented databases are deceptively simple to use, and you can often get a system loading and saving objects within an hour or two. There's no catch: As I said in the previous chapter, they *are* that easy. Let's start by looking at the overall context and the relationships we need to represent.

Object Relationships and XML Relationships

XML documents represent relationships between pieces of information. Objects in memory use different techniques to represent relationships. Table 11.1 summarizes some of the ways that relationships might map into each other; they are described in more detail in the text that follows.

Containment

The most obvious relationships are *sequence* and *containment*. For example, a chapter might *contain* a *sequence* of paragraphs.

Table 11.1 Representing Relationships

XML RELATIONSHIP	OBJECT REPRESENTATION
Containment	Child pointers; uses; recursive (so usually *not* "has-a" object containment)
Sequence	Linked lists; arrays; `fby` pointers
Has (attributes or child element)	Object properties, or as for containment
Is-A (element type)	Pointer to base element type definition; sometimes done with inheritance
Refers To (ID/IDREF)	Often not directly represented; lookup table of IDs

Containment can be recursive:

```
<!ELEMENT ListOfPoints
    (Item*)
>
<!ELEMENT Item
    (paragraph|ListOfPOints)+
>
<!ELEMENT paragraph
    (#PCDATA)*
>
```

This allows the following markup:

```
<ListOfPoints>
    <Item>
        <Paragraph>Item One</Paragraph>
    </Item>
    <Item>
        <Paragraph>Item Two has sub-items:</Paragraph>
        <ListOfPoints>
            <Item><paragraph>height</paragraph></Item>
            <Item><paragraph>width</paragraph></Item>
        </ListOfPoints>
    </Item>
</ListOfPoints>
```

Consider the following C++ representation (in pseudocode):

```
class ListOfPoints {
    public:
        Item myItems[6]; // allocate space for 6 children
};
```

Unfortunately, although this looks neat and tidy, we can't do the same thing for Item:

```
class Item {
    public:
        paragraph myparas[6];
        ListOfPoints myPoints[6];
};
```

because this doesn't represent the order in which the paragraphs and lists occur (we'll discuss Sequence next). For now, consider the storage size of a ListOfPoints object. Instead of including six Item objects inside a ListOf-Points object, the ListOfPoints object needs to have pointers (or references) to its children.

```
class ListOfPoints {
    public:
        Item *myItems[6];  // array of pointers to children
};
```

In specific cases, where you know your document structure is very fixed, you might represent XML containment as object containment, but it's very unusual:

```
<Employee Number="89120">
    <firstname>Liam</firstName>
    <initials>R. E.</initials>
    <lastName>
</Employee>

class Employee {
    String firstName;
    String lastName;
    int employeeNumber;
}
```

This representation requires that the programmer have detailed knowledge of the problem domain. Even then, there may be problems. I've lost count of the number of times (especially in North America) where an electronic filing system dictates that I can only have one middle initial in my name. If you have a long name, or if your telephone number contains letters (extension 301) or your address needs six lines, you quickly come to value flexible software design and dynamic storage.

So in general, containment is best represented by a pointer or reference. If your XML does not nest very deeply, and does so only in a controlled way, you can use object containment instead of references.

Sequence

The containment examples used an array of six children. This is broken, of course; there is no reason to suppose that an element will always have exactly six children.

In a relational environment it's tempting (but inefficient) to give each child a node number, and use SORTBY whenever you retrieve content. It's sometimes faster to store a list of children in a single VARTEXT field, and sort them in the client instead of the server.

In an object-oriented environment, the obvious ways to represent an ordered sequence of objects are with vectors or arrays. If you are using the C++ programming language, the Standard Template Library provides these; there are standard libraries or classes for most other languages as well. Unfortunately, you may find you need to use classes that your database vendor supplies—the examples in this section generally use pseudocode to suggest this.

We need to investigate two specific issues before using a container class: *size overhead* and *loading behavior*.

Size Overhead

Pointers (or references in Java) are more expensive in an object-oriented database than in the raw language. In the worst case, following a pointer can involve a database query behind the scenes. More important for size considerations, a pointer might be stored in a format that's larger than you expect—pointers of 128 bits or larger are not uncommon. This lets the pointer in the database store additional information, such as a server ID, if the object has been migrated, or a globally unique object ID.

It's worth making a linked list with a few hundred thousand entries to see how large the database gets. You should also time the operation, and watch the memory footprint. The *rusage* command on many Unix systems is used for this; in C, consult the manual page for *end* or *etext*.

Some list container classes are fairly expensive, with both forward and reverse links and sometimes additional fields. Others are fast and cheap. If you need to access the *n*th element of a list or vector, a doubly linked list and an *n* field can halve the average access time, but at a space overhead. If your average document contains a million list items, an overhead of 20 megabytes per document may be unacceptable.

Loading Behavior

After designing your test program that creates a few hundred thousand objects in a list, write a program that traverses the list and looks at each object in turn, but does not keep a reference to them. You may find that the entire database is loaded into memory as you do this. Worse, you might find that accessing any element of the list causes the entire list to be read into memory.

Some database vendors provide container classes that are carefully written to avoid loading more objects into memory than necessary. I have not provided a list of such vendors because it may change, and because you should do experiments yourself to test memory usage of classes. It's important not to believe marketing claims or technical documentation in determining how your system works. Measure it.

Representing Sequences of Text and Elements

If you have *mixed content*, in which text and elements are intermixed, you can choose whether to store that content (including the markup) as an uninterpreted string or to make each stretch of uninterrupted text be a node in your object tree.

For example, a book title might contain a superscript. It's rare, but not unknown. Most systems ignore this fact, but a professional bibliographic system must take this into consideration. You might choose to keep a plain text title field in your database, and allow it to contain strings such as "The `<i>e</i>` = `<i>mc</i><sup>2</sup>` Revolution". This might hamper searching; but on the other hand, searching for the implied structure is harder, especially from within a "book title" text field in a dialogue box. A compromise is to store a *surrogate field*, such as `"The e = mc2 Revolution"`, and to apply the same transformation on queries.

If you do store the text completely, you may have performance issues; yes, you'll need to write a string matcher that copes, but life will be a lot more fun. You might look at XQL, discussed in Chapter 14, "XQL, XLink, XPath, and XPointer Explained"; there are freely available XQL implementations. We'll look at a sample class structure in this chapter, too.

Sometimes you need the full generality of being able to do any query against any part of any document, and you simply have to pay the price.

Has-A

This is simply XML containment—a chapter has a title, which is usually content, although it could conceivably be an attribute. There is nothing special here; it's mentioned because it is important in object-oriented design methodologies.

Is-A

This is the fundamental building block of both an object-oriented system and of an XML system. When you declare an element type *t* in an XML Document Type Definition, whether you use a Schema or a DTD, you are saying that every element of type *t* is a *t*. In other words, every `<para>` is-a *para*. If that sounds trite, it isn't. The idea is that every element marked as being a *para* has some set of shared characteristics. In the same way, every object that is a member of a particular class has shared characteristics.

This similarity leads many people to represent the XML is-a relationship in an object-oriented database as class membership, with each paragraph being a member of a *para* class. This is generally inappropriate because:

- It's easy to edit an XML DTD, but difficult to change an object class hierarchy and the associated code.
- There may be a large performance overhead (especially with Java over a network).

- The relationship does not imply commonality of *behavior* in XML. The same XML element may behave quite differently in different contexts, although one can use namespaces to help clarify this somewhat.

- You will have problems storing documents from multiple document types, since elements with the same name in two different DTDs are in fact entirely unrelated, except by chance.

The result is that you end up with an object representing the declaration in the DTD, and the individual element instances all having an is-a pointer to that object. If you are using C++, you probably need to avoid "smart" or dual-direction pointers, otherwise referencing the DTD object will cause every single element instance object to be loaded into memory, too. You can get around that, if you need to, by having an even "smarter" pointer that uses a small intermediate object.

Refers To

Any XML element can have one or more attributes of type IDREF. The value of this attribute may (and in a valid document, will) correspond exactly to the value of an ID attribute on some element, possibly the same element. This is a simple way of creating links.

One way to represent this is with a pointer; another is to keep a hash table of all ID values found in a document and point to the corresponding elements. If you do this, you may need to store an intermediate object in the hash table, so that looking at the hash table doesn't load the entire database into memory.

If you use a pointer, you may have problems if the object at the other end is deleted, or if its ID-valued attribute is changed (the pointer would go to the wrong element). This is not insurmountable, but it does need to be handled.

The Other Way

I'm going to pause here to talk about the case when, instead of representing or storing XML in an object-oriented database, you already have an object-oriented database or a set of objects in memory, and you want to represent the objects in XML.

Containment and References

If you're trying to represent objects in XML, perhaps to export them, you'll find that they don't usually form a tree. A doubly linked list, a back reference, a loop, or a tree with parent pointers can all occur. As a result, you should represent only direct object containment in XML, and use ID/IRDREF or XLink to represent pointers or references.

Classes and Types

Type information could be transmitted using element names, but make sure that your object type names will fit. In C++, a type name can be fairly complex, and can include punctuation. It is better to store the name as either a string or as a marked-up structure. You could store `"int  *ip"` as `<pointer-to><int>ip</int></pointer-to>`, but this quickly gets unwieldy with `"int *(* f(int, char *)[]"`; and when you add class inheritance to the picture, the simple string begins to look pretty interesting.

If you did represent type names like that, assuming you had access to the necessary information to do so, you could use XQL to ask questions about your variable types, which might be useful.

Similar reasoning applies to other aspects of your data, and you'll always have to make the same trade-offs between size, complexity, and usefulness.

Serialization

If you are saving objects as XML, you might be able to use a Visitor Pattern and a serialization interface. If you use Java's built-in serialization, remember that you have to quote markup, turning `&` into `&amp;` and `<` and `>` into `&lt;` and `&gt;` respectively; otherwise, an XML parser reading the output will go wrong.

You may be inclined to use XML CDATA marked sections, because these seem to promise to contain arbitrary data. In fact, the data must still be textual, not binary, and a CDATA section cannot contain the string `]]>`. This means you have to check for it, and, if you find it, end the CDATA section, emit `]]&gt;`, and then start a new CDATA section. If you're doing that, you might as well have escaped `&`, `<`, and `>` in the first place—it's usually easier to escape three different characters than one three-character sequence.

Where Does the Behavior Live?

It's tempting to try to represent an entire application in XML, with the idea to enable nonprogrammers to write code. But let's face it, if they could do that, they'd be programmers. The following example shows an attempt to do this:

```
<program>
  <variable name="i" id="var001" />
  <foreach var="i" start="1" end="20">
    <if>
        <condition>
            <comparison op="greater-than">
                <varref name="i" />
                <constant>2</constant>
            </comparison>
        </condition>
        <then>
            i is &i; and is getting large
        </then>
        <else>
            This is the first one.
        </else>
    </if>
  </foreach>
</program>
```

In short, let programming languages do what they are good at, and let XML do what it's good for. The behavior is not in the data.

You may also think about trying to use XML design methodologies to model applications. A class becomes an element type, perhaps, or a Document Type Definition. This doesn't work either. Believe me. However, there *is* often value in tying actions to specific elements. You might do this through the use of fixed attributes, which in the SGML world are known among the jargon-loving as *architectural forms*:

```
<!ATTLIST StockPrice
    onValidate CDATA #FIXED "is-valid-ticker-symbol($content)"
>
```

You then write an application that understands the presence of the onVali- date attribute to imply special processing. This model implies that you have control over your document type definitions but not over the markup itself; that adding to the DTD is possible, but altering the instance is difficult, impractical, or impossible.

You could, of course, *modify* or *transform* the markup, moving the architectural form out of the data and into the application. The fixed-attribute approach is good for interchange, where a group of people agree on a set of architectural forms and can then exchange markup whose elements have different names, as long as the structure is identical. If your interchange architecture has a different structure from your actual DTD, the fixed-attribute approach fails, and you end up having to do transformations.

The preceding example is procedural, with an action to be done in a certain place, but it could just as easily have been declarative, as here:

```
<!ATTLIST StockPrice
    is-a CDATA #FIXED "ticker-symbol"
>
```

Now the behavior is back in the application, where it belongs, but it is *triggered* by the data. This is much more elegant, and it works well in practice, too.

XML has another mechanism that can help with introducing behavior: *namespaces*. You could declare a namespace for stock trading, for example, then refer to that within the marked up document:

```
<ST:Price ST:company="V. A. Linux Inc.">384</ST:Price>
```

This, again, requires either marked up data or transformations, but the behavior is still in the application.

One interesting system that uses XML to represent applications is Entity; it uses embedded Perl fragments for the behavior, and XML to describe the user interface. This seems to be an excellent combination. You can find Entity at www.advogato.org under Projects, or at www.gnome.org.

Whichever route you take, if you are reading this book you will almost certainly end up wanting to *do* things with the XML. The trick is to avoid wired-in behavior wherever possible; you need to *decouple* the data from the behavior. Having a `StockPrice` class in your code might be fine, because that's a general sort of object you might need in an e-commerce application. Turning every element type into a separate class is generally overkill, and a change to the document structure can quickly become a coding nightmare. Expect your document structures to change.

Generic XML Repository with External Application

In a general-purpose XML repository storing any XML document for any reason, there should be no element-specific behavior: The client application should do it. In the database, however, you could store associations between XML elements and behavior, either by using attributes in a DTD or (probably better) using a Schema.

NOTE
Don't forget that you may need to store images, text files, and perhaps XML files with errors—an XML editor that won't let you save an incomplete document is not going to be very popular!

Application-Specific Repository with Wired-In Behavior

The other extreme is to build your database to match a single DTD or set of DTDs. The element classes can then do more than just generic get-content and set-content functions. But with this approach, you often end up with a system that is brittle and hard to change; it breaks later when requirements are proved wrong, as they inevitably are. Guard against that by using *interfaces* and avoiding inheriting behavior. See William Brown's book *AntiPatterns: Refactoring Software, Architectures, and Projects in Crisis* (Wiley, 1998) for more details on this and other similar problems.

As you work with a system in which the object semantics are tightly coupled to XML elements, over time you may find one of two things happening:

- A move away from XML internally, with conversion routines on import and export, so that XML becomes an interchange or backup format.
- A move toward decoupling the XML from the object semantics, ending up with a more general repository underneath with a middle layer to map between actions and information.

An example of moving away from XML might be to store a date attribute as a system date object instead of as an XML string.

Decoupling deserves a clearer explanation. Consider a separate mapping file that, in essence, says that in a particular type of document, when you see *this* element in *this* context, do *this*; for example, it might warn that in an element called date the content is not a plausible date. With such a file in place (let's hope the file is itself an XML document!), you can change the way XML information is treated without having to change either the XML itself or the application code.

The next step is to support a scripting language such as Perl or Python in the mapping file. If you do that, you are probably moving past the merely useable and into the realm of the *way cool*.

Class Designs

This section gives some possible class designs. Although they work, you'll want to customize them for a specific application or for a specific database or language; that is build a prototype, measure its performance, separate the easy-to-do from the hard-to-do tasks, and try to build a replacement that adds as few features as possible.

The code samples here use pseudocode that you'll have to translate into the language you are using. They are closest to C++, and were tested in C++, then translated because, as explained, you need to use the container classes that come with your database, and to design the class hierarchy to suit your own application. No amount of boilerplate code can substitute for even five minutes of analysis.

The first step is to think about an XML element. An XML document is logically composed of a tree of elements, so we'll need our element to be a tree node; we can arrange this by saying that the contents of an element consist of a list of elements:

```
class Element { // incomplete
    private:
        String elemtype;
        ListOfElements contents; // wrong, see below
        AttributeList attributes;
    public:
        String getElemType() { return elemtype; }
        String setElemType(String newValue) {
            if (elemtype) { delete elemtype; }
            elemtype = newValue;
            return elemtype; // for convenience
        }
};
```

Unfortunately, this minimal (and very incomplete) class can't represent text content. Most documents have at least a little text content somewhere, so we need to fix this. Furthermore, our list of contents will need to hold a mixture of text and elements; in this way, we can represent *mixed content* as sequences of alternating text and elements:

```
<p>This is <emphasis>mixed content</emphasis> with some text</p>
```

Here, the p element is represented as having three children: (1) the Unicode string `"This is "`, (2) an `emphasis` element, and (3) the Unicode string `"with some text"`.

NOTE

For our list to contain both text and elements, generally (depending on the language) they both need to inherit from a single superclass, representing things that can occur in content.

```
class XMLnode
    public:
    // Since #PCDATA has no children, we might not want Children here.
    // We will later add serialization and support a
    // validate() visitor.
        String getText();
};
```

In addition, we want an element name to be a reference to the DTD or a pointer to an XML Schema instance. The same applies to attribute names.

```
class XMLelement : public XMLnode {
    public:
        char *getName();
```

```
        char *setName();
        XMLnode *getChildren(); // normally supply an iterator here
    private:
        XMLNode *children; // for representing the hierarchy
        XMLNode *next; // for representing sequence
        XMLAttributes *attributes;  // again, add ways to get at these
        String name;
}
```

The important point to understand about this example is that an element contains references (pointers) to children and attributes, and that it does not allow direct access to them, so you can change the representation later.

Some designs, including the Document Object Model, the W3C DOM, have a getParent() method; it restricts the implementation to a tree, otherwise a node could have multiple parents. There seems to be no good reason for this restriction, other than short-sightedness.

The next pointer here is one way of representing the fact that, apart from the single outermost document element, the children always form a list. You could use an STL list instead, or whatever container classes your database provides.

External Entities

Any part of any XML document could be contained in one or more external entities. The XML rule is that an external entity always forms a tree, though, so we can represent it easily as another sort of XMLNode:

```
class CMLExternalEntity : public XMLNode {
    public:
        char *getSystemIdentifier();  // etc., accessors as before
    private:
        char *SystemIdentifier; // a (possibly relative) URL
};
```

A sample structure we might build is shown in Figure 11.1. The corresponding XML document follows:

```
<?xml version="1.0" ?>
<!DOCTYPE People [
    <!ENTITY Simon SYSTEM "http://www.holoweb.net/xmldb/ent/simon.xml">
]>
<People>
    <Person>
        <Name>Helen Bostock</Name>
        <Born>1963-01-24</Born>
    </Person>
    &Simon;
</People>
```

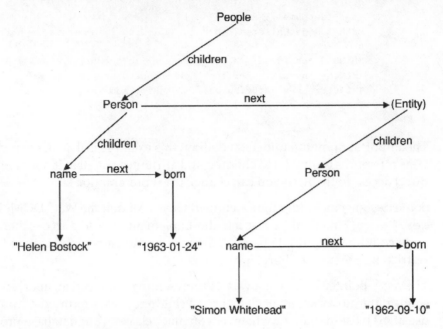

Figure 11.1 Sample object structure.

The `simon.xml` file looks like this:

```
<?xml version="1.0">
<Person>
    <Name>Simon Whitehead</Name>
    <Borm>1962-09-10</Borm>
</Person>
```

Another way to handle external entities would be to use annotated pointers to represent the children relationship, in which case clients that navigated the tree would not need to know about entities. You'd manage that by having a separate pointer object that could have an Entity subtype. Whether that makes sense for you depends on the sorts of clients you expect for your classes. It might simplify interoperability with DOM applications, if that is a goal.

Text

At this point we have represented elements; now we need to add text (#PCDATA) and internal entities. Text is easy, but we have to remember it's Unicode, not ASCII, and to include a length count. Characters that are 16 bit can have either byte set to 0, which turns into a 0 byte, the C string terminator. That's not an issue in Java; and in C++, you should normally use a Unicode-aware string class if your database supports one.

```
class XMLText : public XMLNode {
   private:
       char *theText; // might use wchar_t in C++
       int length;
};
```

Accessor methods include a way to get the text, set the text if appropriate, and also perhaps search it.

You have to consider text entities embedded in #PCDATA, too. Another representation might be to give #PCDATA a list of children, which would alternate between text and internal entities, but that doesn't solve the problem for internal entities containing elements:

```
<!ENTITY Myers "Myers Rubber Door Company">
<!ENTITY Logo "The <i>only</i> Rubber Door supplier in town!">
. . .
<P>We are &Myers;, &Logo;</p>
```

Making a search for *"Myers, the only"* match this paragraph is a challenge. The best way might be to give XMLNode a match() function that can hide the implementation details, and perhaps that builds a plain text representation of each element's content. It's not an easy problem to solve, but most people don't need it solved here. If you find yourself trying to work this out, consider using a text retrieval package alongside your object-oriented database.

Summary

This chapter presented ideas for using an object-oriented database to store XML, really just opening the door on the topic. It is such a large field that an entire book could be written about it. Regard this chapter as a useful guide, pointing out some of the common pitfalls, and giving you enough information to get started.

The next chapter discusses a very different sort of database that's particularly useful where speed of retrieval is an issue.

## CHAPTER 12

Dynamic Hashing: *ndbm*

This chapter introduces a form of database that's very different from any mentioned so far—*dynamic hashing, libraries,* the fastest and simplest sort of database we have discussed. Excellent open source implementations are available, in several versions, including *dbm, sdbm, db,* and *ndbm*; there is also a GNU version called *gdbm*. These names are not acronyms, although the *db* is generally intended to suggest database, and the *g* at the start of *gdbm* is for the GNU project (GNU is *Not Unix*). Most of the time, these implementations are interchangeable except for license restrictions; their main differences are summarized at the end of the chapter. The term *ndbm* has been used to mean both the specific package called *ndbm* and any compatible replacement. The only incompatible version is the much older *dbm* package.

These databases are supplied in the form of C libraries that you link against. You can also use them with Perl, tcl, or Python, and with native methods for use with Java. Most versions of Unix include at least one version of *ndbm*.

First, we'll discuss the fundamental aspects of dynamic hashing, to help you decide whether you are interested in them. Then we'll describe how they work with some sample Perl and C code. Finally, we'll talk about the different versions.

NOTE

The examples in this chapter have been tested on FreeBSD 3.3, Solaris 2.6 (SPARC), and Red Hat Linux 6.0. I've used these and similar programs on machines ranging from a VAX 11/750 under BSD 4.1 through SPARC servers under SunOS 4 and Solaris 2, HP/UX, AIX, OSF/1, Ultrix, and many other Unix variants. This is the most portable of the C-level technologies discussed in this book, and the Perl interface takes that one step further.

What Does *ndbm* Do?

Dynamic hashing libraries perform three main functions:

Store an unordered set of key-value pairs.

Retrieve any value based on its key.

Iterate over all the keys.

You use the libraries when you have a lot of values that you look up based on a single value, whether a number or a string. Though this description is very succinct, it's not at all clear, so let's discuss these three features one at a time.

Store an Unordered Set of Key-Value Pairs

You can associate an arbitrary binary value with a string. The string is actually a binary value, too, so it can be a Unicode string, or an integer, or anything else. The value usually has to be smaller than a kilobyte or so, but this is more than enough for a filename or for a single database field. The newer libraries have a larger limit on the size of a value, or no limit at all.

The Network Information System (NIS, formerly known as Yellow Pages) usually uses *ndbm* to store the map between usernames and password file entries: The network username is the key, and the corresponding password file entry is the value. Some versions of the X Window system use *ndbm* to store a database of color maps; you can think of it as a simple two-column database table:

```
+-----------+----------+
| Name      | Color    |
+-----------+----------+
| red       | #FF0000  |
| green     | #00FF00  |
| dim brown | #220303  |
| blue      | #0000FF  |
| .   .   . |          |
+-----------+----------+
```

In Perl, you might write $Colors{red} = "#FF0000"; and the Perl runtime library would take care of the database write for you. The C API is slightly more complex, because *ndbm* stores arbitrary binary data and not just NUL-terminated strings, but it's still pretty easy.

NOTE NUL is the ASCII code for a byte whose value is 0, not to be confused with NULL, the zero-valued word. On a 64-bit machine, NULL is usually 8 bytes, all of which are zero, where NUL is a single zero byte.

Since the *ndbm* library has a very short code and small memory footprint, and is very fast, it's often used where a relational database would be overkill. Furthermore, since until relatively recently there were no freely available relational databases, *ndbm* was often a major cost saver. It's still worth using today even without the cost savings.

Retrieve Any Value by Key

The original *dbm* library's documentation claimed that *dbm* could return the value associated with any key using at most two file system accesses. This was after you had opened the database, but that's a pretty fast operation since the database must be on a locally accessible file system. Later, after I show you how to use *ndbm*'s major functions, we'll do a quick benchmark.

Iterate over All Keys

Although *ndbm* doesn't usually support queries such as finding all keys greater than 267 in a numeric comparison, it does let you look at every key in turn, one by one, and fetch the values. The *db* library supports sorted b-tree access, which could be used as the basis for a relational database implementation.

You could, for example, implement "find all keys larger than 27" with (in pseudocode):

```
foreach key k:
    if k > 27:
        add k to the result set
```

If your database is large, this isn't going to be fast enough. It will, however, work for copying a database; and the iteration has very low overhead (typically doing a single disk access for every 20 to 50 items) so it's a fast way of dumping an *ndbm* database. It's also the only way to dump an *ndbm* database, unless you have an external list of keys.

When Not to Use *ndbm*

Though the *ndbm* library has a very small storage overhead, it has no support for transactions, rollback, journaling, or multiphase commit. If the system crashes in the middle of a write operation, your database will fail.

Therefore, in general, you should use *ndbm* as a fast cache, not as an authoritative repository for your data. The example in Chapter 15, "Hybrid Approaches," uses an XML document as the master, and builds the *ndbm* database by reading the XML document.

NOTE
The *db* package mentioned earlier has a backward compatibility option to let it emulate *ndbm*, although slowly. It also supports some more traditional "database" features. See the *db* section below.

How *ndbm* Works

The *ndbm* library, and most of its variants, use a technique called *dynamic hashing*. An *ndbm* database is (conceptually at least) a disk file organized as an array of disk blocks. The database size is always a power of two blocks; as a result, *ndbm* can use a fixed number of bits to access any block. The database starts out empty, then expands to use 1 bit, so that blocks 0 and 1 are reachable. When either of those two blocks fills up, the database expands to use 2 bits, allowing blocks 0, 1, 2, and 3, and using 2 bits for the address.

NOTE
For a complete understanding of dynamic hashing, read Don Knuth's *The Art of Computer Programming, Volume 3: Sorting and Searching* (Addison-Wesley, 1998). If you are not familiar with hashing, turn to *Compilers: Principles, Techniques, and Tools* by Alfred V. Aho, Ravi Sethi, and Jeffrey D. Ullman (Addison-Wesley, 1985), which is informally known as the "Dragon Book" because of its cover illustration.

To store an item, *ndbm* first makes a hash of the key (to get a 32-bit integer, for example). It then looks at the least-significant bit, or, if the database is using 6 bits, the least significant 6 bits, of the hash. This gives it a block address, so *ndbm* fetches that block. If there is room to store the data item, in it goes. If not, *ndbm* has to expand the size of the database to 7 bits. Doing this is a fairly slow process, as *ndbm* has to look at every key, and potentially move it to the correct new block. Once this is done, the item can be stored.

To retrieve an item, *ndbm* computes the hash as before, fetches the correct block, and scans through to see if the item is there. Since the blocks are usually fairly small (1 to 8 kilobytes, depending on the implementation and compile-time options), this is very fast.

Some versions of *ndbm* have two separate files to store the database; others have just one. Some versions cope with the instance of a key or value that is too large to fit in a single block, and others don't. They are all excellent at storing a lot of small keys with corresponding small values. A good use might be to map from titles of encyclopedia entries into filenames or article numbers. As you will see in the *Performance* section later in the chapter, *ndbm* can store hundreds of items per second—for example, a run to store 10,000 items took 17 seconds on a Pentium II at 266MHz, and 0.385 seconds on a 400MHz SPARC system.

Using *ndbm*

The following sections describe, using simple sample code, how to use *ndbm*. It's a good idea to start by compiling and trying these small examples to work out which version of *ndbm* you have installed and how to use it.

After presenting the examples, I'll explain the different *ndbm* versions, then show you how to compile the example code with some of them.

Creating a Database and Saving a Value

The model is this: You first open a database with dbm_open(); this returns a handle, usually of type DBM *, which you then pass to all of the other dbm_* functions.

```
DBM *myDB = dbm_open("james", O_RDWR|O_CREAT, 0766);
```

This will open a database called james for reading and writing. If the database does not already exist, the O_CREAT flag tells dbm_open() to create it, using file permission mode 0766 (in octal, so the leading 0 is important). (See the manual page for open in Section 2 of the Unix Programmers' Manual for more details of these flags and modes.) The constants O_RDWR, O_RDONLY, and O_CREAT are defined in the <fcntl.h> header file.

Once you have opened a database, you can store a value in it using a data type called a *datum*, which is usually defined in the <ndbm.h> header file like this:

```
typedef struct {
    char *dptr;
    int dsize;
} datum;
```

The dbm_* functions are unusual in that they often take one or more datum structs as arguments, not pointers to them; they can also return such structs. If you learned C by reading the first (pre-ANSI C) edition of Brian W. Kernighan and Dennis M. Ritchie's excellent book, *The C Programming Language*, be aware that passing structs as arguments and returning them was added to C after that book was published (as was the enum type). The second edition, *The C Programming Language, 2nd Edition* (Prentice Hall, 1988), also written by Kerningham and Dennis, revised for ANSI C, does discuss these features of the language.

To store a value under a given key, you first store both the key and the value in separate datum objects in memory. Here is how you might store a string under the integer key 3:

```
datum key, content;
int i = 3;
key.dptr = (char *) &i;
key.dsize = sizeof(int);
content.dptr = "Simon";
content.dsize = 6; /* S i m o n \0 */
dbm_store(myDB, key, content, DBM_REPLACE);
```

The return value of dbm_store() is used in the complete example that follows to work out whether the store succeeded or not. The DBM_REPLACE flag tells *ndbm* to replace an existing value if it's there. You can also use DBM_INSERT, in which case an existing value is not changed.

You can compile this example into a C program that takes a database name, a key, and a value, and stores the value under the given key, in the database that you name. The database is created if necessary.

```
#include <errno.h>
#include <string.h> /* strings.h on some systems */
#include <stdio.h>
#include <fcntl.h> /* for O_RDWR */

#include <ndbm.h>

/* save database key value
 * saves the given key
 */

char *progname = "save";

static char *systemError();
```

```
int
main(
    int argc, char *argv[]
)
{
    int createmodes = 0644;
    DBM *theDBM;

    /* save the program name for error reporting */
    progname = strrchr(argv[0], '/');
    if (progname) {
        progname++; /* step over the "/" */
    } else {
        progname = argv[0];
    }

    if (argc != 4) {
        fprintf(stderr, "%s: usage: %s dbmfile key value\n",
            progname, progname
        );
        exit(1);
    }

    theDBM = dbm_open(argv[1], O_RDWR|O_CREAT, createmodes);
    if (!theDBM) {
        fprintf(stderr, "%s: failed to open database %s: %s\n",
            progname, argv[1], systemError()
        );
    }

    /* store the value, or try to: */
    {
        datum theKey;
        datum theContent;
        int status;

        theKey.dptr = argv[2];
        theKey.dsize = strlen(argv[2]) + 1; /* include the \0 */

        theContent.dptr = argv[3];
        theContent.dsize = strlen(argv[3]);

        status = dbm_store(theDBM, theKey, theContent, DBM_REPLACE);

        switch (status) {
        default:
        case -1:
            fprintf(stderr,
                "%s: insert into %s of key %s failed, code %d\n",
                progname, argv[1], theKey.dptr, status
            );
```

```
                /* not all versions of ndbm let us work out what the
                 * error was exactly; see the manual page for ndbm on
                 * your system.
                 */
                exit(1);

        case 0: /* OK */
        case 1: /* it was already there, value replaced */
            dbm_close(theDBM);
                /* NOTE: dbm_close() is declaerd as having no
                 * return value, even thouh the close could potentially
                 * fail if the disk was full. The Berkeley db
                 * interface corrects this.
                 */

        }
    }

    exit(0);
}

static char *
systemError()
{
    return strerror(errno);

    /* Not all systems have strerror(); if yours doesn't,
     * you may have this instead:
     *     extern char *sys_errlist[];
     *     extern int sys_nerrs;
     * you have to check errno < sys_nerrs, and, if so,
     *     return sys_errlist[errno]
     *     else return "unknown error"
     * There may also be a dbm_error(), which returns
     * an integer of some sort to describe the most recent
     * error; it's probably an errno sort of integer.
     */
}
```

Save this example in a file called `save.c` (or download it from this book's companion Web site) and compile it, perhaps with:

```
$ cc -o save save.c -lndbm
```

If you are using Windows, both *sdbm* and *db* have been ported to Windows; see the following section *Versions of ndbm*.

Then run the example:

```
$ ./save cities "Paris" "North of France. Traffic hectic."
$
```

There is no output if the operation succeeded, as is usual on Unix.

```
$ ls -l cities*
-rw-r--r--  1 liam  liam  16384 Dec 31 03:57 cities.db
$
```

You may find that you have two files, `cities.dir` and `cities.pag`, with some versions of *ndbm*.

The next section shows you how to retrieve the value later.

NOTE

In Chapter 18, "Sketches from the Forge: Sample Applications," you will see an example that uses an *ndbm* database to store link targets in order to serve an XML file over the Web with links inserted on the fly.

Reading a Value

You can retrieve a value with `dbm_fetch( )` like this:

```
datum key, value;
int i = 3;

key.dptr = (char *) &i;
key.dsize = sizeof(i);

content = dbm_fetch(myDBM, key);
```

Note that `dbm_fetch()` is returning an entire struct, not just a pointer or scalar value. If the item is not found, `content.dptr` will be 0 (NULL). In some implementations, `content.dptr` will also be 0, but this cannot be relied upon.

The `dptr` pointer is pointing to static memory within the *ndbm* library; you will need to copy the value before calling any *ndbm* functions again. More recent implementations (notably *db*) use `malloc()` to store the value, and thereby help to make a thread-safe version. If you are using threads with *ndbm*, you'll need to write a set of wrapper functions around them to handle locking.

The following example program fetches a value back from a database:

```
#include <errno.h>
#include <string.h> /* strings.h on some systems */
#include <stdio.h>
#include <fcntl.h> /* for O_RDONLY */

#include <ndbm.h>

/* usage: fetch database key
 * fetches the given key from the named database
 */

char *progname = "fetch";
```

```
static char *systemError();

int main(
    int argc, char *argv[]
)
{
    int createmodes = 0; /* value never actually used */
    DBM *theDBM;

    /* save the program name for error reporting */
    progname = strrchr(argv[0], '/');
    if (progname) {
        progname++; /* step over the / */
    } else {
        progname = argv[0];
    }

    if (argc != 3) {
        fprintf(stderr, "%s: usage: %s dbmfile key\n",
            progname, progname
        );
        exit(1);
    }

    theDBM = dbm_open(argv[1], O_RDONLY, createmodes);
    if (!theDBM) {
        fprintf(stderr, "%s: failed to open database %s: %s\n",
            progname, argv[1], systemError()
        );
        exit(1);
    }

    /* store the value, or try to: */
    {
        datum theKey;
        datum theContent;
        int status;

        theKey.dptr = argv[2];
        theKey.dsize = strlen(argv[2]) + 1; /* include the \0 */

        theContent = dbm_fetch(theDBM, theKey);

        if (theContent.dptr == NULL) { /* not found */
            fprintf(stderr, "%s: key %s not found\n",
                progname, theKey.dptr
            );
            exit(1);
        }

        if (theContent.dsize == 0) {
```

```
                    /* found but had zero length, or
                     * in some implementations, not found
                     */
                    fprintf(stderr, "%s: key %s empty\n",
                        progname, theKey.dptr
                    );
                    exit(0);
                }

                printf("%*.*s\n",
                    theContent.dsize,
                    theContent.dsize,
                    theContent.dptr
                );
                dbm_close(theDBM);
                /* NOTE: dbm_close() is declared as having no
                 * return value, even though the close could potentially
                 * fail if the disk was full. The Berkeley db
                 * interface corrects this.
                 */
            }

        exit(0);
    }


    static char *systemError()
    {
        return strerror(errno);
        /* see comments in save.c for this routine */
    }
```

Save this in `fetch.c` and compile as for `save.c`:

```
$ cc -o fetch fetch.c -lndbm
```

You can use it like this:

```
$ ./fetch cities "Paris"
North of France. Traffic hectic.
$
```

You can store any number of values with the save program and fetch them in the same way.

Some versions of *ndbm* place limits on the maximum length of a key or value; there are also some other size restrictions.

Deleting a Value

If you want to delete all values, and there are no processes using the database, it's sometimes easiest to remove the file(s). You can remove an individual entry with the `dbm_delete()` function:

```
datum key, value;
int i = 3;

key.dptr = (char *) &i;
key.dsize = sizeof(i);

dbm_delete(myDBM, key);
```

The return value from dbm_delete() is -1 if there was an error, or if the item was not present. You can use dbm_error() to distinguish between the two cases on systems that provide it.

The following program lets you delete a key-value pair from a database by specifying the key:

```
#include <errno.h>
#include <string.h> /* strings.h on some systems */
#include <stdio.h>
#include <fcntl.h> /* for O_RDWR */

#include <ndbm.h>

/* usage: delete database key
 * deletes the given key and associated content
 */

char *progname = "delete";

static char *systemError();

int main(
    int argc, char *argv[]
)
{
    DBM *theDBM;

    /* save the program name for error reporting */
    progname = strrchr(argv[0], '/');
    if (progname) {
        progname++; /* step over the "/" */
    } else {
        progname = argv[0];
    }

    if (argc != 3) {
        fprintf(stderr, "%s: usage: %s dbmfile key value\n",
            progname, progname
        );
        exit(1);
    }

    theDBM = dbm_open(argv[1], O_RDWR, 0);
```

```
            if (!theDBM) {
                fprintf(stderr,
                    "%s: failed to open database %s for writing: %s\n",
                    progname, argv[1], systemError()
                );
            }

            {
                datum theKey;
                int status;

                theKey.dptr = argv[2];
                theKey.dsize = strlen(argv[2]) + 1; /* include the \0 */

                (void) dbm_delete(theDBM, theKey);
                /* although dbm_delete returns a value, it does not
                 * distinguish between the cases where a delete failed,
                 * or the item was not there.
                 */

                dbm_close(theDBM);
            }

            exit(0);
        }

        static char *systemError()
        {
            return strerror(errno);
        }
```

Compile `delete.c` in the same way as before, and run it:

```
$ ./delete cities Paris
$ ./fetch cities "Paris"
fetch: key Paris not found
$
```

Reading All Values

You can dump out all the values in a database with the following program:

```
#include <errno.h>
#include <string.h> /* strings.h on some systems */
#include <stdio.h>
#include <fcntl.h> /* for O_RDONLY */

#include <ndbm.h>

/* usage: printall database
 * prints all keys and values in the database
 */
```

```c
char *progname = "printall";

static char *systemError();

int main(
    int argc, char *argv[]
)
{
    int createmodes = 0; /* value not used */
    DBM *theDBM;

    /* save the program name for error reporting */
    progname = strrchr(argv[0], '/');
    if (progname) {
        progname++; /* step over the "/" */
    } else {
        progname = argv[0];
    }

    if (argc != 2) {
        fprintf(stderr, "%s: usage: %s dbmfile\n",
            progname, progname
        );
        exit(1);
    }

    theDBM = dbm_open(argv[1], O_RDONLY, createmodes);
    if (!theDBM) {
        fprintf(stderr, "%s: failed to open database %s: %s\n",
            progname, argv[1], systemError()
        );
        exit(1);
    }

    /* print all values */
    {
        datum theKey;
        datum theContent;
        int status;

        for (theKey = dbm_firstkey(theDBM);
            theKey.dptr != NULL;
            theKey = dbm_nextkey(theDBM)
        ) {
            theContent = dbm_fetch(theDBM, theKey);

            if (theContent.dptr == NULL) { /* not found */
                fprintf(stderr,
                    "%s: internal error: key %s not found\n",
                        progname, theKey.dptr
```

```
                        );
                        exit(1);
                }

                if (theContent.dsize == 0) {
                        /* found but had zero length, or
                         * in some implementations, not found
                         */
                        fprintf(stderr, "%s: key %s empty\n",
                            progname, theKey.dptr
                        );
                } else {
                        printf("[%d] %*.*s\t%*.*s\n",
                            theKey.dsize,
                            theKey.dsize,
                            theKey.dsize,
                            theKey.dptr,
                            theContent.dsize, theContent.dsize,
                            theContent.dptr
                        );
                }
        }
        dbm_close(theDBM);
        /* NOTE: db_close() is declared as having no
         * return value, even though the close could potentially
         * fail if the disk was full.  The Berkeley db
         * interface corrects this.
         */
    }

    exit(0);
}

static char *systemError()
{
    return strerror(errno);
}
```

Compile this and run it:

```
$ cc -o printall printall.c -ldbm
$ ./printall cities
[14]  Godmanchester      nothing ever happens in Godmanchester
[10]  Cambridge Lots of twiddly bits here
[6]   Paris     Ah to be in Paris in the Springtime
[8]   Toronto   Where I live.
[7]   Mumbai    Where the sewers don't all have lids
```

The numbers in brackets indicate the length of the key to enable you to see if there are hidden spaces. A more general design would just print out the keys, one per line; then you could get the values like this:

```
$ printall cities | xargs -n 1 fetch cities   # does not work as written
```

There are lots of other possibilities, but, again, these examples are just intended to get you started. For a small number of values (fewer than 100, say), you could use Unix filenames instead, but after that, performance often suffers, whereas *ndbm* remains fast even for millions of entries.

Performance

How fast is fast? A sample program that called dbm_store() in a loop managed to store a little more than 10,000 items a minute on a low-end Pentium-based system (233 MHz) with 16 MBytes of RAM under FreeBSD with the *db* library. The *sdbm* library is generally a lot faster, storing 10,000 items in 17 seconds on the same system. A Sun SPARC Server running Solaris 2.6 took 0.385 seconds for the same task, and stored 100,000 items in under a minute, using the *ndbm* library supplied with the system; the resulting file for the 10,000-item test was a little over a megabyte.

But because *ndbm* has to copy data repeatedly as a database grows, insertion time suffers from occasional hiccups; the result is that the average insertion time increases logarithmically with database size. You can improve this greatly using the native *db* interface, because you can specify an anticipated database size, thereby avoiding unnecessary copying. The chart in Figure 12.1 shows times measured with the sample program for database sizes from 10,000 up to 320,000 items. Keys were the integers as ASCII strings, values "testing with 21". The largest database, with 320,000 items, listed at 66 megabytes; but because not all pages were used, it actually occupied only 19 megabytes.

NOTE Confusingly, the documentation for *ndbm* is found on the manual page for dbm_clearerr **on Solaris 2;** man -k dbm **is usually a good way to find it both on Solaris and elsewhere.**

Here is the sample program:

```
#include <errno.h>
#include <string.h> /* strings.h on some systems */
#include <stdio.h>
#include <fcntl.h> /* for O_RDWR */

#define EXTCONST /* may need this if you use the sdbm built with perl */

#include <sdbm.h>
```

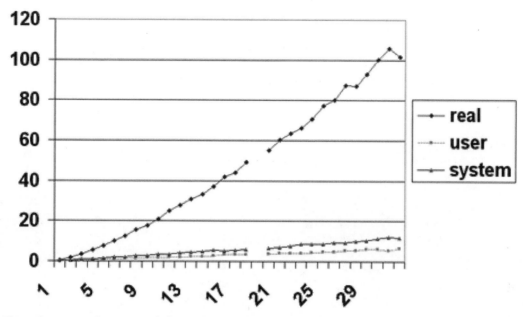

Figure 12.1 Performance of *db* as the database size grows.

```
/* usage: ./speed database n value
 * saves the given value n times, so you can measure
 * how long it took.
 */

char *progname = "speed";

static char *systemError();

int main(
    int argc, char *argv[]
)
{
    int createmodes = 0644;
    DBM *theDBM;
    int max;

    /* save the program name for error reporting */
    progname = strrchr(argv[0], '/');
    if (progname) {
        progname++; /* step over the / */
    } else {
        progname = argv[0];
    }
```

```
    if (argc != 4) {
        fprintf(stderr, "%s: usage: %s sdbmfile key value\n",
            progname, progname
        );
        exit(1);
    }

    theDBM = sdbm_open(argv[1], O_RDWR|O_CREAT, createmodes);
    if (!theDBM) {
        fprintf(stderr, "%s: failed to open database %s: %s\n",
            progname, argv[1], systemError()
        );
    }

    max = atoi(argv[2]);
    if (max <= 0) {
        fprintf(stderr, "%s; n must be anumber greater thann 0, not %s",
            progname, argv[2]
        );
        exit(1);
    }

    /* store the value, or try to: */
    {
        datum theKey;
        datum theContent;
        int status;
        char number[40];
        int n;

        theContent.dptr = argv[3];
        theContent.dsize = strlen(argv[3]);

        for (n = 0; n < max; n++) {
            (void) sprintf(number, "%d", n);
            theKey.dptr = number;
            theKey.dsize = strlen(number) + 1; /* include the \0 */

            status = sdbm_store(theDBM,
                theKey,
                theContent,
                DBM_REPLACE
            );

            if (status < 0) {
                fprintf(stderr,
                    "%s: insert into %s of key %s failed, code %d\n",
                    progname, argv[1], theKey.dptr, status
                );
                /* not all versions of ndbm let us work out what the
                 * error was exactly
```

```
                          */
                      exit(1);
                  }


              }
          }

      sdbm_close(theDBM);
          /* NOTE: sdbm)close() is declared as having no
           * return value, even though the close could potentially
           * fail if the disk was full. The Berkeley db
           * interface corrects this.
           */

      exit(0);
  }


  static char *systemError()
  {
      return strerror(errno);
  }
```

Compile this with

```
$ cc -o speed speed.c -lsdbm
```

(assuming that you have *sdbm* installed) and run it like this:

```
$ time ./speed-sdbm sdbm 10000 'this is a test with sdbm'
real    0m17.473s
user    0m0.403s
sys     0m1.080s
$ time ./speed sdbm 10000 'this is a test with db .'
real    0m48.467s
user    0m0.363s
sys     0m1.670s
$ ls -l sdbm*
-rw-r--r--  1 liam  liam  1101824 Jan  3 22:17 sdbm.db
-rw-r--r--  1 liam  liam     4096 Jan  3 22:27 sdbm.dir
-rw-r--r--  1 liam  liam  6028288 Jan  3 22:27 sdbm.pag
$
```

The sdbm.db file is from *db,* and the other two are from *sdbm.* You can see how *sdbm* has been compiled to use larger blocks—it makes a bigger file, but goes much faster. Both of these are running much faster than a relational database would, though, because they are not offering the same guarantees. Note that the *sdbm* file has holes in it (not every block is used). You can check this with ls -s to see how many blocks a file is using; the result might be in 512 byte units, 1024 byte units, or something else altogether, so check against a regular file to make sure.

A similar test for retrieval time can use the *printall* program much earlier in this chapter. To compile with *sdbm*, change every dbm_* function to sdbm_, and change ndbm.h to sdbm.h:

```
$ time ./printall sdbm | wc
   10000   80000  348890

real    0m0.389s
user    0m0.218s
sys     0m0.028s
```

The output of the *wc* command shows there were 10,000 lines of output, which is what we expect since we stored 10,000 identical items, under 10,000 different keys. The retrieval took about a third of a second (0.389s), which is pretty fast. Using the output in this way is more reasonable than retrieving the items and not printing them. With *sdbm*, results are still good, but not as fast:

```
$ time ./printall-sdbm sdbm | wc
   10000   80000  348890

real    0m2.231s
user    0m0.314s
sys     0m0.187s
```

You can configure *sdbm* to have a different block size and get it to be faster, but in general, *db* is faster at retrieval, and *sdbm* is faster at creating and updating the database. If you use the native (non-*ndbm*) interface to *db*, you can improve performance considerably.

Using *ndbm* in Perl

Following the Perl tradition of "there's more than one way to do it" (TMTOWTDI), there are three main ways to use *ndbm* in Perl, all of which involve making a Perl hash a reflection of an *ndbm* database.

The first way, used with versions of Perl older than 5, is to use the dbmopen and dbmclose functions:

```
my %users;
dbmopen %users, "userfile", 0644
    or die "could not open users dbm file: $!";

$users{"liam"} = "Liam Quin"; # save a value

dbmclose %users;
```

The Perl documentation for *perlfunc*:

```
$ perldoc perlfunc
```

will show it to you, as will (for a correct installation)

```
$ man perlfunc
```

The second way is to use *tie* to connect a hash and a database:

```
use Fcntl;  # for O_RDWR etc.
use NDBM_File;

my %users;
tie(%users, NDBM_File, "userfile", O_RDWR|O_CREAT, 0644);

print $users{liam} . "\n";
untie %users;
```

The deprecated `dbmopen` and `dbmclose` functions shown previously are actu-ally implemented in terms of `tie` and `untie`.

This second method would be the best way to use *ndbm* but for one problem: The package called *ndbm* is not free, but is available only as part of certain commercial versions of Unix. This is what spawned all of the replacements such as *sdbm*, in an excellent demonstration of how closed source can lead to market fragmentation. Nonetheless, the need for Perl scripts to work regard-less of the *ndbm* clone available gave rise to the third method—using the `Any-DBM_File` module.

The `AnyDBM_File` module looks first for `NDBM_File`, then for `DB_File`, `GDBM_File`, `SDBM_File`, and finally `ODBM_File`. You can change the order, too:

```
@AnyDBM_File::ISA = qw(DB_File SDBM_File);
```

Here is a sample from the documentation of `AnyDBM_File` that reads an *ndbm* database and writes it out as a *db* database:

```
use POSIX;  # for O_CREAT and O_RDWR
use NDBM_File;
use DB_File;

# try to open the old database first:
tie(%oldhash, NDBM_File, $old_filename, O_RDONLY, 0) ||
    die "could not open ndbm database $old_filename: $!";

# reasonable chance of success, so let's create
# the output file:
tie(%newhash, DB_File, $new_filename, O_CREAT|O_RDWR) ||
    die "could not create db file $new_filename: $!";

while (($key, $value) = each %oldhash) {
    $newhash{$key} = $value;
}

untie(%oldhash);
```

Instead of the loop, you may be tempted to write a simple assignment (as was the author of `AnyDBM_File` in some versions of the documentation), like this:

```
%newhash = %oldhash;
```

This will work, but it involves having the entire old database in memory at once. For a large database, using `each` is more efficient.

Whichever of the three methods you use, you always end up with what appears to be a normal Perl hash object, but is actually kept inside an *ndbm* hash database. The `exists()` and `defined()` functions both work as normal, as does `keys()`; but be aware of the caveats that follow.

Caveats

Be aware of these issues while using *ndbm* in Perl:

- If Perl crashes while you are using a database that you have open for writing, the database may be corrupted; you may need to remove it altogether and start from scratch.

- Not all installations of Perl have all the *ndbm* variants; you should use `AnyDBM_File` if you want your Perl program to run on other systems. The `dbmopen()` and `dbmclose()` functions are deprecated.

- Check the return value from `tie()`, otherwise an error in opening the database will make your program appear to work normally, but it will not be saving anything! The documentation, including *Programming Perl* by Larry Wall, Tom Christiansen, and Randal L. Schwartz, (O'Reilly & Associates, 1996), is not always careful to do this in the examples.

- Although the normal `keys()` and `values()` work as you expect, as does referring to a tied hash in a list context, the resulting array is constructed by loading the entire database into memory. This is inefficient at best, and may fail altogether if the database is larger than the amount of virtual memory available. You should use each to iterate over all keys in a database, like this:

```
    while (($key,$val) = each %users) {
print "$key => $val\n";
    }
```

Despite these caveats, *ndbm* is a very powerful facility, and it is particularly easy to use in Perl.

Versions of *ndbm*

Later versions of *ndbm* provide four main kinds of new features:

- Freely available source.

- Better performance, usually through caching.

- Raising or removing limits, such as those on the sizes of keys and values.

- Improving the API, including supporting access to more than one open database.

The main variants are described in the following sections, and summarized in Table 12.1.

dbm

Perl calls this version *odbm*, presumably for "old dbm." This was the very first version on Unix, and was limited, in that you could only use one database at a time. The design is also not thread-safe, and *odbm* is not often used today. It is, however, still included in Solaris 2, if you compile with `-I/usr/include/rpcsvs` and link with `-lnsl`; but the manual page tells you not to use it. The *dbm* library was included in 4.1 BSD Unix in 1981, and possibly in Version 7 Unix before that. The source is commercial and is not publicly available.

As with most later versions, a *dbm* database generally contains "holes"—unused blocks that are not allocated. These holes do not take up any space on disk, but if you copy a database with *cp* or *mv*, or back it up to tape with *cpio* or *tar*, the holes may suddenly turn into full blocks of zeros in the copy. Some versions of *tar* have an option to treat blocks of zeroes specially so as not to make the file use more space when extracted. More important, a block of zeros may be interpreted as an end of tape mark with some broken tape drivers. Such drivers would report an early end of file, and *tar* would complain about an incomplete file.

NOTE
The *dbm* library has a slightly different API from *ndbm*; see the manual page for it if you have to use it.

ndbm

This version was the "new dbm" that appeared in BSD Unix in the early 1980s. It is still commercial, and now BSD Unix uses the *db* library (described in the following list) as a freely available replacement. It remains one of the most widely distributed versions of *dbm*.

You need to be aware of a number of limitations with *ndbm* beyond the license and unavailability of source code:

- Every key-content pair must fit into a single 1024-byte disk block; this renders *ndbm* unsuitable for storing XML documents—although, as we will discuss, it is still useful to us.

- All key-content pairs that hash together (that is, have the same 32-bit hash value, which is very rare in practice) must fit into the same block.

- There are no locks: If multiple processes try to access the same database, with one or more trying to write, expect confusion. You can use an external lock file, or open the database with O_RDWR | O_EXCL for exclusive access to try to work around this.

- The *ndbm* library returns pointers to static data, and therefore is not thread-safe.

The *ndbm* library is used by Sun's Network Information System, by most versions of the X Window System to map color names, such as *red* to hex values like #FF0000, and even by the password management system on some versions of BSD Unix. It is very solid, and, within its limitations, very robust.

sdbm

The *sdbm* library is small and fast. It was written in 1989 by Ozan Yigit, then of York University, Toronto, as a publicly available replacement; since then, it has been very widely ported. It shares the size restrictions of the *ndbm* package, but by default uses 4096-byte blocks instead of 1024-byte ones, considerably reducing the likelihood of problems.

The *sdbm* library is included as part of the Perl distribution so that Perl always has at least one *ndbm*-style database available.

The *sdbm* functions all begin with sdbm_ instead of dbm_, and the include file is <sdbm.h>.

gdbm

This is the GNU version of *ndbm*. As you might expect, it has many features, one of which is that you can specify the block size when you create the database. This version copes with items larger than a block, so the only reason for changing the block size is to tune the size and performance of the database, but because the entire raison d' être for *ndbm* is performance, this is pretty useful.

Be sure to check the *gdbm* license before linking against it. Early versions were distributed with the GNU Public License (GPL) and not the GNU Library License, so that you could only use *gdbm* if your program was under the GPL.

The files produced by *gdbm* do not contain holes, and therefore do not use more space when copied with *cp* or *tar*. And although the *gdbm* functions all begin with gdbm_, there is an *ndbm* compatibility mode for use with old programs.

db

When the BSD team needed a free replacement for *ndbm*, and were unable to use *gdbm* because of its license, they created their own. Ozan Yigit (who had previously written *sdbm*), Margo Seltzer, and, later, Keith Bostic all worked on it, producing a library that is fast and flexible, supports a much richer API than *ndbm*, yet retains C-level compatibility.

Like *gdbm*, the *db* package does not have limits on the sizes of keys or content. Files created with *db* can be moved between platforms. Also, like *gdbm* files, they do not contain holes, and therefore can easily be copied with *cp* or *tar*.

There is a b-tree interface, as well as a strict hashing one, and even a facility to map text files into arrays of lines. A commercial version of the *db* library is available from its authors (they have been adding transaction support and other more traditional database features). The free version, distributed under the BSD license, is still actively supported.

One of the more interesting features of the *db* library is that if you pass a NULL pointer (or *undef* in Perl) as a filename when you open or create a database, the package uses memory instead of a file. This gives you the flexibility to use the same code both in in-memory transient data and in persistent file-based data.

The *db* library is harder to port to a new version of Unix than most others, but since it has already been ported almost everywhere, this probably won't affect you. FreeBSD installs *db* by default, as do some of the Linux distributions.

If you want the best performance, use the native interface to db. See the manual entries for *db*, *dbopen*, and *dbhash* for more details; the following example may also help:

```
#include <errno.h>
#include <string.h>
#include <stdio.h>
#include <fcntl.h>
#include <sys/types.h>
#include <limits.h>
#include <db_185.h>  /* or db.h */

/* save database key value
 * saves the given key
 */

char *progname = "savelots";
```

```c
static char *systemError();

int
main(
    int argc, char *argv[]
)
{
    int createmodes = 0644;
    DB *theDB;
    HASHINFO H;
    int N = 0;
    int i;
    DBT theKey;
    DBT theContent;
    char keybuf[40];

    /* save the program name for error reporting */
    progname = strrchr(argv[0], '/');
    if (progname) {
        progname++; /* step over the "/" */
    } else {
        progname = argv[0];
    }

    if (argc != 4) {
        fprintf(stderr, "%s: usage: %s dbmfile N value\n",
            progname, progname
        );
        exit(1);
    }

    N = atoi(argv[2]);
    if (N < 1) {
        fprintf(stderr,
            "%s: 2nd argument must be a number > 0, not \"%s\"\n",
            progname, argv[2]
        );
        exit(1);
    }

    H.bsize = 4096;
    H.ffactor = 100; /* max items per block */
    H.nelem = N;
    H.cachesize = 1 * 1024 * 1024; /* 1 MB cache */
    H.hash = 0; /* default */
    H.lorder = 0; /* default */

    theDB = dbopen(argv[1], O_RDWR|O_CREAT, createmodes, DB_HASH, &H);
    if (!theDB) {
        fprintf(stderr, "%s: failed to open database %s: %s\n",
            progname, argv[1], systemError()
```

```
        );
    }

    theContent.data = argv[3];
    theContent.size = strlen(argv[3]);

    /* store the value, or try to: */
    for (i = 0; i < N; i++) {
        int status;

        (void) sprintf(keybuf, "%d", i);
        theKey.data = keybuf;
        theKey.size = strlen(keybuf) + 1; /* include the \0 */


        status = theDB->put(theDB, &theKey, &theContent, 0);

        switch (status) {
        case -1:
            fprintf(stderr,
                "%s: insert into %s of key %s failed, code %d\n",
                progname, argv[1], theKey.data, status
            );
            exit(1);
        }
    }

    theDB->close(theDB);

    exit(0);
}

static char *
systemError()
{
    return strerror(errno);
}
```

This code is very similar to earlier examples, except that you have to use the
returned DB structure to get at the various functions. It runs between 20 and

Alternative Versions

There are several other *ndbm*-compatible libraries, although they seem to be
used only rarely now. One of the more common was *dbz*, which had the smallest
database files but was slowest. A newer version is *cdb*; a search on www
.freshmeat.net may turn up others.

100 times faster than the same library in *ndbm* emulation mode. Based on this fact, you may conclude that the *ndbm* emulation mode is poorly implemented, but it simply appears to use defaults that, for most databases, will involve a lot of copying of data.

Summary of Features

Table 12.1 is based on part of the Perl AnyDB documentation (with some changes and additions), and summarizes the features of the more common *ndbm* variants.

The *ndbm* Library and XML

By this point in the chapter, you probably have lots of ideas about how to make use of the *ndbm*-style packages with XML documents. Here are some samples.

Cross-References

Suppose you have cross-reference markup like this:

```
See <xref what="chapter" idref="chap12" />
```

Table 12.1   Features of ndbm Variants

FEATURE	ODBM	NDBM	SDBM	GDBM	DB
Often included with Unix	yes	yes*	no	no	no
Ported to non-Unix systems	N/A	N/A	yes	yes	?
Code Size	small	small	small	big	big
Database Size	?	?	small	big?	ok**
Speed	okay	okay	fast	okay	fast
Licensing restrictions	yes	yes	no	yes	no
Freely available source	no	no	yes	yes	yes
Files contain holes	yes	yes	yes	no	no
Size limits	1k	4k	1k***	none	none
Run-time control over block size	no	no	no	yes	yes
Byte-order independent files	no	no	no	no	yes

*On mixed-universe machines, *dbm* and *ndbm* may be in the BSD compatibility library, which is often shunned.

**The code size can be trimmed if you compile for one access method. In any case, since *db* is generally configured as a shared library and used by other applications, this may not be an issue.

***By default, but can be redefined.

You would like to present this to a user on a screen or paper as: *See Chapter 12, "Running Barefoot Is Healthier,"* but the individual chapters are stored in separate files. The trick is to write a program (perhaps a Perl script) that reads all of the chapters and builds an *ndbm* database in which the keys are the XML IDs and the values are the corresponding chapter titles. You then write another script that reads a single chapter, replacing the preceding markup with something like this:

```
See <xref what="chapter"
    idref="chap12">Running Barefoot Is Healthier</xref>
```

With a little work, you can make it so that the script will *replace* any content that's already in the `xref` element, so that the same script can be run repeatedly on the same input, for when the chapter title changes.

Keeping the information in a *ndbm* database is especially convenient for large documents, where you may have tens or hundreds of thousands of cross-references. It's tempting to use a relational database to keep track of them, but remember that the XML documents may be authoritative. The throwaway *ndbm* file doesn't create a future integrity problem when data is changed in one place but not the other, and it's quick enough to create that nobody minds.

Links between Files

We will need to keep track of the filename we used for each glossary entry, so that we can generate cross-references not from explicit markup, but from terms used in the body of the glossary. Keeping a mapping between titles and filenames can make that process considerably easier. The mapping is built up as HTML files are generated, and a second pass retrofits the links.

The production code keeps all the information in an in-memory Perl hash table, but the program takes several seconds to run; moving the hash to *ndbm* might make it fast enough to generate HTML on the fly when it's requested. That in turn makes it easier to support per-user "themes," generating the same content in different styles.

Summary

This chapter introduced a very fast, persistent hash-based lookup mechanism. It's not as robust as a regular database by far, but it is ideal for applications where fast retrieval is needed on small pieces of slowly changing information.

I included a lot of detail about *ndbm* here, because other books on XML and on databases don't seem to cover it. It's a tool that can make a small job possible in a short time, and well worth knowing about.

In the next chapter, we'll go one step further away from relational databases, and look at text retrieval systems.

## CHAPTER 13

Text Retrieval Technology Overview

The popularity of World Wide Web search pages is a good indication of how text retrieval systems can provide a significant value to almost any document-oriented system. In this chapter, you'll get an overview of a text retrieval system; you'll learn how they work and what they can do, and you'll be given guidelines to help you decide when you might want to use one. The information in this chapter may also help you later, if you want to implement one yourself, which is a lot of fun, but also a lot of work.

What Is Text Retrieval?

Text retrieval is a subset of *information retrieval*, in which an index is generated automatically to assist in finding pieces of text at a later time. A well-known example of a text retrieval system is that used by AltaVista, which enables users to search for documents on the World Wide Web.

In general, information retrieval is a difficult and therefore poorly understood field. The main goal is to find information automatically; that is, to answer a user's request. For example, a user might need to find bed and breakfast accommodation in Wirral, England. Another user might be scanning 1937 issues of the *Wall Street Journal* looking for incidences of bankruptcy in the footwear industry. A third user might be interested in pictures of Milan

Cathedral or in a film demonstrating how to shave safely. But these retrieval capabilities are beyond the scope of a book on XML. We will focus on retrieving *textual* information.

The main difficulty facing the developers of textual information retrieval software is that the computer has no understanding of the actual information it stores, which is central to all retrieval applications. Since the computer does not understand the text, either the text must be categorized by human researchers, or *brute force and ignorance* must be applied.

The sections that comprise this chapter introduce the various ways to categorize documents (we'll return to this topic in more detail in Part Four, "Links and Metadata"), including the so-called brute-force methods, which have served AltaVista and others so well.

Categorizing Documents

It is possible to mark each document in a collection with one or more keywords or phrases that identify the broad topic of discourse in that document. The topics are generally arranged in a hierarchy of increasing specialization, such as clothing, clothing/footwear, and clothing/footwear/socks. There are standardized hierarchies of topics created so that people can search across collections created by different organizations. Most people are familiar with the Dewey decimal classification scheme used in many public libraries, but for a private collection, a domain-specific hierarchy may be more effective.

Unfortunately, there are several difficulties with marking text by category:

It must be done by hand. If we could mark text by category automatically by computer, we wouldn't need to do it at all (except as an optimization) because we wouldn't have the problem any more. Classification is costly and slow, because a specialist must read the text and decide where to place it. Nevertheless, it is also very valuable (witness Yahoo! www.yahoo.com/).

A single text may be in multiple categories and different parts of a long text may be about entirely unrelated topics. Consider the *Encyclopaedia Britannica* entry for Canada, which includes sections on history, geography, economics, geology, anthropology, and possibly beer. Splitting long texts into sequences of smaller texts can help here; chapters or sections often form cohesive units for the purpose.

The list of categories is determined by experts, not by the users who do the searching. If you are looking for books on fly-fishing, but have to trawl through the categories of, say, sporting, hunting, water activities, the scheme is of little help. Worse, if you later discover that fly-fishing was listed under string and twine, the categories actively hindered your search.

Extensive categorization schemes for published information already exist. The Dewey decimal classification system is probably the best known. Nevertheless, it, too, can cause confusion, as everyone can attest who has visited a library to look for a book on the Web or on word processing only to find it along with other information technology books under mathematics and numerical systems.

Electronic items can be in more than one place at a time. An electronic categorization system has a major advantage over one for purely physical objects: It's easy for a digital object to appear in more than one place in a hierarchy. If you're not sure where to put *The Lord of the Rings*, for example, you can put it under both adult and teen fiction, as well as under jewelry.

Automatic classification of text is an active research area, but has not yet reached a point where it can be used reliably; see Chapter 23, "Further Reading" for pointers to more in-depth resources on this topic.

Uncategorized Information

Because classification is difficult, it is common that an information retrieval system has to deal with a large mass of heterogeneous data with no classification information available. The computer has no real understanding of the information, so we must use cruder techniques; the most commonly used is to simply ask, "Which documents contain the same words as the query?"

If you are looking for the famous paper on algebraic topology by Canary and Green, but you can't remember the title, searching the World Wide Web for "Green and Canary" is not what you should do! You need to find a more specific database that indexes only mathematics. If Web pages had an *author* element, you could search for papers by those two authors. This kind of embedded metadata is the subject of Part Four, "Links and Metadata."

In the absence of useful metadata, an information retrieval system will generally compare the words in the query with those in each document, and return the documents that contain those words most often. This can be refined (for example, using a thesaurus to find "money" when "coins" are mentioned), but they still just compare words. This approach becomes less useful for a more specialized collection of information, because more documents will share a common vocabulary. Thus, technical or specialized information is probably best searched with *phrase-aware systems*, described in the next section.

Queries

The search entered by a user is termed a *query*. The sorts of query you need to handle will play a large part in determining how to implement the actual search engine. There are several types of basic query, some of which are described in the following sections.

Character Search

This is a search for all documents containing a string of literal characters (typically user-supplied). As a bonus, we might offer case-sensitive and case-insensitive searching. Some systems (including the author's *lq-text* system, first released in 1989) also support *hypercase searching*, where lowercase letters in the query match any case in the documents, but uppercase letters in the query match only uppercase letters.

With a character search, the query "to be or not to be" would not retrieve any of Shakespeare's plays, because this phrase does not occur as just shown. It's usually written, "To be, or not to be," with commas and an uppercase "T" at the start. Furthermore, it might not all be on one line in the ASCII or XML document that stores it, and the space in the query would fail to match the newline in the input. Obviously, a good search engine should do better than this, once the authors perceive the problem.

You can implement a character search with Unix *grep*, but this is likely to be slow if you have many files or a large amount of data. People tend to get impatient after only a couple of seconds, so an index is generally used. You can store *n*-grams in an index to speed up a character search: For example, one list might store every occurrence of t followed by h followed by e; another list might store every occurrence of h followed by e followed by a space, in which case, a search for "the" would find weather as well as theory. You can then filter out the matches you don't want before presenting them to the user. Of course, people don't often search for the, and a more plausible search such as ankle involves intersecting the index entries for ank, nkl and kle. If you include a token for a word boundary, \b for example, you can also include \ban and le\b to ignore ankles and thankless, should that be desired. Probably it isn't. You can also handle query expansion, letting `foot` match `feet`, by searching for both words and merging the results.

Regular Expressions

If we allow regular expressions (or patterns) in queries, life becomes a little more interesting. The intrepid researcher can try `"to[ \n]+be[, \n]+or[ \n]+not[ \n]+to[ \n]+be"` to match the well-known quote from *Hamlet*. Most regular expression implementations are line-oriented, although in the XML world, it makes more sense to be element-oriented, with the caret (`^`) and dollar sign (`$`) matching the beginning and end of a container, as implemented in some commercial SGML and XML software. The publicly available *sgrep* utility is useful here, as is Perl.

Regular expression syntax isn't for everyone. Searching for "She walked with a weary foot" won't work if you misremember it as "She walks with weary feet," unless you are extraordinarily careful with your regular expressions!

On the other hand, a search engine that supports wildcards or full regular expressions is likely to be appreciated by the more sophisticated users. But such users also tend to be both the most demanding and have the most complex needs, so these options are worth considering carefully.

One problem with many open source projects is that the programmers create the design, and they are not always the end user of the system. A programmer is usually willing to tolerate a very complex environment in exchange for extra power, whereas someone not interested or less knowledgeable in technology probably doesn't want anything that doesn't intuitively and immediately help to get a job done.

Word Sequences

If the user's query is treated as a sequence of words, with the software taking care of white space, we will find more of the documents we are seeking. In the terminology of text retrieval, *recall* is higher. See, for example, Gerard Salton's *Automatic Text Processing* (Addison-Wesley, 1989) for formal mathematical definitions of recall and precision.

Once we treat a query as a sequence of words, we become free to consider changing the words, allowing "sock" to retrieve "socks" and "foot" to retrieve "feet." The more we expand the query to include other word forms, the more results we will get; but we will also start to find things the user didn't want or expect. In the jargon of text retrieval research, *precision* is lower.

Given a query such as "Ealing Green," we might first retrieve all documents that contain either word, anywhere in the document, perhaps sorting the results so that documents that contain lots of the word Ealing many times, or Green many times, will appear first. It would be better to list first those documents containing the word Ealing immediately followed by the word Green, since humans naturally read juxtaposition of words in a query as implying sequence. Nonetheless, the information retrieval community appears to have been slow to embrace the idea of searching based on phrases.

In informal experiments, I found that allowing word order to be significant in queries increased user satisfaction. Sometimes that's almost as important as getting the right answer; and if you can do both at once, you win. It's particularly useful with technical information; if you watch MetaSpy or the other Web query engine monitors, or log referrers to your Web site, you will quickly see that a lot of people search for phrases. People *want* to do this, so why not enable it?

One way to implement a phrase-aware search engine is to make an *inverted index* of all the words in all the data, and, for each occurrence, remember where it was. You might, for example, store the fact that "banana" occurred as the 3,127th word in a particular document. If someone searches for "banana republic," you'll look in the index of all the bananas, compare it to the index of all republics, and look for a pair with adjacent word numbers in the same file. The need to store word numbers (or byte offsets, but that's even more data) means that the index is larger, and creating the index is a little slower—which may be why many systems don't do it.

Algebraic Queries

It is possible to define a *little language* (in the sense used by Jon Bentley in his *Programming Pearls* books (see Chapter 23) for expressing a search. For example, you might say, "find all documents containing the word elephant but not containing the word custard near the word banana." You have to be careful to avoid surprises, however; there are systems in which the query "to be or not to be" is treated as a Boolean expression and returns all of the documents in the database being searched!

Regular expressions are themselves a little language; many systems use more than one little language, although it is a significant benefit to users if those languages can share concepts wherever possible. This approach is particularly suited to sophisticated users, and is easily extensible to cover XML-specific searching.

Here are some simple examples that various commercial products use (including Interleaf Panorama, www.interleaf.com, and Synex ViewPort, www.synex.se):

```
"1976" within <PartNo>
```

This means find all occurrences of 1976 within a PartNo element; for many, this is the be-all and end-all of XML-aware searching. You could implement this with a hybrid system consisting of a text retrieval engine and a representation of structure, as we'll see in Chapter 15, "Hybrid Approaches."

Boolean expressions like this next example can use a lot of memory to implement, if you end up reading all of the matches for all three words and then combining them:

```
("Gretna Green" AND "married") NEAR "elope"
```

An optimization is to store the matches for each word in sorted order, so that you can apply the expression as you read the matches off the disk. This may also let you deliver the first few matches immediately, unless you sort the results by "quality" or "ranking":

```
<Para ID="j30015">
```

Software implementing attribute searching must (obviously) store attribute values. One way would be to store them as words along with the main text in the database.

Query Expansion

When users are unfamiliar with the contents of the archive being searched, or when the search is more general than looking for a specific word or phrase, it's useful to have the information retrieval system search for *more* than the user requested. You might incorporate *ranking*, to try to sort the results so that the most likely documents or matches appear near the start of the list.

Two ways to expand the search are to use *stemming*, in which words with a common prefix or derived from a common etymological or grammatical root are considered equivalent, and to implement a thesaurus to search for all words of similar meaning to those in the query.

Stemming

In early information retrieval systems, *stemming* involved simply removing the ends of the words to get a stem (or root), so that walked, walking, and walker would all be found by looking for walk; and fly, flier, and fling would (less smoothly) go together. The downside is that stemming generally reduces precision, but improves recall—you are more likely to find things, but you are also more likely to find things you didn't expect. Since most retrieval systems do not have any way to determine actual parts of speech, all words that end in -sses, -os, and so on are likely to be considered to be plurals, so that SunOS and Jesus are thought to be plural. With broader systems, the town of Dorking is full of people who dork a lot. Hence, any search for Jesu finds Jesus (probably acceptable) and any search for dork finds Dorking (probably a little surprising).

Automatic part-of-speech detection can help to reduce false hits, for example by deducing that Dorking is a noun and hence not conflating it with the (putative) verb to dork (that is, not assuming that dork and Dorking come from the same root). Such detection tends to be computationally expensive. Accuracy can be over 85 percent with probabilistic models, but, unfortunately, the words that it fails on may be exactly the ones that are unusual, and that people are more likely to include in their queries.

Experiments with semantic nets, such as the publicly available WordNet package (www. cogsci.princeton.edu/~wn/) are promising but still in early stages. They generally analyze the query to determine part-of-speech information, and try to do the same to the indexed text.

Term Replacement and Thesauri

Another way of improving searches is to use some kind of thesaurus, so that a search for "coins" can also find documents containing "money." This improves recall, finding more of the documents in the database that might be relevant to the query, but it reduces precision, forming a blunt instrument that retrieves many irrelevant documents. Worse, the user might have no way of knowing why a particular document was retrieved, which can be very bewildering.

NOTE

A public domain thesaurus is available from Project Gutenberg (http://promo.net/pg/), another from the WordNet project (www.cogsci.princeton.edu/~wn/), another with the Moby Project (www.dcs.shef.ac.uk/research/ilash/Moby/), and a list of free lexical resources at http://sp.shinshu-u.ac.jp/~mutiyama/dict.html. A number of commercial systems use some kind of thesaurus.

Automatic thesaurus generation, in which the text is scanned for words that are commonly used together, is sometimes helpful. One way to do this is to look for phrases that differ by a single word, so that if a user sees "to milk dry" and "to suck dry," he or she knows that to milk can sometimes mean to suck. More sophisticated algorithms are more discriminating. Unfortunately, automatic thesaurus generation generally involves going to a lot of trouble for a very small improvement in search quality.

With XML documents, you could use a per-element type of thesaurus, so that the contents of `<PlaceName>`, `<Description>`, and `<Keywords>` could all be treated differently. This becomes much more important for multilingual documents, too. I once worked with a group of people making dictionaries; they spent an entire week running a spell-check, carefully pressing Ignore for each fragment of pronunciation or etymology. A context-sensitive checker would have saved them several days each time.

Similarity and Feedback

The late Gerald Salton of Cornell University described an idea called *document similarity* in which a person decides that two documents are similar to each other if they have a lot of words in common. The words are weighted by their expected frequency to derive a numerical distance vector. A user can give relevant feedback to the information retrieval system by choosing one or more documents and saying "find other documents like this one."

Similarity algorithms work best on collections that have varied subjects (so that there are documents with widely differing vocabularies) and that tend to be entirely about a single topic. Variations include per-paragraph similarity and using phrases instead of words, both of which can give dramatic improvements in some cases.

However, few users are willing to take the time to say, "I liked this document, get more like it," which limits the effectiveness of this technique.

Multiple Languages

There are two situations to discuss here: first, a heterogeneous collection of documents (with some documents in Urdu and some in Welsh, for example) or multilingual documents with multiple languages in the same document; second, the issue of users whose first language is not the same as that of the document collection.

Both of these are relevant to XML; the second is especially important with distributed or Web-based applications.

Heterogeneous Collections

Some systems can search across documents in multiple languages by translating the query into the appropriate word or words for each language. This seems to work best in specific domains, such as Bible search software.

Searching multiple languages involves many subissues, some of which can be very specialized. Stemming is a particularly difficult one because different languages use different rules; even determining word boundaries is tricky in some languages, such as Japanese. This is not likely to be a feature that is easy to add to an existing system, especially if it means changing the internal representation of queries to allow for on-the-fly translation.

A major issue for XML documents is the handling of special characters, whether they are marked up using character references, elements, entities, or inserted as Unicode or other special characters. In Quebec, for example, accents are retained in uppercase French words, but in France they are generally dropped. Another issue is how to handle accented characters and ligatures that may occur in foreign phrases quoted in English verse. Accented characters are generally best ignored in searches unless linguistic processing is performed, but this does not mean deleting accented characters from queries! On the other hand, `&eacute;` should certainly not be treated as a word division by the indexing or searching software.

Unicode and wide character support is another important issue, particularly as XML mandates Unicode support.

Multiple Locales

The second multilingual situation occurs when the users speak different languages, making an internationalized interface imperative. Furthermore, translations of summaries or entire documents may be made available. In such an environment, there must be a way to indicate the language of a query, and the list of results should show the language of each document.

Implementation Issues

Before you decide to write your own text retrieval engine, consider both the freely available systems and the commercial packages; pointers to get you started are offered in Chapter 22, "Databases, Repositories, and Utilities," in the section titled *Information Retrieval Databases*.

If you do decide to write your own, consider starting with one of the existing free packages, such as my *lq-text* system, to save work. The following sections describe some possible components you can use to make the issues clearer.

Making an Index

To provide reasonable response time, you'll generally want to build some sort of persistent index that you can read off disk. Chapter 23, "Further Reading" lists references that address different sorts of indexes, so we'll only discuss two main variants here.

Signatures

For each block of input, make a hash of all the words. For example:

```
for each input document d
    hashes[d] <- 0;
    for each word w in d
        hashes[d] |= hash(w);  // i.e. bitwise or
```

To see if a given document contains the word *ankle*, first compute the hash of *ankle*, then see if all of the bits in the word's hash are set in the document's hash:

```
searchfor(word)
    hw <- hash(word);
    for each document d
        if ((hashes[d] & hw) == hw)
            retrieve d
```

This algorithm will retrieve documents that do not contain the query word (*w*, say) sometimes, if it should happen that some other words have set all the same bits as *w* does in the document's hash. You may therefore need to scan the documents later to check for false matches.

Inverted Index

Building an inverted index is described in most books on text retrieval. Here's a simple algorithm:

```
Read the input and split it into words
For each input word w,
    reduce w to its root
    (e.g. turn "feet" to "foot", "running" to "run")
    print
        the word root,
        the document number
        the word number within the document
```

This produces a stream like this:

```
this 1 1
produces 1 2
a 1 3
stream 1 4
```

and so on.

You can then sort that output first by the word, and, then, for lines in which the words are the same, by document number numerically and finally by word number numerically.

Join all of the occurrences of each word together:

```
a 1 3 19 27; 2 205 211 291 . . .
aaron 5 1792 1983
barefoot 1 271962 271978 272011
```

You can see that you could save space by storing the first entry for each file, then the *increment* since the previous value:

```
a 1 3 16 8; 2 205 5 80
aaron 5 1792 191
barefoot 1 271962 16 33
```

In practice, this saves considerably more space than the example might suggest. A file like this will be quite large (perhaps larger than your original data) and it can't easily be updated without rewriting it. The next step is a binary representation.

STAIRS, the first text retrieval system, put the matches for each word in a separate file. To make the resulting mind-bogglingly large directory manageable, it used a separate directory for each two-letter prefix. Under this scheme, the example words would be stored under `a/a`, `aa/aaron`, and `ba/barefoot`, respectively.

Measurements show that each word occurs, on average, approximately 10 times, in most bodies of text. The most popular 10 words generally account for over 25 percent of all the occurrences of all the words. As a result, storing matches in files will generate a lot of small files. A database starts to look inviting, but remember that the average word is only six characters long, including a space and the occasional punctuation mark. If your database uses 4 bytes to store an integer, and you are storing word number, document number, and a word identifier to tie the relation together, you're storing 12 bytes. Add the overhead of the database block structure and b-tree index, and this approach usually ends up using between 3 and 10 times the storage space of the original documents. I've seen one implementation that was noticeably slower than *grep* on fast SCSI disks.

Perhaps after reading the previous chapter, you're contemplating using *ndbm* to store the matches for each word. You could do that with the BSD *db* package, but most others have relatively small limits on what you can store under a single key. The compromise used in *lq-text* is to use *ndbm* to map from a word to a unique number; this number is used as an offset into a file of 32-byte fixed-sized records. A larger file is used to store overflows from the 32-byte records.

A further optimization is to store numbers in binary, using *arithmetic encoding*. For convenience and efficiency, *lq-text* uses an 8-bit encoding, in which the number is encoded in the least significant seven bits of each byte, and the top bit is used to indicate that another byte of value follows. This is shown in Table 13.1.

Table 13.1   Representing Numbers with Arithmetic Encoding

NUMBER	STORAGE
0 – 127	1 byte, value 0– 27
128 – 16383	2 bytes, the first also having the top bit set
16384 – 2097151	3 bytes, the first two also having the top bit set
2097152 – 268435455	4 bytes, the first three with the top bit set
268435456 – 4294967295	5 bytes, the first four having the top bit set

The use of *delta coding* for sequences, in which you store the difference from the previous value, works particularly well in conjunction with variable-byte storage of numbers, because most numbers then end up stored in a single byte. The result is that *lq-text* manages to store the following information for each match in an average of three bytes:

FIELD	DESCRIPTION
FID	File Identifier: a unique number for each document.
Block	Block in File, or Structure Pointer, described in text.
WIB	Word in Block, starting at 0. Refers to natural language words, not machine words.
Flags	Various flags for this word, including PLURAL, POSSESSIVE, NUMBER.
PrevFlags	Flags for the space between this word and the previous, including PUNCTUATION, EXTRA_SPACE, SKIPPED_COMMON.
NextFlags	The *PrevFlags* value for the next word that was seen in the input.
Distance	The distance between this word and the previous, to a maximum of 15.

The matches are stored in sorted order first by FID, then by Block, then by Word in Block. Furthermore, a sequence of matches for the same file is preceded by a count, to avoid repeating the FID. The Flags and Distance are stored together in a single byte; but if that byte has the same value as the byte for the previous match in the sequence, a single bit is set in the Block to indicate that it is not stored.

The input is normally divided into arbitrary blocks; these are 4096 bytes long by default, but for indexing SGML or XML it's logical to use a different Block Number for each piece of text content. You would then need a way to map that Block Number (or Structure Identifier) into an element path, in order to handle XML-sensitive queries.

Another way to handle XML queries is to treat `<Name` and `</Name` as words in the index. For many types of documents, this will work fine; the most likely problem will be performance. A secondary problem is searching attributes; perhaps adding an IN_ATTRIBUTE flag might help, along with using a special syntax for attribute names, such as `<<Name` or `<Element.AttributeName`.

Another practical issue is users who want to find "boy" inside a section title, for example. If you have multiple document types, this may involve searching `H1`, `H2`, and `H3` in one set of documents, `Title directly within Section` in another, and `T` in a third set. Worst, the first set might use a `T` element to mean something entirely different.

One approach to this problem is to provide a "virtual document type," and map the elements in each actual document onto that virtual DTD. Technical solutions to this vary from architectural forms (which require modifying each DTD) to external text files or database entries.

Whether users search a single actual document type, a virtual one, or multiple disparate ones, a user interface giving a picklist of elements with a brief description of each is clearly worthwhile. Most users fall into the category of people whom Alan Cooper calls *perpetual intermediates*, users who never become experts. See Alan Cooper's book, *About Face: The Essentials of User Interface Design* (IDG Books, 1995); Alan Cooper designed Microsoft's Visual Basic, a widely used scripting language.

Phrase-level elements such as emphasis are generally insignificant (`<emph>in</emph>significant`)—they don't cause a word break. The same goes for entities such as `&eacute;`. On the other hand, you may want to search for inline phrase-level elements such as `PlaceName`, `Art-Gallery`, or `Date`.

Presenting the Results

You need to give users enough information to let them decide which documents to view, or whether to try a new query altogether. One way is to provide a document title. More technically savvy researchers or people more familiar with the data may want to see a few words on either side of each match, so that they can see the context in which the words were used.

In either case, the results should be sorted. If there is a single logical order in which people expect to see documents, such as by date for email, you can index the documents in the right order and avoid sorting results when the query is run. Other common sorting orders include statistical ranking, Boolean ranking, and document similarity.

Statistical Ranking

The idea of statistical ranking is that words that occur unexpectedly and frequently in a document are more significant than words that occur at their normal, average frequency. This can also be applied to a document query, so that unusual words in a query are weighted more heavily than common words. A simple summary of an algorithm to do that is as follows:

1. For each document d, count the number of times each query word occurs in d, and divide that by the size of d.

2. Compare that to the frequency of the word in the collection as a whole, divided by the collection size.

3. If the word occurs unusually often in d, rank d nearer the start of the list.

This algorithm does not work well for words that occur much less often than once per document on average, because a single rare word in a query will cause all other words in the query to be (in effect) ignored.

Boolean Ranking

If the user's query is "uncontrolled laughter", a Boolean system might treat the query as, "find all documents containing the word 'uncontrolled' and also containing the word 'laughter.'" Since it's clearly better to find the two words when they are adjacent, as a phrase, let's consider the query "uncontrolled AND laughter."

An effective approach to sorting results is generally to first list all documents containing all of the keywords in the query, then those containing all but one, then all but two, and so on. Even more effective is to first list those documents that contain the phrase ("uncontrolled laughter" in this case), then documents containing both words, then other documents.

Document Similarity

You could take an entire document and use it as a query, rank the results using one of the methods described, and say that the top-ranked document was the most "similar" to the starting document. To do this, you need efficient query processing.

You can apply the same reasoning with a query, and ask users to enter a sample paragraph, perhaps using copy and paste from some other source.

The main problem is that if you use a statistical ranking, your query is a very small document, so all the words in it occur more frequently per kilobyte than the average, and the weighting returns odd results. If you can do a "normal" result, and get the user to select documents he or she wanted but that weren't quite right, you can use the selected documents to home in on the right one. There is a lot of literature describing this type of approach (for example, Salton's SMART system developed by Chris Buckley and others at Cornell University). In practice, most users don't have the patience or interest, and would rather simply repeat their original search with slightly different keywords.

I have experimented with a similarity ranking that uses the sum of rankings for each subphrase in the query. This seems to be good for finding similar passages, but is slow.

Returning Results to a Program

One obvious use for a text retrieval system is to augment another program. You might have a Web page that lets people search a Postgres database, for example, written using PHP. Most queries are best handled with SQL in this case, but queries for natural language phrases could be passed off to an external text retrieval system.

You then have to deal with the question of what exactly to return: an entire document, a list of point locations indicating matches, the smallest containing section element, and so on. The next chapter takes this question a little further, talking about XML-specific query languages.

Summary

In general, a word-level search is likely to be more useful than a character-level one. Text retrieval systems provide a way of searching documents very quickly, turning an $O(n)$ operation into roughly $O(1)$ at the expense of using additional disk storage space. Freely available text retrieval packages are described in Chapter 22, "Databases, Repositories, and Utilities," in Part Five, "Resource Guide." Some of the code techniques described in this chapter are also useful in other applications.

In the next chapter, we'll look at XML query languages in more detail.

## CHAPTER 14

XQL, XLink, XPath, and XPointer Explained

This chapter introduces four important XML-related standards that involve linking and searching of XML documents. XQL and XLink are used to relate one XML document with another, or to point into other documents. XPath and XPointer are ways of referring to specific locations within a single XML document.

NOTE At the time of writing, these standards were not published, except as drafts.

Why So Many Standards?

It may seem odd that there are so many different XML-related ways of pointing at things when the Web makes do with Uniform Resource Locators and Names (URLs and URNs). There are two main reasons for this. First, people are doing things with XML that were not commonly done with HTML; second, the standards are broken out so that XQL, XLink, XSL, and other high-level standards can make use of XPointer and XPath. This is similar to the way in which many other standards documents (including XML 1.0) refer to the URL specification, rather than inventing a new pointer mechanism.

The next section contains a brief summary of the standards, after which the standards are each examined in a little more detail, together with notes about how they might relate to database management systems, or to how you might store links in a database.

NOTE Before reading the more detailed sections, you might want to check out www.w3.org/XML in case the specifications have been published or have changed completely. These standards are too important to omit from this book, but not final enough to use.

There are Perl modules and Java classes to implement most or all of this, and there are at least fragments in C, C++, Python, and other languages, too.

How the Standards Interrelate

XPath is used by both the XML Style Transformation Language (XSLT) and by XPointer; XLink and XQL use XPointer. The value of having multiple standards that share a single way of linking is that people learn it once and implement it once.

XPath Overview

XPath is the XML Path Language for addressing (referring to) parts of an XML document. XPath is used by XPointer and by the XML Style Transformation Language, XSLT. Rather than attempting to cover it in detail here, a few examples will suffice. The standard is quite readable, and is included on this book's companion Web site at www.wiley.com/combooks/quin.

NOTE The XPath standard is published at www.w3.org/TR/xpath. The version referred to here is available at www.w3.org/TR/1999/REC-xpath-19991116 in both HTML and XML.

XPath is a simple expression language. The expressions match part of a document. For example:

```
/screenplay/act[2]/scene[5]
```

matches the fifth scene in the second act of a screenplay. If you wanted to match any actor element, anywhere inside a scene but not in the introduction, you might use:

```
//scene/*/actor
```

There is also a more verbose expression language, with statements like this:

```
self::node()/descendant-or-self::node()/child::para
```

It's a little difficult to justify having used a non-XML syntax for all this, but we're stuck with it now.

XPointer Overview

XPointer is the language used as a fragment identifier for any URI reference that locates a resource of Internet media type `text/xml` or `application/xml`.

NOTE

XPointer is published as a working draft at www.w3.org/TR/xptr; the latest version at the time of writing was available at www.w3.org/TR/1999/WD-xptr-19991206 in both HTML and XML.

Consider the following URL:

```
http://www.holoweb.net/~liam/xmldocs#xpointer(id(simon12))
```

Here, the `#xpointer(id(simon12))` part is a fragment using XPointer.

The actual syntax of the *fragment identifier* (the # and everything following it) is defined by XPath, although XPointer also extends XPath. If multiple `xpointer()` expressions are given, they are evaluated in turn from left to right.

When a Web browser fetches a URL using HTTP, the fragment identifier is not sent to the server. Instead, the browser fetches the entire document and only then processes the fragment identifier. An alternative is to use an HTTP *query*, perhaps to a Perl or Java servlet or to a CGI script:

```
http://www.fictional.eg/documents/britannica.xml?xptr=xpointer(id("Wales
")/descendant::P[1]
```

This usage is not defined by the XPointer Specification, however, and the XML Query Language (shown later) might be more appropriate.

An XPointer fragment can refer to XML ID attributes, as in the example, or to other attributes, element names, or even textual content. Note that without access to a schema or DTD, the browser interpreting the pointer can't tell which attributes are of type ID. Two ways around this are to use the attribute name instead or the HTML compatibility mode. The next example uses an HTML-style XPointer:

```
http://www.holoweb.net/~liam/xmldocs#simon12
```

The next example uses two XPointers, the first of which searches for an attribute of *type* ID, the second of which searches for an attribute of *name* ID. Assume that only one will succeed:

```
http://www.holoweb.net/~liam/
xmldocs#xpointer(id(simon12))xpointer(//*[@id="simon12"])
```

As with XPointer, the latest version of the specification is on the companion Web site, and the current version is at the World Wide Web Consortium's (W3C) site.

XLink Overview

XLink is, as the name suggests, an XML-based way of linking between documents.

NOTE These notes are based on the latest draft of XLink at www.w3.org/TR/2000/WD-xlink-20000221. The latest version can be found at www.w3.org/TR/xlink in both HTML and XML. XLink is not a published standard at the time of this writing.

To date, there is little software available to support XLink directly. Nonetheless, the concepts are important, and XLink is a good way of transporting link information between databases. Once XLink is published as a standard, there will probably be support both in browsers and at the library level. Expect to see support in Perl, Python, Java, C++, and other languages.

XLink uses XML syntax to create structures that can describe both HTML-style unidirectional hyperlinks and much more powerful multiway linking constructs. XLink is activated by a *namespace declaration* like this:

```
<bibliography xmlns:xlink="http://www.w3.org/1999/xlink">
    content that uses links
</bibliography>
```

This example allows the content of the bibliography element to contain XLink hypertext links. You could put the `xmlns:xlink` attribute on the outermost document element if you wanted, to enable XLink in the entire document.

NOTE Like all XML names, the namespace identifier is case-sensitive, and must appear in lowercase, as in the previous example.

Simple HTML-Style Links

XLink defines a *simple link* to be a "two-ended inline link." Here, inline means that the markup for the link is at one end of a link; *two-ended* means that it's a link with two ends, of course. HTML examples include A and IMG. In the case of an IMG element, one end of the link is the document containing the IMG markup, and the other end is the image.

A minimal simple link might look like this:

```
<A xlink:type="simple"
   xlink:href="sock-weaving-patterns.xml"
>Here are my Sock Weaving Patterns!</A>
```

If you are always using a validating XML parser, so that the DTD (or schema) is always read, you could use attribute defaults:

```
<!ELEMENT A
   (#PCDATA)
>
<!ATTLIST A
   xlink:type CDATA "simple"
>
```

The xlink:type attribute can take any of the following six values:

Simple. The markup is a simple link, as in the preceding example.

Extended. The markup is an extended link, as described in the next section.

Locator. A *locator* is part of an extended link.

Arc. An *arc* is the imaginary line connecting two end-points of a link; arcs have a direction.

Resource. A *resource* is something pointed to by a link.

Title. A *title* can be used to describe a link, rather like alt text for an HTML image.

The actual markup used will probably have changed by the time this book is published; the draft used here is on the companion Web site, but see www.w3.org for the latest version.

Extended Links

Extended links are all nonsimple links. In particular, an extended link doesn't need to be in the same document as either end of a link, and is not restricted to having two ends. You can use extended links to make a file that, when parsed, causes links to appear between two entirely different documents.

If software were available to handle extended links, you could use a database to store all of your links, and create an XML file on the fly that used XLink to represent them. Each link would use XPointer to refer to specific points in the target document.

NOTE

If you research XLink in other books, check first to ensure that the material is up to date. A good online tutorial is that of Rusty Harold at http://metalab.unc.edu/xml/ books/bible/updates/16.html.

XQuery Overview

The XML Query Language, XQuery, is a database query language for XML like SQL, but at the time of writing, there isn't even a public draft for it. Members of the working group have made sample implementations, and there is an interesting Java implementation by Howard Katz, (howardk@fatdog.com). The Web site at http://metalab.unc.edu/xql/ has a pointer to a mailing list and mentions more implementations, and the tutorial at http://metalab.unc .edu/xql/xql-tutorial.html is quite helpful.

NOTE

XQuery is also called XQL, although at one time XQuery, XML Query, and XQL were three different proposals.

The XML Query Language is actually very like XPath, already described. The differences, although minor, are intended to make it possible to use XQuery.

The tutorial contains the following example, which shows how multiple conditions can be combined with and to form a more complex query:

```
front/author='Theodore Seuss Geisel'[@gender='male' and
@shoesize='9EEEE']
```

The example might match the following XML fragment:

```
<front>
    <title>....</title>
    <author
        gender="male"
        socks="argyle"
        shoesize="9EEEE"> Theodore Seuss Geisel</author>
    . . .
</front>
```

The current XML Query syntax is not very SQL-like; a more SQL-like approach might be:

```
SELECT front FROM docs
    WHERE front.author LIKE ' Theodore Seuss Geisel'
    AND front.author.attr.gender = 'male'
    AND front.author.attr.shoesize = '9EEEE';
```

Unfortunately, SQL doesn't easily handle the ideas of containment and sequence, and doesn't have the concept of a value being different from an attribute value. Using the same syntax as other XML standards is probably more important than using something similar to, but not the same as, SQL.

If you are considering implementing a query interface to an XML database, you should look at XML Query before inventing your own language.

Related Standards

A number of other XML-based standards have to do with linking; the most useful and widely implemented is the Resource Description Framework (RDF). Several of these standards are listed in this section for reference. (We will return for more detail on RDF in Part Four, "Links and Metadata.")

The Resource Description Framework (RDF)

RDF is important because it is widely used and implemented, and though the specification is difficult to understand, the idea is simple. An RDF document describes relationships between a group of other documents or resources. The description can be hierarchical, and can represent relationships between groups of documents. Some typical relationships are *Author*, *Table of Contents For*, *Entitled*, and *Contains*. But note, RDF is not intended as a way of marking up hypertext links, so it does not compete with XLink. Its original purpose was to describe a Web site in sufficient detail for visualization tools, such as the Cyberbolic Map used by SoftQuad HoTMetaL and the expanding pane on the left side of a Microsoft Internet Explorer screen. It has since been incorporated by Web search engines, by the Red Hat Linux package manager, by Netscape, and in a host of other applications.

HyTime

The International Organization for Standards (ISO) produced HyTime, a standard method of representing links using SGML. The standard is complex, difficult to read, and, as for all ISO standards, you must pay for a paper copy (available from your national standards body, for approximately $200). HyTime has not been widely adopted, but some of the ideas behind it have become influential; it is far more powerful than any of the other approaches mentioned here.

Topic Maps

The ISO Topic Maps standard is an offshoot of the large and complex ISO Hypertext and Time-based multimedia standard, HyTime. Topic maps use a small subset of HyTime links to accomplish much the same thing as RDF. But in practice, topic maps seem unlikely to displace RDF, since they offer little extra functionality and are not an open standard. As an ISO standard, you must purchase the Topic Map specification from your local standards body.

Links and Databases

This section discusses ways to use XML links and databases together.

Automatic Linking

Suppose you've just been given an encyclopedia to convert to XML and publish on the Web. You could convert each article to XML using a combination of Omnimark and Perl, but the result would be fairly boring. You want to insert links, so that whenever an article title is mentioned, it becomes a link to that article, but there are 96,000 articles, so you don't want to edit the articles by hand.

One solution is to build a database of all the article titles, then, for each article, scan for each article title in turn and mark it up as a link wherever it occurs. There are two problems with this approach. First, it's slow; second, and more important, most of the links will be wrong! An encyclopedia entry for "Green" doesn't mean every occurrence of "Green" should be a link.

For a transcription of the eighteenth-century dictionary of thieving slang, used for earlier examples in the book, I experimented, using an in-memory hash table. For an Internet Relay Chat (IRC) glossary, which gets updated on the fly, I used a text retrieval package. For an encyclopedia, a database of article titles might be converted to an *ndbm* database for the purpose of linking, with text retrieval used for adding links. The following two sections consider both of these approaches.

Dealing with Incorrect Links

For the purposes of this discussion, we will leave the problem of incorrect links unsolved, but the following offer some possible approaches to consider:

- Mark articles as not suitable as targets for inserted links.
- Check that the articles have some keywords in common, and flag those that don't for human review.
- Check category names and mark links between categories as requiring intervention.

In both the dictionary of thieving slang and the IRC glossary, the wrong links did not pose a problem, because the material was designed to be browsed randomly, and a few random links add to the fun.

AutoLinker in Memory

The Perl script here reads the file dict.xml, generates an HTML page for each dictionary entry, and adds links to the HTML wherever it can. A sample entry from the dictionary is shown in Figure 14.1. The HTML for this entry is shown in Figure 14.2, as rendered by Netscape's browser.

The following is most of the Perl that accomplishes this. The full code can also be found at www.holoweb.net/~liam/dict/, if you're interested. There is enough here for you to reuse in your own projects, with a few tedious details removed to save space:

```perl
#! /usr/local/bin/perl -w
use strict;

sub main
{
    # convert dict.sgml into HTML files.
    #
    # there are several steps:
    #
    # (1) read dict.sgml and build in-memory index and entries hashes
    #       (this currently does not use XML::Parser but should)
```

```
<entry><title>BACON</title>
<p>the Prize, or whatever kind
which Robbers make in their Enterprizes.
<eg>He has saved his Bacon</eg>; i.e. He
has himself escaped with the Prize,
whence it is commonly used for any
narrow Escape.
<eg>The Cove has a bien
squawl to maund Bacon</eg>; i.e. he has a
good Voice to beg Bacon; used to jeer
a bad Voice, or an indifferent Singer.
<eg>The Bacon Sweard rakes in his Throttle</eg>;
<i>i.e.</i> the Sweard of the Bacon sticks in
his Throat; used to a person who has
Hoarseness, or one, who at their Merry-Meetings, excuses himself from
Singing, on pretence of a Cold.</p></entry>
```

Figure 14.1 BACON, in a 1736 dictionary.

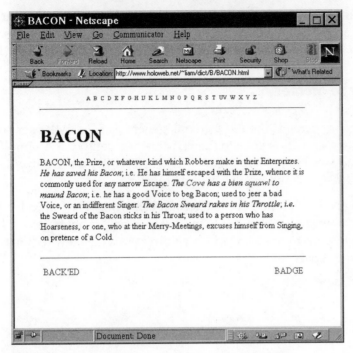

Figure 14.2 The dictionary entry converted to HTML.

```
    #
    process_dict_file();

    # (2) create a directory structure,
    #     with html in subdirectories A B C... H, IJ, K.. T, UV, W,...Z
    #
    create_directory_structure();

    # now write the indexpages for categories
    write_category_pages();

    # (3) process the entries to insert links between pages
    # (4) write out the HTML (these two steps are combined,
    # because they are done on an entry-by-entry basis)
    write_html_with_links();

    # (5) write out the index pages in each subdirectory
    #
    write_index_pages();

    # (6) write out the top-level page, index.html
    #
    write_index_html();
}
```

The subroutine `main( )` is called from the very end of the script, after all of the initialization is done.

The next section of code handles reading the dictionary. The `letters` array stores the letters of the alphabet, because the dictionary uses the eighteenth-century collating sequence in which I and J sort together, as do U and V:

```perl
my @letters = (
    "A", "B", "C", "D", "E", "F", "G", "H", "IJ", "K", "L", "M",
    "N", "O", "P", "Q", "R", "S", "T", "UV", "W", "X", "Y", "Z"
);

my %entries = ();
my %InCategory = ();

sub process_dict_file()
{
    my $thisLetter = "-";
    while (<>) {
        # remove comments
        s/<!--.*?-->//g;

        if (!/<entry/i) {
            # capture the title(s) for the entry
            if (/<letter[^<>]*>\s*<title>([^<>]+)<\/title>/) {
                $thisLetter = $1;
                $thisLetter =~ s/[^A-Z]//g;
                next;
            }

            if (/./) {
                if (/<\/letter>\s*$/) {
                    next;
                }
            }
            next;
        }

        # build the entry up into a string:
        s/^.*(<entry)/$1/;
        my $entry = $_;
        while ($entry !~ /<\/entry/i) {
            chomp($entry);
            $entry .= ' ';
            my $rest = <>;
            if (!defined($rest)) {
                die "end of file inside entry";
            }
            $entry .= $rest;
        }
        chomp($entry);
```

```
        $entry =~ s@(</entry>).*$@$1@i;
        saveEntry($entry, $thisLetter);
    }
}
```

A couple of utilities for file handling: **create_directory_structure**

```
sub create_directory_structure()
{
    foreach (@letters) {
        mkdir("$_", 0755) || die " can't create directory $_: $!";
    }
}

my %Seen = ();
my %SortKey = ();
my %Letter = ();

sub mkFileNameFromTitle
{
    # this is a fairly common thing to do: given the content of
    # an XML element, make a unique filename.

    my ($title, $sortas) = @_;
    my $file = $title;

    # trim leading/trailing spaces:
    $file =~ s@^\s+@@;
    $file =~ s@\s+$@@;

    # remove italic prefix or suffix:
    $file =~ s@^<i>.*?</i>\s*([^<>].*)$@$1@;
    $file =~ s@^(.*?)<i>.*?</i>\s*$$@$1@;

    # strip tags:
    $file =~ s@<[^<>]*>@-@g;

    # turn unacceptable characters to minus signs:
    $file =~ s@[^a-zA-Z0-9.]@-@g;

    # remove trailing, leading and multiple minus signs:
    $file =~ s@--+@-@g;
    $file =~ s@^-+@@;
    $file =~ s@-$@@;

    # remove leading to, a or the
    $file =~ s@^(a|the|to|an)-@@i;

    # ensure that the filename is unique
    my $n = 0;
    my $name = $file;
    while (exists($Seen{$name})) {
```

```perl
        $n++;
        $name = $file . "-${n}";
    }

    # remember the name so we don't recreate it:
    $Seen{$name} = $title;

    if (!defined($sortas)) {
        $sortas = $name;
    }
    $sortas =~ tr/UuIi/VvJj/;
    $SortKey{$name} = $sortas;
    return $name;
}


sub saveEntry($$)
{
    my ($entry, $thisLetter) = @_;

    # my $useBrace = ($entry =~ /title brace=\"right\"/);

    my @targets = ($entry =~ /<target[^<>]*>(.*?)<\/target>/g);
    my @titles;
    while ($entry =~ /<title([^<>]*)>(.*?)<\/title>/g) {
        my ($atts,$text) = ($1, $2);
        # an ignored entry isn't a target for links:
        if ($atts !~ /link=\"ignore\"/) {
            push @targets, $text;
        }
        push @titles, $text;
    }

    if ($#titles < 0) {
        die "missing title in $entry";
    }

    # expand XML entities (&amp; etc.) in the titles:
    @titles = map { handleEntities($_) }  @titles;

    my $sortas = undef;
    if ($entry =~ /^<entry[^<>]* sortas="([^<>"]+)"/) {
        $sortas = $1;
    }

    if ($entry =~ m@^\s*(?:as[,;:\s]*)?<eg>(.*?)</eg>@) {
        push @targets, $1;
    }

    my $filename = mkFileNameFromTitle($titles[0], $sortas);

    my $text = $entry;
```

```
$text =~ s@^.*?<p>(.*)</entry>@$1@;
$text =~ s@^\s*@@;
$text = handleEntities($text);

# save the body, the titles and the filename
my %h = (
        'body' => "$text",
       'titles' => [ @titles ],
      'targets' => [ @targets ],
     'filename' => $filename
);

foreach (@targets) {
    addPattern($_, $filename);
}

push @{$entries{$thisLetter}}, \%h;
}
```

XML text content can (and often does) include entity references like &amp, so we have to handle it. It's convenient to handle other inline elements here, too, although it might be better to use XSL to do that, or to have a hash table to map start/end elements into HTML.

```
sub handleEntities($)
{
    my ($text) = @_;

    # entities and non-html elements mapped to html:
    $text =~ s@\&stress;@\'@g;
    $text =~ s@\&hy;@\xad@g;
    $text =~ s@\&c;@<i>\&amp;c.</i>@g;

    $text =~ s@<eg>@<i class="eg">@g;
    $text =~ s@</eg>@</i>@g;
    $text =~ s@<meaning>@<i class="meaning">@g;
    $text =~ s@</meaning>@</i>@g;

    return $text;
}
```

Writing out the HTML with the embedded links is the most interesting part. This algorithm turns each entry's title into a Perl substitute statement that, when executed, replaces the title with a link to the file containing the corresponding definition. We then run each of the substitutions in turn over every defintion.

For performance, we compile the regular expression that will be used to match titles in entry bodies only once; getReadyForPatterns() in the following example does that:

```perl
sub write_html_with_links()
{
    my $letter;

    getReadyForPatterns();

    foreach $letter (@letters) {
        my $i;
        my @entryList = @{$entries{$letter}};
        for ($i = 0; $i <= $#entryList; $i++) {
            writeOneFile($letter, $entryList[$i]);
            $prev = $h;
        }
    }
}


my $putLinksInto;

sub writeOneFile($$$$)
{
    my ($letter, $this, $prev, $next) = @_;

    open(OUT, "> $$this{filename}") ||
        die "can't create $$this{filename}: $!";

    $this->{body} = &$putLinksInto($this, $$this{filename});
    mkheader(\*OUT, $$this{titles}[0]);

    definitionBody(\*OUT, $this);

    print OUT "</body></html>\n";

    close(OUT) || die "can't close $$this{filename}: $!";
}
```

In this excerpt, most of the work of creating HTML folders for each definition, with index.html files pointing to all the words, is not shown, but it's in the working code if you want it. Note that mkheader() creates the start of an HTML document:

```perl
sub mkheader($$)
{
    my ($file, $title) = @_;

    print $file <<EOF;
<html><head><title>${title}</title></head><body
    bgcolor="#EEDDAA"
    text="#330000"
    link="#009900"
    vlink="#CC9999"
    alink="#FF6666"
```

```
><blockquote>
EOF
}


sub definitionBody($$)
{
    my ($file, $h) = @_;

    my $body = $h->{body};
    my $title = $h->{titles}[0];
    my $titlesep = ', '; # comes after the title, before body
    my $insideTitle = $title;
    if ($#{$h->{titles}} > 0) {
        $insideTitle = join ', ', @{$h->{titles}};
        $titlesep = '; ';
    }
    print $file "<h1>$title</h1>\n";
    print $file "<p>
        <span class=\"headword\">${insideTitle}</span>";
    print $file "${titlesep}$body</p>\n";
}


sub mkIndex($$)
{
    # not shown, makes index.html
}


my %phrases;

sub addPattern($$)
{
    my ($pattern, $file) = @_;
    $pattern = lc $pattern;
    $pattern =~ s/-/[^a-z]/;
    $pattern =~ s@</?i>@@g;
    $pattern =~ s/'s/(['e]?#)?/g; # turn 's into optional, use # for s
    $pattern =~ s/'d/(['e]?d)?/g; # turn 's into optional
    $pattern =~ s/s\b/s?/i;       # allow missing trailing S
    # now turn # back into an s:
    $pattern =~ tr/#/s/;

    # some definitions use "to run", "a sword",
    # but those prefixes (to and a)
    # would not appear in an actual sentence.
    if ($pattern =~ /^(?:to|a|an|the)\s+[a-z]/) {
        $pattern =~ s/^(?:to|a|an|the)\s+//;
    }

    # finally, munge whitespace into a pattern to recognize whitespace:
    $pattern =~ s/\s+/\\s+/g;
```

```
        if (defined($phrases{$pattern})) {
            print STDERR "duplicate: $pattern: $phrases{$pattern}, $file\n";
            return;
        }

        $phrases{$pattern} = $file;
}


# fixLinks:
# the problem:
# dimber-damber turned into:
# <a href="../D/<a href="../D/DIMBER.html"
# >DIMBER</a>-<a href="../D/DAMBER.html">Damber</a>.html">
# <a href="../D/DIMBER.html"
# >Dimber</a>-<a class="x" href="../D/DAMBER.html">Damber</a></a>
#
# i.e. the links nested...
# the solution:
# <a class="x" href="../D/DIMBER-Damber.html">Dimber-Damber</a>
#

sub fixLinks($)
{
    my $text = shift;

    # first, remove markup from href attributes:
    while ($text =~ /href="[^"<]*<a/) {
        $text =~ s{
            <a([^<>]*)href="([^<"]*)<a[^>]*>(.*?)</a>
        }{<a${1} href="$2$3}xg;
    }

    # now, nested anchors
    while ($text =~ m@<a[^<>]*>([^<]|(<[^a/]))*<a@) {
        $text =~ s@(<a[^<>]+>)([^<>]*)<a[^<>]*>(.*?)</a>@$1$2$3@g;
    }

    return $text;
}


sub getReadyForPatterns()
{
    # build up a perl subroutine called putLinksInto, in a text
    # variable, then eval that variable to define the subroutine.
    # The effect is as if xthe subroutine was in the source, with
    # all 1500 titles, e.g.s#bacon#<a href="bacon.html">bacon</a>g#
    # This means the expressions only get compiled once, for a huge
    # performance increase.

    my @patterns = sort {
```

```
        # put longer patterns first
        length($b) <=> length($a) ||
        $a cmp $b
} keys(%phrases);

my $sub = "\$putLinksInto = sub {\n";
$sub .= 'my ($entry, $file) = @_;' . "\n";
$sub .= 'my $text = $entry->{body}; ' . "\n";
$sub .= 'study $text;' . "\n";

foreach (@patterns) {
    print STDERR ".";
    $sub .= "if (\"$phrases{$_}\" ne \$file) {" . "\n";
        $sub .= '$text =~ s@\b' . ${_} .
            '\b(?!###)@<a class="x" href="../' .
            $phrases{$_} .
            '">$&</a>###@gsmi;' . "\n";
    $sub .= '}' . "\n";
}

$sub .= '$text =~ s/###//g;' . "\n";

# sometimes we substitute inside a link by mistake:
$sub .= 'return fixLinks($text);' . "\n";
$sub .= '}' . "\n";

# now evaluate the string to define &putLinksInto():
eval($sub);
}

# at the end of all definitions, call main():
main();
```

AutoLinker with Text Retrieval

This uses two kinds of databases, and is therefore a *hybrid* solution. The idea is to use text retrieval to find all the article titles in a given article, then turn the result into XLink or HTML link markup. It's harder to set up, but more powerful. I describe this in more detail in the next chapter.

Visualizing Relationships

If you have all of your links (or RDF relationships) stored in a database, it's not too difficult to start drawing graphical representations of them. You could use the Perl GD module to generate data for a Java applet, perhaps.

Figure 14.3 shows the links in a glossary of terms used in Internet Relay Chat conversations. The glossary is at www.valinor.sorcery.net/glossary/, with links inserted automatically using my text retrieval package, *lq-text*. In this case, the Java `GraphLayout` demo was used (`GraphLayout` is part of the Java software development kit), and the links were generated by a Perl CGI script that looked at the HTML, rather than a database.

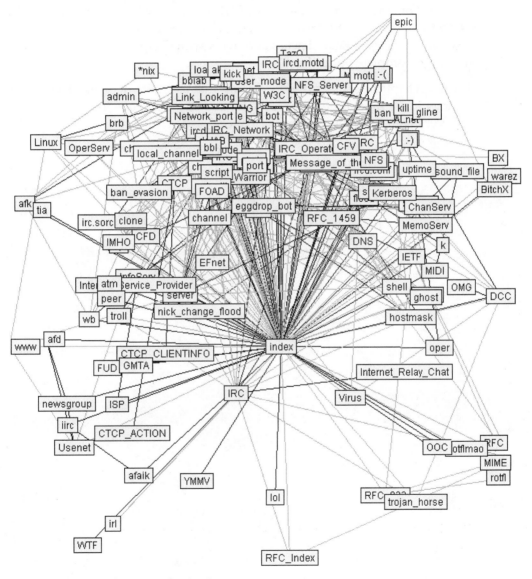

Figure 14.3   Links between glossary items.

Summary

Links in XML can involve more than one arc and more than two ends; and they can be more powerful than HTML links with only slightly more complex markup. The standards that state how the links work were still evolving at the time of this writing, but may be final by the time you read this book, so it's worth checking. Since XML links can be external to the documents involved, you can store them in a database. The Perl code showed one way to add links to documents on the fly, using a database (an in-memory hash table in this case) of link targets. We'll discuss another way in Chapter 18, "Sketches from the Forge: Sample Applications."

The next chapter discusses hybrid systems that use more than one database or strategy at the same time. These systems can be a challenge to create, but can give very high flexibility and performance.

## CHAPTER 15

Hybrid Approaches

In previous chapters, I explained ways of using XML together with a single type of database. In this chapter, I describe how to combine multiple techniques. There are those who want to see everything as an XML document, and others who prefer to view the world as composed of relational tables or of objects. The real world is not an elegant, abstract concept, so it is no surprise that no one of these models solves all needs.

A *hybrid* approach is one that incorporates more than one technology. You might, for example, combine *dbm* and a relational database or an object-oriented database and a text retrieval package. Hybrid systems are sometimes more difficult to maintain, and may require more expertise to create, but as this chapter will demonstrate, they offer many advantages.

Files and Databases

The fastest commercial SGML repositories have been around much longer than XML itself. Of these, the fastest store data in *flat files*. That doesn't make much of a repository, though, so other software is added. One interesting approach is to use a relational database to store *metadata* such as filename, permissions, author, and title, but to keep the actual documents in external files. The external files can be accessed with the Network File System (NFS), through a Web server, or with another (generally proprietary) mechanism. There are a number of difficulties with this approach, but fortunately, they can all be surmounted.

The primary difficulty is a *referential integrity* problem, as database people call it. In this situation, you have two sets of information that are interrelated, but that can be updated independently. Consider, then, what if you delete a file that's still listed in the database? What if you change the title in the database but don't edit the document? What if you rename a file? What if a file changes while you're backing up the database, or the database changes while you're backing up files?

The obvious way to surmount this is to deny users all access to the files except through your software, and write a server that controls all aspects of file management. And where there is derived information stored in the database, you make sure that it is updated only by actually reading and parsing a document file.

A second potential problem is that a file system may be less robust than a database. Since databases are stored on the same disks used for file systems, this is generally a nonissue. All you have to do is back up all of your data daily and weekly, and use high-quality external hardware RAID storage if the data is important.

A known problem is that if you need to do a lot of structure-based searches on your XML data, you'll end up representing the XML structure in the database and lose the biggest advantage of this strategy: speed. If, say, you are planning to ask for a listing of all retail stores in a certain geographical region that sell magazines that in turn contain articles describing socks manufactured in your Aberdeen factory, this isn't the way to go. If you need XML-sensitive searching at all, refer to the upcoming section, *Databases and Text Retrieval*, for a solution.

All this is further complicated by the variation in support for external files in different databases. Some databases (including Oracle 8i) have support for backing up a database and external files together so that no data is lost, but this level of support is the exception rather than the rule.

Another possibility is to use a text management system such as Revision Control System (RCS) or Concurrent Versions System (CVS) to store the documents, and keep metadata (see Part Four, "Links and Metadata") in the relational database. If you are not familiar with RCS and CVS, check them out—they are pretty useful. I keep all of my text and configuration files in RCS. The next section explores this in more detail.

Using RCS and a Relational Database

RCS stores text files. Each time you change the file, you "check it in" to RCS. RCS then stores the changes. As a result, the size of an RCS log file grows slowly, yet RCS can quickly show you the differences between any two versions. The following log shows checking a file out, making changes, and then asking RCS what the changes were:

```
@
bash-2.03$ mkdir RCS
bash-2.03$ ci -u Morality.html
RCS/Morality.html,v  <--  Morality.html
enter description, terminated with single '.' or end of file:
NOTE: This is NOT the log message!
>> a poem by Matthew Arnold
>> .
initial revision: 1.1
done
bash-2.03$ co -l Morality.html
RCS/Morality.html,v  -->  Morality.html
revision 1.1 (locked)
done
bash-2.03$ (edit the file Morality.html here)
bash-2.03$ rcsdiff -c Morality.html
===================================================================
RCS file: RCS/Morality.html,v
retrieving revision 1.1
diff -c -r1.1 Morality.html
*** Morality.html      2000/03/02 21:36:02      1.1
--- Morality.html      2000/03/02 21:45:57
***************
*** 10,15 ****
--- 10,18 ----
  <p>
  We cannot kindle when we will<br>
  The fire that in the heart resides,<br>
+ <!--* http://www.library.utoronto.ca/utel/rp/poems/arnold2b.html
+     * has which instead of that
+     *-->
  The spirit bloweth and is still,<br>
  In mystery our soul abides:<br>
    But tasks in hours of insight will'd<br>
***************
*** 21,28 ****
  We dig and heap, lay stone on stone;<br>
  We bear the burden and the heat<br>
  Of the long day, and wish 'twere done.<br>
!   Not till the hours of light return<br>
  All we have built do we discern.<br>
  </p>
```

```
--- 24,66 ----
  We dig and heap, lay stone on stone;<br>
  We bear the burden and the heat<br>
  Of the long day, and wish 'twere done.<br>
!   Not till the hours of light return,<br>
  All we have built do we discern.<br>
  </p>

bash-2.03$ ci -u Morality.html
RCS/Morality.html,v  <--  Morality.html
new revision: 1.2; previous revision: 1.1
enter log message, terminated with single '.' or end of file:
>> added the rest of the verses, fixed a typo,
>> and commented a difference.
>> .
done
```

The lines after prompts set in boldface indicate what I typed; I've also shown the changed lines in the *diff* output in bold. A plus sign at the start of a line marks an added line, and an exclamation point (!) indicates a changed line. Had there been any deleted lines, they would have been marked with a hyphen.

The *rcsdiff* command can compare any two versions of the file, with the -r option:

```
rcsdiff -r1.2 -r1.9 Morality.html
```

It would be fairly easy to write a CGI script, perhaps using PHP, which checked a file into RCS and updated the database. You might keep a simple table like this:

```
+-----+-----+----+-----------+---------+--------------------------+
|DocID|Owner|Rev |ModDate    |File     |Title                     |
+-----+-----+----+-----------+---------+--------------------------+
|104  |james|1.14|2000-03-14 |r419.xml +Book Review: MySQL & mSQL |
+-----+-----+----+-----------+---------+--------------------------+
```

Your script could extract title and other information from the file each time it's changed, and update the database. You would be able to do title, owner, and date searches quickly, and retrieve any version of any document.

The main reason to put files into the database is to be able to back up your data safely. If the data is external, you may need to shut down the database in order to ensure that no files change during the operation.

The main advantages to having the files external are:

Database size. Most databases have a larger storage overhead than the file system.

Performance. The database may go slowly when there's a lot of stored data.

External access. You could make a text retrieval index of the files, for example, or do a read-only CVS fetch of a project without having to use the database.

The ability to find documents based on words or phrases found within them is very useful. A hybrid system that stores files externally and indexes them with a text retrieval package is described in the next section, but even the ability to use the Unix *grep* command should not be undervalued.

Databases and Text Retrieval

Most text retrieval systems work with files, not database fields. If you want to provide the most powerful searching possible, you may end up with one of two hybrid solutions: relational databases and text retrieval, or object-oriented database and text retrieval.

Whichever sort of database you are using, the simplest technique is to generate an external file that corresponds to each document, and hand the files to the text retrieval package to index. Give the files significant names, perhaps composed of a document number and a revision number. When you use the text retrieval package to search, it will give you a list of filenames that match your query. You can then map these filenames back to internal objects or database rows, carefully checking document access permissions before returning the number of matches and document list to the user.

My *lq-text* package has been used in this way, as have many commercial packages. At the time of this writing, there are no open source text retrieval packages that handle XML. Commercial vendors such as Open Text and Verity have support for SGML and/or XML searching.

The following is an example of a query result using *lq-text*. The format is entirely configurable, and is shown here in a SQL-like format:

```
+---+----------------------+-------------+----------------------------+
|Doc|Prefix                |Match        |Postfix                     |
+---+----------------------+-------------+----------------------------+
|12 |nal) the "XForms" X11 |user interface|toolkit. You need to have a |
|12 |on a freely distributed|user interface|toolkit called the XForms L|
|13 |w programming language.|User interface|design. MPI was designed af|
|96 |r PostgreSQL (Graphical|User Interface|) 9. Integrated Development|
|96 |r PostgreSQL (Graphical|User Interface|) PostgreSQL has Tcl/Tk int|
+---+----------------------+-------------+----------------------------+
```

```
+---+----------------------------+--------------+
|Doc|Filename                    |Location      |
+---+----------------------------+--------------+
|12 |PCMCIA-HOWTO                |/usr/doc/HOWTO |
|13 |Parallel-Processing-HOWTO   |/usr/doc/HOWTO |
|96 |PostgreSQL-HOWTO            |/usr/doc/HOWTO |
+---+----------------------------+--------------+
```

The results are returned as lines of text using the command-line API; alternatives include using the C API to extract individual fields or using a unique separator string between the fields and then extracting them from text. One way to do this would be to generate XML; *lq-text* can already escape tags in several ways. The following example shows a possible XML rendition of the same matches:

```
<Results>
  <File Name="/usr/doc/HOWTO/PCMCIA-HOWTO">
    <Match>
      <Before>tem before you begin: · A 2.0.*, 2.1.*, or 2.2.* series
kernel source tree. · An appropriate set of module utilities.
(Optional) the ''XForms'' X11 </Before>
      <Text>user interface</Text>
      <After> toolkit. You need to have a complete linux source tree for
your kernel, not just an up-to-date kernel image. The driver
modules</After>
    </Match>
    <Match>
      <Before>module "misc/serial", "serial_cs" This package includes an
X-based card status utility called cardinfo. This utility is based on a
freely distributed</Before>
      <Text>user interface</Text>
      <After> toolkit called the XForms Library. This library is
available as a separate package with most Linux distributions. If you
would li</After>
    </Match>
  </File>
  <File Name="/usr/doc/HOWTO/Parallel-Processing-HOWTO">
    <Match>
      <Before>nd parallel file I/O. Are these things useful? Of course
they are... but learning MPI 2.0 is a lot like learning a complete new
programming language. </Before>
      <match>User interface</match>
      <After> design. MPI was designed after PVM, and clearly learned
from it. MPI offers simpler, more efficient, buffer handling a</After>
    </Match>
  </File>
  <File Name="/usr/doc/HOWTO/PostgreSQL-HOWTO">
    <Match>
      <Before>reater than 200 Gig 7. How can I trust PostgreSQL ?
Regression Test Package builds customer confidence 8. GUI FrontEnd Tool
for PostgreSQL (Graphical </Before>
      <Text>User Interface</Text>
      <After>) 9. Integrated Development Environment Tools for
PostgreSQL (GUI IDE) 10. Interface Drivers for PostgreSQL 10.1 ODBC
Driver</After>
    </Match>
    <Match>
      <Before>ge MAY not be supported by PostgreSQL!! You may need to
```

```
verify those and add it to regression package. 8. GUI FrontEnd Tool for
PostgreSQL (Graphical </Before>
      <Text>User Interface</Text>
      <After>) PostgreSQL has Tcl/Tk interface library in the
distribution called 'pgTcl'. Tcl/Tk is a Rapid Application Development
tool and is</After>
    </Match>
  </File>
</Results>
```

To give an idea of how a text retrieval package might be coerced into cooperating in that way, the command used to generate the previous list is shown here:

```
#! /bin/sh

echo "<Results>"

lqphrase "$@"
lqkwic \
    -S '<File Name="${FileName}">\n' \
    -A '</File>\n' \
    -s '<Match>
            <Before>${TextBefore}</Before>
            <Text>${MatchedText}</Text>
            <After>${TextAfter}</After>
        </Match>\n'\
    -f -

echo "</Results>"
```

The *lqkwic* program substitutes the ${TextBefore} and other variables given in the -s option for each match, and uses the -S and -A values before and after each group of matches for a given file. Other options (not shown here) support the replacement of XML entities and encoding of < and & in the output. This is a pretty complex example, and the purpose isn't to teach *lq-text* commands, but to give an idea of how it can be fairly easy to integrate a text retrieval package into other software at the Unix (or NT) shell level.

Issues to Consider

Not all text retrieval packages can cope with documents that change, unless you build a new index of all document, often a very lengthy process. If this is an issue for you, check first. The *lq-text* package can "unindex" a file, if you still have the original. Space in the index is made available for reuse, but the index never actually shrinks, so it's a good idea to rebuild it completely once a month or so.

Most text retrieval databases are unavailable, or give incomplete answers, while the index is being rebuilt. If it takes several hours to rebuild the index, that would make your service unavailable for a long time. The simplest way to avoid the downtime is to build a new index alongside the current one; you keep using the current index until the new one is ready, then switch.

Some packages can handle compressed or gzip'ed files, and some can't. Some can handle them at retrieval time but not at indexing time, oddly.

Most text retrieval packages can write a database to a networked drive, but do so very slowly. A factor of 10 or more performance loss is not at all unheard of. It's therefore common to run indexing software on the server even if the retrieval is done on a client.

You should always consider a text retrieval package to be a sort of cache—it is not the primary repository for your data, and often doesn't store the data itself at all. As with all caches, there are consistency problems. One is that the text retrieval package may grant access to information about documents even if the user doing the query should not be able to see the data. This is how the Dead Sea Scrolls were leaked: Someone had access to a text retrieval index and was able to piece the documents together word by word! Another issue is that the text retrieval system might not notice that a document has been changed, and give incorrect results.

When you are choosing (or implementing) a text retrieval system, note that the more documents you have, the more you will value precise and correct answers. Higher precision usually means storing more information; consequently, more accurate retrieval packages tend to have larger indexes—often larger than the actual data. If you also need temporary storage to build the index, and enough room for a spare copy of the index while it's being rebuilt, remember to budget for the extra disk space. Usually, the more memory you have, the faster indexing goes, so having extra memory on the server may be useful.

Using *ndbm* as a Cache Manager

Relational databases are very slow compared to most other storage technologies. Few databases can handle a paltry 100,000 transactions per second even on a Pentium or SPARC system. If you are serving up data from a database onto the Web, you may find things are too slow, taking several seconds to send a complete Web page. Users will generally wait three seconds or so for a response, but not 10 or 20 unless they really need the information.

One way to speed performance is to design your database so that as few SQL JOIN statements are needed as possible. Sometimes, performance constraints mean you end up abandoning the third normal form that we mentioned in Chapter 3, "Just Enough SQL."

If the database isn't your own, or if you decide that you need to keep the current schema, you could speed things up by keeping a copy of recently accessed documents. This copy is called a *cache*, which is very difficult to implement, for these reasons:

- If the database changes, documents in the cache become incorrect.

- If multiple processes write to the cache at the same time, it may be come corrupt.

- Different users might get different views of the database; the cache must take this into account.

- In a multiuser server environment, the documents in the cache itself must be protected so people can't look at what other users are reading.

- Problems in the database code become hard to debug, because you have to work out whether the document you see was from the cache or was freshly generated. A separate interface that bypasses the cache can help, as can a program to give a detailed table of contents of the cache itself.

The easiest way to implement a cache in the HTTP environment is to cache the generated HTML pages, making sure that the URL of a page is sufficient to generate the page. Some sites use cookies or the HTTP Realm-based "401 Authentication" described briefly in Chapter 2, "Client/Server Architecture," and generate user-specific pages for a given URL based on the realm or cookie. Don't do this. Put a session identifier into the URL if you have to, otherwise the browser's own cache will make debugging early impossible.

Once you've made your URLs unique, you can use Apache's cache (www .apache.org); or investigate Squid (www.squid-cache.org). Figure 15.1 shows this architecture.

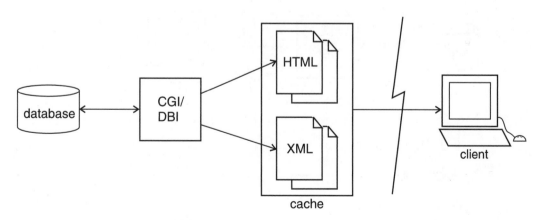

Figure 15.1   An external HTTP-based cache.

If the URL is not sufficient to produce the correct page, you will have to use a different technique. You may want to do this anyway if you build up pages by assembling fragments, because caching the fragments may be more efficient or easier to implement. For example, if a fragment changes, you will know which parts of the cache to delete. Figure 15.2 shows where this cache goes in the architecture.

If you have a lot of very small files, you'll end up with a lot of wasted disk space, because each file has to be stored in an integral number of blocks on disk. The size of a disk block varies depending on the type of disk and the operating system. Most Unix systems can use disk blocks as small as 512 bytes even on a large disk, whereas Microsoft Windows systems tend to use 16 Kbyte or larger blocks. For a million files of 500 bytes each, you would lose 15 gigabytes of space.

In a Client/Server environment, a server can keep track of the latest version of an object, and can often avoid going to the database at all if it's asked for the same object twice. You have to remember to check permissions, of course; even if it's the same user, the database permission table might have been updated.

One way to implement a cache is to use the Berkeley *db* package (see Chapter 12, "Dynamic Hashing: *ndbm*," for more on *ndbm* and related packages), which is what some versions of Netscape use. You use the URL or document path as a key. The corresponding value might be the data itself or it might be a structure that describes the data. If you store the data in the *db* file, the benefits are

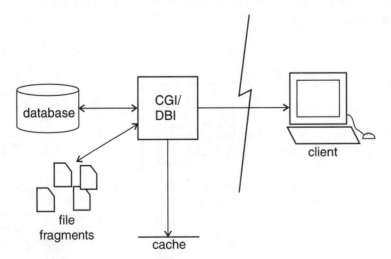

Figure 15.2 An internal cache.

that you lose less file system space and gain faster access; the disadvantage is that it's more difficult to control the size of the cache.

Other Hybrid Applications with *db*

Earlier in the chapter, we discussed the AutoLinker example, which adds hypertext links and annotations to documents on the fly. The example used an in-memory database built by reading an XML file. An alternative is to split the process into two parts. The first part reads the XML file or uses DBI to perform a database query, and saves the results in an *ndbm* (or *db*) database. The second part can then be run at any time on any document, without the overhead of having to scan for possible targets. A variation of the AutoLinker, described in Chapter 18, uses a text retrieval database to add links to documents in a similar two-stage strategy.

Documents as Objects

A number of XML-based systems use an object-oriented database to store XML, usually representing each element as an individual object. An alternative is to consider an entire document to be an object. The object could be stored externally, on the file system or in a different database, with the object-oriented database holding a "surrogate object" that represents the actual document. This is similar to the approaches already described with relational databases.

Document Management and Workflow

If you have a team of people working on the same document, it might *sound* useful to allow anyone to edit any element. In practice, however, people usually want to edit a chapter or a section, not just a single emphasis element. This lets you make an optimization and store the "editable objects" as single objects, either internal to the database or externally.

Once someone has edited an object, he or she may need to get approval from management before the object can be published. Clearly this can be automated, perhaps by sending email to the manager, as well as storing a "needs approval" state for the object.

Document management and workflow are two large, related subject areas on which entire books have been written. What's important to point out here is that currently there are few open source content management systems; but that is changing. Chapter 22, "Databases, Repositories, and Utilities," in Part Five, "Resource Guide," has pointers to more, and the companion Web site for this book may list more when they appear.

Error Handling

Error handling is one of the most difficult tasks to do well when creating a hybrid system. Each component will probably report errors in its own way, and you will need to trap the failures and report the detailed system-level information, but in a way that helps the user to diagnose the problem.

One system I've used issues the error "You may have too many process running," whenever one of the components dumps core or crashes. A better message might be "The program start-revision crashed; it was called from internal task: Copy configuration to make new revision, as part of revising document DZ40196 from revision 4 to revision 5." Then the users and staff would have a clue about where to start debugging.

It is worth spending a *lot* of time on a user interface, because that's *all* the user sees. The user rarely looks at the code itself. Error handling is an important part of that interface, and a difficult one.

Summary

Though short, this chapter addressed some of the most important ideas in the book. Combining the strengths of two or more systems leads to a stronger one.

It isn't always easy to combine packages; there are issues relating to backup, to integrity, to security, and to error reporting. But these issues are worth overcoming, because hybrid systems have the best performance and the greatest range of features.

Part Four, "Links and Metadata," gives an overview of related standards and ends with some sketches of sample applications.

Links and Metadata

Part Four is about *metadata*; that is, information about information.

Chapter 16, "Just Enough Metadata." Introduces some of the more common metadata standards, in particular the Dublin Core and the Resource Description Framework (RDF).

Chapter 17, "Storing Links and Metadata." Discusses storing metadata in a relational database, and explains reasons for doing so.

Chapter 18, "Sketches from the Forge: Sample Applications." Delves into one example in detail (the AutoLinker), and another more briefly (BookWeb).

## CHAPTER 16

Just Enough Metadata

I n this chapter, you'll learn what metadata is and what its most common uses are. Subsequently, you'll be introduced to working with metadata in XML. The next chapter builds on this introduction by discussing ways to implement metadata and citing examples of why you might want to do so.

To begin this chapter, I present a little historical background of metadata on the Web, because it will help to relate the various specifications with one another.

Metadata Defined

Simply, *metadata* is information about data. To expand on that brief definition, metadata is anything not necessarily derived from data, but associated with it. Examples of metadata include the name of the author of a Web page, the publication date of a book, or my shoe size. Sometimes metadata may be derived from the data itself, but stored separately for convenience. An example of this is a file size in bytes, stored by most operating systems alongside more "traditional" metadata such as a filename and a creation date.

Because metadata is information, it can itself be used as data. Information about that data is in turn metadata (not "meta-metadata"). If you make a list of all the authors of all the books in your library, the name of that list is metadata about the list itself.

For the purposes of this book, we'll focus on metadata for XML documents and for the Web. We'll also discuss other data that's stored in XML but is about physical objects.

History: HTML META and LINK Tags

Very early in the history of the World Wide Web, HTML supported a HEAD element that could contain metadata, and a BODY element for the actual document, just as it does today. The HTML HEAD element can contain a document title, any amount of metadata using META and LINK elements, and, more recently, some style and scripting information.

META Elements Introduced

The META elements typically look like this:

```
<HEAD>
    <TITLE>History of Sock Weaving in Lancashire, 1790 to 1815</TITLE>
    <META NAME="Keywords"
        CONTENT="Sock Weaving,History,Lancashire,Socks">
    <META NAME="Description"
        CONTENT="A fascinating study of Sock Weaving in the late
Eighteenth and early Nineteenth centuries; an often overlooked topic in
the history of the County of Lancashire">
</HEAD>
```

The idea is that a Web search engine might display the title and description in its results list. Unfortunately, commercial sites often misuse the keywords field in particular to display their competitors' product names! Nonetheless, this simple metadata has some interesting properties. It is contained in the HTML document directly, making it easier to manage if you have a small number of documents, though harder to manage for a large site—if your company name changes, you may have 150,000 Web pages to edit. Perl to the rescue, but the point remains. If you generate your HTML from a database, or use scripting facilities such as Templates, the Perl Mason package (www.cpan.org), or WebMacro (http://webmacro.org), you can store this metadata in a database, sharing keywords automatically where appropriate.

HTML META elements are empty (in XML the end of the META tag would be />) and have attributes to store the values. Why? Because of a rule that states the first piece of text content must end an HTML header; but it causes problems. You can't have elements inside attributes (neither in HTML nor in XML), so you can't use mathematical expressions such as $E = mc^2$ in the metadata. Perhaps we should be glad people can't put fonts and colors into search engine result lists (and <BLINK>!), but this limitation is a major disadvantage for many people.

A less obvious property is that there is no way to identify who wrote a Web page, nor to distinguish that from who *typed* the Web page.

LINK Elements Introduced

The second metadata innovation on the Web was the LINK element, late in 1989. This element is not widely used today, mostly because the leading HTML browsers didn't support it. By 1995, there were only two or three browsers that made any use of LINK; I helped write an IETF RFC in an attempt to encourage it, but this too failed. The concepts returned in RDF, as we will see. Still, some uses of LINK remain, so let's take a quick look at it:

```
<HEAD>
    <TITLE>History of Sock Weaving in Lancashire, 1790 to 1815</TITLE>
    <META NAME="Keywords"
        CONTENT="Sock Weaving,History,Lancashire,Socks">
    <META NAME="Description"
        CONTENT="A fascinating study of Sock Weaving in the late
Eighteenth and early Nineteenth centuries; an often overlooked topic in
the history of the County of Lancashire">
    <LINK REL="stylesheet" HREF="argyle.css" TYPE="text/css">
    <LINK REV="made" HREF="mailto:liam@holoweb.net">
    <LINK REL="TOC" HREF="../index.html">
</HEAD>
```

REL is an abbreviation for relationship. The first LINK element in the example shows how to connect an HTML document to a style sheet (which you probably already knew); the second shows a REV (for reverse) relationship—the target resource *made* this Web page, perhaps by typing it. The Lynx browser has a command to send email to the person listed in a "made" link. The third LINK element, TOC, shows an example that says that the index.html document in the parent directory is a table of contents that includes this document.

NCSA Mosaic and some commercial help viewers add a toolbar icon automatically whenever a TOC link is found, so that the user can get to a table of contents quickly. Unfortunately, those browsers are in the minority, so not many Web sites use REL and REV for this.

NOTE In the Web architecture documents at www.w3.org, you can read about other kinds of links, including guided tours and "agrees/disagrees" disputation and commentary. These ideas have not been widely implemented.

The Dublin Core

The first International World Wide Web Conference was held in Europe in the spring of 1994. The second conference was in Chicago in November 1994. (The host hotel staff were amazed that the conference was so popular—hence over-booked—that people who had never met before were sharing rooms.) In a hallway in that hotel at that conference, Yuri Rubinsky (the late president of SoftQuad, then a leading SGML company), Joseph Hardin of NCSA, and Stu Weibel of OCLC, the library cataloguing organization, were lamenting the fact that there was no way to do a Web search by author. In fact, if you knew the author, date, and title of a document, an old-fashioned library card catalog was far more useful in many ways than any search engine.

The result of that hallway meeting was a workshop in Dublin, Ohio, to try to estab-lish a card catalog for the Web. After several more workshops, a core set of metadata (known as the Dublin Core) and a set of guidelines for their use, were developed.

The main guiding principles for the Dublin Core set of metadata interchange elements were as follows:

- All Dublin Core elements are optional and repeatable. That is, you can have zero or more of any of them.

- All values are strings, and they are expected to be in English unless other-wise stated.

- The Dublin Core elements must be simple enough that people who are not professional cataloguers can create and use them.

The Dublin Core version 1.1 elements are described at http://purl.org/DC. Table 16.1 summarizes the elements.

The Dublin Core can be used in an HTML document using META elements, or can be used with RDF, as we will discuss later in the chapter. Here's our HTML HEAD with some Dublin Core elements added:

```
<HEAD>
    <TITLE>History of Sock Weaving in Lancashire, 1790 to 1815</TITLE>
    <META NAME="Keywords"
        CONTENT="Sock Weaving,History,Lancashire,Socks">
    <META NAME="Description"
        CONTENT="A fascinating study of Sock Weaving in the late
Eighteenth and early Nineteenth centuries; an often overlooked topic in
the history of the County of Lancashire">
    <META NAME="dc.Creator" CONTENT="Andrew Weaver">
    <META NAME="dc.rights"
        CONTENT="Copyright Andrew Weaver, All rights reserved.">
    <META NAME="dc.contributor.photographer"
        CONTENT="James Weaver">
</HEAD>
```

Table 16.1   Dublin Core Elements Summary

NAME	DEFINITION	COMMENTS
Title	The formal name or title of the resource	Typically, a Title will be a name by which the resource is formally known: a complete book title or a placename, perhaps.
Creator	An entity primarily responsible for making the content of the resource	Examples of a Creator include a person, an organization, or a service.
Subject	The topic of the content of the resource	Typically, a Subject will be expressed as keywords, key phrases, or classification codes that describe a topic of the resource, preferably a value selected from a controlled vocabulary or formal classification scheme.
Description	An account of the content of the resource	Description may include, but is not limited to: an abstract, table of contents, reference to a graphical representation of content, or a free-text account of the content.
Publisher	An entity responsible for making the resource available	Examples of a Publisher include a person, an organization, or a service.
Contributor	An entity responsible for making contributions to the content of the resource	Examples of a Contributor include a person, an organization, or a service.
Date	A date associated with an event in the life cycle of the resource	Typically, Date will be associated with the creation or availability of the resource. The date should be in ISO 8601 format, YYYY-MM-DD.
Type	The nature or genre of the content of the resource	Type includes terms describing general categories, functions, genres, or aggregation levels for content. There is a draft list of Dublin Core Types intended as a basis for a shared controlled vocabulary for this field. An example might be *fiction* but not *paperback*, as that's the Format instead.
Format	The physical or digital manifestation of the resource	Format might include the MIME Media Type or dimensions of the resource. Format may be used to determine the software, hardware, or other equipment needed to operate the resource. Examples of dimensions include size and duration.
Identifier	An unambiguous reference to the resource within a given context	Example formal identification systems include the Uniform Resource Identifier (URI) the (including Uniform Resource Locator (URL)), the Digital Object Identifier (DOI), and the International Standard Book Number (ISBN).
Source	A reference to a resource from which the present resource is derived	The present resource may be derived from the Source resource in whole or in part. You might give the ISBN of a book here from which a transcription was made, for example.

continues

Table 16.1 *Continued*

NAME	DEFINITION	COMMENTS
Language	A language of the intellectual content of the resource	The value should be a language tag taken from RFC 1766: a two-letter ISO 639 Language Code followed, optionally, by a two-letter ISO 3166 Country Code. Examples include "en" for English, "fr" for French, or "en-uk" for English as used in the United Kingdom.
Relation	A reference to a related resource	This should be a string or number conforming to a formal identification system such as a URL or ISBN.
Coverage	The extent or scope of the content of the resource	Coverage will typically include spatial location (a place name or geographic coordinates), time period (a period label, date, or date range), or jurisdiction (such as a named administrative entity). Recommended best practice is to select a value from a controlled vocabulary (for example, the Thesaurus of Geographic Names at http://shiva.pub.getty.edu/tgn_browser/) and that, where appropriate, named places or time periods be used in preference to numeric identifiers such as sets of coordinates or date ranges.
Rights	Information about rights held in and over the resource	Typically, a Rights element will contain a rights management statement for the resource or reference a service providing such information. Rights information often encompasses intellectual property rights (IPR), copyright, and various property rights. If the Rights element is absent, no assumptions can be made about the status of these and other rights with respect to the resource.

Notice how any Dublin Core element can be qualified to be more precise, as in the case of the photographer. The general principle is that you can use any qualifier you like, but people using the metadata can ignore the qualifiers. You must therefore avoid changing the meaning of the base element with a qualifier. If you ignore the word photographer, James still contributed to this document.

NOTE

The syntax for including Dublin Core elements in HTML is defined by RFC 2731, which can be found at www.ietf.org/rfc/rfc2731.txt, along with all other IETF standards.

Other Groups

At the same time the Dublin Core work was underway, another group was developing a way to label a Web site as unsuitable for children. The Platform for Internet Content Selection (PICS) group published a standard that used a LISP S-Expressions syntax `(very (much (like (this))))` for representing that metadata. This standard *is* used on the Web, but the people who use it generally just assume that if a site has a PICS rating, it is not suitable for viewing by children; they don't actually attempt to read the rating itself.

Another group was working independently on ways of associating digital signatures with lists of HTML documents (manifests, as such lists are often called). A fourth group was trying to establish methods of representing a Web site so that graphical maps could be drawn.

The PICS, digital signatures, manifests, and map groups combined in 1996 to work on a generic Resource Description Framework (RDF). This group became the World Wide Web Consortium's Metadata Activity (www.w3.org/Metadata/Activity.html). The groups have converged on XML as a standard, and on the RDF where possible.

The Resource Description Framework

The main ideas behind RDF emerged at the very earliest "Web collection" meetings. But as we all know, coming up with ideas is the easy part; formulating the *syntax* is difficult.

RDF consists of a set of *statements* that *resources* have certain *properties*. This is very similar to other metadata specifications. Examples of properties are: *is the author of*, *was published in the year*, and *wears socks of this color*. As you can see, the properties can be about anything, not just Web pages, although you have to use a Uniform Resource Identifier (URI) to identify the resource. Most people use a Uniform Resource Locator, or URL, although other types of URI are defined. We'll stick to URLs for now.

Suppose I have a simple Web site for a glossary, consisting of a table of contents that mentions each definition, and a separate HTML file for each definition. I can say who wrote each definition (it's not always me; people submit them to me) and that the table of contents is a `TOC` for the definition. I could do this much with the `REL`/`REV` attributes mentioned earlier, but with RDF, I can have a separate file that does it. A search engine or a Web site explorer could download the RDF instead of having to march through all the files.

NOTE
The RDF Specification is at www.w3.org/TR/REC-rdf-syntax in both HTML and XML. The information given here is based on the version found at www.w3.org/TR/1999/ REC-rdf-syntax-19990222, which was published as a W3C Recommendation, the W3C equivalent of a standard.

Definitions

RDF can be intimidating because of the formal definitions, but it's actually quite easy to interpret.

Resources

All things described by RDF expressions are called *resources*. A resource may be:

- An entire Web page, such as the HTML document www.w3.org/ Overview.html
- Part of a Web page, such as a specific HTML or XML element within the document source
- A collection of pages, such as an entire Web site
- An object that is not directly accessible via the Web, such as a printed book

Resources are always named by URIs and optional anchor IDs. Anything can have a URI; the extensibility of URIs allows the introduction of identifiers for any entity imaginable.

NOTE The URI Specification is at www.ietf.org/internet-drafts/draft-fielding-uri-syntax-04.txt.

Properties

A *property* is a specific aspect, characteristic, attribute, or relation used to describe a resource. Each property has a specific meaning; defines its permitted values, the types of resources it can describe, and its relationship with other properties. The RDF Specification itself does not address how the characteristics of properties are expressed (for more information, refer to the RDF Schema Specification).

NOTE The RDF Schema Specification is at www.w3.org/TR/PR-rdf-schema, and is described in more detail later in this chapter.

Statements

A specific resource together with a named property and the value of that property for that resource is an RDF *statement*. These three individual parts of a statement are called the *subject*, the *predicate*, and the *object*, respectively. The object of a statement (the property value) can be another resource or it can be a *literal* (a resource specified by a URI, a simple string, or another primitive datatype defined by XML). In RDF terms, a literal may have content that is XML markup but is not further evaluated by the RDF processor. (There are some syntactic restrictions on how markup in literals may be expressed; see Section 2.2.1 of the RDF Specification.)

An RDF Example

Here is a simple example that says that Liam Quin created the glossary index page at www.valinor.sorcery.net/glossary/ using RDF with the XML syntax:

```
<?xml version="1.0"?>
<rdf:RDF
    xmlns:rdf="http://www.w3.org/1999/02/22-rdf-syntax-ns#"
    xmlns:dc="http://purl.org/dc/elements/1.0/">
    <rdf:Description about="http://www.valinor.sorcery.net/glossary/">
        <dc:Creator>Liam Quin</dc:Creator>
    </rdf:Description>
</rdf:RDF>
```

Hold on to your socks, it's not as bad as it looks! We'll take it one step at a time. First, we have the XML Declaration that says this is an XML document. We then have an `rdf:RDF` element that introduces the `rdf:` and `dc:` *namespace prefixes*. You can read more about namespaces at www.w3.org/XML/ but for now, a namespace is a way of associating an element prefix such as `rdf:` with a URL. The bold typeface shows the namespace syntax:

```
<?xml version="1.0"?>
<rdf:RDF
    xmlns:rdf="http://www.w3.org/1999/02/22-rdf-syntax-ns#"
    xmlns:dc="http://purl.org/dc/elements/1.0/">
    <rdf:Description about="http://www.valinor.sorcery.net/glossary/">
        <dc:Creator>Liam Quin</dc:Creator>
    </rdf:Description>
</rdf:RDF>
```

You can think of the `xmlns:rdf` attribute as similar to a `#include` in C, a *use* statement in Perl, or, better, an *import* in Java. It adds the RDF semantics to the content of the element to which it's associated. I have used the Dublin Core URL to introduce the Dublin Core properties, and I've used `dc` as a prefix. There is no significance to the prefix value here; I could have used `wf:` for Warwick Framework (so called after a syntax meeting at Warwick University), as long as I used the right URL in the namespace attribute.

The actual description part of the example is very simple. There are three parts: a *resource*, given by the URL `http://www.valinor.sorcery.net/glossary/`, a *property*, Creator, and a *value*, `Liam Quin`. The meaning of the value is determined by the owner of the Creator property, in this case `http://purl.org/DC/` because of the `dc:` prefix.

Here is the example again, with the single RDF statement about that page in bold:

```
<?xml version="1.0"?>
<rdf:RDF
    xmlns:rdf="http://www.w3.org/1999/02/22-rdf-syntax-ns#"
    xmlns:dc="http://purl.org/dc/elements/1.0/">
    <rdf:Description about="http://www.valinor.sorcery.net/glossary/">
        <dc:Creator>Liam Quin</dc:Creator>
    </rdf:Description>
</rdf:RDF>
```

As you can see, it's pretty simple. I could add some more statements, too:

```
<?xml version="1.0"?>
<rdf:RDF
    xmlns:rdf="http://www.w3.org/1999/02/22-rdf-syntax-ns#"
    xmlns:dc="http://purl.org/dc/elements/1.0/">
    <rdf:Description about="http://www.valinor.sorcery.net/glossary/">
        <dc:Creator>Liam Quin</dc:Creator>
        <dc:Title>Glossary of Internet Relay Chat Terms and
Abbreviations</dc:Title>
    </rdf:Description>
    <rdf:Description about="http://www.valinor.sorcery.net/clients/">
        <dc:Creator>Liam Quin</dc:Creator>
        <dc:Title>List of Internet Relay Chat Client Software</dc:Title>
    </rdf:Description>
</rdf:RDF>
```

This is verbose, but clear, and it compresses well with *gzip* or *compress*. The prefixes make explicit where each property is defined.

NOTE The RDF Specification contains an example very similar to this one, except that it uses an `s:` prefix to refer to the RDF Schema Specification, and then uses `s:Creator`. This appears to have been done under the assumption that the RDF Schema Specification defined the Dublin Core properties; but in fact, it doesn't, probably because the Schema Specification wasn't finished when RDF itself was published.

The result of running the RDF Visualization tool at www.w3.org/RDF/Implementations/SiRPAC/ on this simple example is shown in Figure 16.1. It's a little difficult to read, but the online version lets you drag nodes around, which is helpful. SiRPAC also validates your RDF, so it's worth checking out. The source code is available, as well.

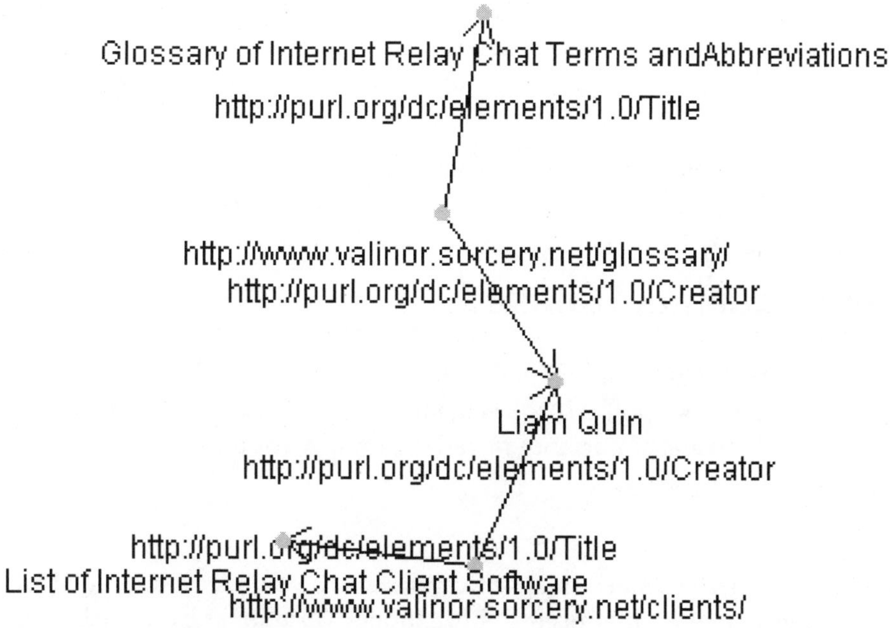

Glossary of Internet Relay Chat Terms andAbbreviations
http://purl.org/dc/elements/1.0/Title

http://www.valinor.sorcery.net/glossary/
http://purl.org/dc/elements/1.0/Creator

Liam Quin
http://purl.org/dc/elements/1.0/Creator

http://purl.org/dc/elements/1.0/Title
List of Internet Relay Chat Client Software
http://www.valinor.sorcery.net/clients/

Figure 16.1   SiRPAC visualization of the RDF example.

The RDF Schema Specification

The RDF Schema Specification at www.w3.org/TR/PR-rdf-schema (the version used here is at www.w3.org/TR/1999/PR-rdf-schema-19990303 in both HTML and XML) defines a simple class system for RDF, with terms such as SubClassOf and SubPropertyOf. You could use RDF Schema to say that a sock is a subtype of footwear, that a boy is a kind of animal, or that a photographer is a kind of contributor.

This capability lets RDF model much of the same sort of typology for which ISO HyTime Topic Maps were designed, as the *ISO Topic Maps* section, upcoming, describes.

Who Uses RDF?

The World Wide Web Consortium's RDF page at www.w3.org/RDF/ lists some 30 RDF-based projects, but it's incomplete. Red Hat Linux uses RDF to describe the relationships among software packages, for example, Netscape's

Open Source browser, Mozilla (www.mozilla.org) uses RDF extensively. Dave Beckett's list of RDF projects at www.cs.ukc.ac.uk/people/staff/djb1/research/metadata/rdf.shtml gives pointers to yet more lists or RDF projects, documents, and resources.

If you are planning to use metadata, you should investigate RDF and the Dublin Core first. If they meet your needs, travel no further.

Other Metadata Standards

There are a large number of standards for representing metadata. Of the three given in this section, MARC is the most widely used; Finding Aids are a good example of metadata about metadata; topic maps are very new.

MARC

The MARC version 21 specification can be found online at http://lcWeb.loc.gov/marc/; it is used (with national variations) by libraries throughout the world. Its full name is MARC 21 Format for Bibliographic Data, and it is as large and complex as its name. It is also very powerful, although it's primarily oriented toward describing physical objects such as books, journals, articles, and videotapes. MARC is not XML-based, and although there are SGML and XML representations available, they assume knowledge of the several hundred MARC fields.

If you are interested in bibliographical work, MARC is a wonderful resource for ideas and information.

Finding Aids to Archival Collections

A Finding Aid is a guide to a collection that is held by a museum, an art gallery, a library, or other institution. The Encoded Archival Description (EAD) is an SGML or XML format for exchanging Finding Aids. The home page for Finding Aids in XML is www.loc.gov/ead/ead.html, and there are more details at www.oasis-open.org/cover/ead.html on Robin Cover's excellent site.

This example is included as one of literally hundreds of other metadata standards for specific domain areas. This book does *not* attempt to list them!

ISO Topic Maps

The International Organization for Standardization (ISO, www.iso.ch) has published a standard ISO/IEC 13250:2000 Information technology—SGML Applications—Topic Maps. This standard can be purchased from your national standards body or directly from ISO. It appears to compete with RDF, but in a closed ISO environment.

Topic Maps let you categorize resources and specify types and subtypes, very much like RDF Schema except with HyTime links instead of the RDF syntax.

Summary

To repeat: Metadata is information about information. The leading standards for metadata in the XML and Web arenas are the Dublin Core and RDF. Other standards for metadata have existed for many years, especially in the library community; some of those standards are available on the Web. Many of the specifications are a little dry, but the RDF example given here and the various tutorials at the Web sites mentioned throughout will help.

The next chapter, "Storing Links and Metadata," discusses ways to store metadata in a database.

## CHAPTER 17

Storing Links and Metadata

The previous chapter introduced ways to represent metadata at a markup level. Building on that, this chapter explains how to store metadata in a database and the reasons for doing so, many of which have been alluded to earlier in the book. Finally, this chapter offers suggestions on how to implement these approaches.

Links as Links and as Metadata

A *link* is a relationship between two resources, often represented by explicit markup, for example by an `<A>` element in HTML or by using XLink. The fact that the link exists is metadata about the link, and about the two resources; the relationship itself is metadata about the two resources. The following examples illustrate this more clearly.

The markup `<a href="toc.html">Table of Contents</a>` in an HTML document (`chapter12.html`, say) represents a link between a document and a table of contents that mentions that document. The statement, "There is a link between `chapter12.html` and `toc.html`," is itself a piece of metadata, because it's information about information.

If I use XPath and XLink to store the link markup in a separate database instead of the actual file, perhaps using `"Table of Contents"` as a string to search for, I have muddied the waters. I have stored metadata (the fact that there is a link) and the data itself (in this case, the link markup) together. As someone who likes to splash about barefoot in the mud, I don't have a problem with this, but it means that the term metadata can be confusing.

NOTE
In this chapter, the term metadata is used to include stored information about links.

If I add to the link markup in my HTML file the fact that it's a link to a table of contents, I have created some inline metadata, showing that metadata doesn't need to be stored separately:

```
<a href="toc.html" REL="TOC" TITLE="Contents">Table of Contents</a>
```

I have added `REL` to show the relationship between the document containing the link (`chapter12.html`) and the remote resource (`toc.html`). That's information about the link, of course. I've also added a Title attribute giving the title of the remote resource—although strictly speaking, that's a Microsoft Internet Explorer feature.

Storing Metadata in a Database

There are many reasons to store metadata (including links) in a database. The following sections describe some of them, and offer implementation suggestions.

Searches and Queries

One of the more obvious reasons to put information into a database is so that you can get it back out again, in a different order if you so desire. The following query might find all documents that were written by Liam Quin and that contain a link to a picture whose title (in the metadata database) is "splashing barefoot through muddy puddles." You could take this one step further and find all other images on the same page and list their titles.

```
SELECT (url, title) FROM docs, links
   WHERE docs.author LIKE 'Liam Quin'
     AND docs.id = links.id
     AND links.mimetype LIKE 'image/%'
     AND links.title LIKE 'splashing barefoot through muddy puddles'
   ;
```

The syntax here is deliberately vague, because in practice, you'd use multiple tables. Let's explore this in more detail. For now, let's suppose we are storing a range of XML documents on a Web site and delivering XML using XSL. We'll store the following information about each document:

- The filename and location (separately, so we can move files around)
- The document's author and creation data (not the same as the file creation data)
- The document's title and keywords
- A MIME media type for each document (`text/xml` or `image/jpeg`, for example)
- A unique ID, for efficient joins

In addition, we'll make a separate "links" table, storing:

- A link type (table of contents or annotation, for example)
- A pair of linked documents

A multiway link with three end-points would have *two* rows in the links table, one for each arc.

NOTE If you allow a URL instead of a filename and location, you will need to use a VAR-TEXT or VARCHAR field that allows at least 2048 bytes for the URL, as some browsers accept them that long. Other, older, browsers truncate at 1024 characters. The original Web architecture allowed only 72 characters, since HTML had a MIME media type of `text/html`, and text files had a 72-character line length restriction. However, I'm not aware of any software that ever enforced this.

The next decision is how to obtain the data. Since we've said it's in our XML files, we could run an XML parser over them, perhaps using Perl and a SAX-based parser or *sgrep*. That means we are considering the XML files, not the database, to be authoritative. (This is an unusual way of thinking for many database programmers, so expect to have to explain it carefully, to make sure everyone involved understands.)

It's not generally possible to search images for keywords, so you'll have to make a separate database for those or link to an external asset management system if you have one. Be careful to separate the parts of the database that are derived from external data from those that contain authoritative data that was entered directly into the database.

Once you have the data entered, you can easily start playing with queries, such as that in the example at the start of this section. You could also use PHP, or Apache's mod_perl and DBI, to write a Web-based search interface. Be careful not to let people type arbitrary SQL, since DELETE and INSERT can change your database! If you do support SQL directly, perhaps for debugging, use an account that doesn't have write access, and handle the errors in your interface.

Link Visualization

Another reason for using metadata in a database is so that you can draw pictures of it. This can really help people to explore the data or to fix errors. I made a picture of my IRC glossary (mentioned in Chapter 15, "Hybrid Approaches") and discovered some clusters of terms that were not linked well to other related terms. This had not been obvious by looking at individual glossary entries, but was clear from the map. In that case, there was no database involved: A CGI script in Perl generated an HTML page on the fly by reading the HTML glossary; the HTML page in turn invoked a Java applet to show the result. The following Perl script does this (note, it could be made simpler and faster by using DBI and a link database, and shorter by using the Perl HTML::LinkExtor from CPAN).

The code here assumes that it's in the same directory as the GraphLayout demo included with the Java Development Kit (JDK) from Sun. You may need to recompile the demo with larger values in the node and arcs arrays. You can try this out at www.valinor.sorcery.net/applets/javagloss.cgi (or find Ankh on irc.sorcery.net and ask him where it moved, if it's gone).

```perl
#! /usr/local/bin/perl -w
use strict;

sub main
{
    print "Content-type: text/html\r\n\r\n";

    print <<EOF;
<html><head>
<title>Valinor: Wobbly Glossary</title>
<body bgcolor="#000000" text="#CC9977">
<h2>Valinor's Wobbly Java IRC Glossary</h2>
EOF
    makeAppletTagsfromLinks();
    exit(0);
}

sub fail
{
    my ($str) = @_;

    print "<h2>dithathter!</h2>\n";
    print "<p>$str</p>\n";
    exit(0);
}
```

```
######

sub makeAppletTagsfromLinks
{
    my $links = getGlossLinks();
    print <<EOF;
<applet code="Graph.class" width=900 height=800>
 <param name=edges value="${links}">
 <param name=center value="index">
</applet>
<hr>
EOF
}

sub getGlossLinks()
{
    my %arcs;
    my %seen;
    my %linkCounts;

    my $glossDir = "/usr/home/liam/public_html/valinor/glossary";
    my $glossFile = "${glossDir}/index.html";

    open(GLOSS, "< $glossFile") ||
        fail("Can't read glossary index file $glossFile: $!");

    $seen{"index.html"} = 1;

    # read the main index.html file and process all the links in it
    while (<GLOSS>) {
        while (m/<a[^<>]+href="([^"]+)"/ig) {
            # for each link...
            my $other = $1;

            # ignore all except relative links to files:
            next if ($other =~ m@/@);

            # process each file only once:
            next if ($seen{$other});
            $seen{$other} = 1;

            # Process the linked file.
            # This is not recursive, so we will only ever include files
            # linked to from index.html or directly from those files:
            # the goal was to look at just the glossary.
            open(OTHER, "< ${glossDir}/$other") || next;

            $other =~ s/\.html//;
            $arcs{ "index" . "/" . $other } = 1;

            while (<OTHER>) {
```

```
            while (m/<a[^<>]+href="([^"]+)"/ig) {
                my $end = $1;
                next if ($end =~ m@/@) {
                $end =~ s/\.html//;
                next if (exists $arcs{ $end . "/" . $other});
                $arcs{ $other . "/" . $end } = 1;
                ++$linkCounts{$other};


            }
        }
        close(OTHER);
    }
}
close(GLOSS);

# now build up a list of arcs with distances apart to draw them:
my $result = ""; my $pair;
foreach $pair (keys %arcs) {
    # generate "node1,node2/d,node1,node3/d,node3,node4/d....."
    # where d is the perferred line length in pixels for each arc
    $pair =~ tr{-/}{_-}; # remove - and turn / into -
    my $distance;
    if (/index\b/) {  # long links to spread the glossary out
        $distance = int(rand(200)) + 175;
    } else {          # shorter links between items
        $distance = int(rand(100)) + 50;
    }
    $result .= ",$pair/$distance";
}
$result =~ s/^,//;
return $result;
}


# now do the real work:
main();
```

You can see that most of this short piece of Perl is devoted to extracting HTML links out of files. I've left it in this form because it's easy to play with and to understand. You could convert it to use DBI by combining it with one of the examples from Part One, and perhaps use the link extraction code to populate a database. The important point here is that you can use a mixture of tools to glue components together—in this case, a bunch of HTML files, a Java applet, and some Perl.

If you are familiar with Java, you could modify the GraphDemo applet directly to contact a database, perhaps using a servlet. As I said in the "Introduction," I'm not assuming a knowledge of Java. But the GraphDemo is easy to edit and quite fun. We've gone from a fairly pedestrian set of SQL tables to a state-of-the-art Java representation of links between documents with hardly a blink.

NOTE

Many link visualization tools are available. Petros Demetriades and Alexandra Poulo-vassilis described one at the Seventh International World Wide Web Conference in 1998 (www.dcs.kcl.ac.uk/pg/petros, and links). Another was described by Andrew Wood, B. Hendley, and R. Beal (*HyperSpace: Web browsing with visualisation*, Poster presented at Technology, Tools and Applications, the Third International World Wide Web Conference, April 10–14,1995, Darmstadt, Germany). There is a Java demo at www.cs.bham.ac.uk/~amw/hyperspace/java/enhanced.html. A quick Web search at www.metacrawler.com will yield many more visualization tools.

There have also been SQL-like languages proposed (and implemented) for reasoning about hypertext, some using object-oriented database, others traversing flat files, still others using relational databases. You can also find research papers at Brown University (http://landow.stg.brown.edu/HTatBrown/BrownHT.html) and elsewhere. Hypertext research started in earnest in the 1960s and has been going strong ever since.

Once you've put metadata into a database, you should be able to mine the data in many useful ways.

Groups of Related Documents

If you have a database of topics, you can present the documents in "virtual folders" by category. I used this approach for the dictionary of eighteenth-century slang that I've been using as an example throughout this book. Each dictionary entry was marked up with one or more category keywords and virtual indexes were created showing all matching pages. (Note: The Perl AutoLinker described in Chapter 14 did not show this.)

You can take this *clustering* approach further by analyzing the words in the documents; this is a common technique in text retrieval, as the many research papers on the subject will attest. Chapter 23, "Further Reading," in Part Five, "Resource Guide," can give you pointers to them; and Doug Pederson and others at Xerox have published some helpful papers (available online) on the subject.

Extra Link Functionality

Although HTML links are familiar to millions of people, XML links are more powerful, as Chapter 14, "XQL, XLink, XPath, and XPointer Explained," demonstrated. If you generate HTML or XML on the fly from a database, perhaps with XSLT or PHP, you can use the stored metadata to generate extra links. The next two sections give some examples.

What's Related

As Jakob Nielsen notes in his excellent book *Designing Web Usability* (New Riders, 2000), a set of further links at the end of a Web page can help people who find the wrong document as well as those who want to know more. If your database stores information about which documents are about related topics, or are about topics that are often confused one with another, you can generate further reading and what's related links easily. I tried this with the Internet Relay Chat glossary I mentioned earlier, and noticed people staying on the site much longer, following the links to related material, and often bookmarking it.

You can do this on almost any Web site, if you have access to the *httpd* log files. To begin, enable the more detailed log format that includes browser and referring page. You can use the browser to spot search engines and robots, and ignore them. Then use the Referrer field to see when people came from one of the big search engines. If you sort the log first by the address of the client requesting the page, then by their browser, then by time, you tend to see a whole session at a time. Figure 17.1 shows the Web Reports tool I used to do this (you can get Web Reports from www.holoweb.net/~liam if you want to try this on your own site).

When an Internet Explorer 5 (IE5) user bookmarks a page, IE5 tries to fetch `favicon.ico` from that directory and then, if it's not found, `/favicon.ico`; this lets you have an idea of how many people are bookmarking a page.

Multiway Links

If your link structure is held in a database, you can generate different markup on the fly as appropriate. XML users can have multiway links with popup menus to let them choose which branch to follow. HTML users can have document layers or windows that pop up with JavaScript, or multiple `<A>` elements.

Navigational Aids

If you are generating HTML or XML for online viewing, it's a good idea to make navigational tools to help users. For example, you could generate information showing the position of the current page in a stream. Figure 17.2 shows a possible graphic for the IRC glossary, showing linked terms.

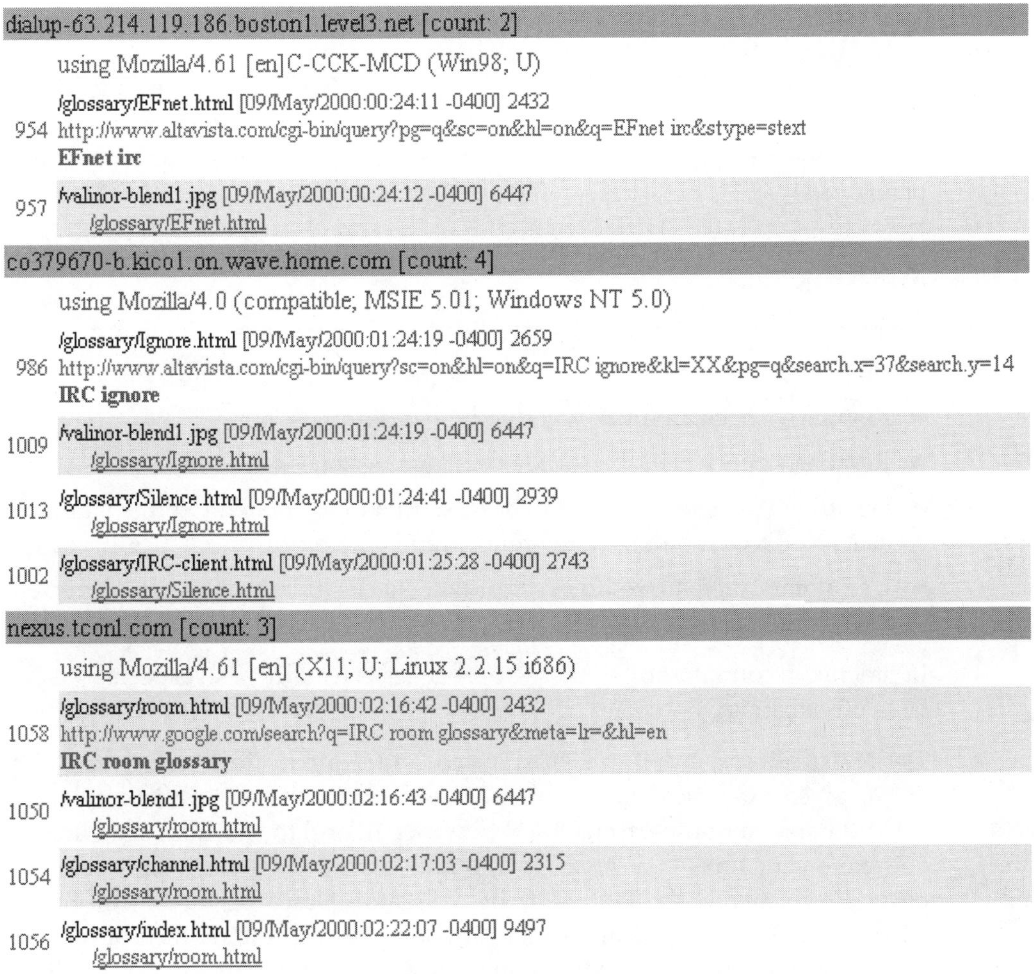

dialup-63.214.119.186.boston1.level3.net [count: 2]

using Mozilla/4.61 [en]C-CCK-MCD (Win98; U)

/glossary/EFnet.html [09/May/2000:00:24:11 -0400] 2432
954 http://www.altavista.com/cgi-bin/query?pg=q&sc=on&hl=on&q=EFnet irc&stype=stext
EFnet irc

957 /valinor-blend1.jpg [09/May/2000:00:24:12 -0400] 6447
/glossary/EFnet.html

co379670-b.kico1.on.wave.home.com [count: 4]

using Mozilla/4.0 (compatible; MSIE 5.01; Windows NT 5.0)

/glossary/Ignore.html [09/May/2000:01:24:19 -0400] 2659
986 http://www.altavista.com/cgi-bin/query?sc=on&hl=on&q=IRC ignore&kl=XX&pg=q&search.x=37&search.y=14
IRC ignore

1009 /valinor-blend1.jpg [09/May/2000:01:24:19 -0400] 6447
/glossary/Ignore.html

1013 /glossary/Silence.html [09/May/2000:01:24:41 -0400] 2939
/glossary/Ignore.html

1002 /glossary/IRC-client.html [09/May/2000:01:25:28 -0400] 2743
/glossary/Silence.html

nexus.tconl.com [count: 3]

using Mozilla/4.61 [en] (X11; U; Linux 2.2.15 i686)

/glossary/room.html [09/May/2000:02:16:42 -0400] 2432
1058 http://www.google.com/search?q=IRC room glossary&meta=lr=&hl=en
IRC room glossary

1050 /valinor-blend1.jpg [09/May/2000:02:16:43 -0400] 6447
/glossary/room.html

1054 /glossary/channel.html [09/May/2000:02:17:03 -0400] 2315
/glossary/room.html

1056 /glossary/index.html [09/May/2000:02:22:07 -0400] 9497
/glossary/room.html

Figure 17.1　An excerpt from a WebReports page.

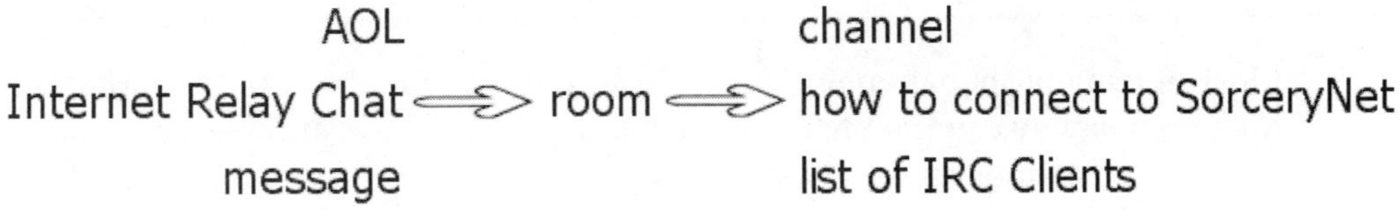

AOL　　　　　　　　　channel

Internet Relay Chat ⟹ room ⟹ how to connect to SorceryNet

message　　　　　　　list of IRC Clients

Figure 17.2　Second-level links for navigation.

Link Management and Analysis

Link management sounds formal, but it can be thought of as encompassing much of the previous examples (link visualization, mentioned earlier, is a form of analysis).

Link Checking

An ongoing frustration of Web users is links that go astray. There are several approaches to preventing this problem, including the following:

- Regularly check all links, whether by hand or by script.
- Regularly check HTTP error logs (surprisingly useful).
- Generate Web sites from a database, so that every generated link starts out as a NOT NULL database reference, and is therefore automatically correct.
- Use an intermediate redirect script that checks links and gives a corrected URL if necessary.

In practice, a combination of these approaches is usually best, especially if you have off-site links.

The Perl Cookbook, by Tom Christiansen and Nathan Torkington (O'Reilly, 1998), gives examples (in Chapter 20) of using the Perl LWP::Simple and HTML::Parser modules from CPAN (www.cpan.org) to check for stale links. If you have your links in a database, though, you need to check each link only once. *Programming the Perl DBI*, by Alligator Descartes and Tim Bunce, (O'Reilly, 2000) is a good investment if you want to combine the approaches. But if you bought this book thinking you wouldn't also have to buy all the others, not to worry; just read the online documentation for the various Perl modules with the *perldoc* command.

Its also might be an interesting exercise to see what analysis you can do. If, for example, you load your Apache *httpd* Web server logs into a database, you can use SQL and database visualization tools to explore it.

Document Management

Most document management systems store metadata about users and about documents; they can then handle permissions, workflow, and searching. Document management is a large part of the focus of Part Two of this book. Storing metadata in a database and the document externally is often a good way to start building a document management system. Later, you can evolve to offering the W3C Document Object Model API (DOM) to customers or users.

Summary

Once you start putting information in databases, you can have all sorts of fun analyzing it and generating different views of it. That is, after all, much of the value of a relational database. Determine what sort of questions you can answer with these tools. Then go and answer them!

The next chapter brings together many of the concepts discussed throughout the book, and outlines two sample applications, both of which involve manipulating metadata, including information about links. After that, it's time to write applications of your own!

## CHAPTER 18

Sketches from the Forge: Sample Applications

This chapter introduces two worked examples that tie together earlier discussions. The first is a version of the AutoLinker that uses text retrieval to insert links into generated XML or HTML documents on the fly. The second is a discussion of the BookWeb application introduced in Chapter 3, "Just Enough SQL."

This book is intended as a *toolkit*, not an *application shelf*. I had to decide between giving complete, but tiny, examples, and giving a higher-level view of entire applications, broad enough to be interesting. I chose a compromise. The printed examples are not complete, but the fragments given show how to fit components together and use technology.

The AutoLinked Glossary

The AutoLinker adds hypertext links automatically and generates HTML, taking phrase-definition pairs that might have come from a database, an XML document, or even a plain text file. When a definition mentions a term that's defined, the AutoLinker adds a definition to that term. I've shown you a Perl version of the AutoLinker, written to handle a dictionary marked up in XML. In that application, the text was static—the dictionary was published in 1736.

The AutoLinker is particularly useful for a glossary that is updated from time to time. When a new entry is defined, we want any other entries that mention that term to be linked automatically. For example, the entry for "electronic mail" might also mention Usenet. If, later, a definition is added for Usenet, we need to go back and change the entry for electronic mail to contain a *link* to the entry to Usenet, not just a reference. The AutoLinker will do that for us, automatically. All we have to do is enter a plain text definition of Usenet, and everywhere Usenet is mentioned, a link will appear.

On occasion, however, this can be disconcerting. The AutoLinker doesn't check for words with multiple meanings, so the phrase "file this away for future reference" could end up having links to computer storage (file) and maybe even to online stock trading (future). In a small glossary, this wouldn't matter much—people enjoy exploring the links even if they're a little unexpected sometimes, because they learn as they do so. In a large glossary, in contrast, you'd need to prevent certain of the links from being inserted. The Perl AutoLinker, at www.holoweb.net/~liam/xmldb/, supports an XML attribute on an entry to state, in essence, "This entry is never a target for an automatic link"; it also supports markup around a phrase to state, "Don't link this phrase anywhere," or, "Link this phrase *here*."

Use Cases

The following use cases give the main ways in which the glossary was originally expected to be used. In fact, most people visiting the glossary do so because they conducted a Web search to find an explanation of a word or phrase. As a result, the glossary index is consulted much less often than I had anticipated, and links within the glossary items are followed more often. The use cases here don't reflect that, except for a mention of What You Might Have Wanted links that were added to the glossary after observing how it was used.

The use cases are described informally rather than in any specific notation. There are formal methodologies for determining use cases, and for a large project you should investigate them. A useful book is Putnam Texel's and Charles Williams' *Use Cases Combined with Booch/OMT/UML: Process and Products* (Prentice-Hall, 1997).

USE CASE: VIEW THE INDEX

1. The user sees a list of all glossary terms.

2. The definition terms are highlighted as links.

3. Optionally, the index may be split alphabetically.

4. The definitions are not shown.

The index is shown in Figure 18.1.

IRC Glossary

valinor | policy | bots | clients | staff | [glossary] | search | new

*	*nix
:	:-(:-)
A	admin afaik afd afk akill atm
B	ban ban evasion bbiab bbl BitchX bot brb BX
C	CFD CFV channel channel mode channel operator channel takeover ChanServ clone CTCP
D	DALnet DCC DNS domain
E	EFnet eggdrop bot epic
F	file server flood FOAD frown fserv FUD
G	ghost gline GMTA
H	HNG hostmask
I	IAB ib IETF Ignore iirc IMHO InfoServ Internet Service Provider IP IRC IRC admin IRC client IRC Network IRC Operator IRC Server IRC Warrior irc.sorcery.net ircd ircd.conf ircd.motd ircII ircle irl ISP
J	j/k
K	k Kerberos kick kill kline
L	Link Looking Linux load average local channel lol
M	Macintosh mask MemoServ Message of the day MIDI MIME mIRC motd
N	netsplit Network port newsgroup NFS NFS Server nick NickServ
O	OMG OOC op oper OperServ
P	peer pirch port
R	RFC RFC 1459 RFC 822 RFC Index room rotfl rotflmao
S	script server Service shell Silence smile SorceryNet sound file
T	tia trojan horse troll
U	Undernet Unix uptime Usenet user mode
V	Virus
W	W3C warez wb WTF www
Y	YMMV

Figure 18.1   Glossary index.

USE CASE: VIEW AN ENTRY

1. The user views the Index, as in the previous example.

2. The user chooses an entry by following a link from a highlighted term.

3. The definition of that term is shown, as follows:

   a. The term being defined or explained is clearly marked.

   b. The definition is shown.

   c. Within the definition, any terms that are themselves defined in the glossary are highlighted as links to the corresponding definitions.

   d. There is a navigational link back to the index.

   e. There may also be links called What's Related or You Might Have Wanted in a list following the definition. These links must be clearly marked so they are not mistaken for part of the definition.

Figure 18.2 shows a sample glossary entry.

USE CASE: EDIT AN ENTRY

1. The user views an entry.

2. The user activates an Edit button or link.

3. The definition is presented in an editable HTML form, such as that shown in Figure 18.3.

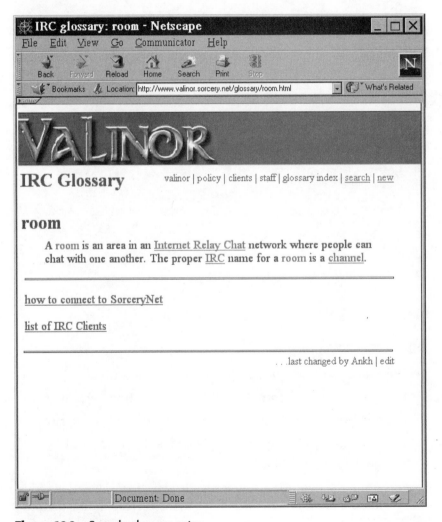

Figure 18.2   Sample glossary entry.

4. The user makes any desired changes, including adding links.

5. The user activates a Save Changes button or link.

6. The server saves the updated glossary entry.

7. If the term being defined was changed, links in other entries to the old term are removed and links to the new term are added where necessary.

8. Links are added to the new definition.

9. If necessary, the index page is changed.

10. The user is presented with the new definition or with the updated index page (implementation choice).

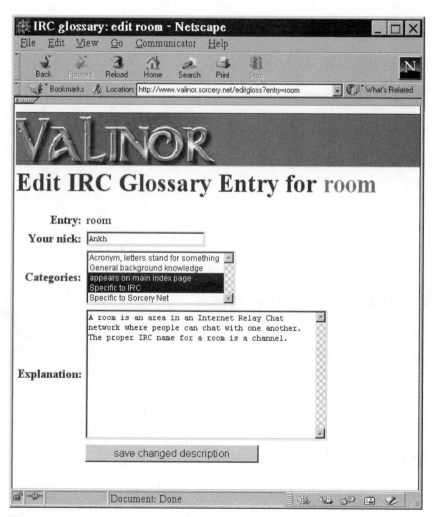

Figure 18.3   Editing a glossary entry.

USE CASE: CREATE AN ENTRY

1. The user views the index (to determine if the entry is already there).

2. The user selects a New Entry button or link.

3. A blank HTML form is presented.

4. The user creates the entry.

5. The user activates a Save Changes button or link.

6. The new entry is checked for required fields and to make sure it doesn't already exist; if incorrect, an error is issued. The user is returned to step 4, retaining data.

7. The entry (having passed all required checks) is saved; links are added to this term in all other entries mentioning the term.

8. Links are added to the new entry.

9. The user is presented with the new definition or with the updated index page (implementation choice).

USE CASE: DELETE AN ENTRY

1. The user views the entry to be deleted.

2. The user activates a Delete Entry link or button.

3. The user confirms the action.

4. The entry is deleted.

5. Links to that entry are removed from other definitions.

6. The user is presented with a confirmation message and returned to the index.

Implementation Overview

Most of the glossary is a pretty standard Web application. The obvious tools to use include the various Perl CGI modules from CPAN or a Java servlet with session tracking. My implementation used Perl, but it predated the CGI module. The glossary terms could be stored in an SQL database, in a flat file, or even in a *dbm*-style database. If you choose to use a flat file or *dbm*, make regular backups, and ensure that the files were not open for writing while a backup was taking place. Another implementation might use an XML file for each glossary entry.

The use cases implied that links were inserted whenever an entry was saved. In fact, it could be done at any time before showing the entry to the user, so another option is to insert links on the fly. You can easily support customized "themes" that way, too, to share a glossary among multiple sites. The main difficulty is making sure that Web search engines still index all of your glossary terms. Search engine crawlers often don't follow links that include .cgi in the URL, so you will need to hide the fact you are using CGI scripts. This is not a problem with servlets, of course; and you could also use a script alias or a CGI script that uses a QUERY_PATH parameter.

Here, I assume that you will generate static XML pages containing all of the links, just to have something concrete to describe; these XML pages will then be converted to HTML on the fly for browsers that don't support XML directly. Other browsers see XML with an XSL style sheet.

NOTE
The Internet Relay Chat glossary used as an example makes static HTML files, partly to save load on the server and partly because the implementation predates XML being published as a specification (though you can't tell that from the outside).

Implementation One Step at a Time

The next few sections will show how a text retrieval database (my own *lq-text*) is used to insert the links. The details of the CGI interface to view and store entries are not shown, so you might find it helpful to consult the online documentation for *lq-text* while you read this chapter, but it's not necessary to understand this material. You can find it at www.holoweb.net/~liam/lq-text/.

Extract Text and Make an Index

When the AutoLinker is started from scratch, it needs a text retrieval database. Each plain text (or XML) glossary entry is saved to a separate file in a temporary directory. The filenames used, however, are those intended for the final glossary URLs. A list of files is made and fed to the indexing program, *lqaddfile*. This makes an index (in a binary format) of all the words in all of those files. The *lq-text* configuration file used looks like this:

```
IndexNumbers On
MinWordLength 1
MaxWordLength 20
IgnoreHTMLhead True
DOCPATH /usr/home/liam/public_html/valinor/tmp.gloss:.
common /dev/null
```

The `IgnoreHTMLhead` entry directs *lq-text* not to index words found until the start of the document body or until a special marker. The other entries should be self-explanatory, or can be ignored if you aren't actually doing this yourself.

After this has been accomplished, it's not necessary to rebuild the entire index when a single entry is added or changed. Instead, *lqunindex* can be run on the old entry, if there was one, and then *lqaddfile* run on the new one.

To prevent the index from becoming too fragmented or large, a monthly *cron* job could be used. It would have to use a lock file to keep the CGI applications waiting while it renamed the *lq-text* index directory; it could then remove the files inside the directory safely while the AutoLinker built a new one.

Since *lq-text* does not need to refer to the text files once the index is built (for this application at least), they can be removed. You might want to keep them, though, as described in the upcoming section *Search the Glossary*.

Insert Links into One Document

The AutoLinker inserts links into a copy of one of the temporary files. If you remove the temporary files after making the index, you'll need to re-create it at this stage. It must be byte-for-byte identical to the version you fed the AutoLinker to be indexed.

The AutoLinker is given a list of all of the possible link targets (the terms being defined); it runs each term as a query to see if it occurs in the document of interest. The result at this stage is a list of matches that occur in the document being linked; the matches for each term look like this:

```
2 1 120 33 ChanServ.html
2 1 116 37 EFnet.html
2 1 113 46 IRC-Network.html
2 2 0 48 IRC-Server.html
2 1 119 52 IRC.html
2 2 0 52 IRC.html
2 2 31 64 MemoServ.html
. . .
```

The fields are Number of Words in Phrase (two in this case, because these are all matches for the phrase IRC Network); Block in File and Word in Block (which locate the match), File Number, and Filename. The actual phrase is appended to each match using *sed*, giving a list of all the matches for each glossary term. This long list is then sorted by file number so that all the matches for a given document (MemoServ.html, for example) appear together, rather than all of the matches for a given glossary term.

Next, hypertext links are added to this list of matches, using a short Perl script that also removes overlaps (described shortly). The result is a list of matches like this:

```
2 1 120 33 ChanServ.html #<a href="ChanServ.html">##</a>
2 1 116 37 EFnet.html   #<a href="EFnet.html">##</a>
```

```
2 1 113 46 IRC-Network.html  #<a href="IRC-Network.html">##</a>
2 2 0 48 IRC-Server.html  #<span class="glossref">##</span>
2 1 119 52 IRC.html  #<a href="IRC.html">##</a>
2 2 0 52 IRC.html  #<a href="IRC.html">##</a>
2 2 31 64 MemoServ.html  #<a href="MemoServ.html">##</a>
 . . .
```

Next, we use the *lqsed* program to combine the list of matches with the original document. This is a program that reads matches augmented with left and right replacement strings, and prints a copy of the matched document with each match surrounded by the corresponding left and right strings. This produces the following result for the entry IRC Server (which contains the phrase "IRC network"):

`<DL><DT><span class="glossref">`IRC Server`</span></DT>`

`<DD>`A `<a  href="server.html">`server`</a>` (q.v.) that is part of an `<a href="IRC-Network.html">`IRC network`</a>`; most `<span class ="glossref">` IRC servers`</span>` are on computers running some version of the `<a href="Unix.html">`Unix`</a>` operating system, such as `<a href="Linux.html">`Linux`</a>`, FreeBSD or Sun's Solaris. The most common `<span class="glossref">`IRC Servers`</span>` are from `<a href ="EFnet.html">`EFnet`</a>`, `<a href="Undernet.html">`Undernet`</a>` and `<a  href="DALnet.html">`DALnet`</a>`, and are called hybrid, ircu and `<a href="ircd.html">`ircd`</a>` (or "Bahamut") respectively.`</DD>` `</DL>`

There's a lot of markup there, and you can see why you wouldn't want to maintain it by hand!

Overlapping Matches

An important problem to avoid is illustrated by the case where you have an entry for Internet Relay Chat and another for Chat Server. The resulting markup might look like this:

```
<a href="internet-relay-chat.html">Internet
Relay <a href="chat-server.html">Chat</a> Server</a>
```

This is not good, since overlapping hypertext links are not allowed in HTML at all, and are at best confusing. Avoid adding the markup shown in bold.

Fortunately, *lqkwic* can generate byte offsets in the match list, and this makes it easy to remove overlapping matches. Another approach is to use an option to the *lqsed* command to prevent overlaps.

NOTE

If you are not using *lq-text*, the same scheme should still work, but you may have to reimplement the *lqsed* program.

One or All?

It doesn't take long to process the entire glossary every time an entry is added or changed, so that's what the AutoLinker does for the glossary example. For other data, it may be faster to update just a single document. If performance is a real issue, most text retrieval packages support a C or C++ API.

Search the Glossary

Once you've built an index to all of the files, you might as well use it! Modern text retrieval packages might already include Web interfaces; or it might take only an hour or two to write one.

Other AutoLinker Applications

Although an interactive Web-based glossary is a fun example and makes it possible for you to go and try it out, there are many other applications where mining data for links can be useful.

Document Conversion

I was once faced with the problem of converting an encyclopedia into SGML, including all the cross-references. The cross-references were generally marked with "See" or "See Also," and a Perl script easily found them. The problem was how to find the right entry. In most cases, it was unambiguous—the "See Also:" marker might be followed by "France" or "Sock Manufacture." But in a few thousand cases, there were multiple words after the marker, most of which required human intervention.

Text retrieval showed which of the several candidate entries had the most words in common with the source containing the marker, and the candidates were sorted accordingly. As a result, the handwork was reduced drastically—the correct link was almost always the first one.

Textual Analysis

Consider the possibilities of being able to answer questions such as: "Which of the companies mentioned in this annual report have high stock values today?" "Which cities are mentioned in our survey but have no database entry?","Which links to repair tasks point to tasks with no words in common with the paragraph containing the link?" Some of these questions can be answered with tools such as Perl and Omnimark; others can be answered using text retrieval.

AutoLinker Summary

Links between a database and a text retrieval system enable entire areas of exploration that are difficult with only one or the other technology. The capability of the text retrieval system to find embedded phrases very quickly is a good complement to the database's ability to sort and select from items based on exact values.

BookWeb

BookWeb is a database application for identifying books based on names mentioned in them. People submit lists of names from books, and as these are added to the database, the application's utility grows.

This book addresses only a fraction of the ideas behind BookWeb. The software is evolving as well; design changes may mean the actual application is implemented differently.

At the time of this writing, BookWeb uses a relational database (MySQL) to store the tables given in Part One. A Web interface uses PHP for database queries.

XML is used in two areas:

- To store book reviews and other longer prose.
- To store the lists of names that users enter, until a human moderator approves them.

The XML in both cases is stored outside the database. The lists are written by a PHP script and (once approved) are processed using a Perl program with XML::Parser and the Perl DBI module.

Users can search BookWeb to see which books mention a particular name, or browse by author. In addition, links to book reviews and other items are added to database results on the fly by including external files. This application uses a mixture of a relational database, flat files, text retrieval, and XML parsing, glued together by Perl and/or PHP scripts.

A Perl script processes saved XML book reviews, use the Perl DBI module to connect to MySQL, and checks and expands references to books before the human moderator sees the review, adding links in much the same way as the AutoLinker. This saves the moderator time and helps to create a richer Web, with more hypertext links, when the reviews are published.

Experiments are also under way to use a "network of trust" system (see www.advogato.org for an example of this) in which reviewers can be granted trusted status by other reviewers, to increase the number of people able to add content to the database.

Storing linked documents as XML can provide great flexibility in how the information is used and delivered. A good text retrieval package belongs in your toolkit, alongside a working knowledge of SQL, even if you don't use it every day. An understanding of how to use the tools *together* to process links and metadata is even more useful.

NOTE

Note, BookWeb is currently undergoing a name change, and this book's companion Web site, www.wiley.com/compbooks/quin, will have a pointer to the current name and URL.

Summary

We have looked in some detail at the AutoLinker, because it's an unusual application. At this point, you can probably go out and write similar projects in an afternoon. Now is the time to do that!

This chapter marks the end of the main book. The chapters in Part Five, "Resource Guide," contain pointers to additional reading, online material, screenshots, program documentation, and much more.

Resource Guide

Part Five is where the references and tools live. You'll find pointers here to software, documentation, conferences, mailing lists, tutorials, newsgroups, IRC channels, and additional writings.

Chapter 19, "Open Source Licenses." Explains some of the goals of Open Source development, and describes the more common licenses that are used for free software (meaning you are free to change it). Before incorporating software into commercial or other projects, you need to make sure the licenses of all components are suitable. This chapter also reprints some of the more common licenses, to help you understand them.

Chapter 20, "Installing and Configuring Downloaded Software." Offers tips about how to install software you'll find on the Net, and gives pointers to additional information. If you are already familiar with building software, including tools such as *apt-get*, *gnorpm*, *configure*, and *make*, you can safely skip this chapter.

Chapter 21, "XML Parsers, Editors, and Utilities." Overviews the more common XML libraries and tools you can use, including browsers and formatting software.

Chapter 22, "Databases, Repositories, and Utilities." References relational, object-oriented, and text retrieval databases; includes a section on *ndbm*-style hashing databases. Document and content management systems are mentioned too, although most of these are commercial.

Chapter 23, "Further Reading." Lists various sources where you can find out more about the topics discussed throughout this book, including online documentation, books, magazines, and mailing lists.

## CHAPTER 19

Open Source Licenses

How software is distributed and licensed has become very important. Some packages are distributed complete with source, some are not; you can resell some and not others; some are free of charge, and others are not. It is important to understand the license terms of software you use, particularly if you are building a product out of other components. This chapter starts with a brief overview of each license, and then gives the text of some of the more common ones. The remainder of the chapters in this part of the book, "Resource Guide," mentions the license used for each product, wherever possible, so that you can check it easily.

A couple of caveats before we begin:

- A number of these licenses are not intended to be easy to read by people who (like me!) are not lawyers. If you are making a product to sell, hire professional legal advice. None of the material in this chapter should be regarded as legal advice.

- Most software licenses are written in the United States. This means that they may or may not carry any legal weight outside the United States. Many commercial licenses state that by opening an envelope you agree to the terms of the license, for example. This has not been tested in courts in the United Kingdom; and in Canada, at least one piece of commercial software was ruled to be protected neither by its license nor by copyright law.

The best way to approach any license is probably as an indication of how the author or supplier of the software would like it to be treated. The following sections summarize the main distribution terms in use today.

What Is Open Source?

Eric Raymond, author of the widely read article "The Cathedral and the Bazaar" on software development, has been a vocal champion for Open Source. He (and others) realized that the concept of free software needed to be marketed, and so created the "brand name" Open Source along with the Web site, www.opensource.org/. An account of this is given in the book *Open Sources: Voices from the Open Source Revolution*, edited by Chris DiBona, Sam Ockman, and Mark Stone (O'Reilly, 1999).

The Open Source Definition given at the opensource.org Web site is an attempt to nail down exactly what is meant by Open Source; in addition, you can get copies of most or all of the licenses in this chapter there. It is based on a document called "The Debian Free Software Guidelines," written by Bruce Perens in 1997 for the Debian Linux project.

The version here (1.7) is reprinted from www.opensource.org/ with the permission of Eric Raymond. And, note, the OSD and Rationale sections have been combined, with excerpts from the latter set in italics.

Open Source Definition (Version 1.7)

The intent of the Open Source Definition is to write down a concrete set of criteria that we believe capture the essence of what the software development community wants "Open Source" to mean—criteria that ensure that software distributed under an open-source license will be available for independent peer review and continuous evolutionary improvement and selection, reaching levels of reliability and power no closed product can attain.

For the evolutionary process to work, we have to counter short-term incentives for people to stop contributing to the software gene pool. This means the license terms must prevent people from locking up software where very few people can see or modify it.

When software developers distribute their software under OSI approved software licenses, they can apply the "OSI Certified" mark to that software. This certification mark informs users of that software that the license complies with the intent of the Open Source Definition. More information about our certification mark and program is available [on the Web site].

Open source doesn't just mean access to the source code. The distribution terms of open-source software must comply with the following criteria:

1. Free Redistribution

The license may not restrict any party from selling or giving away the software as a component of an aggregate software distribution containing programs from several different sources. The license may not require a royalty or other fee for such sale.

By constraining the license to require free redistribution, we eliminate the temptation to throw away many long-term gains in order to make a few short-term sales dollars. If we didn't do this, there would be lots of pressure for cooperators to defect.

2. Source Code

The program must include source code, and must allow distribution in source code as well as compiled form. Where some form of a product is not distributed with source code, there must be a well-publicized means of obtaining the source code for no more than a reasonable reproduction cost—preferably, downloading via the Internet without charge. The source code must be the preferred form in which a programmer would modify the program. Deliberately obfuscated source code is not allowed. Intermediate forms such as the output of a preprocessor or translator are not allowed.

We require access to unobfuscated source code because you can't evolve programs without modifying them. Since our purpose is to make evolution easy, we require that modification be made easy.

3. Derived Works

The license must allow modifications and derived works, and must allow them to be distributed under the same terms as the license of the original software.

The mere ability to read source isn't enough to support independent peer review and rapid evolutionary selection. For rapid evolution to happen, people need to be able to experiment with and redistribute modifications.

4. Integrity of the Author's Source Code

The license may restrict source code from being distributed in modified form only if the license allows the distribution of "patch files" with the source code for the purpose of modifying the program at build time. The license must explicitly permit distribution of software built from modified source code. The license may require derived works to carry a different name or version number from the original software.

Encouraging lots of improvement is a good thing, but users have a right to know who is responsible for the software they are using. Authors and maintainers have reciprocal rights to know what they're being asked to support and protect their reputations. Accordingly, an open-source license must guarantee that source be readily available, but may require that it be distributed as pristine base sources plus patches. In this way, "unofficial" changes can be made available but readily distinguished from the base source.

5. No Discrimination Against Persons or Groups

The license must not discriminate against any person or group of persons.

In order to get the maximum benefit from the process, the maximum diversity of persons and groups should be equally eligible to contribute to open sources. Therefore we forbid any open-source license from locking anybody out of the process.

Some countries, including the United States, have export restrictions for certain types of software. An OSD-conformant license may warn licensees of applicable restrictions and remind them that they are obliged to obey the law; however, it may not incorporate such restrictions itself.

6. No Discrimination Against Fields of Endeavor

The license must not restrict anyone from making use of the program in a specific field of endeavor. For example, it may not restrict the program from being used in a business or from being used for genetic research.

The major intention of this clause is to prohibit license traps that prevent open source from being used commercially. We want commercial users to join our community, not feel excluded from it.

7. Distribution of License

The rights attached to the program must apply to all to whom the program is redistributed without the need for execution of an additional license by those parties.

This clause is intended to forbid closing up software by indirect means such as requiring a nondisclosure agreement.

8. License Must Not Be Specific to a Product

The rights attached to the program must not depend on the program's being part of a particular software distribution. If the program is extracted from that distribution and used or distributed within the terms of the program's license, all parties to whom the program is redistributed should have the same rights as those that are granted in conjunction with the original software distribution.

This clause forecloses yet another class of license traps.

9. License Must Not Contaminate Other Software

The license must not place restrictions on other software that is distributed along with the licensed software. For example, the license must not insist that all other programs distributed on the same medium must be open-source software.

Distributors of open-source software have the right to make their own choices about their own software.

Yes, the GPL is conformant with this requirement. GPLed libraries "contaminate" only software to which they will actively be linked at runtime, not software with which they are merely distributed.

The following text is also from the OSD Web page, but is not part of the actual Open Source Definition.

We think the Open Source Definition captures what the great majority of the software community originally meant, and still mean, by the term "Open Source." However, the term has become widely used and its meaning has lost some precision. The OSI Certified mark is OSI's way of certifying that the license under which the software is distributed conforms to the OSD; the generic term "Open Source" cannot provide that assurance, but we still encourage use of the term "Open Source" to mean conformance to the OSD. For information about the OSI Certified mark, and for a list of licenses that OSI has approved as conforming to the OSD, see www.opensource.org/licenses/ certification-mark.html.

Bruce Perens wrote the first draft of this document as "The Debian Free Software Guidelines," and refined it using the comments of the Debian developers in a month-long e-mail conference in June, 1997. He removed the Debian-specific references from the document to create the "Open Source Definition."

Send questions or suggestions about this page to webmaster@opensource.org.

The Licenses

The following sections briefly describe each license. The more important are then reprinted in full, so that, if necessary, you can delve into them in some detail.

Public Domain Software

In the early days of Unix, software was shared freely among sites that held source licenses for the operating system. Many people distributed add-on software with no restrictions whatsoever, placing it in the public domain. You can do anything you like with public domain software; you can even say you wrote it, and although that's somewhat reprehensible, the author has no recourse against you.

Public domain software is not licensed, of course, but like anything else published, published software is copyrighted unless it *explicitly* says that it is in the public domain.

Unfortunately, someone can take a piece of public domain software, improve it, and refuse to distribute the source to the improved version. The software is then restricted, and in that sense is no longer free. Most open source software licenses are an attempt to prevent this.

The GNU Copyleft (GPL, GPV)

When Richard Stallman started the Free Software Foundation (FSF) and its "GNU is not Unix" project, he wanted information to have the "right" to be "free," that is, to be unimpeded by restrictions. As a consequence, he said that people could not charge money for his software, and must always give the source away so that the recipients could make any changes they wanted to.

The first version of the GNU Public License went even further, and said that if you used GNU software as part of a larger project, even just distributing it on the same tape, the entire of the larger project became covered by the GNU license. For this reason, you will still see people sometimes refer to it as the GNU Public Virus, the GPV.

The second version of the GNU Public License is much less virulent, and GNU programs can now coexist with other software more or less problem-free. The GPL, as it's known to its friends, is the license that implements Richard Stallman's idea of so-called Copyleft (a pun on copyright), ensuring that software can be changed by anyone. Furthermore, if you make a changed version of GNU software, you must redistribute the changes under the same terms and conditions.

The GNU Library License (LGPL)

If you take a piece of code covered by the GNU Public License and include it in another program, whether by copying the code or by linking against a library, the resulting program is covered by the GPL. This is clearly not acceptable for system libraries such as *libc*, and so the Library GNU License (LGPL) was developed. It's very similar to the GPL, except that it doesn't spread to other software so easily.

You can link a piece of code against a library covered by the LGPL and then sell the resulting code.

The Perl Artistic License

Larry Wall wanted Perl to be free of restrictions, but also wanted people to be able to use Perl in commercial projects, so rather than use the GNU Public License, he wrote his own, which is short and easy to understand.

The BSD License

The University of California at Berkeley was an early adopter of the Unix operating system. It modified Unix to support a more efficient virtual memory system (demand paging), and distributed its changes freely to other Unix license holders. Eventually, it produced a version of the Berkeley Software Distribution (BSD) that was entirely free of proprietary Unix code; and 4.4 BSD was released under the BSD license.

This license lets you do pretty much anything you want with the code, though earlier versions of it required that you display a notice giving due credit to the Regents of the University of California. For this reason, many people use either the MIT X License (described later), or a later (or modified) BSD license when they release free software. The latest versions of the BSD license do not have the "advertising clause," and are now very similar to the X Window System license.

The MIT (X Window System) License

The X Window System (popularly, but incorrectly, called X Windows) was developed at the Massachusetts Institute of Technology and released publicly to encourage widespread adoption. This policy succeeded: The technically superior but non-free Sun NeWS system is now history. If you modify a program distributed under the MIT X license, you can keep your modified version to yourself or sell it, which is not possible with a program distributed under the GPL. This means that manufacturers of video cards can keep their drivers secret and still support the X Window system; it is also useful for other software. The MIT license is one of the easiest to understand.

My *lq-text* package is distributed under the Barefoot License which is based on the C-News license by Henry Spencer and Geoff Collyer, which in turn derives from the BSD and X licenses.

The Mozilla Public License

This license is included here for two main reasons. First, it is widely used, even though that is not always appropriate. Second, Mozilla is one of the most influential recent open source projects, and is an excellent example of a large software company releasing their source code.

The license was created specifically for Mozilla, the Open Source version of Netscape's Web browser. It is complex, however, because Netscape's existing browser had complex licensing issues, so be sure to look at the BSD, X, and GNU licenses for new code. If you are considering using Mozilla or other code using the "MPL" in your own project, though, you may well end up using the MPL for the entire project.

The Barefoot License

The final license covered here is that used by me for software I have released. It is based on the MIT and BSD licenses, but requires that people contact the author before making commercial use of the software. A proposed version requires licensees to take their shoes off, mostly to test whether anyone actually reads licenses.

The GNU General Public License

Version 2, June 1991, Copyright (C) 1989, 1991 Free Software Foundation, Inc. 675 Mass Ave, Cambridge, MA, 02139, USA. Everyone is permitted to copy and distribute verbatim copies of this license document, but changing it is not allowed.

Preamble

The licenses for most software are designed to take away your freedom to share and change it. By contrast, the GNU General Public License is intended to guarantee your freedom to share and change free software—to make sure the software is free for all its users. This General Public License applies to most of the Free Software Foundation's software and to any other program whose authors commit to using it. (Some other Free Software Foundation software is covered by the GNU Library General Public License instead.) You can apply it to your programs, too.

When we speak of free software, we are referring to freedom, not price. Our General Public Licenses are designed to make sure that you have the freedom to distribute copies of free software (and charge for this service if you wish), that you receive source code or can get it if you want it, that you can change the software or use pieces of it in new free programs; and that you know you can do these things.

To protect your rights, we need to make restrictions that forbid anyone to deny you these rights or to ask you to surrender the rights. These restrictions translate to certain responsibilities for you if you distribute copies of the software, or if you modify it.

For example, if you distribute copies of such a program, whether gratis or for a fee, you must give the recipients all the rights that you have. You must make sure that they, too, receive or can get the source code. And you must show them these terms so they know their rights.

We protect your rights with two steps: (1) copyright the software, and (2) offer you this license, which gives you legal permission to copy, distribute, and/or modify the software.

Also, for each author's protection and ours, we want to make certain that everyone understands that there is no warranty for this free software. If the software is modified by someone else and passed on, we want its recipients to know that what they have is not the original, so that any problems introduced by others will not reflect on the original authors' reputations.

Finally, any free program is threatened constantly by software patents. We wish to avoid the danger that redistributors of a free program will individually obtain patent licenses, in effect making the program proprietary. To prevent this, we have made it clear that any patent must be licensed for everyone's free use or not licensed at all.

The precise terms and conditions for copying, distribution and modification follow.

Terms and Conditions for Copying, Distribution, and Modification

0. This License applies to any program or other work which contains a notice placed by the copyright holder saying it may be distributed under the terms of this General Public License. The "Program," below, refers to any such program or work, and a "work based on the Program" means either the Program or any derivative work under copyright law; that is to say, a work containing the Program or a portion of it, either verbatim or with modifications and/or translated into another language. (Hereinafter, translation is included without limitation in the term "modification.") Each licensee is addressed as "you."

   Activities other than copying, distribution, and modification are not covered by this License; they are outside its scope. The act of running the Program is not restricted, and the output from the Program is covered only if its contents constitute a work based on the Program (independent of having been made by running the Program). Whether that is true depends on what the Program does.

1. You may copy and distribute verbatim copies of the Program's source code as you receive it, in any medium, provided that you conspicuously and appropriately publish on each copy an appropriate copyright notice and disclaimer of warranty; keep intact all the notices that refer to this License and to the absence of any warranty; and give any other recipients of the Program a copy of this License along with the Program.

   You may charge a fee for the physical act of transferring a copy, and you may at your option offer warranty protection in exchange for a fee.

2. You may modify your copy or copies of the Program or any portion of it, thus forming a work based on the Program, and copy and distribute such modifications or work under the terms of Section 1 above, provided that you also meet all of these conditions:

   a) You must cause the modified files to carry prominent notices stating that you changed the files and the date of any change.

   b) You must cause any work that you distribute or publish, that in whole or in part contains or is derived from the Program or any part thereof, to be licensed as a whole at no charge to all third parties under the terms of this License.

   c) If the modified program normally reads commands interactively when run, you must cause it, when started running for such interactive use in the most ordinary way, to print or display an announcement including an appropriate copyright notice and a notice that there is no warranty (or else, saying that you provide a warranty) and that users may redistribute the program under these conditions, and telling the user how to view a copy of this License. (Exception: If the Program itself is interactive but does not normally print such an announcement, your work based on the Program is not required to print an announcement.)

   These requirements apply to the modified work as a whole. If identifiable sections of that work are not derived from the Program, and can be reasonably considered independent and separate works in themselves, then this License, and its terms, do not apply to those sections when you distribute them as separate works. But when you distribute the same sections as part of a whole which is a work based on the Program, the distribution of the whole must be on the terms of this License, whose permissions for other licensees extend to the entire whole, and thus to each and every part regardless of who wrote it.

   Thus, it is not the intent of this section to claim rights or contest your rights to work written entirely by you; rather, the intent is to exercise the right to control the distribution of derivative or collective works based on the Program.

In addition, mere aggregation of another work not based on the Program with the Program (or with a work based on the Program) on a volume of a storage or distribution medium does not bring the other work under the scope of this License.

3. You may copy and distribute the Program (or a work based on it, under Section 2) in object code or executable form under the terms of Sections 1 and 2 above provided that you also do one of the following:

   a) Accompany it with the complete corresponding machine-readable source code, which must be distributed under the terms of Sections 1 and 2 above on a medium customarily used for software interchange; or,

   b) Accompany it with a written offer, valid for at least three years, to give any third party, for a charge no more than your cost of physically performing source distribution, a complete machine-readable copy of the corresponding source code, to be distributed under the terms of Sections 1 and 2 above on a medium customarily used for software interchange; or,

   c) Accompany it with the information you received as to the offer to distribute corresponding source code. (This alternative is allowed only for noncommercial distribution and only if you received the program in object code or executable form with such an offer, in accord with Subsection b above.)

   The source code for a work means the preferred form of the work for making modifications to it. For an executable work, complete source code means all the source code for all modules it contains, plus any associated interface definition files, plus the scripts used to control compilation and installation of the executable. However, as a special exception, the source code distributed need not include anything that is normally distributed (in either source or binary form) with the major components (compiler, kernel, and so on) of the operating system on which the executable runs, unless that component itself accompanies the executable.

   If distribution of executable or object code is made by offering access to copy from a designated place, then offering equivalent access to copy the source code from the same place counts as distribution of the source code, even though third parties are not compelled to copy the source along with the object code.

4. You may not copy, modify, sublicense, or distribute the Program except as expressly provided under this License. Any attempt otherwise to copy, modify, sublicense or distribute the Program is void, and will automatically terminate your rights under this License. However, parties who have

received copies, or rights, from you under this License will not have their licenses terminated so long as such parties remain in full compliance.

5. You are not required to accept this License, since you have not signed it. However, nothing else grants you permission to modify or distribute the Program or its derivative works. These actions are prohibited by law if you do not accept this License. Therefore, by modifying or distributing the Program (or any work based on the Program), you indicate your acceptance of this License to do so, and all its terms and conditions for copying, distributing or modifying the Program or works based on it.

6. Each time you redistribute the Program (or any work based on the Program), the recipient automatically receives a license from the original licensor to copy, distribute, or modify the Program subject to these terms and conditions. You may not impose any further restrictions on the recipients' exercise of the rights granted herein. You are not responsible for enforcing compliance by third parties to this License.

7. If, as a consequence of a court judgment or allegation of patent infringement or for any other reason (not limited to patent issues), conditions are imposed on you (whether by court order, agreement or otherwise) that contradict the conditions of this License, they do not excuse you from the conditions of this License. If you cannot distribute so as to satisfy simultaneously your obligations under this License and any other pertinent obligations, then as a consequence you may not distribute the Program at all. For example, if a patent license would not permit royalty-free redistribution of the Program by all those who receive copies directly or indirectly through you, then the only way you could satisfy both it and this License would be to refrain entirely from distribution of the Program.

If any portion of this section is held invalid or unenforceable under any particular circumstance, the balance of the section is intended to apply and the section as a whole is intended to apply in other circumstances.

It is not the purpose of this section to induce you to infringe any patents or other property right claims or to contest validity of any such claims; this section has the sole purpose of protecting the integrity of the free software distribution system, which is implemented by public license practices. Many people have made generous contributions to the wide range of software distributed through that system in reliance on consistent application of that system; it is up to the author/donor to decide if he or she is willing to distribute software through any other system and a licensee cannot impose that choice.

This section is intended to make thoroughly clear what is believed to be a consequence of the rest of this License.

8. If the distribution and/or use of the Program is restricted in certain countries either by patents or by copyrighted interfaces, the original copyright holder who places the Program under this License may add an explicit geographical distribution limitation excluding those countries, so that distribution is permitted only in or among countries not thus excluded. In such case, this License incorporates the limitation as if written in the body of this License.

9. The Free Software Foundation may publish revised and/or new versions of the General Public License from time to time. Such new versions will be similar in spirit to the present version, but may differ in detail to address new problems or concerns.

   Each version is given a distinguishing version number. If the Program specifies a version number of this License which applies to it and "any later version," you have the option of following the terms and conditions either of that version or of any later version published by the Free Software Foundation. If the Program does not specify a version number of this License, you may choose any version ever published by the Free Software Foundation.

10. If you wish to incorporate parts of the Program into other free programs whose distribution conditions are different, write to the author to ask for permission. For software that is copyrighted by the Free Software Foundation, write to the Free Software Foundation; we sometimes make exceptions for this. Our decision will be guided by the two goals of preserving the free status of all derivatives of our free software and of promoting the sharing and reuse of software generally. NO WARRANTY.

11. BECAUSE THE PROGRAM IS LICENSED FREE OF CHARGE, THERE IS NO WARRANTY FOR THE PROGRAM, TO THE EXTENT PERMITTED BY APPLICABLE LAW. EXCEPT WHEN OTHERWISE STATED IN WRITING, THE COPYRIGHT HOLDERS AND/OR OTHER PARTIES PROVIDE THE PROGRAM "AS IS" WITHOUT WARRANTY OF ANY KIND, EITHER EXPRESSED OR IMPLIED, INCLUDING, BUT NOT LIMITED TO, THE IMPLIED WARRANTIES OF MERCHANTABILITY AND FITNESS FOR A PARTICULAR PURPOSE. THE ENTIRE RISK AS TO THE QUALITY AND PERFORMANCE OF THE PROGRAM IS WITH YOU. SHOULD THE PROGRAM PROVE DEFECTIVE, YOU ASSUME THE COST OF ALL NECESSARY SERVICING, REPAIR, OR CORRECTION.

12. IN NO EVENT UNLESS REQUIRED BY APPLICABLE LAW OR AGREED TO IN WRITING WILL ANY COPYRIGHT HOLDER, OR ANY OTHER PARTY WHO MAY MODIFY AND/OR REDISTRIBUTE THE PROGRAM AS PERMITTED ABOVE, BE LIABLE TO YOU FOR DAMAGES, INCLUDING ANY GENERAL, SPECIAL, INCIDENTAL, OR CONSEQUENTIAL DAMAGES ARISING OUT OF THE USE OR INABILITY TO USE THE PROGRAM (INCLUDING BUT NOT LIMITED TO LOSS OF DATA OR DATA BEING RENDERED INACCURATE OR LOSSES SUSTAINED BY YOU OR THIRD PARTIES OR A FAILURE OF THE PROGRAM TO

OPERATE WITH ANY OTHER PROGRAMS), EVEN IF SUCH HOLDER OR OTHER PARTY HAS BEEN ADVISED OF THE POSSIBILITY OF SUCH DAMAGES.

END OF TERMS AND CONDITIONS

The GNU Lesser General Public License (LGPL)

Version 2.1, February 1999 (The master copy of this license lives on the GNU Web site [http://www.gnu.org/copyleft/lesser.html]).

Copyright (C) 1991, 1999 Free Software Foundation, Inc. 59 Temple Place, Suite 330, Boston, MA 02111-1307 USA.

Everyone is permitted to copy and distribute verbatim copies of this license document, but changing it is not allowed.

[This is the first released version of the Lesser GPL. It also counts as the successor of the GNU Library Public License, version 2, hence the version number 2.1.]

Preamble

The licenses for most software are designed to take away your freedom to share and change it. By contrast, the GNU General Public Licenses are intended to guarantee your freedom to share and change free software—to make sure the software is free for all its users.

This license, the Lesser General Public License, applies to some specially designated software packages—typically libraries—of the Free Software Foundation and other authors who decide to use it. You can use it too, but we suggest you first think carefully about whether this license or the ordinary General Public License is the better strategy to use in any particular case, based on the explanations below.

When we speak of free software, we are referring to freedom of use, not price. Our General Public Licenses are designed to make sure that you have the freedom to distribute copies of free software (and charge for this service if you wish); that you receive source code or can get it if you want it; that you can change the software and use pieces of it in new free programs; and that you are informed that you can do these things.

To protect your rights, we need to make restrictions that forbid distributors to deny you these rights or to ask you to surrender these rights. These restrictions translate to certain responsibilities for you if you distribute copies of the library or if you modify it.

For example, if you distribute copies of the library, whether gratis or for a fee, you must give the recipients all the rights that we gave you. You must make sure that they, too, receive or can get the source code. If you link other code with the library, you must provide complete object files to the recipients, so that they can relink them with the library after making changes to the library and recompiling it. And you must show them these terms so they know their rights.

We protect your rights with a two-step method: (1) We copyright the library, and (2) we offer you this license, which gives you legal permission to copy, distribute and/or modify the library.

To protect each distributor, we want to make it very clear that there is no warranty for the free library. Also, if the library is modified by someone else and passed on, the recipients should know that what they have is not the original version, so that the original author's reputation will not be affected by problems that might be introduced by others.

Finally, software patents pose a constant threat to the existence of any free program. We wish to make sure that a company cannot effectively restrict the users of a free program by obtaining a restrictive license from a patent holder. Therefore, we insist that any patent license obtained for a version of the library must be consistent with the full freedom of use specified in this license.

Most GNU software, including some libraries, is covered by the ordinary GNU General Public License. This license, the GNU Lesser General Public License, applies to certain designated libraries, and is quite different from the ordinary General Public License. We use this license for certain libraries in order to permit linking those libraries into nonfree programs.

When a program is linked with a library, whether statically or using a shared library, the combination of the two is legally speaking a combined work, a derivative of the original library. The ordinary General Public License therefore permits such linking only if the entire combination fits its criteria of freedom. The Lesser General Public License permits more lax criteria for linking other code with the library.

We call this license the "Lesser" General Public License because it does less to protect the user's freedom than the ordinary General Public License. It also provides other free software developers less of an advantage over competing non-free programs. These disadvantages are the reason we use the ordinary General Public License for many libraries. However, the Lesser license provides advantages in certain special circumstances.

For example, on rare occasions, there may be a special need to encourage the widest possible use of a certain library, so that it becomes a de-facto standard. To achieve this, non-free programs must be allowed to use the library. A more frequent case is that a free library does the same job as widely used non-free libraries. In this case, there is little to gain by limiting the free library to free software only, so we use the Lesser General Public License.

In other cases, permission to use a particular library in non-free programs enables a greater number of people to use a large body of free software. For example, permission to use the GNU C Library in non-free programs enables many more people to use the whole GNU operating system, as well as its variant, the GNU/Linux operating system.

Although the Lesser General Public License is less protective of the users' freedom, it does ensure that the user of a program that is linked with the Library has the freedom and the wherewithal to run that program using a modified version of the Library.

The precise terms and conditions for copying, distribution and modification follow. Pay close attention to the difference between a "work based on the library" and a "work that uses the library". The former contains code derived from the library, whereas the latter must be combined with the library in order to run.

Terms and Conditions for Copying, Distribution, and Modification

0. This License Agreement applies to any software library or other program which contains a notice placed by the copyright holder or other authorized party saying it may be distributed under the terms of this Lesser General Public License (also called "this License"). Each licensee is addressed as "you".

   A "library" means a collection of software functions and/or data prepared so as to be conveniently linked with application programs (which use some of those functions and data) to form executables.

   The "Library", below, refers to any such software library or work which has been distributed under these terms. A "work based on the Library" means either the Library or any derivative work under copyright law: that is to say, a work containing the Library or a portion of it, either verbatim or with modifications and/or translated straightforwardly into another language. (Hereinafter, translation is included without limitation in the term "modification".)

   "Source code" for a work means the preferred form of the work for making modifications to it. For a library, complete source code means all the source code for all modules it contains, plus any associated interface definition files, plus the scripts used to control compilation and installation of the library.

Activities other than copying, distribution and modification are not covered by this License; they are outside its scope. The act of running a program using the Library is not restricted, and output from such a program is covered only if its contents constitute a work based on the Library (independent of the use of the Library in a tool for writing it). Whether that is true depends on what the Library does and what the program that uses the Library does.

1. You may copy and distribute verbatim copies of the Library's complete source code as you receive it, in any medium, provided that you conspicuously and appropriately publish on each copy an appropriate copyright notice and disclaimer of warranty; keep intact all the notices that refer to this License and to the absence of any warranty; and distribute a copy of this License along with the Library.

   You may charge a fee for the physical act of transferring a copy, and you may at your option offer warranty protection in exchange for a fee.

2. You may modify your copy or copies of the Library or any portion of it, thus forming a work based on the Library, and copy and distribute such modifications or work under the terms of Section 1 above, provided that you also meet all of these conditions:

   a) The modified work must itself be a software library.

   b) You must cause the files modified to carry prominent notices stating that you changed the files and the date of any change.

   c) You must cause the whole of the work to be licensed at no charge to all third parties under the terms of this License.

   d) If a facility in the modified Library refers to a function or a table of data to be supplied by an application program that uses the facility, other than as an argument passed when the facility is invoked, then you must make a good faith effort to ensure that, in the event an application does not supply such function or table, the facility still operates, and performs whatever part of its purpose remains meaningful.

   (For example, a function in a library to compute square roots has a purpose that is entirely well defined independent of the application. Therefore, Subsection 2d requires that any application-supplied function or table used by this function must be optional: If the application does not supply it, the square root function must still compute square roots.)

   These requirements apply to the modified work as a whole. If identifiable sections of that work are not derived from the Library, and can be reasonably considered independent and separate works in themselves, then this License, and its terms, do not apply to those sections when you distribute them as separate works. But when you distribute the same sections as part of a whole which is a work based on the Library, the distribution of the whole must be on the terms of this License, whose permissions for other licensees extend to the entire whole, and thus to each and every part regardless of who wrote it.

Thus, it is not the intent of this section to claim rights or contest your rights to work written entirely by you; rather, the intent is to exercise the right to control the distribution of derivative or collective works based on the Library.

In addition, mere aggregation of another work not based on the Library with the Library (or with a work based on the Library) on a volume of a storage or distribution medium does not bring the other work under the scope of this License.

3. You may opt to apply the terms of the ordinary GNU General Public License instead of this License to a given copy of the Library. To do this, you must alter all the notices that refer to this License, so that they refer to the ordinary GNU General Public License, version 2, instead of to this License. (If a newer version than version 2 of the ordinary GNU General Public License has appeared, then you can specify that version instead if you wish.) Do not make any other change in these notices.

    Once this change is made in a given copy, it is irreversible for that copy, so the ordinary GNU General Public License applies to all subsequent copies and derivative works made from that copy.

    This option is useful when you wish to copy part of the code of the Library into a program that is not a library.

4. You may copy and distribute the Library (or a portion or derivative of it, under Section 2) in object code or executable form under the terms of Sections 1 and 2 above provided that you accompany it with the complete corresponding machine-readable source code, which must be distributed under the terms of Sections 1 and 2 above on a medium customarily used for software interchange.

    If distribution of object code is made by offering access to copy from a designated place, then offering equivalent access to copy the source code from the same place satisfies the requirement to distribute the source code, even though third parties are not compelled to copy the source along with the object code.

5. A program that contains no derivative of any portion of the Library, but is designed to work with the Library by being compiled or linked with it, is called a "work that uses the Library." Such a work, in isolation, is not a derivative work of the Library, and therefore falls outside the scope of this License.

However, linking a "work that uses the Library" with the Library creates an executable that is a derivative of the Library (because it contains portions of the Library), rather than a "work that uses the library." The executable is therefore covered by this License. Section 6 states terms for distribution of such executables.

When a "work that uses the Library" uses material from a header file that is part of the Library, the object code for the work may be a derivative work of the Library even though the source code is not. Whether this is true is especially significant if the work can be linked without the Library, or if the work is itself a library. The threshold for this to be true is not precisely defined by law.

If such an object file uses only numerical parameters, data structure layouts and accessors, and small macros and small inline functions (ten lines or less in length), then the use of the object file is unrestricted, regardless of whether it is legally a derivative work. (Executables containing this object code plus portions of the Library will still fall under Section 6.)

Otherwise, if the work is a derivative of the Library, you may distribute the object code for the work under the terms of Section 6. Any executables containing that work also fall under Section 6, whether or not they are linked directly with the Library itself.

6. As an exception to the Sections above, you may also combine or link a "work that uses the Library" with the Library to produce a work containing portions of the Library, and distribute that work under terms of your choice, provided that the terms permit modification of the work for the customer's own use and reverse engineering for debugging such modifications.

You must give prominent notice with each copy of the work that the Library is used in it and that the Library and its use are covered by this License. You must supply a copy of this License. If the work during execution displays copyright notices, you must include the copyright notice for the Library among them, as well as a reference directing the user to the copy of this License. Also, you must do one of these things:

a) Accompany the work with the complete corresponding machine-readable source code for the Library including whatever changes were used in the work (which must be distributed under Sections 1 and 2 above); and, if the work is an executable linked with the Library, with the complete machine-readable "work that uses the Library," as object code and/or source code, so that the user can modify the Library and then relink to produce a modified executable containing the modified Library. (It is understood that the user who changes the contents of definitions files in the Library will not necessarily be able to recompile the application to use the modified definitions.)

b) Use a suitable shared library mechanism for linking with the Library. A suitable mechanism is one that (1) uses at run-time a copy of the library already present on the user's computer system, rather than copying library functions into the executable, and (2) will operate properly with a modified version of the library, if the user installs one, as long as the modified version is interface-compatible with the version that the work was made with.

c) Accompany the work with a written offer, valid for at least three years, to give the same user the materials specified in Subsection 6a, above, for a charge no more than the cost of performing this distribution.

d) If distribution of the work is made by offering access to copy from a designated place, offer equivalent access to copy the above specified materials from the same place.

e) Verify that the user has already received a copy of these materials or that you have already sent this user a copy.

For an executable, the required form of the "work that uses the Library" must include any data and utility programs needed for reproducing the executable from it. However, as a special exception, the materials to be distributed need not include anything that is normally distributed (in either source or binary form) with the major components (compiler, kernel, and so on) of the operating system on which the executable runs, unless that component itself accompanies the executable.

It may happen that this requirement contradicts the license restrictions of other proprietary libraries that do not normally accompany the operating system. Such a contradiction means you cannot use both them and the Library together in an executable that you distribute.

7. You may place library facilities that are a work based on the Library side-by-side in a single library together with other library facilities not covered by this License, and distribute such a combined library, provided that the separate distribution of the work based on the Library and of the other library facilities is otherwise permitted, and provided that you do these two things:

a) Accompany the combined library with a copy of the same work based on the Library, uncombined with any other library facilities. This must be distributed under the terms of the Sections above.

b) Give prominent notice with the combined library of the fact that part of it is a work based on the Library, and explaining where to find the accompanying uncombined form of the same work.

8. You may not copy, modify, sublicense, link with, or distribute the Library except as expressly provided under this License. Any attempt otherwise to copy, modify, sublicense, link with, or distribute the Library is void, and will automatically terminate your rights under this License. However, parties who have received copies, or rights, from you under this License will not have their licenses terminated so long as such parties remain in full compliance.

9. You are not required to accept this License, since you have not signed it. However, nothing else grants you permission to modify or distribute the Library or its derivative works. These actions are prohibited by law if you do not accept this License. Therefore, by modifying or distributing the Library (or any work based on the Library), you indicate your acceptance of this License to do so, and all its terms and conditions for copying, distributing or modifying the Library or works based on it.

10. Each time you redistribute the Library (or any work based on the Library), the recipient automatically receives a license from the original licensor to copy, distribute, link with, or modify the Library subject to these terms and conditions. You may not impose any further restrictions on the recipients' exercise of the rights granted herein. You are not responsible for enforcing compliance by third parties with this License.

11. If, as a consequence of a court judgment or allegation of patent infringement or for any other reason (not limited to patent issues), conditions are imposed on you (whether by court order, agreement, or otherwise) that contradict the conditions of this License, they do not excuse you from the conditions of this License. If you cannot distribute so as to satisfy simultaneously your obligations under this License and any other pertinent obligations, then as a consequence you may not distribute the Library at all. For example, if a patent license would not permit royalty-free redistribution of the Library by all those who receive copies directly or indirectly through you, then the only way you could satisfy both it and this License would be to refrain entirely from distribution of the Library.

If any portion of this section is held invalid or unenforceable under any particular circumstance, the balance of the section is intended to apply, and the section as a whole is intended to apply in other circumstances.

It is not the purpose of this section to induce you to infringe any patents or other property right claims or to contest validity of any such claims; this section has the sole purpose of protecting the integrity of the free software distribution system, which is implemented by public license practices. Many people have made generous contributions to the wide range of software distributed through that system in reliance on consistent application of that system; it is up to the author/donor to decide if he or she is willing to distribute software through any other system and a licensee cannot impose that choice.

This section is intended to make thoroughly clear what is believed to be a consequence of the rest of this License.

12. If the distribution and/or use of the Library is restricted in certain countries either by patents or by copyrighted interfaces, the original copyright holder who places the Library under this License may add an explicit geographical distribution limitation excluding those countries, so that distribution is permitted only in or among countries not thus excluded. In such case, this License incorporates the limitation as if written in the body of this License.

13. The Free Software Foundation may publish revised and/or new versions of the Lesser General Public License from time to time. Such new versions will be similar in spirit to the present version, but may differ in detail to address new problems or concerns.

Each version is given a distinguishing version number. If the Library specifies a version number of this License which applies to it and "any later version," you have the option of following the terms and conditions either of that version or of any later version published by the Free Software Foundation. If the Library does not specify a license version number, you may choose any version ever published by the Free Software Foundation.

14. If you wish to incorporate parts of the Library into other free programs whose distribution conditions are incompatible with these, write to the author to ask for permission. For software which is copyrighted by the Free Software Foundation, write to the Free Software Foundation; we sometimes make exceptions for this. Our decision will be guided by the two goals of preserving the free status of all derivatives of our free software and of promoting the sharing and reuse of software generally. NO WARRANTY.

15. BECAUSE THE LIBRARY IS LICENSED FREE OF CHARGE, THERE IS NO WARRANTY FOR THE LIBRARY, TO THE EXTENT PERMITTED BY APPLICABLE LAW. EXCEPT WHEN OTHERWISE STATED IN WRITING THE COPYRIGHT HOLDERS AND/OR OTHER PARTIES PROVIDE THE LIBRARY "AS IS" WITHOUT WARRANTY OF ANY KIND, EITHER EXPRESSED OR IMPLIED, INCLUDING, BUT NOT LIMITED TO, THE IMPLIED WARRANTIES OF MERCHANTABILITY AND FITNESS FOR A PARTICULAR PURPOSE. THE ENTIRE RISK AS TO THE QUALITY AND PERFORMANCE OF THE LIBRARY IS WITH YOU. SHOULD THE LIBRARY PROVE DEFECTIVE, YOU ASSUME THE COST OF ALL NECESSARY SERVICING, REPAIR OR CORRECTION.

16. IN NO EVENT, UNLESS REQUIRED BY APPLICABLE LAW OR AGREED TO IN WRITING, WILL ANY COPYRIGHT HOLDER, OR ANY OTHER PARTY WHO MAY MODIFY AND/OR REDISTRIBUTE THE LIBRARY AS PERMITTED ABOVE, BE LIABLE TO YOU FOR DAM-

AGES, INCLUDING ANY GENERAL, SPECIAL, INCIDENTAL, OR CONSEQUENTIAL DAM-
AGES ARISING OUT OF THE USE OR INABILITY TO USE THE LIBRARY (INCLUDING BUT
NOT LIMITED TO LOSS OF DATA OR DATA BEING RENDERED INACCURATE OR LOSSES
SUSTAINED BY YOU OR THIRD PARTIES OR A FAILURE OF THE LIBRARY TO OPERATE
WITH ANY OTHER SOFTWARE), EVEN IF SUCH HOLDER OR OTHER PARTY HAS BEEN
ADVISED OF THE POSSIBILITY OF SUCH DAMAGES.

END OF TERMS AND CONDITIONS

The Artistic License

This license is used for the Perl interpreter, and is therefore commonly known
as the Perl Artistic License.

Preamble

The intent of this document is to state the conditions under which a Package
may be copied, such that the Copyright Holder maintains some semblance of
artistic control over the development of the package, while giving the users of
the package the right to use and distribute the Package in a more-or-less cus-
tomary fashion, plus the right to make reasonable modifications.

Definitions

- "Package" refers to the collection of files distributed by the Copyright
  Holder, and derivatives of that collection of files created through textual
  modification.

- "Standard Version" refers to such a Package if it has not been modified, or
  has been modified in accordance with the wishes of the Copyright Holder.

- "Copyright Holder" is whoever is named in the copyright or copyrights
  for the package.

- "You" is you, if you're thinking about copying or distributing this Package.

- "Reasonable copying fee" is whatever you can justify on the basis of
  media cost, duplication charges, time of people involved, and so on. (You
  will not be required to justify it to the Copyright Holder, but only to the
  computing community at large as a market that must bear the fee.)

- "Freely Available" means that no fee is charged for the item itself, though
  there may be fees involved in handling the item. It also means that recipients of the item may redistribute it under the same conditions they
  received it.

1. You may make and give away verbatim copies of the source form of the Standard Version of this Package without restriction, provided that you duplicate all of the original copyright notices and associated disclaimers.

2. You may apply bug fixes, portability fixes, and other modifications derived from the Public Domain or from the Copyright Holder. A Package modified in such a way shall still be considered the Standard Version.

3. You may otherwise modify your copy of this Package in any way, provided that you insert a prominent notice in each changed file stating how and when you changed that file, and provided that you do at least ONE of the following:

    a) Place your modifications in the Public Domain or otherwise make them Freely Available, such as by posting said modifications to Usenet or an equivalent medium, or placing the modifications on a major archive site such as ftp.uu.net, or by allowing the Copyright Holder to include your modifications in the Standard Version of the Package.

    b) Use the modified Package only within your corporation or organization.

    c) Rename any nonstandard executables so the names do not conflict with standard executables, which must also be provided, and provide a separate manual page for each nonstandard executable that clearly documents how it differs from the Standard Version.

    d) Make other distribution arrangements with the Copyright Holder.

4. You may distribute the programs of this Package in object code or executable form, provided that you do at least ONE of the following:

    a) Distribute a Standard Version of the executables and library files, together with instructions (in the manual page or equivalent) on where to get the Standard Version.

    b) Accompany the distribution with the machine-readable source of the Package with your modifications.

    c) Accompany any nonstandard executables with their corresponding Standard Version executables, giving the nonstandard executables nonstandard names, and clearly documenting the differences in manual pages (or equivalent), together with instructions on where to get the Standard Version.

    d) Make other distribution arrangements with the Copyright Holder.

5. You may charge a reasonable copying fee for any distribution of this Package. You may charge any fee you choose for support of this Package. You may not charge a fee for this Package itself. However, you may distribute this Package in aggregate with other (possibly commercial) programs as part of a larger (possibly commercial) software distribution provided that you do not advertise this Package as a product of your own.

6. The scripts and library files supplied as input to or produced as output from the programs of this Package do not automatically fall under the copyright of this Package, but belong to whomever generated them, and may be sold commercially, and may be aggregated with this Package.

7. C or Perl subroutines supplied by you and linked into this Package shall not be considered part of this Package.

8. The name of the Copyright Holder may not be used to endorse or promote products derived from this software without specific prior written permission.

9. THIS PACKAGE IS PROVIDED "AS IS" AND WITHOUT ANY EXPRESS OR IMPLIED WARRANTIES, INCLUDING, WITHOUT LIMITATION, THE IMPLIED WARRANTIES OF MERCHANTIBILITY AND FITNESS FOR A PARTICULAR PURPOSE.

The End

The BSD License

The following is a BSD license template. To generate your own license, change the values of OWNER, ORGANIZATION, and YEAR from their original values as given here, and substitute your own. The version here is as distributed at www.opensource.org/licenses/, so as to encourage people to use the same wording.

OWNER = Regents of the University of California

ORGANIZATION = University of California, Berkeley

YEAR = 2000

In the original BSD license, the first occurrence of the phrase "COPYRIGHT HOLDERS AND CONTRIBUTORS" in the disclaimer read "REGENTS AND CONTRIBUTORS."

License Template

Copyright (c) YEAR, OWNER, All rights reserved.

Redistribution and use in source and binary forms, with or without modification, are permitted provided that the following conditions are met:

- Redistributions of source code must retain the above copyright notice, this list of conditions and the following disclaimer.

- Redistributions in binary form must reproduce the above copyright notice, this list of conditions and the following disclaimer in the documentation and/or other materials provided with the distribution.

- Neither name of the organization nor the names of its contributors may be used to endorse or promote products derived from this software without specific prior written permission.

THIS SOFTWARE IS PROVIDED BY THE COPYRIGHT HOLDERS AND CONTRIBUTORS "AS IS" AND ANY EXPRESS OR IMPLIED WARRANTIES, INCLUDING, BUT NOT LIMITED TO, THE IMPLIED WARRANTIES OF MERCHANTABILITY AND FITNESS FOR A PARTICULAR PURPOSE ARE DISCLAIMED. IN NO EVENT SHALL THE REGENTS OR CONTRIBUTORS BE LIABLE FOR ANY DIRECT, INDIRECT, INCIDENTAL, SPECIAL, EXEMPLARY, OR CONSEQUENTIAL DAMAGES (INCLUDING, BUT NOT LIMITED TO, PROCUREMENT OF SUBSTITUTE GOODS OR SERVICES; LOSS OF USE, DATA, OR PROFITS; OR BUSINESS INTERRUPTION) HOWEVER CAUSED AND ON ANY THEORY OF LIABILITY, WHETHER IN CONTRACT, STRICT LIABILITY, OR TORT (INCLUDING NEGLIGENCE OR OTHERWISE) ARISING IN ANY WAY OUT OF THE USE OF THIS SOFTWARE, EVEN IF ADVISED OF THE POSSIBILITY OF SUCH DAMAGE.

The MIT License

Copyright (c) 2000 Copyright Holders

Permission is hereby granted, free of charge, to any person obtaining a copy of this software and associated documentation files (the "Software"), to deal in the Software without restriction, including without limitation the rights to use, copy, modify, merge, publish, distribute, sublicense, and/or sell copies of the Software, and to permit persons to whom the Software is furnished to do so, subject to the following conditions:

The above copyright notice and this permission notice shall be included in all copies or substantial portions of the Software.

THE SOFTWARE IS PROVIDED "AS IS", WITHOUT WARRANTY OF ANY KIND, EXPRESS OR IMPLIED, INCLUDING BUT NOT LIMITED TO THE WARRANTIES OF MERCHANTABILITY, FITNESS FOR A PARTICULAR PURPOSE AND NONINFRINGEMENT. IN NO EVENT SHALL THE AUTHORS OR COPYRIGHT HOLDERS BE LIABLE FOR ANY CLAIM, DAMAGES OR OTHER LIABILITY, WHETHER IN AN ACTION OF CONTRACT, TORT OR OTHERWISE, ARISING FROM, OUT OF OR IN CONNECTION WITH THE SOFTWARE OR THE USE OR OTHER DEALINGS IN THE SOFTWARE.

The Mozilla Public License Version 1.0

1. Definitions

1.1. "Contributor" means each entity that creates or contributes to the creation of Modifications.

1.2. "Contributor Version" means the combination of the Original Code, prior Modifications used by a Contributor, and the Modifications made by that particular Contributor.

1.3. "Covered Code" means the Original Code or Modifications or the combination of the Original Code and Modifications, in each case including portions thereof.

1.4. "Electronic Distribution Mechanism" means a mechanism generally accepted in the software development community for the electronic transfer of data.

1.5. "Executable" means Covered Code in any form other than Source Code.

1.6. "Initial Developer" means the individual or entity identified as the Initial Developer in the Source Code notice required by Exhibit A.

1.7. "Larger Work" means a work which combines Covered Code or portions thereof with code not governed by the terms of this License.

1.8. "License" means this document.

1.9. "Modifications" means any addition to or deletion from the substance or structure of either the Original Code or any previous Modifications. When Covered Code is released as a series of files, a Modification is:

A. Any addition to or deletion from the contents of a file containing Original Code or previous Modifications.

B. Any new file that contains any part of the Original Code or previous Modifications.

1.10. "Original Code" means Source Code of computer software code which is described in the Source Code notice required by Exhibit A as Original Code, and which, at the time of its release under this License is not already Covered Code governed by this License.

1.11. "Source Code" means the preferred form of the Covered Code for making modifications to it, including all modules it contains, plus any associated interface definition files, scripts used to control compilation and installation of an Executable, or a list of source code differential comparisons against either the Original Code or another well known, available Covered Code of the Contributor's choice. The Source Code can be in a compressed or archival form, provided the appropriate decompression or de-archiving software is widely available for no charge.

1.12. "You" means an individual or a legal entity exercising rights under, and complying with all of the terms of, this License or a future version of this License issued under Section 6.1. For legal entities, "You" includes any entity which controls, is controlled by, or is under common control with You. For purposes of this definition, "control" means (a) the power, direct or indirect, to cause the direction or management of such entity, whether by contract or otherwise, or (b) ownership of fifty percent (50%) or more of the outstanding shares or beneficial ownership of such entity.

2. Source Code License

2.1. The Initial Developer Grant

The Initial Developer hereby grants You a world-wide, royalty-free, non-exclusive license, subject to third party intellectual property claims:

(a) To use, reproduce, modify, display, perform, sublicense and distribute the Original Code (or portions thereof) with or without Modifications, or as part of a Larger Work; and

(b) Under patents now or hereafter owned or controlled by Initial Developer, to make, have made, use and sell ("Utilize") the Original Code (or portions thereof), but solely to the extent that any such patent is reasonably necessary to enable You to Utilize the Original Code (or portions thereof) and not to any greater extent that may be necessary to Utilize further Modifications or combinations.

2.2. Contributor Grant

Each Contributor hereby grants You a world-wide, royalty-free, non-exclusive license, subject to third party intellectual property claims:

(a) To use, reproduce, modify, display, perform, sublicense, and distribute the Modifications created by such Contributor (or portions thereof) either on an unmodified basis, with other Modifications, as Covered Code or as part of a Larger Work; and

(b) Under patents now or hereafter owned or controlled by Contributor, to Utilize the Contributor Version (or portions thereof), but solely to the extent that any such patent is reasonably necessary to enable You to Utilize the Contributor Version (or portions thereof), and not to any greater extent that may be necessary to Utilize further Modifications or combinations.

3. Distribution Obligations

3.1. Application of License

The Modifications which You create or to which You contribute are governed by the terms of this License, including without limitation Section 2.2. The Source Code version of Covered Code may be distributed only under the terms of this License or a future version of this License released under Section 6.1, and You must include a copy of this License with every copy of the Source Code You distribute. You may not offer or impose any terms on any Source Code version that alters or restricts the applicable version of this License or the recipients' rights hereunder. However, You may include an additional document offering the additional rights described in Section 3.5.

3.2. Availability of Source Code

Any Modification which You create or to which You contribute must be made available in Source Code form under the terms of this License either on the same media as an Executable version or via an accepted Electronic Distribution Mechanism to anyone to whom you made an Executable version available; and if made available via Electronic Distribution Mechanism, must remain available for at least twelve (12) months after the date it initially became available, or at least six (6) months after a subsequent version of that particular Modification has been made available to such recipients. You are responsible for ensuring that the Source Code version remains available even if the Electronic Distribution Mechanism is maintained by a third party.

3.3. Description of Modifications

You must cause all Covered Code to which you contribute to contain a file documenting the changes You made to create that Covered Code and the date of any change. You must include a prominent statement that the Modification is derived, directly or indirectly, from Original Code provided by the Initial Developer and including the name of the Initial Developer in (a) the Source Code, and (b) in any notice in an Executable version or related documentation in which You describe the origin or ownership of the Covered Code.

3.4. Intellectual Property Matters

(a) Third Party Claims. If You have knowledge that a party claims an intellectual property right in particular functionality or code (or its utilization under this License), you must include a text file with the source code distribution titled "LEGAL" which describes the claim and the party making the claim in sufficient detail that a recipient will know whom to contact. If you obtain such knowledge after You make Your Modification available as described in Section 3.2, You shall promptly modify the LEGAL file in all copies You make available thereafter and shall take other steps (such as notifying appropriate mailing lists or newsgroups) reasonably calculated to inform those who received the Covered Code that new knowledge has been obtained.

(b) Contributor APIs. If Your Modification is an application programming interface and You own or control patents which are reasonably necessary to implement that API, you must also include this information in the LEGAL file.

3.5. Required Notices

You must duplicate the notice in Exhibit A in each file of the Source Code, and this License in any documentation for the Source Code, where You describe recipients' rights relating to Covered Code. If You created one or more Modification(s), You may add your name as a Contributor to the notice described in Exhibit A. If it is not possible to put such notice in a particular Source Code file due to its structure, then you must include such notice in a location (such as a relevant directory file) where a user would be likely to look for such a notice. You may choose to offer, and to charge a fee for, warranty, support, indemnity or liability obligations to one or more recipients of Covered Code. However, You may do so only on Your own behalf, and not on behalf of the Initial Developer or any Contributor. You must make it absolutely clear that any such warranty, support, indemnity or liability obligation is offered by You alone, and You hereby agree to indemnify the Initial Developer and every Contributor for any liability incurred by the Initial Developer or such Contributor as a result of warranty, support, indemnity or liability terms You offer.

3.6. Distribution of Executable Versions

You may distribute Covered Code in Executable form only if the requirements of Section 3.1-3.5 have been met for that Covered Code, and if You include a notice stating that the Source Code version of the Covered Code is available under the terms of this License, including a description of how and where You have fulfilled the obligations of Section 3.2. The notice must be conspicuously included in any notice in an Executable version, related documentation or collateral in which You describe recipients' rights relating to the Covered Code. You may distribute the Executable version of Covered Code under a license of Your choice, which may contain terms different from this License, provided that You are in compliance with the terms of this License and that the license for the Executable version does not attempt to limit or alter the recipient's rights in the Source Code version from the rights set forth in this License. If You distribute the Executable version under a different license You must make it absolutely clear that any terms which differ from this License are offered by You alone, not by the Initial Developer or any Contributor. You hereby agree to indemnify the Initial Developer and every Contributor for any liability incurred by the Initial Developer or such Contributor as a result of any such terms You offer.

3.7. Larger Works

You may create a Larger Work by combining Covered Code with other code not governed by the terms of this License and distribute the Larger Work as a single product. In such a case, You must make sure the requirements of this License are fulfilled for the Covered Code.

4. Inability to Comply Due to Statute or Regulation

If it is impossible for You to comply with any of the terms of this License with respect to some or all of the Covered Code due to statute or regulation then You must: (a) comply with the terms of this License to the maximum extent possible; and (b) describe the limitations and the code they affect. Such description must be included in the LEGAL file described in Section 3.4 and must be included with all distributions of the Source Code. Except to the extent prohibited by statute or regulation, such description must be sufficiently detailed for a recipient of ordinary skill to be able to understand it.

5. Application of this License

This License applies to code to which the Initial Developer has attached the notice in Exhibit A, and to related Covered Code.

6. Versions of the License

6.1. New Versions

Netscape Communications Corporation ("Netscape") may publish revised and/or new versions of the License from time to time. Each version will be given a distinguishing version number.

6.2. Effect of New Versions

Once Covered Code has been published under a particular version of the License, You may always continue to use it under the terms of that version. You may also choose to use such Covered Code under the terms of any subsequent version of the License published by Netscape. No one other than Netscape has the right to modify the terms applicable to Covered Code created under this License.

6.3. Derivative Works

If you create or use a modified version of this License (which you may only do in order to apply it to code which is not already Covered Code governed by this License), you must (a) rename Your license so that the phrases "Mozilla", "MOZILLAPL", "MOZPL", "Netscape", "NPL" or any confusingly similar phrase do not appear anywhere in your license and (b) otherwise make it clear that your version of the license contains terms which differ from the Mozilla Public License and Netscape Public License. (Filling in the name of the Initial Developer, Original Code or Contributor in the notice described in Exhibit A shall not of themselves be deemed to be modifications of this License.)

7. DISCLAIMER OF WARRANTY

COVERED CODE IS PROVIDED UNDER THIS LICENSE ON AN "AS IS" BASIS, WITHOUT WARRANTY OF ANY KIND, EITHER EXPRESSED OR IMPLIED, INCLUDING, WITHOUT LIMITATION, WARRANTIES THAT THE COVERED CODE IS FREE OF DEFECTS, MERCHANTABLE, FIT FOR A PARTICULAR PURPOSE OR NON-INFRINGING. THE ENTIRE RISK AS TO THE QUALITY AND PERFORMANCE OF THE COVERED CODE IS WITH YOU. SHOULD ANY COVERED CODE PROVE DEFECTIVE IN ANY RESPECT, YOU (NOT THE INITIAL DEVELOPER OR ANY OTHER CONTRIBUTOR) ASSUME THE COST OF ANY NECESSARY SERVICING, REPAIR OR CORRECTION. THIS DISCLAIMER OF WARRANTY CONSTITUTES AN ESSENTIAL PART OF THIS LICENSE. NO USE OF ANY COVERED CODE IS AUTHORIZED HEREUNDER EXCEPT UNDER THIS DISCLAIMER.

8. TERMINATION

This License and the rights granted hereunder will terminate automatically if You fail to comply with terms herein and fail to cure such breach within 30 days of becoming aware of the breach. All sublicenses to the Covered Code which are properly granted shall survive any termination of this License. Provisions which, by their nature, must remain in effect beyond the termination of this License shall survive.

9. LIMITATION OF LIABILITY

UNDER NO CIRCUMSTANCES AND UNDER NO LEGAL THEORY, WHETHER TORT (INCLUDING NEGLIGENCE), CONTRACT, OR OTHERWISE, SHALL THE INITIAL DEVELOPER, ANY OTHER CONTRIBUTOR, OR ANY DISTRIBUTOR OF COVERED CODE, OR ANY SUPPLIER OF ANY OF SUCH PARTIES, BE LIABLE TO YOU OR ANY OTHER PERSON FOR ANY INDIRECT, SPECIAL, INCIDENTAL, OR CONSEQUENTIAL DAMAGES OF ANY CHARACTER INCLUDING, WITHOUT LIMITATION, DAMAGES FOR LOSS OF GOODWILL, WORK STOPPAGE, COMPUTER FAILURE OR MALFUNCTION, OR ANY AND ALL OTHER COMMERCIAL DAMAGES OR

LOSSES, EVEN IF SUCH PARTY SHALL HAVE BEEN INFORMED OF THE POSSIBILITY OF SUCH DAMAGES. THIS LIMITATION OF LIABILITY SHALL NOT APPLY TO LIABILITY FOR DEATH OR PERSONAL INJURY RESULTING FROM SUCH PARTY'S NEGLIGENCE TO THE EXTENT APPLIC-ABLE LAW PROHIBITS SUCH LIMITATION. SOME JURISDICTIONS DO NOT ALLOW THE EXCLUSION OR LIMITATION OF INCIDENTAL OR CONSEQUENTIAL DAMAGES, SO THAT EXCLUSION AND LIMITATION MAY NOT APPLY TO YOU.

10. U.S. GOVERNMENT END USERS

The Covered Code is a "commercial item," as that term is defined in 48 C.F.R. 2.101 (Oct. 1995), consisting of "commercial computer software" and "commercial computer software documentation," as such terms are used in 48 C.F.R. 12.212 (Sept. 1995). Consistent with 48 C.F.R. 12.212 and 48 C.F.R. 227.7202-1 through 227.7202-4 (June 1995), all U.S. Government End Users acquire Covered Code with only those rights set forth herein.

11. MISCELLANEOUS

This License represents the complete agreement concerning subject matter hereof. If any provision of this License is held to be unenforceable, such provision shall be reformed only to the extent necessary to make it enforceable. This License shall be governed by California law provisions (except to the extent applicable law, if any, provides otherwise), excluding its conflict-of-law provisions. With respect to disputes in which at least one party is a citizen of, or an entity chartered or registered to do business in, the United States of America: (a) unless otherwise agreed in writing, all disputes relating to this License (excepting any dispute relating to intellectual property rights) shall be subject to final and binding arbitration, with the losing party paying all costs of arbitration; (b) any arbitration relating to this Agreement shall be held in Santa Clara County, California, under the auspices of JAMS/EndDispute; and (c) any litigation relating to this Agreement shall be subject to the jurisdiction of the Federal Courts of the Northern District of California, with venue lying in Santa Clara County, California, with the losing party responsible for costs, including without limitation, court costs and reasonable attorneys fees and expenses. The application of the United Nations Convention on Contracts for the International Sale of Goods is expressly excluded. Any law or regulation which provides that the language of a contract shall be construed against the drafter shall not apply to this License.

12. RESPONSIBILITY FOR CLAIMS

Except in cases where another Contributor has failed to comply with Section 3.4, You are responsible for damages arising, directly or indirectly, out of Your utilization of rights under this License, based on the number of copies of Covered Code you made available, the revenues you received from utilizing such rights, and other relevant factors. You agree to work with affected parties to distribute responsibility on an equitable basis.

EXHIBIT A

"The contents of this file are subject to the Mozilla Public License Version 1.0 (the "License"); you may not use this file except in compliance with the License. You may obtain a copy of the License at http://www.mozilla.org/MPL/.

Software distributed under the License is distributed on an "AS IS" basis, WITHOUT WARRANTY OF ANY KIND, either express or implied. See the License for the specific language governing rights and limitations under the License.

The Original Code is _____.

The Initial Developer of the Original Code is _____.

Portions created by _____ are Copyright (C)

_____.

All Rights Reserved.

Contributor(s): _____."

The Barefoot License

This copyright statement and license is used for my *lq-text* package. It has not been reviewed by a copyright lawyer, so you should probably not use it for your own software. It's given here as an example of a typical free software license.

Copyright *date* Liam R. E. Quin. All rights reserved.

Written by Liam Quin.

This software is not subject to any license of the American Telephone and Telegraph Company or of the Regents of the University of California, or of the X Consortium, or of the Free Software Foundation.

Permission is granted to anyone to use this software for any purpose on any computer system, and to alter it and redistribute it freely, subject to the following restrictions:

1. The author is not responsible for the consequences of use of this software, no matter how awful, even if they arise from flaws in it.

2. The origin of this software must not be misrepresented, either by explicit claim or by omission. Since few users ever read sources, credits must appear in the documentation.

3. Altered versions must be plainly marked as such, and must not be misrepresented as being the original software. Since few users ever read sources, credits must appear in the documentation.

4. Permission must be obtained for any commercial use of this software, which involves resale of all or part of the software, whether modified or not.

5. This notice may not be removed or altered.

6. The individuals for whom and by whom this software is installed must go entirely barefoot for 36 continuous hours, entirely at their own risk, starting within ten days of the first successful use of the package. If this clause cannot be met, a commercial version of the license may be available as an alternative.

This product contains software developed by the University of California, Berkeley, and its contributors.

In particular, see copyright notices in lq-text/src/liblqtext/lqsort.c and in the directories lq-text/src/db and lq-text/src/bsdhash, if they are present.

[Acknowledgment is made to Henry Spencer for permission to modify and use his and Geoff Collyer's C News copyright notice.]

## CHAPTER 20

Installing and Configuring Downloaded Software

P eople are sometimes discouraged from downloading free Unix software because it seems difficult to install; and on occasion, it *is* difficult, but more often, it's a case of their not knowing what to do. That's the point of this short chapter: to give you some general guidelines, tell you where to look for more information, and present an example of how to run *configure*.

Most commercial Microsoft Windows applications use the InstallShield program to make a graphical installer, the sort of installer that requires you to be sitting in front of the console when you run it–which is inappropriate for a server in an air-conditioned machine on a cold floor. Many Unix servers don't have graphical consoles at all, and in any case, the familiar "You must now restart your computer to complete the installation" is entirely inappropriate on an ftp server with 500 users logged in.

Free software is usually distributed in one of four ways:

A binary snapshot, which you simply unpack and use, but can't configure very easily and can't uninstall reliably.

A binary package, such as an RPM for Red Hat Linux, a "pkg" for Solaris or FreeBSD or a "package" for Debian Linux, which detects other packages it needs automatically and can be uninstalled.

A source package, such as an SRPM for Red Hat, a Debian Linux source package, or a Port for FreeBSD.

A source tarball, which you must configure and compile yourself, but is the most flexible.

We'll look at each of these in turn shortly. Only the fourth is at all complicated, and even it's not as bad as having your teeth pulled out by a goat. In fact, it's preferable. But before we can install anything, we have to download it.

Finding Packages

Suppose you are looking for a C or C++ library to parse XML files. You might start in one of two or three places:

- A search at www.altavista.com/ for C *parse XML.*
- A search at www.metacrawler.com/ for *"parse XML" C;* this will search AltaVista and several other search engines at the time, but only gives the first few results.

You are more likely to get somewhere with a search at www.freshmeat.net/, as this is a specialized repository for information about open source software. A freshmeat record for my *lq-text* package is shown in Figure 20.1.

It Doesn't Have to Be Difficult

There are programs designed to search for software packages and install them. A few of them are described in this section. Usually, you will need to run them as *root* so that they can write to system directories. Programs using the X Window system may also need to be given permission to access your own display, odd though it may seem. You can use the *xhost* program to do this:

```
$ xhost +'hostname'
```

But note that doing this has the unfortunate side effect of giving everyone on the Internet access to your display, too. See your system's manual pages for *xhost* and xauth for more secure approaches.

Red Hat and Mandrake

Red Hat and Mandrake Linux users can run this under the X Window system; it's a front end to the Red Hat *rpm* system, which we'll discuss under Binary Packages shortly. You can use *gnorpm* to search for packages to install, as shown in Figure 20.2; *gnorpm* can also install them, and will identify other packages you need that are not yet installed.

Since *gnorpm* uses the Gnome Project libraries (www.gnome.org), you will need to have Gnome installed. You can run *gnorpm* like this:

```
# gnorpm
```

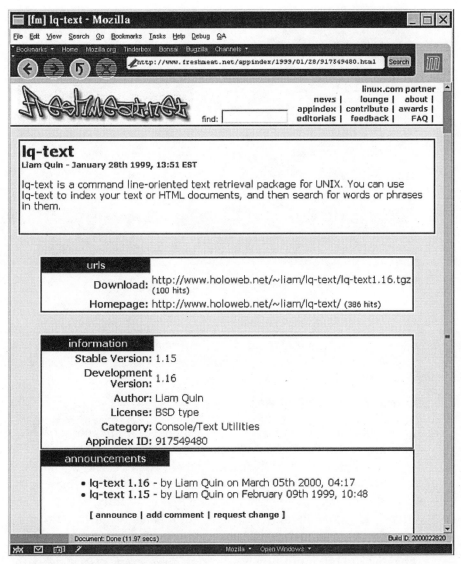

Figure 20.1 A *freshmeat* record.

Figure 20.2 also shows *gnorpm* in use. The Web Find icon on the main toolbar is probably the most useful button to start with, but you can also use *gnorpm* to install packages from a CD-ROM, or that you have downloaded with *ftp*.

The most common problem with *gnorpm* is that it might fail to download files because the remote server is too full. The terminal window from which you started *gnorpm* will usually display a message to that effect. Your best strategy then is one of three: wait for another time; use *ftp* as described shortly; or change *gnorpm*'s preferences to use a different mirror site.

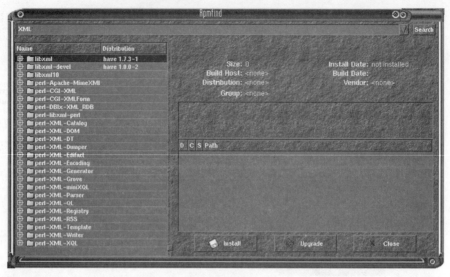

Figure 20.2 Searching for packages with *gnorpm*.

If you are not using the X Window system, you can use the *rpm* command; run *rpm—help* or read the manual page (*man rpm*) to see the options. It's simplest to use *ftp* (shown shortly) to pick up a package and then use *rpm -i* to install it.

Debian Package Utilities

The Debian Linux Distribution was designed with the intent of integrating as much Linux software as possible into the Debian package system. The packages are all stored centrally, making them easier to find. There are around 4500 software packages in the Debian system, provided by a team of more than 500 volunteer developers. As with Red Hat Linux, any of these packages can be downloaded and installed automatically, including any required dependencies.

The powerful but unintuitive *dselect* and *dpkg* programs are the basic package management utilities for Debian Linux. The complex interface of *dselect* and *dpkg* has led to the development of other tools, which generally still use *dpkg* internally, but provide an easier-to-use interface. The most widely used interface is called A Package Tool (*apt*). Others include *console-apt* and *gnome-apt*. Figure 20.3 shows *console-apt* in use; compare this to Figure 20.4, which shows the KDE installer *kpackage*.

If you are not using the X Window system, you can search for packages with the command

```
$ dpkg -l '*pattern*'
```

```
         Pri Package       Section  Avail.ver  Inst.ver   PkgSZ  InstSZ   Descripti
  [-] Opt libxml-dev       devel    1.8.5-1    1.8.5-1    257    1385     Development
  [-] Opt libxml1          libs     1.8.5-1    1.8.5-1    133    368      GNOME XML
  [+] Req libc6            base     2.1.3-7    2.1.3-7    1861   9572     GNU C Li
  [+] Opt lintian          devel    1.11.2     1.11.2     155    595      Debian pac
  [+] Opt luci             devel    0.1.1-1    0.1.1-1    111    208      LUCI is a
  [+] Opt memprof          devel    0.3.0-3    0.3.0-3    153    372      memory pro
  [+] Opt mesag-dev        devel    3.1-15     3.1-15     569    1814     Development
  [+] Opt mesag-widget     devel    3.1-15     3.1-15     55     190      Development
  [+] Opt nasm             devel    0.98-3     0.98-3     548    1460     General-pu
  [+] Opt orbit            devel    0.5.0-3    0.5.0-3    114    354      A CORBA OR
  [+] Opt perl-byacc       devel    2.0-1      2.0-1      88     170      The Berkel
  [+] Opt pkglist          devel    0.3        0.3        17     89       Package Li
libxml-dev     installed, upgraded: unchanged
XML is a metalanguage to let you design your own markup language.
A regular markup language defines a way to describe information in
a certain class of documents (eg HTML). XML lets you define your
own customized markup languages for many classes of document. It
can do this because it's written in SGML, the international standard
metalanguage for markup languages.

Install this package if you wish to develop your own programs using
the GNOME XML library.
024% Development files for the GNOME XML library               [         ]
```

Figure 20.3   Debian Linux Terminal-based *console-apt* installer.

There is also a complete package listing and search engine on the Debian Web site (www.debian.org).

The following log shows how you might use *apt* to download and install a library:

```
# apt-get install libxml-dev
Reading Package Lists... Done
```

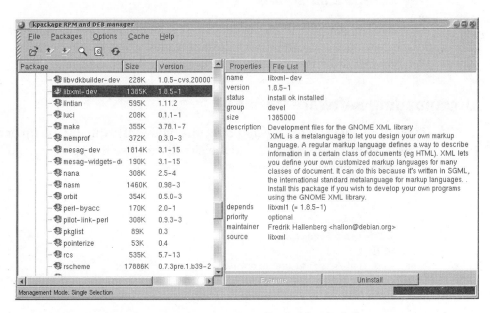

Figure 20.4   Debian Linux KDE *kpackage* installer for the X Window system.

```
Building Dependency Tree... Done
The following NEW packages will be installed:
  libxml-dev
0 packages upgraded, 1 newly installed,
0 to remove and 0 not upgraded.
Need to get 264kB of archives. After unpacking 1418kB will be used.
Get:1 http://http.us.debian.org unstable/main libxml-dev 1.8.5-1 [264kB]
Fetched 264kB in 1s (144kB/s)
Selecting previously deselected package libxml-dev.
(Reading database ...)
Unpacking libxml-dev (from .../libxml-dev_1.8.5-1_i386.deb) ...
Setting up libxml-dev (1.8.5-1) ...
#
```

The FreeBSD and NetBSD Ports Collection

If you are lucky enough to be running one of these two operating systems, you will find that the /usr/ports directory tree contains install information for thousands of packages. Find a package you want, go to its directory and, as root, type:

```
# make install
```

You'll see that the software is downloaded automatically, patched if necessary, compiled, and installed.

Free Software on Solaris

A hundred or so of the more popular free packages have been built into binary Solaris packages and can be downloaded from www.sunfreeware.com/ with a Web browser or by ftp; there are instructions at that site.

Downloading Software With FTP

If you were given an ftp site and directory, you will normally use *ftp* or a Web browser such as *netscape* to go to the site. If you use the *ftp* command, make sure that you enable "binary mode":

```
$ ftp ftp.somewhere.org
[messages about being connected]
user: anonymous
password: your@email.here
[more messages]
ftp> cd /pub/waycool/version3.2
CD SUCCESSFUL
ftp> dir
[ftp responds with a long file listing]
ftp> bin
```

```
BINARY MODE ENABLED
ftp> get waycool-3.2.rpm
ftp: opening data connection, type I
ftp: transfer ok, waycool-3.2.rpm -> waycool-3.2.rpm, 801K/sec
ftp> quit
$
```

Once you have downloaded the package, see the upcoming section *Installing a Binary Package*.

Installing a Binary Package

This is the easiest thing to do. Some packages have a custom installer that you have to run, and come packaged as a *tar* archive containing a file called README or INSTALL. Most, however, come as RPM, APT, or PKG files.

Table 20.1 shows the most common operating systems and what you need to install packages. Note that a Solaris 2 *pkg* file is *not* usually suitable for use on FreeBSD, despite having the same command and extension.

Installing a Source Package

Source packages are programs that need to be compiled before they are installed. Although binary distributions are common on Linux, many administrators prefer to download the source, so that they know it has not been tampered with in any way. On FreeBSD and NetBSD, there is a mechanism for downloading source packages, which includes an MD5 digital signature, to verify the files have not been tampered with.

Source Packages on Red Hat Linux and Mandrake

A Red Hat Linux source *package* file usually ends in the extension like `.srpm`; you can use *gnorpm* to install it, but installing a source package creates an RPM file (whose name ends in `.rpm`) that you then have to install. The command-

Table 20.1 Installing a Package on Various Operating Systems

OPERATING SYSTEM	FILE	INSTALL WITH
Solaris	PKG	pkgadd
FreeBSD	PKG	pkgadd
Red Hat Linux	RPM	gnorpm, rpm
Debian Linux	APT	apt-get, apt, deselect

line *rpm* program has options to check, unpack, build and install source RPMs. They usually end up under the /usr/src directory.

Source Packages on FreeBSD and NetBSD

These operating systems have a /usr/ports directory; go into the directory for the package you want to install, and type, as root:

```
# make install
```

The package will be downloaded, and its digital signature will be checked. If that works, the source will be unpacked, and any operating-specific "patches" will be applied; then it will be compiled and installed. In addition, if the package needs any other packages to run properly, they will be automatically downloaded and installed in the same way.

Because the packages are installed in /usr/local, once built, you will need to make sure that you have enough disk space there.

Debian Linux

You can use *apt-get* to install from source, as shown here:

```
# mkdir /usr/src/xmlstuff
# cd /usr/src/xmlstuff
# apt-get source libxml-dev
Reading Package Lists... Done
Building Dependency Tree... Done
Need to get 884kB of source archives.
Get:1 http://http.us.debian.org stable/main libxml 1.8.5-1 (dsc) [668B]
Get:2 http://http.us.debian.org stable/main libxml 1.8.5-1 (tar) [877kB]
Get:3 http://http.us.debian.org stable/main libxml 1.8.5-1 (diff) [928B]
Fetched 884kB in 9s (91.3kB/s)
dpkg-source: extracting libxml in libxml-1.8.5
#
# ls -l
total 871
drwxr-sr-x  8 root    src     2048 Mar 10 04:25 libxml-1.8.5/
-rw-r--r--  1 root    src      928 Jan 25 13:55 libxml_1.8.5-1.diff.gz
-rw-r--r--  1 root    src      668 Jan 25 13:55 libxml_1.8.5-1.dsc
-rw-r--r--  1 root    src   877033 Jan 25 13:55 libxml_1.8.5.orig.tar.gz
# cd libxml-1.8.5/
# debian/rules binary
. . .
dpkg-deb: building package 'libxml1'
    in '../libxml1_1.8.5-1_i386.deb'
dpkg-deb: building package libxml-dev'
    in '../libxml-dev_1.8.5-1_i386.deb'
#
```

Installing a Source Tarball

When you install a source package, you generally follow these steps:

1. Find the right version.
2. Download it.
3. Unpack the archive.
4. Read the documentation.
5. Configure.
6. Make.
7. Test.
8. Install.

The first two steps are the same as any other package, and have already been covered. Most likely, you'll fetch a distribution from one of the servers listed in Chapter 23, "Further Reading." Probably it will be a file like libxml-3.2.tgz or lq-text1.16.tar.gz, and the first thing you need to do is to look inside it. Although there are front ends to *tar* rather like *winzip* on Windows, we'll use the command-line version, because it's installed everywhere.

WARNING

Do *not* build source distributions as *root*. Doing this could compromise the security of your system. The slightest mistake can corrupt your entire system, and a malicious or faulty source distribution can easily wreak havoc. Build as an unprivileged user, and only install as root when necessary.

Unpacking the Archive

You can check the *tar* archive first like this:

```
$ tar ztvf libfun-3.2.tgz
```

You should see lots of output, rather like *ls -l*. The important thing to note is that it works at all, and that the files all start with libfun-3.2/, meaning they will be extracted into a directory of that name.

If the files just have names like README, with no common directory prefix, you will need to make a directory, move the archive into it, and unpack it from there:

```
$ mkdir libfun-3.2
$ mv -i libfun-3.2.tgz libfun-3.2
$ cd libfun-3.2
```

If *tar* says that "z" is an unknown option, use this command instead:

```
$ gunzip < libfun-3.2.tgz | tar tvf -
```

The trailing minus sign tells *tar* to read its standard input.

If you get a message such as "gunzip not found," you'll have to install the GNU unzip program first; you can get a binary Solaris package from www.sunfreeware.com (most other systems include it).

Extract all the source files from the archive by changing the "t" option to *tar* into an "x" like this:

```
$ tar zxvf libfun-3.2.tgz
```

or this:

```
$ gunzip < libfun-3.2.tgz | tar xvf -
```

Reading the Documentation

Don't laugh, you need to do this.

Look for a file called INSTALL and read it. It will tell you how to proceed from there. What follows in this section is an overview, but the details will differ.

Configuring

Sometimes this involves editing a Makefile or C source or header files. If you edit a Makefile, be especially careful to note that a tab is *not* the same as eight spaces. If you or your editor converts tabs to spaces, you will get a message like this when you try to build the software:

```
Make: missing separator on line 312. Stop.
```

WARNING

If you are using a Windows system connected to a Unix system over the Internet, avoid the temptation to download files and edit them locally. Microsoft Windows uses an incompatible format for text files, and you will end up with strange errors.

More commonly, instead of editing files, you run a shell script called *configure*. This may ask you some questions, and will then create a Makefile and maybe other files, too.

Building

Once the software is configured, you usually build it like this:

```
$ make
```

You may see reams and reams of output scroll past as the software is compiled. Eventually, you will get your shell prompt back. If there were no errors, you can install the software. If there were errors, you'll have to work out what they were and try and fix them. Check for INSTALL or README files to see you did everything right.

Testing

Some packages include tests. You usually run them like this:

```
$ make test
```

They should say they passed; or at least, they should not say they failed.

Installing

You normally install a package in two parts: first, see what installation will do, then do the install. You see what the installation will do by running *make* with the -n option, meaning "no action":

```
$ make -n install
```

You should see lines like this:

```
cd src;
install -s -c -m 755 xsockweaver /usr/local/bin
```

If you don't want the software installed where make says it's going to put it, you may need to go back to the configuring stage.

If everything looks okay, *this* is the stage where you become the superuser:

```
$ /bin/su
password: enter password here
# make install
[output from make]
# exit
$
```

You are now ready to run the software. In most cases, you will not have to restart the computer or the windowing system, or even log out.

There are a lot of steps here, but remember: If you don't like the way the program behaves, you can change it yourself! You would need to learn the C programming language or Perl or whatever was used to write the software, but there are no other barriers. The source code is all there. You have everything. This is why the software is called *free*—you are free to change it, something you can never do with a binary package of the sort normally used by commercial software.

Installing a Perl Module

Perl is a scripting language, so all Perl scripts are distributed as source. The easiest way to install something is usually with the Comprehensive Perl Archive Network (CPAN) module included with Perl:

```
$ perl -MCPAN -e shell
```

This places you in an interactive shell. You will be asked some questions, and then you can use the online help; or install packages, for example:

```
cpan> install XML::DOM
```

If you decide not to use the CPAN module, you can install Perl modules manually—it's very easy. You will find almost all of them at www.cpan.org. Download a module, unpack it as described for a source distribution in the preceding section, and then build it as follows:

```
$ cd modfun3.2
$ perl Makefile.PL
$ make
$ make test
$ make install
```

XML Parsers, Editors, and Utilities

It would be impossible to include a complete list of tools in any book, so this chapter describes some of the more commonly used tools to read XML into memory (parsers) and to create and edit XML documents by hand (editors), along with related utilities. For information on other tools, a good place to start looking is at www.xml.com/pub/Guide/XML_Parsers. In addition to being in common use, the tools described here have been chosen because they are likely to be useful if you are working with databases, whether on the World Wide Web or elsewhere.

Parsers: Tools that Read XML into Memory

There are two main models used by XML parsers: *event* and *tree* models. In the *event* model, the start of an XML element (for example) simply calls a function you supply, and doesn't save anything in memory unless you do it yourself. Parsers using the *tree* model build up a complete data structure in memory, and either return it to you (XML::Parser in Perl can do that) or give you an API, usually based on the DOM, to manipulate it. Use the event model for speed and low memory overhead. Use the tree model for compatibility with browsers or other DOM-aware applications, or for simplicity in programming.

Certain XML parsers can work either way. They are split by primary language here, although some, such as *expat*, have been incorporated into other languages and may be mentioned more than once.

C and C++ Parsers

The most widely used tools in C and C++ are those written by James Clark; they are available at www.jclark.com for free download. The license is very open, and the software can be used commercially.

SP

SP is Clark's SGML parser. As its name suggests, it handles the fuller SGML standard. Every valid XML document is also a valid SGML document, and since Clark was a member of the XML working group, and is also on the ISO SGML committee, you should not be surprised to learn that SP handles XML.

The parser is most often used with a C command-line front end (on Windows and Unix), called *nsgmls*, which produces a regular and easy-to-parse text output. The format is an augmented ESIS (an industry standard for SGML) and is easy to process in Perl, *awk*, or other languages.

There is a C++ API for SP, but it is not very clearly documented. SP is a fully validating parser, so it reads all of the declarations in both the internal document type declaration subset and any external DTD files as necessary. There is an enhanced version of SP called OpenSP at openjade.sourceforge.net, available under the same free license terms.

NOTE

SP can also use PUBLIC identifiers through a catalog mechanism; but although this is appropriate for SGML, it's a bad idea in XML, since the required SYSTEM identifier overrides the PUBLIC identifier anyway.

expat

The *expat* parser is written in C, and is easier to work with if you are just using XML, not SGML. Unlike SP, *expat* is not a full validating parser; it won't read declarations in an external DTD. There is an overview of *expat* at www.xml.com/pub/1999/09/expat/ written by Clark Cooper, the current maintainer of the Perl XML::Parser package.

Building expat and SP on Unix

For *expat*, you should end up with a directory structure similar to that shown in Figure 21.1; edit the Makefile that's in the *expat* directory. The changed lines are in bold:

```
CC=gcc
# If you know what your system's byte order is, define XML_BYTE_ORDER:
# use -DXML_BYTE_ORDER=12 for little-endian byte order;
# use -DXML_BYTE_ORDER=21 for big-endian (network) byte order.
# -DXML_NS adds support for checking of lexical aspects of
# the XML namespaces spec
# -DXML_MIN_SIZE makes a smaller but slower parser
CFLAGS=-O2 -Ixmltok -Ixmlparse -DXML_NS
# Use one of the next two lines; unixfilemap is better if it works.
FILEMAP_OBJ=xmlwf/unixfilemap.o
#FILEMAP_OBJ=xmlwf/readfilemap.o
OBJS=xmltok/xmltok.o \
  xmltok/xmlrole.o \
  xmlwf/xmlwf.o \
  xmlwf/xmlfile.o \
  xmlwf/codepage.o \
  xmlparse/xmlparse.o \
  xmlparse/hashtable.o \
  $(FILEMAP_OBJ)
EXE=
```

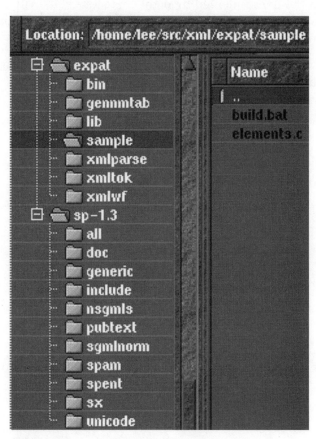

Figure 21.1 Install structure for expat.

```
all: xmlwf/xmlwf$(EXE)

xmlwf/xmlwf$(EXE): $(OBJS)
        $(CC) $(CFLAGS) -o $@ $(OBJS)

clean:
        rm -f $(OBJS) xmlwf/xmlwf$(EXE)

xmltok/nametab.h: gennmtab/gennmtab$(EXE)
        rm -f $@
        gennmtab/gennmtab$(EXE) >$@

gennmtab/gennmtab$(EXE): gennmtab/gennmtab.c
        $(CC) $(CFLAGS) -o $@ gennmtab/gennmtab.c

xmltok/xmltok.o: xmltok/nametab.h

.c.o:
        $(CC) $(CFLAGS) -c -o $@ $<
```

Be sure to note that the lines indented by eight characters start with a tab. If you change them to use spaces, you'll get an error about a "missing separator" or a syntax error from *make*.

Running *make* after editing the Makefile should produce a program called *xmlwf* in the *xmlwf* directory. This program can be run to determine whether an XML file is well formed.

RXP

RXP, a freely available parser in C for Unix and Windows, can be found at www.cogsci.ed.ac.uk/~richard/rxp.html.

Gnome

The XML library for Gnome (http://xmlsoft.org/) supports DOM and SAX. The Gnome project offers one of the more popular desktop environments for the X Windows system, so the software, which is all open source, is very widely used.

Apache

Apache (www.apache.org) is the most widely used Web server on the Internet; it is freely available. The XML support being built in to it will be a major boost for XML. The Apache parser is at xml.apache.org.

Others

Look on this book's companion Web site to find pointers to other C parsers for XML.

- At http://alphaworks.ibm.com you'll find several parsers, although XML4C++ is based on the Apache parser.

- A Web-based validator can be had from www.scripting.com/frontier5/xml/code/xmlValidator.html, and a well-formedness checker (using RXP) at www.cogsci.ed.ac.uk/~richard/ xml-check.html.

- XMLIO is an XML input/output library for C++ applications, distributed under the GPL, at www.fxtech.com/xmlio/.

Python

A Python DOM implementation and several other tools can be found at http://fourthought.com/4Suite/4DOM/.

Lars M. Garshol keeps a page called "Tools for Parsing XML with Python" at www.stud.ifi.uio.no/~larsga/download/python/xml/, which looks quite useful. In March 2000, it listed the following:

saxlib. The Python version of SAX, with drivers.

xmlproc. A validating XML parser.

PyPointers. An XPointer implementation.

dtddoc. A DTD documentation generator.

Java

As noted previously, this is not primarily a Java book, because there are already numerous Java books out there. The following links may be useful, however:

- The SAX event model was designed (at the urging of Peter Murray-Rust) by David Megginson, and was polished and refined on the xml-dev mailing list. It's used by almost all Java-based event-model parsers. You can read more about SAX at www.megginson.com/SAX/, where you'll also find a list of XML parsers.

- The first SAX parser, Ælfred (originally at www.microstar.com), seems unavailable, but David Brownell made a newer version at http://home.pacbell.net/david-b/xml/.

- Sun's Java API for XML is at http://java.sun.com/products/xml.

- Oracle's XML Parser for Java (http://technet.oracle.com/) is one of a number of Java and XML tools released by Oracle.

- The Apache project's Xerces-J parser (http://xml.apache.org/xerces-j/) is open source, and is being widely used; see also xml.apache.org for more information.

- Docuverse DOM SDK is a DOM implementation that claims to be complete, and is available for commercial and noncommercial use without licensing fee.

- XP is James Clark's XML Parser in Java, at www.jclark.com.

- The earliest widely used Java parser was Lark, by Tim Bray (www.textuality .com), but not all the source was distributed.

- IBM's extensive collection of XML tools for Java is at xml.ibm.com or www.ibm.com/xml/.

TeX

Yes, there's even an XML parser written in TeX macros. Though you probably don't want this, I've included it to show that XML parsers are becoming fairly widespread. If you *do* want it, it's on CTAN and is listed on the various archives.

Browsers

The most well-known browser is, of course, Netscape's open source Mozilla project at www.mozilla.org, whose *gecko* rendering engine uses XML extensively. Mozilla uses XML to describe the user interface entirely. Unfortunately, there is no XSL support yet.

The JUMBO browser was written by Peter Murray-Rust, for use in biochemistry. It's at www.vsms.nottingham.ac.uk/vsms/java/jumbo/. It has helped to motivate a lot of XML parser development. There is support for a "hyperglossary," as well as visualization of structures.

Citech has two commercial XML/SGML browsers at www.citec.fi/company/products/, both of which are highly spoken; the older and more mature MultiDoc Pro series of products is based on a toolkit by Synex (www.synex.se) called Viewport. The "doczilla" products use gecko from www.mozilla.org.

Interleaf Panorama (formerly SoftQuad Panorama) may be available from www.interleaf.com; this was the first SGML viewer for the Web, in 1994, but there seems to have been relatively little development since 1997, when the product was bought from SoftQuad by Interleaf.

InDelv claims to have an open source browser that supports XSL, at www.indelv.com.

Finally, no list of XML browsers would be respectable without mentioning that Microsoft Internet Explorer 5 includes XML and XSL support. Currently, IE5 is useful only on Windows (the Solaris version had a lot of problems when I tried it, including turning my root window bright purple by overwriting the default color map, and crashing OpenWindows on Solaris 2.6/SPARC). The Macintosh version is in beta at the time of this writing; and there doesn't seem to be a Linux version.

Transforming Data

The tools in this section transform non-XML text into XML, or XML into other things (including into more, but different, XML).

- If you are generating HTML from XML, or need to transform XML documents, consider XSLT, the XML Style Sheet Transformation mechanism from the W3C (www.w3.org/XML/).

- Ken Holman offers a course on XSL, XPath, and (I think) XSLT, which is said to be very good, at www.CraneSoftwrights.com/training/; but that is commercial. Holman also runs the DSSSL mailing list and is a well-known XML and SGML consultant and trainer, so the material is probably very good indeed, but I have not seen it.

- Jade is James Clark's Amazing DSSSL Engine. DSSSL is the ISO standard for formatting SGML, the Document Style and Semantics Specification Language; it uses the Scheme Language (a dialect of LISP), which has a syntax unfamiliar to most programmers. Jade is free, includes source, and can produce TeX, RTF, and HTML output. Unfortunately, Clark does not seem to be developing it further; instead, another group has taken over. The OpenJade project is at http://openjade.sourceforge.net/, and uses the same open source licensing terms as Jade.

- DSSSL can be used to convert SGML to HTML or to XML, or XML to different XML. But look at XSLT first, because most people find it simpler than DSSSL. XT, also by James Clark, implements XSLT, and is written in Java (www.jclark.com/xml/xt.html).

- Some2XML (www.pault.com) is a small Perl script intended to produce well-formed XML documents from text files that already have some structure.

- Balise from AIS Software (www.us.balise.com) is a programming environment using a Java-like (or C++-like) interpreted language. There is database support, and the software is often used to convert between document formats as well as to extract database data.

- SAXON (http://users.iclway.co.uk/mhkay/saxon/) is an XSL processor that implements XSLT and XPath, unfortunately with a number of incompatible extensions. It includes a Java library that supports a similar processing model to XSL but allows full programming capability, which the authors say you need if you want to perform complex processing of the data or to access external services such as a relational database. SAXON is distributed under the Mozilla Public License.

- Omnimark (www.omnimark.com) is a commercial scripting language; but a free version is available of the interpreter, which is sufficient for most purposes. An RTF-to-XML converter was contributed at www .omnimark.com/develop/contributed/, where you can find many other tools as well. Omnimark is widely used with SGML, and is known for giving clear and helpful error messages.

- At www.alphaworks.ibm.com/tech/DDbE is a Java component library for creating DTDs and Schemas by analyzing XML documents; this can help if you have well-formed XML documents.

- Dave Raggett's HTML Tidy program attempts to convert HTML documents to XML, including correcting common errors. You can find it at: www.w3.org/People/Raggett/tidy/.

- A Python XSLT implementation can be found at http://FourThought .com/4Suite/4XSLT/.

Formatting and Printing

FOP, an Open Source XSL Formatter and Renderer, is a project started by James Tauber, at http://xml.apache.org/fop/, in source form, along with documentation and a mailing list.

Jade and OpenJade were mentioned in the previous section, *Transforming Data*; now there are Windows NT binaries at www.sscd.de/openjade, too.

IBM offers LotusXSL from alphaWorks (www.alphaworks.ibm.com) as a free download. There are also XSL and XML editors at www.alphaWorks.ibm .com/tech/xsleditor.

You can find XML and XSL tutorials at http://zvon.vscht.cz/ZvonHTML/ Zvon/zvonTutorials_en.html.

Editors

A useful list of editors is given at wdvl.internet.com/Software/XML/editors.html, and another at http://xmlsoftware.com/editors/.

- Of the three best-known XML editors, two are commercial (Adept and XMetal) and one (XED) is free.

- Arbortext Adept (www.arbortext.com) has been one of the most widely used SGML editors for many years, and has made the transition to XML. It supports printing and validation, links to databases, and is cross-platform (including Unix).

- SoftQuad added XML support to its successful HoTMetaL Pro HTML editor and called the result XMetaL; it includes a CSS editor. You can order it from www.softquad.com. Figures 21.2 and 21.3 show screenshots of XMetaL. Unfortunately, XMetaL requires a precompiled DTD, so you can't use it with well-formed XML, only with valid XML. In some envi-

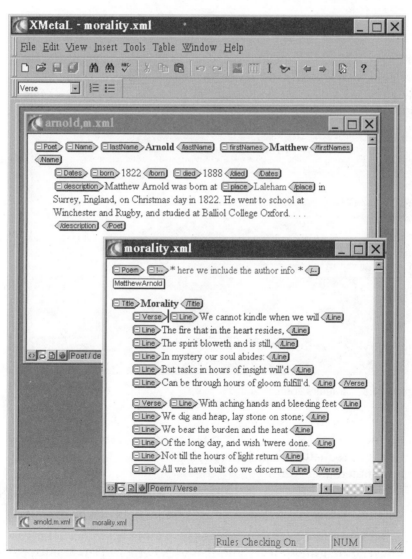

Figure 21.2 XMetaL with tags showing as icons.

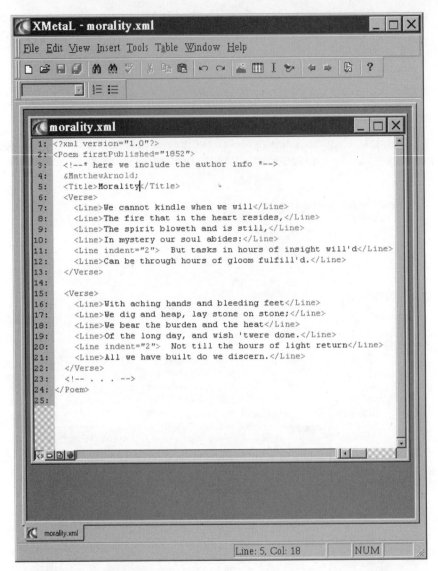

Figure 21.3 XMetal's source view.

ronments, that's good; in others, not so good. The software also seems to be a lot less mature than Arbortext's product, but it is much cheaper and has numerous features.

- Adobe FrameMaker (www.adobe.com) is an excellent tool for creating documentation and books; a Linux version is available.

- XED is currently available as a free beta for noncommercial use at www.ltg.ed.ac.uk/~ht/xed.html; it uses Python/Tk on Linux, Solaris, and Windows, as you can see from Figure 21.4, which shows the pointy brackets. A Macintosh version may also become available.

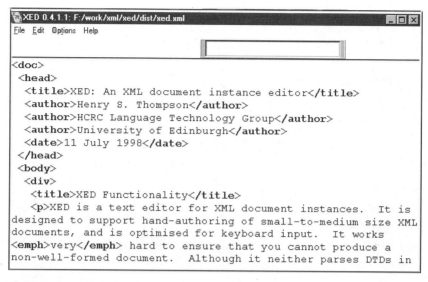

Figure 21.4 XED.

- XML Spy (www.xmlspy.com/) is another commercial XML editor. Figure 21.5 shows a screenshot using the same Poetry example from Chapter 1 that's depicted in XMetaL in Figure 21.2.

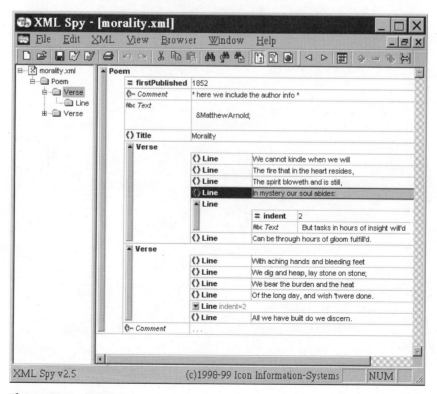

Figure 21.5 XML Spy.

Other XML Editors

Microsoft XML Notepad. www.microsoft.com/xml/notepad.

sxml for emacs. www.inria.fr/koala/plh/sxml.html.

Visual Markup. www.vtopia.com/products/markup/ (commercial; Windows only).

XML Authority. From Extensibility.com.

XMLWriter. www.XMLwriter.net/ (commercial; Windows only, uses Microsoft's XML parser).

XPublish. http://interaction.in-progress.com/xpublish/index (commercial, Macintosh).

Java component library. www.alphaWorks.ibm.com/tech/xsleditor (described in the *Transforming Data* section).

## CHAPTER 22

Databases, Repositories, and Utilities

This chapter gives pointers to relational and other databases and database tools. In particular, go to www.freshmeat .net for free open source Linux/Unix software. You'll find graphical front ends to queries, as well as programming-level tools and modules.

Relational Databases

A good overview site is www.stars.com/Authoring/DB/; another is http://dmoz.org/Computers/Data_Formats/Markup_Languages/XML/Tools/Databases/.

Open Source and Free Relational Databases

You can find a list of free databases at www.freshmeat.net/appindex/daemons/database.html; at one time, "free database" was considered a joke, but today there are solid offerings, including MySQL and PostgreSQL. What's more, some of the major database vendors, including Oracle and Sybase, have ported their commercial databases to free operating systems such as Linux and FreeBSD.

Interbase

Interbase 6 (www.interbase.com) is a new offering. Released by Borland Inc. as an open source project on January 3, 2000, it was a bold move, and the results will be interesting to watch. A beta download for Linux was available at the time of this writing.

MySQL

Although MySQL (www.mysql.com) is limited in functionality, especially in that it does not support transactions or rollback, it is very fast and easy to set up and use. It's also included with Red Hat Linux and possibly other distributions. Good documentation is included, with a helpful tutorial (in the /usr/doc/ directory). Database tables are stored in Unix files, so that a large database will probably hit performance limits, but if you're in the subgigabyte range, MySQL seems a pretty good choice. All of the examples in this book were tested with MySQL under Red Hat Linux.

PostgreSQL

PostgreSQL (www.postgresql.org) is a larger and more sophisticated relational database, with object-relational features. Though somewhat harder to set up, it has many more features. Many small SQL projects seem to migrate from to PostgreSQL (and thence to Oracle). Postgres is distributed under a BSD-style free license, and can thus be used in commercial projects without a fee. The Web page says this:

> PostgreSQL is a sophisticated Object-Relational DBMS, supporting almost all SQL constructs, including subselects, transactions, and user-defined types and functions. It is the most advanced open-source database available anywhere. Commercial Support is also available from PostgreSQL, Inc. (www .pgsql.com) The current version is 6.5.3 and is available at any of the many mirror sites or on CD.

> Interactive PostgreSQL for Windows is a program that allows you to execute PostgreSQL queries; show tables and columns, and history; show and edit tables in grid, and so on. Interactive PostgreSQL for Windows is available at www.zeos.dn.ua.

Commercial Relational Databases

Many of the databases listed here have extensive XML support in one way or another. Oracle in particular has done a lot of work in the XML community.

Some of the products listed here have free downloads for Linux—not just demos but the complete development server. The products are listed in alphabetical order.

NOTE

I have tried to avoid talking about features or SQL extensions that are not widely implemented, because if you use them, you end up locked in to a single vendor.

Empress. Empress has notes on generating XML at www.empress.com/services/ hyperaction/v7/ehtml_xml.html.

IBM DB2 Universal Database. The grandmother of all databases, IBM's flagship DB2 product is now available for Linux as well as many other operating systems, at www-4.ibm.com/software/data/db2/—there's even a Perl driver. IBM also has an extensive set of XML products and downloads at www.ibm.com/xml/, including an XML Extender for IBM DB2 Universal Database. The Extender (www-4.ibm.com/software/data/db2/extenders/ xmlext/) enables you to store and retrieve an XML document as a single column or multiple columns.

Informix. You can download Informix Dynamic Server, Linux Edition Suite, for free at www.informix.com/informix/products/linux/lx.html, but registration is required. You can also order the product on CD. A search for XML on www.informix.com's search interface showed a tutorial using Datablades to store XML poetry in a database, among other things.

Oracle. Widely considered to be the market leader in relational database products, Oracle's version 8i includes extensive support for XML, including a freely redistributable XML Developers Kit (http://technet.oracle.com/ tech/xml/). Oracle has recently ported its database to Linux; but be warned that this is a professional tool, not something to play with. It's a *large* install (plan to allow at least a gigabyte to give you space to use the database), and expect to take several days to install and configure the database. If you walk into almost any computer bookshop, you'll find shelves packed with books on configuring and using Oracle databases.

Ovrimos SQL Server. This is not such a well known product, but it has many features including Web-based administration. It is available commercially on Linux, BSDi, and FreeBSD, as well as on commercial platforms, at www.ovrimos.com/.

Raima. The Raima package (www.raima.com) has been around for many years and has an excellent reputation. Source is available (or was at one time), and it has been very widely ported. There does not seem to be any XML-specific support, however.

Sybase. Sybase Adaptive Server Enterprise is available for Linux; see www.sybase.com/products/databaseservers/linux/ for more details.

Object-Oriented Databases

Object-oriented databases are available for C, C++, Java, and other languages. The projects listed here are mostly commercial, but Poet and eXcelon have free downloads for Java. For reviews of various OODBMS, go to www.dacs.dtic .mil/techs/oodbms2/oodbms-toc.shtml.

eXcelon/Object Design, Inc.

Object Design, Inc. appears to have been renamed eXcelon Corporation (www .excelon.com, www.odi.com). It is offering object-oriented XML repositories as well as its C/C++ and Java object-oriented databases. The Java database can be downloaded and used freely, but you'll have to pay a royalty if you use it in a commercial product. In my experience, this software is solid and performs fairly well; but be prepared to spend some time experimenting to get the most out of it. ObjectStore, the C++ database, has been one of the market leaders in object-oriented databases for many years, and is very solid.

Despite being one of the founding members of the Object Management Group (www.omg.org), ODI has never produced an OQL interface in Java, as far as I know.

There is a Perl interface at www.perl.com/CPAN-local/authors/id/JPRIT/ that supports persistent storage of complex objects.

Poet Software

Although Poet is one of the smaller database companies, its software is good, and it offers very interesting XML support. Poet has a very large user base for its embedded C++ database; the Java interface is newer. Poet also has one of the cleanest and easiest Web sites to navigate. Figure 22.1 shows part of Poet's home page, though this might change at any time, of course. Having the list of products right there is a definite help. Poet is an ODMG member (see Object Design, just described) and implements the Object Query Language, OQL.

Others

Other object-oriented databases of note include these three:

Ardent, at www.ardent.com/ (bought by Informix)

Gemstone, at www.gemstone.com

Versant, at www.versant.com

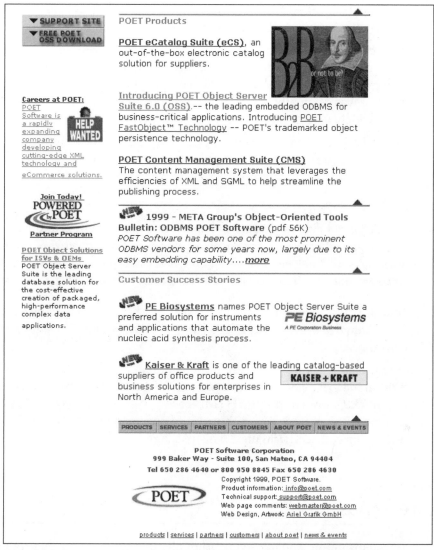

Figure 22.1 Poet Software's home page at www.poet.com.

Repositories and Document Management Systems

The only open source content management system I've seen is Iajitsu; the others described here are commercial.

Astoria. The company name and URL (formerly Crystal; www.chrystal.com) seem to have changed a lot for this high-end commercial object-oriented XML and SGML repository, so you may need to do a Web search. It's built on top of Object Design Inc.'s ObjectStore product, and is gaining an impressive client list. SoftQuad XMetaL and Arbortext's Adept have been integrated into Astoria so that users can edit any part of a document directly.

Interleaf. Interleaf (www.interleaf.com) has several interesting SGML and XML products, including Bladerunner and RDM. These are full-blown applications, rather than tools, and there are other components that can be integrated well. Interleaf was originally known for its Unix-based publishing system, and this is still widely used, although it has perhaps lost ground to Adobe FrameMaker.

Xyvision Parlance. Xyvision is one of the older SGML companies, and its document management and high-end publishing systems are pretty expensive—and powerful—so they're commonly used in heavy industry and large companies.

NOTE

This book has not discussed SGML and XML formatting systems in any detail; Xyvision is mentioned because it has document management. A number of companies provide high-end SGML and XML formatting, and you should examine several and get recommendations from experienced consultants before making a purchase.

Enhydra. This is an open source Java/XML application server; the overview at www.enhydra.org/software/enhydra/documentation/ seems clear and helpful.

Iaijutsu. This is a very interesting open source content management system written in Perl; deus_x on EFnet's #Perl IRC channel is the primary author. Figure 22.2 shows a sample (HTML-based) Web site managed with this system, and Figure 22.3 shows the administration screen. The Iaijutsu URL is www.ninjacode.com/iaijutsu. This package was looking for a new name at the time of writing (Spring, 2000).

Source Repositories

The systems in this category were originally intended for use by programmers to store source code. If you are a programmer and don't use RCS or CVS or a similar system on Windows or the Macintosh, you should start today. Read about RCS and CVS (Unix/Linux), then go try them.

Some of these tools—RCS and CVS in particular—have evolved beyond just source code into more general tools. RCS was illustrated in Chapter 15, "Hybrid Approaches."

Source Code Control System (SCCS)

SCCS was included with Unix System V, and is still found on most commercial Unix systems. Source code is not available, and you can't buy it for other systems,

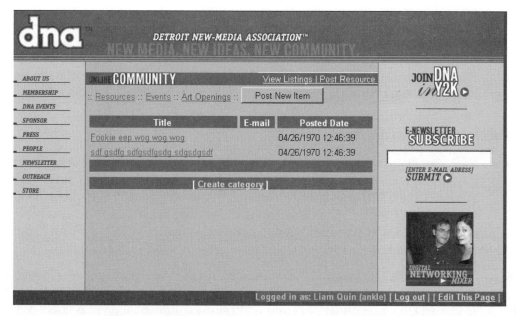

Figure 22.2   Iaijutsu sample Web site.

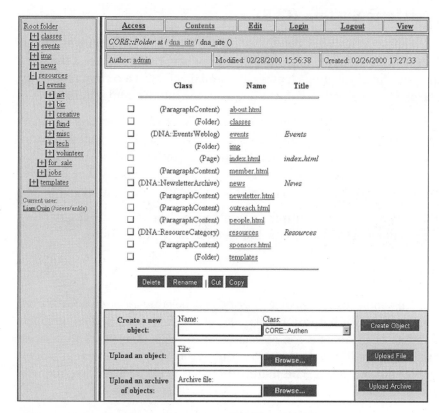

Figure 22.3   Iaijutsu administration "back-end" page.

so RCS is generally preferred. It's mentioned here because you'll see references to it in the documentation of the other systems. SCCS does not use a central repository, but instead stores the master file for each document in a subdirectory.

Revision Control System (RCS)

RCS was distributed as free software in the late 1970s or early 1980s. These days, RCS is distributed under the GNU Public License, and has been very widely ported. RCS does not use a central repository; like SCCS, it uses a directory (called RCS) to store its files. But that directory has to be in the same place as the file under RCS control. This and other features make RCS difficult to use collaboratively.

You can get RCS from any GNU mirror or install it as a package; see Chapter 20, "Installing and Configuring Downloaded Software." RCS is included in most free Unix and Linux systems and in some commercial ones. A good Web page for RCS information is www.cyclic.com/cyclic-pages/rcs.html; you can download RCS from there, too.

Concurrent Versions System (CVS)

Most open source software projects today use CVS, as do a great many commercial projects. CVS is designed to handle the case where two people edit the same file, using a system of merging changes. It maintains files in a central repository, and can be used over a network (including both the Internet and intranets).

Karl Fogel has written a pretty good book on CVS called *Open Source Development with CVS*; its companion Web site at http://cvsbook.redbean.com/cvsbook.html is a good starting point. Another source is Pascal Moli, who maintains a Web site at www.loria.fr/~molli/cvs-index.html that includes the CVS FAQ. Like RCS, CVS may already be installed on your system.

You can download CVS from http://download.cyclic.com/pub/ if you don't have it. You will need to install RCS, too (see the previous section).

/BriefCase

Just before this book was published, /BriefCase became an open source project for Software Configuration Management (www.applied-cs-inc.com). /BriefCase has been on sale commercially since 1992. It appears to address more of the software life cycle than CVS, but as a result may be less useful for (for example) storing XML. The main difference is that /BriefCase requires that developers check out code for editing before they change it.

You can read a comparison of CVS and /BriefCase at www.applied-cs-inc.com/cvs_vs_bc.html (but it may not be very impartial!).

Hashing with *dbm*

Although the original *dbm* and *ndbm* packages are available only as part of a commercial Unix distribution, there are several free versions. The two most widely used are *sdbm* (which is included with Perl) and *db*. Most or all of these can be downloaded from http://linux.about.com/compute/linux/library/metalab/blmeta_libs_db.htm—if you can accurately type this long URL! (Note: This chapter is on this book's companion Web site, to make it easier.)

sdbm. This is a reasonably fast *ndbm* clone, but with limitations on data size of each item and on the number of items than can have the same 32-bit hash value.

gdbm. This is the GNU replacement. As you might expect, it has lots of features, and is not the fastest. This was originally released under the GPL, but may now be under LGPL, meaning you could link a non-GPL program against it.

db. The *db* package was written for BSD Unix, and is fast and well coded. Version 1.85 is the most widely used; there is a version 2.x, but it is distributed under a noncommercial-use license. Version 3.0 was released in November 1999; and, again, if you use the library in a commercial product that you sell, a royalty may apply. *db* also supports a b-tree interface and a line-oriented mode. There is usually support in Perl for *db* on BSD and Linux systems; some other systems have it, too. My own timings indicated that *db*'s "native mode" interface was three or four times faster than its *ndbm* emulation. You can find out more about *db* from www.sleepycat.com.

Hypertext Preprocessor: PHP

PHP is very widely used on the Internet for generating dynamic Web pages. It can generate XML too, and can connect to databases such as MySQL or Oracle. (XML support was added to PHP 4 Beta 4 a week before this book was due at the publisher's, or there would have been a chapter on it!)

You can find out more about PHP and download the latest version (it's free) from www.php.net; there is a lot of good documentation there, too.

Perl DBI

DBI is the DataBase Interface module for Perl that lets Perl connect to many different databases (www.cpan.org). This is mentioned again in the Perl chap-

ter. You can also use DBI with the Apache *mod_perl* module (http://perl
.apache.org/).

Alligator Descartes and Tim Bunce wrote an excellent book on DBI called *Programming the Perl DBI* (O'Reilly, 2000).

Information Retrieval Databases

The simplest searching programs that are of any real use are probably *slocate* and *grep*. There are a great many information retrieval packages available; most of them are not (yet) XML-aware, however.

A good overview and pointers to both free and commercial tools are available at www.searchtools.com/.

Searching without an Index

The tools in this section search files for patterns or search for filenames.

find

The Unix *find* command searches for files whose filename or other properties match a pattern. For example:

```
find /home /usr -name sock.jpg -print
```

will print the full pathname of all files called sock.jpg anywhere under /home or /usr. The *find* command can also handle complex Boolean expressions, but the syntax is somewhat awkward.

locate and slocate

The *locate* command has been replaced by *slocate*, but either may be installed. Both can be found on www.freshmeat.net, and both use the command *locate*. The *locate* command searches a file list that is created nightly, so it's much faster than *find*. You can locate any substring in a path, meaning that:

```
locate sock
```

will find sock.jpg as well as argylesocks.gif and socket.c and a directory called Hassock.

grep

The *grep* command (standard on Unix) searches the *contents* of a list of files for lines that match a regular expression; for example:

```
grep "f[oe]*t" *.txt
```

will print all lines matching the pattern /f[oe]*t/ in the given files. The pattern will match an "f" (anywhere on a line) that's immediately followed by zero or more (*) "o" or "e" characters, and then by a "t."

The *grep* command can be used with *find* and the *xargs* command, as here:

```
find /usr/local/docs -name '*.xml' -print |
xargs grep -n 'barefoot in the snow'
```

This will search all of the XML files that *find* produces for "barefoot in the snow" exactly as given.

NOTE

The xargs command reads filenames on its input and passes them to the given command in batches of 50 or so, running the command multiple times if there are more than 50 files. The command might be run with only one file for the last batch, depending on how many filenames are left over. Since *grep* behaves differently when given only one filename, the –n option was used to force a filename to be printed.

sgrep

The *sgrep* command can use arbitrary delimiters instead of just newlines, and this makes it pretty good at searching XML documents. For example:

```
sgrep -c '"<AUTHOR>" .. "</AUTHOR>" containing "Green"'
```

might find all <AUTHOR> elements containing the string "Green". The pattern syntax seems to have changed slightly with the latest version of *sgrep*, so check the Web page (www.cs.helsinki.fi/~jjaakkol/sgrep.html) or documentation.

Text Retrieval with an Index

Although the query language in *sgrep* is very powerful, even a fairly large SPARC server rarely searches more than 50 megabytes a second using *grep* or *sgrep*; on a PC, you're often lucky to get a tenth of that. In contrast, packages that search an index instead of the actual files can be thousands of times faster, because they can look in a single place to find the names of all files containing a word (*sock*, say) instead of looking at each file in turn.

There are several open source text retrieval packages; a search on www.freshmeat .net should find a few.

lq-text. Originally written by me, *lq-text* is an open source project, available at www.holoweb.net/~liam/lq-text/. It is not currently XML-aware, although that may have changed by the time you read this book. The main distinguishing features of *lq-text* are the capability to index and retrieve compressed files, and an open architecture of separate Unix command that are easy to integrate into shell scripts or to call from Perl CGI scripts.

Open Text. Open Text (www.opentext.com) used to have a search engine called *pat* that was built for the SGML version of the 500-megabyte *Oxford English Dictionary*. This has been rewritten (possibly to avoid license or patent issues?), but the rewrite still handles both SGML and XML. Open Text recently bought an established SGML and XML firm, Microstar, to increase its support for SGML and XML. It also has a content management system, Livelink.

Ultraseek Server. Ultraseek (http://software.infoseek.com/) is a full-text search engine that handles XML. If most of your searches are by experts, with complex Boolean queries and arbitrary element context, Ultraseek Server is not the answer (says the product announcement). But if you want to find, for example, "big blue" in title elements; search for phrases; handle plurals in English, French, and other languages (stemming), then Ultraseek Server is a good fit. Ultraseek Server Content Classification Engine (CCE, http://software.infoseek.com/products/cce/ccetop.htm) is an add-on that organizes large Web sites into topic hierarchies using classification and clustering techniques.

Verity. Verity (www.verity.com) has a powerful and widely used search engine (it's included in some versions of Adobe Acrobat, for example) with SGML support and a range of supporting products.

XRS: XML Retrieval System. The XRS: XML Retrieval System (http://dlb2 .nlm.nih.gov/~dwshin/xrs.html) appears to be free, and has a seminatural-language interface to handle queries like "Get the CHAPTER whose PARAGRAPH contains 'servlet,' 'session', and is written in Java."

Others. Excite and Inktomi (www.excite.com, www.inktomi.com) sell Web search engines that can index XML files; Harvest is a freely available one. And last, www.goxml.com/ has an online index of XML documents found on the Web.

## CHAPTER 23

Further Reading

T his chapter references materials where you can find out more about the topics discussed throughout this book; the sources given include online documentation, books, magazines, and mailing lists.

I had planned to include a list of trade shows and conferences, but decided against it, as they would be out of date by the time this book is published. For example, the function of the former technical GCA SGML conferences has largely been replaced by Markup Technologies and XTech; as far as trade shows, programming conferences, and database gatherings, well, there are just too many to list. My advice is that if you do get involved in open source work, and you want to attend some of these functions, probably the best place to get current info is online.

Books

This book list is arranged as an annotated bibliography, by subject and within the subject, by author. The titles most relevant to this book are shown in **boldface**.

NOTE
I have expressed my opinion of these works bluntly; you may, or may not, agree with my assessments, but they should give you a basis for your own exploration of these sources.

XML and HTML

Ceponkus, Alex, and Faraz Hoodbhoy (1999). *Applied XML*. New York: John Wiley & Sons, Inc.

Includes introductions to the DOM and XSL using Microsoft Internet Explorer.

Chang, Dan, and Dan Harkey (1998). *Client/Server Data Access with Java and XML*. New York: John Wiley & Sons, Inc.

Client/server programming in Java; includes the full DOM API. This book is much more about Java than about XML. It and others like it persuaded me not to include Java in my book.

Dick, Kevin (2000). *XML: A Manager's Guide*. Reading, MA: Addison-Wesley-Longman.

This book is ideal to give to people who need a quick introduction to XML. And you can flatter them by implying they're managers, too.

Flynn, Peter (1998). **Understanding SGML and XML Tools.** Norwell, MA: Kluwer Academic Press.

Although some of the commercial tools described in this book are no longer available or have changed names (DynaText is now sold by Enigma, Panorma by Interleaf, for example) and some of the free tools have been enhanced or supplanted, this is a wonderful book; it is superbly well-written, and gives good introductions to each of the many tools covered.

Goldfarb, Charles, and Paul Prescod (1998). *The XML Handbook*. Short Hills, NJ: Prentice-Hall.

This is really a catalog: individual companies paid money to have their products showcased in it. As a result, there can be little editorial value. The material about freely available XML tools is useful, however. At well over 600 pages, it's also an impressive book to display on the bookshelf in your office.

Graham, Ian S. (1999). **The HTML 4.0 Sourcebook.** New York: John Wiley & Sons, Inc.

This is by far the best of the HTML references I've found. Graham has just finished a new revision, so check for it before buying this one; in it, he covers XHTML, the XML-ified HTML.

Graham, Ian S., and Liam R. E. Quin (1999). **The XML Specification Guide** New York: John Wiley & Sons, Inc.

For obvious reasons, I have to recommend this one. In it, you'll find an introduction to XML, followed by the actual specification reviewed line by line, pointing out ambiguities and potential implementation problems. This book is intended for people working with the specification directly, so it's good if you are working on a parser or creating XML-based languages; it may, however, be more detail than you want if you're just using XML at an API level.

Ibanez, Ardith, and Natalie Zee (1998). *HTML Artistry: More Than Code*. Indianapolis, IN: New Riders.

This is a good introduction to JavaScript and layers. I used it to make a floating help layer for a BookWeb example used in my book.

Lie, Håkon W., and Bert Bos (1997). *Cascading Style Sheets*. Reading, MA: Addison-Wesley-Longman.

Although CSS2 has been published, it has not yet been implemented. In the meantime, this book, written by two people very central to the development of CSS, is a plausible reference to style sheets. Since XSL uses CSS properties, a CSS reference is handy. You may prefer to print out the original 200-page specification, however, from www.w3.org. Ian Graham's book on style sheets (not listed here) is harder to find in stores, but very bluntly states when things don't work in the main browsers.

Maler, Eve, and Jeanne El Andaloussi (1995). *Developing SGML DTDs: From Text to Model to Markup*. Short Hills, NJ: Prentice Hall.

I lost my copy of this book and have been lamenting it ever since. It's the standard work for people who are doing document analysis and creating a DTD to represent their documents. If the book has a downfall, it's that it assumes you are in an authoring environment and have editorial control over your texts and your markup. But since that's the usual case, it's a pretty good book.

Martin, Teresa (1999). *Project Cool: Guide to XML for Web Designers*. New York: John Wiley & Sons, Inc.

Whereas Kevin Dick's book is good to give out as a quick introduction to XML, Martin's book is great for Webheads who need to learn XML.

Navarro, Ann, Chuck White, and Linda Burman (1999). **Mastering XML**. Alameda, CA: Sybex.

This fat monster of a book lists masses of applications. A second edition was in progress at the time of this writing (spring 2000), so make sure you get the newest. The book won't tell you how to program, and has very little detail about any topic, but it offers the best broad coverage.

St. Laurent, Simon, and Robert Biggar (1999). *Inside XML DTDs*. New York: McGraw-Hill.

This book gives clear examples for most of the main uses of XML today. There is a pretty good chapter on metadata, RDF, and the Dublin Core, too.

Walsh, Norm, and Leonard Muellner (1999). *DocBook: The Definitive Guide.* Sebastopol, CA: O'Reilly & Associates.

As more and more projects use the DocBook DTD for documentation, this guide on marking up text will probably become the DocBook bible. The book itself is an excellent example of DTD documentation. A CD-ROM includes style sheets, and the entire book is available in online form. Wow.

Databases

The best reference is the one intended for the specific database you are using. That said, the following three books are particularly useful. Note that I have not listed any PHP books; the reason is, simply, there weren't any useful ones when I started. Now there is one called *Core PHP*, but it seems little more useful than the online documentation, and is less up to date.

Descartes, Alligator, and Tim Bunce (2000). *Programming the Perl DBI.* Sebastopol, CA: O'Reilly.

This came out too late for me to use as a reference, but I think if I'd read it earlier, there would have been more DBI examples in my book.

Stephens, Ryan K., and Ronald R. Plew (1998) *Sams' Teach Yourself SQL in 24 Hours.* Indianapolis, IN: Sams Publishing.

This is a good introduction to SQL and object modeling.

Yarger, Randy Jay, George Reese, and Tim King. (1999). *MySQL and mSQL.* Sebastopol, CA: O'Reilly.

If you are using MySQL, buy this book. If you are using mSQL, upgrade to MySQL, then buy this book.

Information Retrieval and Hypertext

Baeza-Yates, Ricardo, and Berthier Ribeiro-Neto (1999). *Modern Information Retrieval.* Reading, MA: Addison-Wesley-Longman (an ACM Press Book).

This is a very useful overview of the field, which doesn't skimp on implementation notes and references.

Nielsen, Jakob (2000). *Designing Web Usability.* Indianapolis, IN: New Riders.

A truly superb book on designing Web sites that work, written by one of the world's foremost Web usability experts. This book is worth the price just for the pictures, but I'm getting the text read as well, a few wonderful pages at a time.

Landow, George P. (1997). *Hypertext 2.0: The Convergence of Contemporary Critical Theory and Technology.* Baltimore, MD: The Johns Hopkins University Press.

An updated edition of Landow's 1992 book, this gives a useful perspective on hypertext and how it affects content and the way we perceive information.

Wittan, Ian H., Alistair Moffat, and Timothy C. Bell (1944). *Managing Gigabytes: Compressing and Indexing Documents and Images.* New York: Van Rostrand Reinhold.

Look for an updated edition of this book on implementing a text and image retrieval system.

Programming on Unix and Linux

Aho, Alfred A., Ravi Sethi, and Jeffrey D. Ullman (1985). *Compilers: Principles, Techniques, and Tools.* Reading, MA: Addison-Wesley.

This is the book on writing compilers and parsers. Although parsing XML with yacc and lex has problems, this textbook will give you enough theoretical and practical background to write your own tools, if you need to do so.

Bentley, Jon (1985). *Programming Pearls.* Murray Hill, NJ: Addison-Wesley Pub Co.

Originally published as a series of columns in the journal *Communications of the ACM*, this is one of the best books on general programming I have ever encountered. I have not had the opportunity to review the new edition, but look for it. Bentley's insight shows you how to solve real problems with confidence, not just mince around them.

William J. Brown, Raphael C. Malveau, Hays W. "Skip" McCormick, III, and Thomas J. Mowbray (1998). *AntiPatterns: Refactoring Software, Architectures, and Projects in Crisis.* New York: John Wiley & Sons, Inc.

I suggest you read this in conjunction with the Gamma et al. *Patterns* book listed here as well. This book does not tell you that patterns are a bad idea, rather, it describes patterns into which bad projects fall. If you are fixing old code, or you have to make an existing project "talk XML," this book may help back you up when you make cost estimates.

Cooper, Alan (1995). *About Face: The Essentials of User Interface Design.* Foster City, CA: IDG Books Worldwide.

Cooper introduces a lot of seemingly pointless jargon in this book, but with lots of good ideas. His term, "perpetual intermediate," aptly describes most users of most applications.

DiBona, Chris, Sam Ockman, and Mark Stone (eds.) (1999). *Open Sources: Voices from the Open Source Revolution.* Sebastopol, CA: O'Reilly.

This is a very significant collection of chapters about open source software, and is useful for all those who need to explain the open source business model used by companies like Cygnus and Red Hat.

Fogel, Karl (1999). *Open Source Development with CVS.* Scottsdale, AZ: Coriolis Group.

This book tells you how to use CVS and set up a CVS server. It also has chapters on policy for running open source projects. The book has a companion Web site, at http://cvsbook.red-bean.com/cvsbook.html, which includes some of the book content.

Gamma, Erich, Richard Helm, Ralph Johnson, and John Vlissides (1995). *Design Patterns: Elements of Reusable Object-Oriented Software.* Reading, MA: Addison-Wesley-Longman.

This book caused a minor revolution in the software industry, and is now on the list of must-read books for every programmer and software architect. I warn against applying the patterns blindly, however; instead, use the book to help you recognize large-scale "idioms" quickly.

Harlow, Eric (1999). *Developing Linux Applications with GTK+ and GDK.* Indianapolis, IN: New Riders.

Although I include this book, it is now out of date, so you are probably better off with the online documentation. There is another GTK+ book forthcoming from O'Reilly that should be very good indeed. For programming with gnome in general, see Pennington, Havoc, *GTK/GNOME Application Development.*

Kernighan, Brian W., and Rob Pike (1984). *The Unix Programming Environment.* Englewood Cliffs, NJ: Prentice-Hall.

Don't be fooled by the date of this book. If you are doing C or shell programming on Unix, read this book, which was written by two people central to Unix development.

Kernighan, Brian W., and Rob Pike (1999). *The Practice of Programming.* Short Hills, NJ: Prentice-Hall.

Destined to be another classic, this book includes examples in C, C++, Perl, and Java. Like *The Unix Programming Environment* just described, this is a slender volume, but very thought-provoking.

Meyers, Scott (1992). *Effective C++*. Reading, MA: Addison-Wesley.

I don't list many C++ books, but this and its sequel, *More Effective C++*, seem to make it clear that you should avoid C++ for projects unless your developers are all careful and experienced, and communicate well. Use Java, C, or Perl, or maybe Sather (www.gnu.org/software/sather/) instead. There are good reasons for using C++, and these two books will help you think about what they might be.

Pennington, Havoc (1999). *GTK+/Gnome Application Development*. Indianapolis, IN: New Riders.

This is a well-organized account of Gnome programming; it assumes you have read Eric Harlow's book on GTK or the online documentation at www.gtk.org.

Rochkind, Marc J. (1985). *Advanced Unix Programming*. Englewood Cliffs, NJ: Prentice-Hall.

This is an oldie, but good introduction to Unix at the system call level. It still very much applies, both to Linux and to other versions of Unix, although you should be aware that libraries and newer system calls have sometimes replaced the ones mentioned here. Simply check the online documentation (e.g., `man 2 open`; or, on System V and Solaris, `man -s 2 open`) to see if this is true. The book encourages a good style of checking errors.

Stevens, W. Richard (1996). *TCP/IP Illustrated, Vol 3: TCP for Transactions, HTTP, NNTP, and the UNIX Domain Protocols*. Reading, MA: Addison-Wesley.

Though pretty detailed, this is a fairly low-level book. I've listed it because it's useful if you are implementing a server.

Stevens, W. Richard (1998). *Unix Network Programming, Vol 1. Networking APIs: Sockets and XTI*. Reading, MA: Addison-Wesley-Longman.

I used this for Chapter 2, "Client/Server Architecture," although the most common way of writing a server (which I show in the chapter) is not given much prominence in Richard's book for some reason.

Sun Microsystems (1999). *Java Look-and-Feel Guidelines*. Reading, MA: Addison-Wesley-Longman.

If you are programming in Java, learn to work with it, not fight it. This book will help you write cross-platform Java programs and applets. In general, whichever platform and toolkit you use, if you are developing a GUI application, read the user interface style guidelines.

Perl

Christiansen, Tom, and Nathan Torkington (1998). *Perl Cookbook*. Sebastopol, CA: O'Reilly.

This book includes numerous useful examples, including a Web link checker that's easy to understand and still only a few lines of Perl.

Descartes, Alligator, and Tim Bunce (2000). *Programming the Perl DBI.* Sebastopol, CA: O'Reilly.

See my comments for this book under Databases.

Srinivasan, Sriram (1997). *Advanced Perl Programming.* Sebastopol, CA: O'Reilly.

Includes examples on integrating C and Perl, the Perl/Tk toolkit, and networking, among other topics.

Wall, Larry, Tom Christiansen, and Randal L. Schwartz, (1996). *Programming Perl.* Sebastopol, CA: O'Reilly.

This is the best printed reference for Perl (including Perl 5). The second best is the online documentation, which is accessible with the *perldoc* command. There is also a *Learning Perl* book by Randal L. Schwartz and Tom Christiansen, with a foreword by Larry Wall, also published by O'Reilly, if the examples in this book interested you.

Walsh, Nancy (1999). *Learning Perl/Tk.* Sebastopol, CA: O'Reilly.

This book is useful if you want to use Tk and DBI together, for example, to make a graphical user interface to a database. The *Advanced Perl* book listed previously has a short introduction to Perl/Tk; there is also a pocket reference from the same publisher. For Linux, there is a Perl/Gtk module (available from www.cpan.org or www.gtk.org) but no books yet.

Magazines and Journals

The following publications are sorted by title. There are many more, of course, including database magazines.

Linux Journal (monthly). Generally glossy Linux coverage.

Linux Magazine (monthly). Harder to find than *Linux Journal,* but seems to have better technical content.

Markup Languages, Theory and Practice (quarterly). From MIT Press (journals-order@mit.edu). Relatively academic in style, with peer-reviewed articles about SGML, XML, and other markup systems.

The Perl Journal (quarterly). Excellent reading for Perl users.

The Seybold Report (www.syboldreport.com; various frequencies). Offers a range of very high-quality industry newsletters.

SysAdmin (monthly). For people administering Unix systems.

XML Magazine (www.xmlmag.com). The first issue was very general, but the second shows more promise, and is worth a look.

Online Documentation

Many packages come with documentation that gets installed onto your computer. Here are some examples.

- The documentation for the Apache Web server is at www.apache.org, or you may install it. On a default install of Apache, connecting to port 80 of your computer may give you links to documentation, before you reconfigure the server by editing *httpd.conf*.

- MySQL and PHP both have extensive manuals. Look in the `/usr/doc` directory for them on Linux or in `/usr/local` on FreeBSD.

- Perl has a *perldoc* command that's very useful; *man perl* may also help.

- The *man -k* command can search the "synopsis" line of every manual page for keywords.

Web Sites

This is a short list of some of the more important Web sites; it does not include all the sites mentioned in the book.

Community and Catalog

These sites are not for individual packages or projects, but communities where programmers can get together and announce their projects or share knowledge.

Advogato (www.advogato.org). A community of trust, where people can certify other programmers' ability. This site manages to escape being elitist, perhaps because the programmers' diary entries are both entertaining and useful, and because most programmers are less interested in elitism than many other groups.

FreeCode (www.freecode.com). Contains mostly Web tools, such as CGI scripts in various languages.

Freshmeat (www.freshmeat.net). This oddly named site lists thousands of open source projects. Figure 23.1 shows a screenshot.

GeekBoys (www.geekboys.org). A metaportal site! It lets you choose from a huge list of open source and related news sites and see a summary of recent

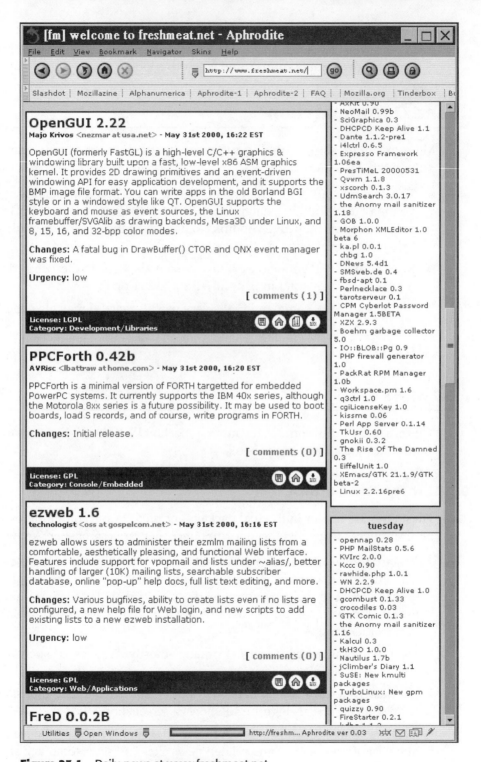

Figure 23.1 Daily news at www.freshmeat.net.

articles. It's great for exploring, because you can look at all the sites they can survey.

Linux Chix (www.linuxchix.org). After listing GeekBoys, I felt I should include this. It has links to the Linux documentation project, among other things.

Server51 (www.server51.net). Like Sourceforge, a host for open source projects.

Slashdot (www.slashdot.org). The only news site that the entire open source community reads every day. If your Web page is mentioned here, expect tens of thousands of hits; if your server crashes, it's said to have been slashdotted.

SourceForge (www.sourceforge.net). A major host of open source projects.

Woven Goods for Linux (www.fokus.gmd.de/linux/). A set of Web pages with information about Linux, plus a collection of applications to build your own Web server on a Linux machine.

XML Sites

These sites have XML resources.

Free XML Tools Page. An extensive list of free XML tools, at www.garshol .priv.no/download/xmltools/.

Goxml.com (http://www.goxml.com/). A search engine for finding XML on the Web.

World Wide Web Consortium (www.w3.org). The XML specifications are at www.w3.org/XML/.

XML dot COM (www.xml.com). A news site for and about the XML industry.

Mailing Lists

Some of these mailing lists get ten or more messages per day, others more than 100 a day. The point is, don't join them all at once! If you find you need to unsubscribe, do *not* post "unsubscribe me," because everyone on the list (10,000 people maybe!) will see your message. Instead, follow the instructions carefully. They are usually sent to you when you join the list, so keep that original message.

dev-xml. A Windows-based XML list for developers; subscribe at dev-xml-subscribe@onelist.com or www.onelist.com/community/dev-xml.

XSL-List (www.mulberrytech.com/xsl/xsl-list). A list for style sheet developers using XSL and XSLT.

XML-APP. A mailing list specifically for those interested in applying the XML technology to real-world applications. It is not a place to discuss general

XML issues, nor is it a place for the naive. You can subscribe by sending a blank message to xml-app-subscribe@sunsite.auc.dk.

XQL (XML Query Language) (http://franklin.oit.unc.edu/cgi-bin/lyris .pl?enter=xql). There is a Frequently Asked Questions (FAQ) file for the list at http://metalab.unc.edu/xql/.

XML-L (http://listserv.heanet.ie/xml-l.html). General discussion of Extensible Markup Language, according to the Web site.

xml-dev (http://xml.org/archives/xml-dev/). This is the XML developer's list, and so can be quite technical and quite busy. It is summarized usefully at http://my.userland.com/viewChannel$1079. List archives are available at http://xml.org/archives/xml-dev/.

Internet Relay Chat

Internet Relay Chat (IRC) is a great way to get information and support. If you have the X Window system installed on Unix/Linux, you can use the *x-chat* program; another popular Unix client is the strangely named BitchX (www.bitchx.com). On Windows, mIRC (www.mirc.com) is the most popular.

Once you have an IRC client, you're ready to connect to a network. You will find programmers at almost any time of day who are prepared to help you, as long as you have taken the trouble to read documentation first.

Debian Linux users can connect to irc.debian.org; Perl users will find EFnet's #perl channel useful. There are HTML, XML, Oracle, and other database channels on EFnet, DALnet, Undernet, and elsewhere.

You can also say hello to me on irc.sorcery.net, where I use the nickname "Ankh."